To my friends
Alan and Lorraine

With Best Wishes

Angelo

15 - 11 - 12

ANGELO

*An Inspiring Autobiography for Those
Determined to Succeed*

Angelo Xuereb

Book Guild Publishing
Sussex, England

First published in Great Britain in 2012 by
The Book Guild Ltd
Pavilion View
19 New Road
Brighton, BN1 1UF

Typesetting in Garamond by
Keyboard Services, Luton, Bedfordshire

Printed in Great Britain by
CPI Group (UK) Ltd, Croydon, CR0 4YY

A catalogue record for this book is available from
The British Library

ISBN 978 1 84624 785 9

I dedicate this book to my mother Marija,
who passed away on 14th January 2011,
and to my father Bertu, who passed away
on 21st January 2012

Contents

Acknowledgments

I thank the Lord for giving me the wisdom of an entrepreneur which is the basis of this book. I thank my parents for my good upbringing which helped me form a strong character. I thank my wife Jessie for her endurance and support throughout my entire hectic life and for caring for our children while I was carrying out my business duties. I thank my children Richard, Claire and Denise for being supportive and for following in my footsteps to carry my business to future generations.

I thank Dr Edward de Bono, originator of lateral thinking, regarded by many to be the leading authority on creative thinking, author of sixty-two books and a good friend, for finding the time in his busy schedule to write a foreword to this book.

I thank Charles Micallef St John for his skills in editing my script, and thanks also go to my personal assistant Caroline Schembri for her patience in typing out my entire handwritten autobiography.

I thank all past and present employees, management and directors of my group of companies. Without their support I could not have achieved success in my business.

Foreword

by Dr Edward de Bono, originator of lateral thinking

This is a remarkable book. It is remarkable for three reasons:

- The first reason is that it is a clear and honest account of a powerful story. It is written as an honest account and not to make any special impression.
- The second reason is that it is actually very interesting. This is not always the case with biographies which have to tell the story as it is. In this book there are difficulties, problems and adventures and the reader does not know what is going to happen. So there is interest in following the story to see what happens – as in all good stories.
- The third reason is that it is indeed a remarkable story. It is the story of a young man who sets out to succeed in business. Propelled by extraordinary determination he succeeds. Starting from nothing he is so successful that at a relatively young age his earnings equal one per cent of the entire GDP of the country in which he lives and works. That is indeed a success story.

There are other aspects of the book which are also of interest. There is the difficulty of dealing with government agencies. In some cases this is even more difficult and uncertain than operating the business to create value.

This book should be an inspiration to all youngsters at an early stage in their lives when they are looking into the future and wondering what it holds for them. The book makes clear that with ambition and determination you can create your own future.

Education is indeed important but the personal characteristics of determination and vision are even more important. As you read through this book you will see how ideas are imagined and then put into action. As a reader you are invited to watch as this happens.

What is perhaps unexpected is that Angelo is not only very good at his business but is also a very good writer. He makes clear not only the circumstances but also his own thinking in those circumstances. The reader can look over his shoulder as events unfold.

It is a powerful book and an inspiring read. Anyone interested in action and success should read it. Description and academic analysis are not enough to make things happen. This book is about making things happen.

Edward de Bono

Introduction

I have never spent much time reading books. Maybe I should be ashamed of myself. In fact, I am a little bit – just enough to proudly declare that I decided to put that right and whilst writing this autobiography in longhand, I also read a novel. I found the book so interesting and relaxing that I've started and finished others as well. When I finish writing this book I'll read it, of course, but it won't count, will it? I just hope it will be as interesting as the others I've read, that's all.

I've had such a hectic life that there was little, if any, time left to enjoy a good book. Maybe as you read what comes after this introduction you will understand better. I had other priorities which left me with no time whatsoever for any hobby, at least for most of my business career.

I'm now fifty-nine and, although retirement is still not on my agenda, I feel now's the time to write my story before my memory starts playing tricks. I'm sure my children, fully grown the three of them, won't begrudge me the luxury of spending my free time at home writing my memoirs while they fill in for me.

I can't know what will happen in the future and what it holds for me and the group I lead. That would be for my children to write about. But this year, while I'm sitting at my desk with a sheaf of blank paper in front of me, I am able to write about my past and how I became an entrepreneur and a proud family man. I can go back and reminisce about my humble beginnings as a young village boy who had a clear vision about what he wanted to do in life.

At times I was scoffed at and many were sceptical about this vision of mine. They thought it was just a dream all young boys get, like wanting to become pope or the first on the moon. But the young village boy knew better. His dream wasn't impossible to bring to reality. All it required was vision, determination and lots and lots of hard work. He remained persistent to the last, overcoming most obstacles thrown in his path to success. Now, here he is, sitting at his desk, scribbling away as though his life depended on it.

I was the eldest son in a family of eleven children, brought up in the farming and later in the construction sectors. It was a hard struggle all the way; my father was very strict and I lived in a mixture of awe and fear of him, which, as you will see, got very close to hatred. To me at the time, it seemed that he deliberately tried to keep me under his control by keeping me poor. I was completely penniless on my wedding day and yet, at the age of forty-five, I had expanded my business so successfully that I was generating around 1% of the National Gross Domestic Product (GDP), leading one of the country's foremost groups diversified in construction, development, tourism and healthcare.

My beginnings coincided with a time when the unemployment rate was high and when young men my age were emigrating in their hundreds. The talk among young people always turned to good jobs in Australia and Canada where the future looked brighter thanks to enlightened governments willing to encourage citizens with initiative. I could easily have been tempted to join the exodus, but I love my country and I love the feel of its rock and soil under my bare feet. I believed that Malta had what it takes to move forward under its own steam with a little help from young entrepreneurs like me. I, therefore, decided to stay because I believed that, even at such a young age, I had a strong enough feeling inside me that with my humble contribution, Malta could truly become the highly polished Jewel of the Mediterranean. Maybe we're not there yet, but we have covered much ground since then and I would like to believe that I have contributed my small share.

I was a very shy village boy, always obedient and never wasted words unless talked to. Yet, years later, I was twice elected mayor of my hometown on an independent ticket and, even later, I was deputy leader of a new political party which contested a general election.

This story is based on facts as they truly happened. It's about a dream that became reality and is written to serve as an example to young people; to inspire dreamers like me who are determined to smash through the difficulties and meet the challenges that could blur their vision head on. It's written for those young people who need to start from scratch and who have the vision to fulfil their dreams. It's written for those young people who face great odds and need an inspiration in order to succeed.

As an entrepreneur I have always looked for new ideas and have never been one to copy what others have done before me. Satisfaction comes from being original and showing others the way forward. This means that the challenges I have had to face were greater, and overcoming them spurned me on to bigger ideas, themselves creating new challenges. But it is this continuous circle that spiralled ever upwards and eventually led to the realisation of a thirteen-year-old boy's dream.

The biggest challenge I had to face throughout the decades in such a small country like Malta was to convince the authorities, politicians and financial institutions that my dreams and visions were practical and feasible. People who didn't share my vision found it difficult to understand and accept my philosophy and this book should serve as an eye-opener for those in power to appreciate the young and upcoming entrepreneurs who are coming forward with what seem to be crazy and revolutionary ideas. These young people hold the future in the palms of their hands and should be encouraged and assisted instead of written off as cranks. In order to achieve progress, all of us – government included – have to appreciate and share the calculated risks that make up most of the ingredients for success. Allowances should be made and the benefit of the doubt should be in favour of the young entrepreneur in order that his or her dream can be realised, especially when they find themselves with their back to the wall with nobody to bail them out except the people in authority. There will always be mistakes, big and small, but mistakes are committed by those who work and toil. Those who just sit back never make mistakes. They just do nothing but criticise.

I have made a number of mistakes throughout my career. One big mistake could have cost me my career and I wouldn't have been here, sitting at my desk, opening a window on my life for all to see. That is why I have always preferred to have a spread of controlled risks rather than a big one that could have proved my undoing. The saying that one must not place all of one's eggs in the same basket is never truer than in a business career.

Some of the readers may never have heard of Malta and where it is situated, let alone anything about its rich history. I have, therefore, included a number of QR codes spread throughout the book to help the reader understand better the places and sites referred to in the following chapters, together with some references to my Group's companies and personal website.

My life has been a stressful one. I can't remember a day when I wasn't making more than one decision at the same time and plugging holes with all my available fingers, but I haven't ever stood alone over the past thirty-seven years; I have always felt the presence of the Almighty hovering somewhere around me to guide me towards the right decisions, not just for me and my business' benefit, but most of all for my family and for the country I love so much. For all this, I thank Him, and for giving me the wisdom to walk the straight road.

It's true that my life has been a success and I'm proud of my achievements. Playing humble at this stage would be hypocritical. But whatever the successes and achievements, I still feel I'm a humble man at heart, at home amongst the humble people I grew up with in the village of Naxxar. They are the people who helped me become what I am today, never making me forget my roots in the narrow streets right in the centre of the old part of Naxxar.

Success has enabled me to travel far and wide and I have been to most countries around the globe, but Malta is my home. This is where my imagination is fuelled. This is where I have visions of a better Malta for our future generations and this is where I feel the determination seeping up from the solid, bare rock beneath my feet to envelop my whole body and mind, and urge me to continue.

The future is beyond this book and no one can see it for the mist that hides it. What is certain is that there are many more challenges awaiting us once the mist lifts, and I intend to face as many of them as possible until God says, 'No more, Angelo. It's now time you took a long, long break.'

1

Parents and Childhood Memories

To understand the significance of my story it is helpful to understand the background and conditions into which I was born. Malta, my nation – of which I am immensely proud – has a long history of foreign domination. In 1800 the leaders of the population invited the British to come in and help drive the French out. Under the wings of the British Empire the population grew. Generally speaking, life improved; Malta, with its splendid deep water port facilities, became a very important part of that Empire. The economy of the island closely mirrored that of Britain; the recession, which hit the mother nation in the 1920s and 30s, was particularly bad for Malta and unemployment was very high.

My parents, Bertu and Maria, both came from traditionally Maltese, large farming families and were born into that world. It was a hard life. My mother at least received a minimal elementary education until she left school at fourteen to help Grandmother raise her ever-growing family. My father, on the other hand, was rather proud of hardly ever having attended school. He preferred helping his father in the fields to sitting at a school desk all day, and he was not alone in his truancy. Feeding the very large families of the time was, and had to be, a priority; every pair of hands that could work were called upon.

Dad never regretted his childhood and youth. In fact, he was proud of it. Having to live by his wits at a time when the highest academic qualification wouldn't have guaranteed employment, his was the best education one could get in the circumstances. He learned the hard way during Malta's lean period between world wars.

During the period of World War II, Malta was hit particularly hard because of her association with the British. Italy declared war on 9th June 1940 and started bombing Malta on the very next day. When the Italian efforts failed, Albert Kesselring, the German Commander in the Mediterranean, declared that he would '*wipe Malta off the map*'. Another eighteen months of continual bombardment followed and food was extremely short. There were over 3,300 air raids during the period and 29,674 homes were destroyed. The inhabitants resolutely withstood the pounding and because of this, King George VI awarded the whole island of Malta the George Cross in 1942. It is the highest award that can be given to civilians. It was the first time such an award had been bestowed on a whole population and it reflected the gallantry shown. The citation stated, 'To honour her brave people I award the George Cross to the Island Fortress of Malta, to bear witness to a heroism and a devotion that will long be famous in history.'

I remember Dad proudly saying that, during World War II, he used to mingle with the soldiers at gun emplacements defending Ta' Qali airfield. This was during air raids while strafing from the dreaded German Stuka bombers whizzed around him! Luckily, he never got hit, and he never knew the inside of a bomb shelter throughout the six-year war.

After the war the whole economy had to be rebuilt and £30,000,000 was granted to Malta for this purpose. Dad took up the challenge and decided to start his own small business, becoming an agricultural agent. This entailed organising small farmers and helping them to grow the crops that his customers wanted to buy, dealing mainly in wheat and barley. He was small fry compared to the established and the experienced, but his war-proven courage served him well. So much so that by the time he was twenty-three in 1949, he considered himself financially strong enough to marry my twenty-two-year-old mother. And the happily married young couple took up residence in a modest town house at 63 St Lucy Street, Naxxar.

Both of my parents were devout Roman Catholics, as were the majority of the Maltese population, and happily and very willingly contributed their share to the baby boom Malta experienced during the first decade after the cessation of hostilities. In my parents' case it seems that this initial momentum carried them well into the second decade as, like their respective parents before them, they set about filling their house to overflowing with children. They had eleven children in thirteen years. There was a gap of only eleven months between a sister and the next!

Speranza (Sperry), the eldest, was born with a Spina Bifida condition. I can now appreciate what my parents must have gone through during the nine long months of my mother's second pregnancy. Speranza ('Hope' in English), in spite of her disability, grew up into a very active person among the community, holding a responsible post as an elected member of the local government – a shining example and inspiration to us all.

After Speranza came Grace. And after Grace it was my turn to see the light of day on 15th June 1952. One can only imagine the pride my mother felt at giving her husband a son, and the pride on my father's face when holding his first-born son in his arms, the natural heir to his slowly growing business. (This was a time when it was unheard of that a daughter would work outside the household.)

Doris and Maryanne (Mary) soon followed, thus forming a thick sandwich of two female layers with me tightly hemmed in between. I was, therefore, the only one Dad could carry along with him wherever he went – the fields, the traditional and quaint village bars, and church.

Then came Joseph (Joe), Albert, Emmanuel (Leli), followed by two other girls, Lucy and Carmen, with the youngest, Paul, closing the final account in 1962. It was customary in those days for couples to name their first two boys and first two girls after the four grandparents. Speranza and I were named after Dad's parents, while Graziella (Grace) and Bertu (Albert) after Mum's.

I started school when I was five years old and my school was

3

in Mosta, run by the Church with teaching nuns. Mum and Dad were almost illiterate and we didn't have money to buy reading books at home, but I was able to get help from my elder sisters if I had a problem with my homework. I remember my father signing his name and writing down numbers, but that was all. He was always busy working and could not get involved in my education. Mum could write some broken words in Maltese and she tried to give me as much support as she could.

When I was thirteen my next brother in line was still only seven, so I was the only one old enough to give Dad a helping hand. At that relatively young age I was already getting first-hand knowledge of the farming industry and Dad's business methods.

Having eleven children in thirteen years was no joke. It was a continuous strain on my mother, who had to do her utmost to keep everybody well fed and healthy, and a strain on my father's finances, however well his business was growing. When this proved not quite good enough to fill so many hungry bellies, Dad turned the front room of our home into a small grocery shop, which my mother used to run. She could only cope for a short time as it was humanly impossible to see to the needs of such a large family and at the same time cope with the few customers who frequented her shop. Furthermore, the income from the shop wasn't large enough to merit the sacrifice and time Mum was forced by circumstances to invest in it.

My parents couldn't afford nannies or helpers. These were luxuries they just dreamed about. But in spite of all this, and in spite of the obvious overcrowding, I can never recall a day when home wasn't always spick and span.

Following the closure of the grocery store Dad had to do something to augment his income. He came up with the idea of breeding a couple of bulls in a barn situated at the far end of our home. It had direct access to Alley number 9.

Encouraged with the success of this experiment, Dad bought a small farm opposite our home in Alley number 10, enabling him to convert the barn into a kitchen and living room, thus enlarging our home which was becoming too small for the growing children.

I clearly remember the two youngest, still toddlers, in two hammocks hung in two corners of the 'new' living room. Dad made the hammocks himself from jute bags and ropes. Thus, the two young ones were kept quiet while gently rocked to sleep.

From the age of five it was my job to cut the top off milk cans and hammer down the sharp edges to use as mugs at tea time. These 'mugs' lasted until they rusted within a couple of weeks and I would then have to do the job all over again. One can only imagine how many milk cans I recycled during this period of family life, but since we were a large family I was never short of raw material. Imagine my happiness when Dad managed to buy some drinking glasses when I was eight years old.

When the grocery shop closed it became my responsibility to do the shopping from other shops in our immediate area. Since we couldn't afford a refrigerator we used to put all perishables and soft drinks in a tin bucket which was lowered all the way down into the well. Bucket and contents, filled to the brim with the cool water, would be left there until required for cooking or drinking. Sometimes, however, if the bucket was let down the well in a hurry, it would tip over and the contents would float away in all directions. Retrieving the contents was never easy and was a sobering reminder that more haste can mean less speed.

Mum was always busy preparing different dishes on different days and always tried to vary our diet as much as possible. We were never short of good meat, however, because Dad was now taking his mature bulls to the abattoir and would bring back their best parts for Mum to cook. He was determined that his children should be given the best food possible and was almost obsessed in his insistence that we eat the most vitamin-laden food. This was, no doubt, because of his memories of near starvation when he was younger.

It had long been a tradition in Malta that Sunday lunch had

to be cooked at the local bakery. No matter how many home-baked lunches were consumed between Monday and Saturday, Sunday's tradition was religiously followed like an eleventh commandment. It used to be the housewives' day of ultimate pride to prepare the nicest dish possible for their large families whatever the financial constraints.

The day always started very early. Between half past four and a quarter to five, the slamming of front doors could be heard all over the village, heralding our housewives' departure to church for the five o'clock Mass. When Mass was over, and after a quick 'good morning' and 'see you at the bakery' on the church parvis, they would all hurry back home to start preparing the most important and biggest dish of the week. Sunday lunches were always big. Very big. In fact, they were too big to fit in the confined space of normal kitchen ovens, which were already quite popular locally. And since they took hours to prepare, so dishes were taken to the local bakery where most of the village housewives congregated outside in long queues, mostly in clusters of four or five, awaiting their turn to hand in their works of art.

Preparation of the Sunday dish wasn't haphazard. Housewives started thinking about it as early as the previous Monday, and when the final decision was made by Wednesday or Thursday, the ingredients were purchased from the various butchers and grocers. Then came the actual preparation after Sunday's five o'clock Mass, and it had to be perfect both in appearance and the preferred added ingredients. This was because the dish had to be paraded all the way from home to the bakery, which could be many alleys and streets away, ultimately to be critically inspected by most of the village housewives.

Then came the long wait in the queue. Not that the women regretted it; it was the only time of the week when they could gossip to their heart's content while eyeing the neighbours' dishes. After this long wait, the baker would examine the dish critically before offering his customary compliments to his customer's satisfaction while handing out a square metal token embossed with a number. This token was all important because it was used to identify the dish on its retrieval a couple of hours later.

Bakers dealt with hundreds of dishes every Sunday morning, many of which looked alike. Dishes varied from macaroni, pork, lamb, chicken and fish, most often accompanied by potatoes and other tasty accessories. (Thanks to my father's business we often had beef on Sundays.) Bakers used to tell them apart by their copy of the square piece of tin. People my age look back with nostalgia at this lost tradition, because food cooked at the bakery tasted much, much better than the modern imitation.

When housewives were not able to make it to the bakery for some reason or other, usually because they were heavily pregnant or had babies to suckle, one of the elder children was delegated for the job. From the age of six it was often my turn because my elder sisters were usually needed to take care of the younger ones. I hated standing in the long queue, listening to the gossip, news and women's talk about children's constant illnesses and inept husbands while my dish was getting heavier by the second. In fact, the women in the queue became so absorbed in their gossip that sometimes I managed to jump the queue without them realising, and return home early to resume games with my brothers and sisters.

Despite the queuing, I always enjoyed retrieving the end result. I used to love waiting my turn inside the bakery and could literally feel the beautiful aroma of perfectly cooked food entering my nostrils and invading my whole body. I remember eyeing each dish hungrily, my mouth watering and my stomach rumbling audibly. On my way home I never managed to resist the temptation to nibble at a dark and crunchy piece of macaroni or a slice of potato from the top of the dish, even when, more often than not, it burned my mouth. Mum never failed to notice the resulting hole on top of the dish, but she never scolded me. Maybe because I was continuing a family tradition set by her.

My arrival back home always brought everybody hungrily to table, all taking their designated places. The table was always laid with the utmost care, usually by one of my elder sisters, with a bottle of wine and a few bottles of soft drinks (our Sunday treat) in the centre surrounded by the best plates in the house (part of Mum's dowry) and all placed carefully on the only tablecloth in the house, reserved solely for Sundays and special feast days.

Life was always hard and busy at home and Mum wouldn't relax until the youngest had been put to sleep and the remaining minor chores delegated to the elder children (myself included). Then, on summer evenings, she would carry her low, wooden, four-legged stool to the adjacent alley where she would meet up with other weary mothers to chat the evening away while playing the traditional tombola (bingo) game.

It was often my evening duty to wash the dishes, cutlery and crockery while Mum spent time with her friends. I was a very well-behaved and quiet boy, and never disobeyed my parents' biddings. I still remember being too short to reach the washing basin in the kitchen and having to stand on a wooden box to carry out my assigned duties. The pride reflected in Mum's smile and eyes, however, was enough for me to look forward to the following evening. But my washing up wasn't always a source of pride for my parents.

They never lost their religious fervour and there wasn't a room in the house that didn't have a holy picture adorning one of its walls. Mum's lifelong wish had always been that one day the family would be financially secure enough to visit Lourdes or Fatima. Next best to fulfilling this wish was the acquisition of souvenirs from those holy places. One day, a friend of hers, on her return from Lourdes, brought her a 6-inch-tall plastic replica of the Our Lady of Lourdes statue filled with water from the miraculous spring at Massabielle. I was too young to realise the significance and importance of this plastic statue for Mum and, after washing the dishes one evening, I noticed for the first time that it was filled with water. Thinking that it must have been filled with tap water by one of my brothers or sisters, and thinking that she wouldn't have liked to see that her precious souvenir was being used as a toy, I emptied it in the sink. Needless to say, Mum wanted to kill me when she realised what I had done. She shouted and chased me all around the house and only Dad's intervention calmed things down. It took her a whole two weeks to start being proud of me again. It seems that the water's miraculous properties became diluted with dishwater and its supernatural powers weren't strong enough to bale me out earlier.

Malta has always been a safe country to live in and this is especially true of our village of Naxxar. People, then, used to leave the front door key in the lock. This saved the time and energy of having to open the front door every time somebody called.

Cars and other vehicles were not as numerous back then. Village streets and alleys were practically free of traffic and served as the village playgrounds; children used to spend hours playing *passju* (hopscotch) or with the popular blue glass marbles all along our streets and alleys. Girls occupied other corners in the alley playing with *żibeġ* (beads) until it was time for us all to attend catechism classes at the church oratory or at the M.U.S.E.U.M, which stands for Magister Utinam Sequatur Evangelium Universus Mundus, translated as 'Divine Teacher, may the whole world follow Your Gospel'. This is a lay Catholic society founded in 1932 by a Maltese priest, now canonised and known as St George Preca specifically to provide children with a proper religious education. These two religious centres were situated in the core of the village, close to the church. On Sunday afternoons, however, we were exempt from lessons. Instead, our instructors used to take the whole group for a walk in the countryside during the winter months, and to the sea in summer.

Owning toys was practically unheard of in those difficult years, but we always managed to construct our own. A popular one among us boys was the wooden scooter made from two discarded ball-bearing wheels and two pieces of wood. Another popular toy was the *karru*, a small wooden platform and three discarded ball-bearing wheels – two to support the *karru* at the back and one in front to support the front steering handle made of a short, narrow strip of wood. To manage the steering handle one had to tie a piece of rope at both ends while another small strip of wood served as a brake lever attached to the back of the *karru*. It was quite a complicated piece of engineering for us young boys, and we were proud of having singlehandedly constructed such a roadworthy contraption. However, more often than not, we returned home bruised all over after constant overturning and crashing into walls. We never blamed our inability to handle the *karru* downhill at high speed; it was always some engineering defect in the three-wheeler, and we used to spend hours correcting what we thought were faults. But it was fun and we always went back to racing them again, ignoring the old, the not-so-old and the fresh bruises that adorned our young bodies.

Another childhood pastime was flying kites. One of my friends came from a long line of sheep-rearing families and his father owned a small flock which was his responsibility to tend. I often kept him company on winter mornings and since we never had much to do except watch for any straying sheep, we whiled away the hours flying kites. Kites weren't so difficult to construct once one knew how. All one required were a couple of thinly cut strips of bamboo, very flimsy coloured paper and string. For glue we used flour mixed with tinned milk and water. Then we would spend the whole morning trying to get our kites to stay aloft the longest and to soar the highest.

The annual village festa was the long-awaited event of the year. In fact, the whole village community's energy was focused solely on one particular date – 8th September. Our Lady of Victories, affectionately known by the Maltese as *il-Bambina*, is also celebrated at Mellieħa and L'Isla (Senglea) in Malta and at Xagħra in Gozo. This is the day when every member of the community dons brand new clothes specially made for the occasion. It's the day when money set aside is happily squandered; the day when children are given some money to spend at their whim; the day when local business booms. It's also the day when people who have given monthly donations throughout the year for new church and street decorations and for fireworks can critically inspect and comment on whether their money has been well spent.

We boys also looked forward to this special day. Not necessarily to enjoy church and street decorations, or to put on our best clothes, or watch the long and slow procession with the beautiful statue of Our Lady wind along the village streets. In fact, we weren't ever anywhere near the hub of the celebrations. My friends and I used to congregate in a field on the outskirts of the village, hiding behind rubble walls, close to where the fireworks were being set off. We were oblivious to the mortal danger to which we were exposing ourselves, interested only in collecting any stray, unexploded pieces. We would prise them open with a knife, mix the different pyrotechnic mixtures together and spread it all around an open space. Then we would set the whole thing alight to enjoy the resulting multi-coloured spectacle, totally ignorant that a particular mixture might not tolerate contact with any other.

We had no fear, even though reports of children blowing themselves up when tampering with unexploded fireworks weren't rare occurrences. We knew about these accidents but never believed that they could ever happen to us. Even today fatal accidents happen all the time when firework factories inexplicably blow up and people die or are maimed for life. Maturity has brought reflection as to how stupid we were, but boys will be boys and danger is sought rather than avoided.

Every rural family, without exception, was practically self-sufficient where food was concerned. Most grew their own produce, raised chickens, rabbits, goats and sheep. Some even baked their own bread and only Sundays saw them anywhere near a bakery. My family was no exception. We couldn't afford to let anything go to waste with so many mouths to feed, and I remember Mum spending hours in the kitchen pickling onions, olives and capers, drying figs, making jam and more. My responsibility in all this was the tending of drying tomatoes and cheeselets. The tomatoes would be spread along the roof parapet for the sun to dry while the cheeselets were kept in hanging cages. My job was to keep birds from getting at them. Regular practice, year in year out, at this job made me an extremely efficient scarecrow.

Summers in Malta can be insufferably hot and sleeping at night in bed under a heat-radiating ceiling feels as comfortable as a dish of macaroni at the bakers. The family still couldn't afford fans. The one and only option was to sleep on the roof under the stars on our hay-filled mattresses and pillows, which we carried up each night, and down on waking up every morning.

The late 1950s saw the first importation of televisions. It was still the black and white era of course but, needless to say, they were an instant sensation. Very few families could afford a set and my family was one of the very many who could not. But clubs, especially band clubs, immediately invested in one. And it immediately started paying high dividends. In fact, the one closest to our house, the Victoria Band Club, would be packed with patrons watching a veritable miracle. The front door would be kept shut as there wouldn't be any more room inside, but the front window would be kept open for those left outside who were tall enough to see over the heads of those sitting inside. There were only two Italian stations transmitting to Malta and since most people couldn't understand a word, the audience inside was very noisy while the few who could understand a few words in Italian would spend the whole evening shushing the majority, probably to emphasise their superior knowledge of foreign languages. The session would turn into a continuous argument with much movement of arms, but with all eyes riveted to the TV screen. Since the window was too high for us boys to reach, we used to take turns standing on one another's shoulders.

The pictures transmitted by these first sets were very grainy (in fact, sometimes it was just grains and no picture), but nothing could have kept us from the club's windows every evening, climbing up and down each other's backs like acrobats.

When I wasn't playing with my friends or doing chores, my father used to take me along with him wherever and whenever possible to reduce (by one) the number of children running around my ever-pregnant mother. I was a very shy boy, and never more so than when he would take me to his favourite bar in the village square for tea or coffee, which were served in glasses. I would sit next to him at his favourite table and he would greet his friends as they walked in. Some would make it to our table and joke with Dad, and sometimes ruffle my hair in friendly greeting. Dad would sometimes start boasting about what a strong boy I was turning out to be and give my bare thigh a slap to emphasise the size of my quadriceps (in those days boys would not start wearing long trousers until well past puberty – a condition still too far away in the future as far as I was concerned). Dad was very strong and an affectionate slap could have easily brought tears to my eyes. But, more often than not, I would cling to his side, seemingly affectionately, to hide the tears I felt overflowing my glazy eyes.

New Year's Day was another favourite date for us children – even more so than Christmas Day. We always referred to New Year's Day as *l-Istrina*, but we never knew what the word meant or its origin; we couldn't care less as long as we received the traditional penny from Dad and some of his friends. This tradition is probably centuries old and seems to vary from some villages to others. But, whatever its origins, it's always the children who end up as beneficiaries. I still recall waking up on every first of January determined to be as good as possible all day and to do nothing untoward that would spoil Dad's good humour and tempt him to break with tradition. Every year he would take me along to the village square where he would meet with most of his friends who, like him, were always accompanied by their own children. Being shy and quiet, I always stuck to Dad's side, but friends of mine, who usually spent their time running around creating mischief, could be seen on this particular day hovering around their fathers, being extra solicitous and very eager to see to their

13

every need. It was the only day of the year when they were as pleasing and well behaved as one could imagine, anxious lest their fathers might have forgotten the significance of the date. The men would act normally, as if the first of January was just a normal day, enjoying the pampering showered upon them by their children and, at the same time, pitying the anxious looks in the children's eyes. They would then laughingly dig in their pockets for the many pennies they had kept ready since early morning and distribute them among all of us. I loved *l-Istina*. I loved to feel the weight of my money box at the end of every New Year's Day.

This tradition lasted well past my childhood and into the early 1970s, when the standard of living was much higher and children were already receiving pocket money every weekend.

Throughout my childhood, Dad's business grew slowly and steadily, and his name became widely known. His popularity in the village grew with his business as did the respect afforded him. His popularity eventually reached other neighbouring villages, and while the locals still continued to affectionately address him as Bertu, new acquaintances from outside the village started addressing him as *Sur* (mister) Bert. At first this unaccustomed title sounded alien to his ears, but he gradually got used to it and eventually began to enjoy the good feeling of having reached the first elusive milestone.

This hard-earned and long-awaited prosperity didn't in any way affect his lifestyle. He remained the person he had always been, enjoying life's simple pleasures and the company of his lifelong friends. But he could now, together with Mum, afford to worry less about making ends meet, and this was reflected in his generosity towards his friends on Sunday mornings.

Even the local church benefitted; Mass was always the start of our Sunday morning together and I remember him waiting his turn to be given a chair by the sexton in charge. The sexton stood just beyond the entrance guarding hundreds of wooden chairs stacked high in rows against the wall. People used to pay him two or three farthings for the hire of a chair. Some just couldn't afford even such a measly amount and would prefer spending a whole hour standing. Dad, however, used to pay him a full penny. A full penny! But a penny went quite a long way in those hard times. In fact, the sexton had to continually be on the lookout for anyone trying to sneak behind him and grab a chair for free.

This 'chair system' enabled everyone, especially the old people, to occupy a favourite spot in church year in year out. And, on someone's death, one would be able to notice a vacant spot during the following Sunday Mass until it was eventually and perpetually taken over by someone else.

The revenue from the hiring of chairs was required for the maintenance of the majestic building and for the sexton's wages. In time, the charge was raised to one penny and the elderly and the poor felt the pinch, especially since they attended Mass every day. This was a time when there was a voluntary segregation of sexes inside the church. Women occupied the middle section while the men were relegated to the sides – undoubtedly a remnant of the strict discipline exerted by the Church until the middle of the twentieth century. It was also the time when women wore black veils to church and the older ones the traditional *għonnella* (faldetta) which was already on its way out. (The *għonnella* was a traditional headdress, but nothing like the familiar veil. It is erroneously referred to in English as 'faldetta'. The *għonnella* covered not just the head, but went all the way down to just below the calves.)

In time, seating in church became more organised with the installation of comfortable benches systematically placed all round the building. Women began opting for a lighter-coloured veil while the *għonnella* vanished completely with the passing away of the older generation. These changes heralded the end of segregation and whole families could be seen attending Mass and praying together.

Malta occupies just 310 square km of land, but with a population of over 400,000, it is one of the world's most densely populated countries. In spite of the island's small size, however, practically every village in Malta and Gozo speaks its distinct dialect. Dialects sound harsher than the 'more rounded' language spoken by city dwellers, but they also sound more musical and villagers are proud of their dialects. They distinguish them from everybody else. Today, villages are no longer isolated; modern transport has shortened distances and industrialisation has contributed to the mixing of villagers and city dwellers at places of work and entertainment. Villagers have learned to speak the city language, but they remain villagers at heart. They are proud of their village heritage reflected in the dialect they speak. And when two from the same village happen to be in mixed company, they happily talk to each other in dialect to the consternation of the others.

All around Malta, names given at baptism are habitually shortened into what sound like pet names. Grazziella is usually shortened to Gracie; Bartholomew to Bertu; Joseph to Żeppu. Mine, Angelo, was shortened to Ġolu. When I was still a young boy everybody called me by the diminutive Ġulinu, more appropriate for a still young Ġolu. While everybody at home called me Ġulinu, Dad started calling me Ġolu from the day I was born. It was only at school, where I was registered by my baptismal name, that I was called Angelo. When I grew older I felt like a person with many aliases. When I was married and settled down, however, I was determined to eliminate all this confusion. But it took me some time and a lot of determination to persuade everybody to address me by the Maltese version of my name – Anġlu.

Malta in World War 2

2

The Village Boy

(1961–1964) 9–12 years

I consider this period a turning point in the fortunes of my family and, more significantly, the period that determined my way forward in life.

Politically, Malta was slowly coming out of a serious constitutional crisis following the Mintoff Labour Government's *en bloc* resignation in 1958. This was brought about by the stalemate in the government's negotiations with its British counterpart regarding financial and political terms that would have sealed Malta's integration with Britain. Our constitution was suspended and there followed four long years of colonial rule from London. As a direct result, investment all but dried up, unemployment figures rocketed while the politico-religious conflict continued to further compound the situation.

All political parties in Malta, especially the two major ones, demanded early general elections. But the British dragged their feet. The infighting that characterised Maltese politics at the time suited their purpose of maintaining the status quo. But the situation couldn't be prolonged indefinitely and at last elections were scheduled for the 17th–19th February 1962. The voters' turnout was high, as always, and Malta regained self-government.

The Nationalists were returned to power after an absence of eight years and Prime Minister George Borg Olivier made it immediately clear that he wanted to start early talks with the British Government, which would lead to Independence.

As children, we were still too young to understand what was going on. Politics were rarely, if ever, discussed at home and never in our presence. We continued to play, attend school and do whatever children our age usually did. However, following the 1962 election, and with Independence not too far off in the future, businessmen and investors started regaining their faith in the country. After Independence a building boom took off. It lasted a number of years, during which ordinary working class people became rich and the rich became richer. It gave new life to the building industry which generated employment and led to further investment in other sectors of the economy and to further new employment.

Dad was not one to wait for Independence to start experimenting in land speculation. His now finely tuned business acumen did not let him down and he started buying fields and barren land at very low prices to resell within months (or sometimes mere weeks or days), albeit at a small profit. The frequency of these transactions increased his income dramatically overnight. The family could now say, at long last, that it had turned the corner.

With more available cash and more in the offing, Dad decided to build a larger farm to house his now-growing herd of bulls and pigs (a later addition) in the outskirts of the village. The transfer to a new and larger farm was imperative as the two sheds where the bulls were housed had become too crowded and the large beasts would very often become nervous with the consequence that they would pull at the ropes round their horns, cut themselves free and escape. Sometimes this would happen in the middle of the night and Dad would be woken up by neighbours knocking on our front door to inform him that his bulls were (again) roaming the streets and alleys of Naxxar and causing panic. Dad would insist that I shouldn't accompany him to the round-up, but I would insist and promise that I would stay in his old pick-up truck at the entrance to the farm to watch the spectacle from a vantage point. Not that it was anything as spectacular as the 'running with the bulls' in Pamplona! Dad and some of his workers would just coax the animals back to the farm and that was that. And in the morning the streets and alleys would stink with bulls' dung!

I vividly remember the transfer of the animals from the old to the new farm, with Dad directing and coaxing the herd through the narrow streets, now completely empty of people who were wise enough to give the animals as wide a berth as possible. With the animals happily accommodated in larger spaces and in a more rural environment, Dad thought that it was his large family's turn to enjoy more elbow room. So he decided to build a new and larger house close to his farm. It was built and made ready for habitation within a couple of months – just in time to welcome Mum from hospital with baby Paul in her arms.

The house was enormous, very similar to a modern, large bungalow, with very large rooms that required some getting used to after a lifetime in confined spaces, but the years I lived in this new house were the happiest of my childhood. Its proximity to the farm meant that Dad was always around and easy for other farmers to reach when they wanted to talk business. Mum could now grow all the vegetables she required and was often assisted by the neighbouring farmhands. It was also safe for us, as we could run about the large terraces and vast fields under the watchful eyes of Mum or Dad. We even had a telephone installed – a real luxury in those days (there were only just over 5,000 private telephones in Malta at that time).

The place was idyllic, surrounded by fields and unspoiled nature. At night, the area was in total darkness and completely isolated, the silence absolute. Apart from the occasional barking of dogs from some distant farms and the isolated bellow of an insomniac bull from our farm, it was so quiet that we could sometimes even hear the swishing sound of snakes as they writhed among stalks of long grass.

On summer evenings we would have our dinner on the front patio which overlooked Mosta with the old capital, Mdina, dominating the skyline. The patio was also the ideal spot to sit on a starry night and watch the fireworks during Malta's long festa season.

Although some of us were no longer small children, Dad still insisted that we should have the best and most nutritious food and Mum would oblige with abundance. She cooked enough to feed a convent and none of us children dared leave an uneaten last morsel, as a sidelong glance from Dad was enough to make us wipe our plates clean.

Although idyllic, a problem we had to face from day one was the much longer distance of our new home from the shops in the village. Those were days when families did their shopping on a daily basis and specifically for the day's requirements. Supermarkets were unheard of and 'freezer' was just a word we learned to spell at school. Dad solved the problem by buying me a sturdy bicycle, ideal to ride over the rough terrain around our house. It was the first non-homemade toy ever to cross our threshold.

I was so proud to fetch the daily shopping and, needless to say, I made the most of this new 'responsibility'; I rode 'my' bicycle every day, over every imaginable street and country lane, up the steepest hill and down the most dangerous rocky valley. The machine became my constant companion. I became an expert rider and the daily strenuous exercise strengthened my leg muscles considerably. No wonder Dad would proudly slap my well-developed quadriceps in the presence of his friends at the village bar.

When I was twelve years old I decided to enter a cycle race during my school's annual sports day, determined to prove my riding abilities. Now much taller and sitting on my bicycle on the starting line, I suppose I must have seemed not a little awkward to the hundreds of students and parents watching from the terraces at the old Empire Stadium in Gżira. And I must have seemed even more so when, all around me, the other competitors were equipped with the latest expensive racers, all larger than the one I was sitting on, complete with multiple changeable gears. Although my mind was fully focused on the race ahead, I can still imagine the smiles and sniggers on both sides of me. But on the word 'go' I started pedalling as if my life depended on it. My legs pumped as never before and soon I found myself in the lead. The low centre of gravity of my bicycle enabled me to speed round the bends more easily than my rivals' large racers and I continued to lead even down the straights. At the end of the third lap around the quarter mile track I still had enough strength left to sprint the final one. However, inexplicably, one of the officials ordered me to stop. I thought I was being disqualified for some infringement I knew nothing about and was on the point of protesting, but he immediately informed me that I had won the race, which I thought was four laps long. I looked back and noticed that the second placed rider was still half a lap behind while a few metres ahead was a cyclist I intended to lap in my final sprint. I can't describe the pride I felt when the American Ambassador presented me with my first trophy.

All around our property there was enough open ground for Dad to teach me to drive a cart and pony. When I became confident and adept enough, he also taught me to ride on the pony's back. This was more fun and even more comfortable than the bicycle along the rough pathways separating the fields.

Growing up on a farm I gained all sorts of skills, including milking sheep, which Mum taught me in the small garden next to the kitchen. Milking sheep was a knack that fascinated me as a young boy and Mum enjoyed teaching me, especially since I would eventually take over this daily chore and she would have that extra hour for the other never-ending work in the house and fields. When I became quite proficient at this new undertaking, I began looking forward to waking up very early each morning. This gave me ample time to furnish the whole family with its daily requirement of milk.

Milking sheep, however, was not my only job; I often gave my father a helping help with the hard work at the farm, but it was a challenge for one so young. He taught me how to mix bulls' feed, but his shovel was too big for me to handle, so I improvised with something handier. Even a half bucketful of dry fodder was too heavy for me and I had to drag it along the ground to the bull shed. At first, Dad wouldn't let me in near the bulls to tip the fodder into the animals' manger as he considered it dangerous for me to squeeze my small body between such enormous beasts. But in time he taught me how to twist an animal's tail to the right to make it turn left and create enough space for me to pass. It was still a dangerous manoeuvre, however, but as a young boy I ignored the danger and enjoyed the adventure. Thinking back, I now realise that I could easily have been killed or maimed for life. A friend of mine had his chin broken by a back kick and the palm of my father's hand was run through by one of his bull's pointed horn. Similar accidents were daily occurrences among cattle breeders.

Dad's bull breeding business required him to wake up as early as four in the morning. This gave him just enough time to coax the previously selected mature bulls onto his truck and drive them all the way to the abattoir. My contribution in bull breeding had been limited to mixing the feed and dragging it to the manger and I eventually thought that it was about time that I learn the whole process to the very end. So I began pestering Dad to wake me up at four on days off from school and take me with him to the slaughterhouse. I used to enjoy the whole process of the efficient and painless killing of bulls and pigs, and of branding and selling the different parts of carcasses to butchers right there on the spot. The whole operation was so fast that I could accompany him even on schooldays and manage to be back in time for school.

After school I used to sow corn along a narrow pathway through which water and drainage from the bulls' sheds oozed slowly down to a nearby field. Being so well irrigated and fertilised, the corn grew fast and strong. Then, once a week, I would harvest some of the still-green stalks and sell them as rabbit feed to nearby villagers. I tied them up in bundles of three or four and placed them in an old pushchair which I pushed all the way to the village. I would walk from door to door, knocking on every one, and ask for three pence a bundle. I learned to haggle with housewives when they considered my price too high compared to the two and a half-penny bundles they bought from a peddler doing his rounds of the village on a horse-drawn cart. I would insist that my corn was thicker and, therefore, contained more food for the rabbits. The women would look down on me with a smile and eventually buy, convinced that they were getting better value for their money. I earned about twenty shillings each time, and at twice weekly I was earning as much as a labourer earned in three or four days. Mum was delighted every time I handed her a full pound Sterling in small change for just a half-day effort.

At this young age I was already drawing plans for rooms which I then constructed in rubble walls in the open grounds around our home. I would draw the plans with different layouts, always with 1.2-metre-high walls and roofed over with long, cane stalks. I was so proud of them that I would ask my parents to let me sleep in one of the rooms I had constructed on different sites around the house. Needless to say, they never let me.

Every winter there was an area close by which would be overgrown with a very tall green species of thorn. I decided that this was to be my secret hideout which no one else would enter unless invited. I even hacked out a passage through the growth and formed various square areas that served as 'rooms' in the very centre where my friends and I would congregate and sit around chatting, unseen by other human eyes. Much later, a developer bought the land and built on it. I felt as though I had been evicted from my property.

All this planning, drawing and construction was the result of my inborn talent for creativity which would shape my future successful career.

After a few weeks in the new house, the realisation dawned on me that I was now living in the very surroundings I used to escape to when I wanted to enjoy the unspoiled open areas and the beauty of nature. I remember hurrying one morning with kite in hand to join my shepherd friend a few fields away from home, when suddenly I stopped in my tracks. I looked back open-mouthed at our house. Then I shifted my gaze towards the village which seemed so distant, with the distant church steeples marking the very centre of an ever-sprawling and crowded cluster of buildings. I then realised that just a few weeks back I had to walk quite a long distance along narrow and winding alleys and past isolated farmhouses beyond the village boundary before I came upon the open fields which were my friend's favourite pasture.

Mum's parents had their home and farm just 500 metres away from ours, so it was now easier to visit them more often. The house was a typical old Maltese rural residence, comprising a large internal courtyard surrounded by all the rooms of the house. This type of building rendered air conditioning superfluous. It fronted on a wide, open public area ideal for outdoor games and I remember the evenings when Nanna Zulla (Grace) invited friends from neighbouring farms. They all used to sit in a semi-circle outside Nanna's front door to play tombola and chat till the late hours. The house has recently been restored to its former magnificence and will probably be scheduled as an authentic Maltese rural residence.

Their farm was typically Maltese, close to their house, and where they raised all kinds of animals. I remember spending hours watching the variety of poultry running around unhindered by fences, pecking away among the pigs in their pen, and the cows, horses, the solitary donkey, ducks, cats and dogs, all running freely around the large area reserved for them. Then the large number of pigeons would suddenly take off in fright at an unexpected grunting of a pig or the barking of a dog. There was also a fish pond with goldfish as long as my forearm. Outside this veritable zoo, Nannu Bertu had his fields where he grew all kinds of fruit and vegetables.

We always enjoyed our visits to Nannu's farm. We were fascinated by the animals and used to sit for long hours watching their antics, games and sometimes fights over favourite food. Even now, fifty years later, I can still visualise the whole scene like a picture on a canvas.

Nannu used to let us walk around with him among the animals while feeding them and recounting stories which, I'm now certain, were his inventions on the spur of the moment. He made us laugh and he laughed with us. I can still picture him now, smiling at us, surrounded by all the animals he loved so much – a latter day Francis of Assisi.

An *ghonnella* wearer, Nanna Zulla was a regular churchgoer, whatever the weather. When eventually the ghonnella died out, everyone realised that a national symbol had *disappeared* for good. It was certainly impractical in modern day Malta, but suddenly everybody realised that the country had lost a custom that could never be resurrected. When later in life I was courting my future wife I had her picture taken wearing Nanna Zulla's *ghonnella*. It was a decision I have never regretted and neither has my wife.

The area close to home was blessed with a quaint country chapel – one of many that Malta and Gozo are dotted with. Most are centuries old and erected either to commemorate the end of some plague, which from time to time depleted the island's population, the deliverance from attacks of African pirates who infested the Mediterranean since time immemorial, or as ex-voto offerings from individuals following religious pledges with particular saints and, more often, with Our Lady under one of her many titles.

In their heydays, these chapels, so far from village centres, were frequented by isolated farmers and hunters. But in time, with villages and towns expanding and transport becoming more efficient, their importance diminished and most were reduced to a bad state of disrepair. Eventually, however, their historical and architectural importance was recognised, and they are now being restored, especially since the introduction of local government in all localities.

Our chapel was dedicated to '*Il-Madonna tax-Xagħra*', literally translated as 'Our Lady of the Barren Land', probably for the infertile, rocky land surrounding it. It was kept closed the year round except on its feast day when the old priest would ask Mum and her friends to give the chapel a good clean up. He would also ask me and my friend to help him prepare for Mass. We used to arrive at the chapel an hour before to ring the bells on the roof and summon the farmers in the area. We used to ring the bells so hard and fast that the din we created would be heard from miles away, but the old priest never reprimanded us. He was either too deaf or too old to bother.

After Easter came the family blessing by the parish priest. He used to do the rounds of every household in the village and its surroundings. In those days, the parish priest would enter every room in the house, blessing every corner with holy water as if to furry out a devil that might be lurking behind some piece of furniture. When the blessing was over, the parish priest would sit down, surrounded by all the members of the family who happened to be in. He would then humbly accept some whisky and a donation for the church while writing down the family details in a notebook, confirming that all the members above the age of seven had abided by the Church precept of receiving Holy Communion at least once a year.

Mum was very strict about this annual household blessing. She made us all stay indoors; all clean and in our best clothes until the blessing was over. Woe upon whoever dared disobey. I enjoyed being sprinkled with holy water, but the long wait for the parish priest was too much when there was so much fun waiting to be had outside. I used to huff and puff and fidget, and complain that the parish priest was taking too long. It was always the same every year; I would go out and stand on the doorstep, gaze towards the village and hope to catch a glimpse of the priest walking down the country lane leading to our house. Then I would look at the rapidly setting sun and at the open ground beckoning me.

'Mum,' I would shout back to where everybody was waiting, 'it seems he won't be coming this year. Can't I just nip outside just for a few –'

'If you step outside just for a second I won't let you out for a whole week,' she would shout back.

I would then literally sprint all the way back to where my brothers and sisters would be waiting. This pantomime would repeat itself a couple of times more, until the sun had all but set, and at last the tired parish priest would walk in. By the time the blessing was over and done with, it would be too dark to venture outside.

Dad had, by now, become the leading farming contractor in our village and surrounding localities. He used to contract farmers to sell him all their wheat as soon as it was sown. Then, when it matured in summer, he would employ extra labourers to harvest the crop with hand scythes. The harvest would then be tied up in bunches and grouped in a centralised field, ready for the harvesting machine. The bundles would then be untied and formed into many heaps. Harvesting was carried out during the night when the straws lose the brittleness caused by the hot summer sun. The operation that followed was a spectacle in itself; a tractor would generate electric power to a number of floodlights on top of the driver's cabin to illuminate a large area of the field and, at the same time, drive its strong wide driving rubber belt that is connected to the large harvesting machine. This, in turn, would move three other belts connected to different specialised parts, which do the actual separating of the wheat crop as it moves inside the machine.

The wheat to be processed was usually collected in a heap on either side of the harvesting machine. Two or three men would stand on top of one of them and throw the crop in tied bunches to two other men standing on the machine, close to the main pinned crushing motor. In one swift movement, these two men would cut loose and throw each bunch into the wide opening of the crushing drum. This part of the operation was dangerous as it was performed at great speed with the sharp spikes rotating extremely fast and close to the completely exposed wide opening. Therefore, the team operating at this end was often rotated to avoid accidents caused by tiredness or lack of concentration.

In the meantime, the actual processing would be taking place inside the harvesting machine, where the crop was separated in three parts – the grain, the stalk and the beards of corn. The two latter parts were automatically and separately carried to the back of the machine where two different, long and moveable outlets literally sprayed the straw into heaps. The grain, in the meantime, was passed through a vibrating sieve on its way to a wide pipe, which ended in two openings as it exited the machine at the side. A worker would be responsible for filling the grain in jute bags while ensuring that one opening was blocked until the first bag was full. The remaining soil and root-entangled small stones ended up underneath the machine. Although safer and more efficient harvesting machines have been developed since then, this harvester was a magnificent invention at the time, and I always followed the whole process with awe and fascination.

This was definitely a job for men, but various women and children would be at hand to do odd jobs that rendered the men's work less strenuous. Some of my friends and I would be standing by to pass hot coffee and water around when required, which the workers would gratefully gulp down in a hurry. In fact, I had to wait until I was fifteen years old to be allowed to participate in the actual harvesting. I worked in all the stages of the process, but the one stage I least enjoyed was the packing of the straws in large, square baskets made from rope, which resembled caskets when full.

We put the beards of corn in jute bags and this was usually carried out on the morrow of the harvesting, when the sun would be very hot. It was hard, hot work, with perspiration literally pouring from our bodies. It would leave us covered from head to toe with dust and tiny particles of straw, turning our skin into fine sandpaper. It required a lot of soap and water to wash everything off, but our skin always ended up all scratched and raw through contact with the brittle straw.

But even after this was completed the day wasn't over; we then had to load it all onto trucks and deliver it to various farms as animal fodder. We would have to unload and empty everything in enclosed sheds and warehouses, which was suffocating work; fine dust and other microscopic particles still managed to find their way into our nostrils and throats in spite of having handkerchiefs covering our faces like cowboy films bandits. Even our heads would be covered with handkerchiefs, knotted at the corners to fit snugly. But it was never enough, as every once in a while we would have to run outside to fill our lungs with fresh air and sometimes to simply cough and retch.

Springtime was another matter completely. It was potato picking time and, as children, we looked forward to the day Dad would ask us to help. We would all run barefoot behind a horse-pulled plough which formed long furrows and exposed the beautiful crop in clusters of four or five. We would vie with each other to pick the largest amount of potatoes until, with arms full, we would race to empty them in the wicker baskets held by our elders. Sometimes one of us would fall in the soft soil, spilling all the potatoes, and everybody would laugh, including the elders. The day would pass and everybody would be happy and tired and ready for a well-deserved dinner, including the horse. Thus, I learned practically all there was to know about potato growing and, later in life, I would play a major role in the whole process from sowing the seed to exporting the final crop. But I shall write about all this in a later chapter

During weekends, farmers wearing their traditional cap (*beritta*) and sandals (*qrieq*) would call at our house to settle their accounts with Dad. He had organised a sort of office with a small desk underneath the staircase. His bookkeeping system consisted simply of small chits of paper on which he jotted down signs and figures only he could understand. Though almost totally illiterate, his memory was such that he was able to state the exact dates and value of produce each farmer delivered, and used to add whole lists of figures as fast as a modern calculator. He dealt mostly in cash, so his contact with banks, at that time, was minimal and he would only engage the services of a qualified bookkeeper during weekends at the peak of the spring season.

I stayed close to him during these business transactions, studying and absorbing his body language, and the way he concluded successful deals. I could see that farmers were quite pleased with the way he dealt with them. Many of them would give me a small tip on their way out and at the end of the day I would deposit all in my money box. Negotiations would be held in a very friendly manner and with jokes flying to and fro. However, I remember one time when a farmer contested a balance in a transaction involving the sum of 20 Maltese liri – a large sum at the time. Neither Dad nor the farmer would give way.

At the end of the inconclusive argument, the farmer smiled and said, 'Ok. No one wins. So I'll give the money to your son!' I was astounded to see that large amount of money in my hands. I just couldn't close my fist over all that paper money and couldn't imagine how I was going to push it through the small slit in my money box. When the farmer left, Dad asked for the money, as it was owed to him. I gave it to him with a deep sigh of relief.

During this period, he was buying and selling fields for agricultural purposes. Sometimes he even dealt in small farmhouses. He would feel proud in buying these properties on a preliminary agreement and resell then to third parties, even if at a small profit, before the actual signing of the final deed. This meant that he made a clear untaxed profit.

All of these profitable business transactions translated into a better quality of life for the family. It also meant that my next brother, Joe, who was only eight or nine at the time, would never go through the experience I had, witnessing the gradual change in Dad's fortunes from his humble beginnings to the very successful businessman he became. My sisters, especially the eldest, had their days full with helping Mum raise the younger children and were never involved in the hard work at the farm (my elder sisters, Sperry and Grace, were now old enough to assist the younger ones during their first years at school – assistance they both missed when they were young since Mum and Dad were practically illiterate and too busy raising a large family). This meant that the experience I gained throughout the years accompanying and helping Dad rendered me the only one with enough knowhow to assist him in the farming business.

In 1964, Malta won her Independence from Great Britain. This freedom was won at a price as we now had to survive without the financial assistance Britain gave us as her colony, and without the expenditure of the thousands of British services personnel stationed in Malta.

In response to this, the government immediately initiated a scheme of grants and subsidies to entrepreneurs willing to invest in five star hotels and factories. These incentives were a success as they attracted massive investment especially from abroad. Overnight Malta found itself on the tourist map and began attracting large, prestigious international conferences. These generated a snowballing effect as many foreigners, especially British, started buying property in Malta to settle permanently or spend their winters away from the freezing temperatures of Northern Europe. This huge influx of investment created a demand for property, and property agents and developers started looking for any kind of land their money could buy, irrespective of whether a building permit would eventually be granted or not. The few local building contractors weren't prepared for the ever-growing demand for their services and heavy investments were made in machinery and employment by both local and foreign building contractors. What followed was a building boom that lasted years and generated thousands of jobs, giving the economy a surge forward.

Dad, whose nose for business opportunities was now very finely tuned, immediately diversified his interests from buying farmland for farming to buying land for speculation. Thus dawned a new era for Malta's economy and for our family fortunes.

 Naxxar Village

3

Teenage Aspirations

(1965–1968) 13–16 years

As the demand for land and property continued at a constant rate, property agents and speculators turned their attention to sites that commanded beautiful panoramas, where prestigious villas could be developed to satisfy up-market clients. Our large, fully detached villa and farm were situated in such an area, and soon enough a new development started to take shape close by. A huge, beautiful villa was quickly being erected for a very wealthy English family. I used to walk over to the site every day to chat with the builders while admiring the beautiful layout of the building with its large, landscaped swimming pool – something completely innovative for a young teenager like me. Soon more villas were taking shape all around our property and my poor rubble-stone rooms quickly became victims of the unforgiving excavator. Although Dad was making large profits from his property business dealings, he wouldn't give up the farming side of his affairs.

I remember one evening around this time that was a massive turning point in my life. I was thirteen and we were all sitting at home during a family gathering to which some of my father's friends were often invited. At one point during the conversation, one of Dads friends turned on me and asked, 'So, Gulino. What would you like to be when you grow up?'

I immediately stood up and very assertively replied, 'A business-man. A successful businessman.'

All smiled at me and at one another, probably because I was usually too shy and withdrawn, and my unequivocal declaration must have pleasantly surprised them. Thinking they could continue with what they must have considered a game, another asked me, 'A businessman? That's good, Gulino. Very good. But what sort of a businessman?'

I shrugged and replied, 'I don't know yet. But I shall definitely become a big businessman.'

Everyone kept looking at me for a few moments. Then somebody changed the subject and I was quickly side-lined and forgotten. It seems, however, that a few of the family friends did not take my answer completely lightly. The sheer determination of my replies and the spontaneity with which I gave them must have set them thinking. Others, however, still kept treating me as Bertu's shy, young son and every once in a while would repeat the question, probably to see how long my 'vocation' would last. They hadn't yet realised that my answers were instinctive. That deep inside me I knew what I wanted to make of my life.

It was at around this time that Dad decided that I should continue my secondary education at Stella Maris College in Gżira. The school was run by the La Salle Christian Brothers and it was then considered one of the best private schools in Malta. I had a lot of catching up to do to keep up with my new class mates, but within a few months I was doing as well as the rest. By the end of the first year I was one of the top students in spite of having to plod along on my own, without any assistance at home and without attending any private lessons.

It was also around this time that Dad decided to enter the potato export market to Holland. This new initiative on my father's part enabled me to experience the complete potato production throughout its stages, from the seeding, cultivation and harvesting, to the screening of the resulting crop into 32-kilo bags and their transport to the harbour for shipment to the distribution contractors in Rotterdam.

Since Dad's English vocabulary didn't go further than 'yes' and 'no', I, at thirteen, was appointed his *de facto* interpreter when he had to deal with the Dutch agents in Malta, and subsequently, when we travelled together to Holland to supervise the auctioning of our product.

Maltese potatoes were in high demand in Holland, but the long sea voyage, coupled with frequent handling along the way, resulted in more than a few rotten potatoes at journey's end. This entailed further selection on the part of the Dutch importers, but our potatoes, easily identified by the licence number boldly stencilled on each bag, always attracted the highest bidders. This was thanks to the high quality of the soil in our area of Naxxar and the care taken during the process of selection and handling of the crop.

The Dutch importers always treated us to dinner on our visits to Rotterdam. Since I was the 'official' interpreter, and since much business talk was carried out during these meals, I invariably ended up barely touching the first course. I always remember how Dad never bothered about the cutlery provided and would use his penknife to my utter embarrassment.

When business in Rotterdam would be over and done with, and with one day to go before our return to Malta, Dad would ask me to take him to a bus station. There we would board a bus (any bus) and ride it to its final destination. The ride would last over one hour. Then we would ride the same bus back to the station, reviewing the same sights we saw an hour earlier. Over the years I suppose I got to see quite a lot of Rotterdam.

The whole potato process starts with seeding time in winter. Mum and other women would spend many long evenings cutting seed potatoes into smaller pieces – usually five. That's already five seeds from one potato. When this slow, manual labour is over, the ploughing process starts. Seeding was simple enough; we tied an open-ended jute bag horizontally and apron-like around our waists, with the openings within easy reach of our hands. To keep the openings from sagging, and to further support the weight of the seeds inside the bag, both ends of the bag were tied to two ends of a short, thin rope which we hung around our necks.

With the bags full of seeds, we walked bare-foot along the furrows with both hands busy collecting the seeds from inside the bag and planting them singly about fifty centimetres apart. We would then press the seeds further down in the soil with our bare feet as we walked along.

This was hard work on cold winter days, with our unprotected feet completely numb since our slow walk along the furrows never generated enough energy to warm our blood and increase its circulation around our bodies. And the situation worsened when it rained with just a plastic bag to protect our heads while our feet sank in the soggy soil. We would stop only when it rained hard and would take whatever scant cover trees or rubble walls could provide.

At lunchtime we would stop for a short rest and a quick snack, which usually consisted of half a loaf of Maltese crusty bread, sliced and spread with oil, fresh tomato, a slice of ham and a chunk of cheese, all sprinkled with salt and pepper. Mum would wake very early each morning to prepare this delicacy so popular among the Maltese. Then we drank almond or orange essence diluted with water. Our hands would be, by then, coal black with soil and potato skin, but with no water anywhere around we would eat our lunches with black hands and all. I always found it funny how, while our hands practically ended up all black, the tips of our fingers never lost their skin colour!

When the plants sprouted we had to nurse them very carefully. Constant weeding by hand would have to be carried out for weeks. To protect the still-fragile plant we would use a hoe to build small mounds of soil around the stalks. This protected them from strong winds, cold spells and the notoriously hot sun.

With the coming of spring, Dad (licensed as number 104 to act as broker between farmers and exporter) was the most popular and successful producer in our region, and he would ask me to take some days off from school to help him cope with his increased responsibilities. He would also take on about a dozen part-timers, mostly women from our area, to do the selection of the crop by hand and place it in jute bags that took 32 kilos. These were supplied directly by the exporter. I would join these helpers on a pickup truck, together with a large number of empty bags, to begin our visits to various fields.

My younger brothers and sisters had, by now, also been recruited by Dad to do their bit. Their job was to print each bag with Dad's licence number with black powder dissolved in water. They used a normal shoe brush and a steel stencil. It was all fun for them, young as they were, to play with brush and paint. And it was even more fun when a sudden, unexpected jolt would overturn the mixture, turning everyone black from head to foot. Mum, of course, wouldn't share in their fun on our return home in the evening.

Arriving at these fields, we would find heaps of scattered potatoes protected from the elements by the plants' own leaves. We would remove the leaves from the top of the heaps and begin the proper selection with the jute bags rolled back at our sides. We would then discard all the very small cherry potatoes and any deformed or damaged ones; these would be the first to rot during the long sea voyage to Holland and even if they survived the trip, they would definitely not be acceptable to the buyer.

When the bags were full, two men would sew the openings with flasks (one short string from a piece of thick rope) with a very large darning needle in readiness for the official weigher who weighed two bags at a time on a special hand tool supported on the shoulders of two strong men.

It was during this time, with my eighteenth birthday a lifetime in the future, that I learnt to drive. I decided I couldn't wait to get behind a steering wheel and Dad's pickup truck's presence was a constant temptation. I could barely reach the foot pedals, but the grey Peugeot's gear lever was attached to the steering column and that made for better control. The large fields we were touring each day were ideal training grounds, though not exactly with the smoothest surface on earth. But with the distant rubble walls and the soft soil as the only obstacles to drive into, I soon became adept enough to be allowed to drive Dad's vehicles on all surfaces, including main roads. I was breaking the law, of course, but in those days road discipline was quite slack and traffic wasn't as heavy as it is today.

When the potato selection was over, and on the eve of the crops' export to Holland, trucks overflowing with bagfuls would start arriving at the harbour from all around Malta. They would form long queues to wait all night for the final inspection in the morning. As many as thirty to forty trucks could be seen at first light with their drivers standing beside them, stretching their cramped joints, eager for a cup of coffee and for the whole business to start. Then, gradually, the first four or five trucks would be ordered to move forward to where the wooden grading trolleys were situated. The official inspector would point at twenty bags at random to be weighed. When satisfied, he orders that two or three bags be opened and their contents emptied on the grader. If they were found to be below the required specifications, more bags from the same truck were sampled and if the contents were again found unacceptable, the truck was turned back so that the whole consignment was unloaded and graded to the inspector's satisfaction. This would waste everybody's time because everybody wanted to get the whole thing over and done with as early as possible.

When the grading was carried out to the inspector's complete satisfaction, the trucks would be unloaded manually and the bags put in the potato shed – a one-storey building open on all four sides for good ventilation. From then on, our potatoes would be the stevedores' responsibility. It would be their job to transfer the bags on to barges and later to the ship. With so much rough handling, even before the produce had left Malta, and the inadequately ventilated cargo ship, it was no wonder that so many potatoes were rotten at their final destination in Holland.

I sometimes accompanied our truck driver Żeppu throughout this exercise, which I enjoyed immensely. During these operations at the docks I met with one of the stevedore contractors, Armando Chircop, with whom I spent a long time talking and joking during the whole operation. He was the person responsible for the cargo from the time of its final inspection to its loading on the ship. To date, after forty-three years, he and his wife Anna are still two of my family's closest friends.

All in all, I enjoyed this whole spring potato process of unpaid family effort.

When I was about fifteen and (although a little nervous) after making sure Dad was in quite a good mood, I told him that I wished to start my own business. I was understandably surprised with his total rejection.

'No!' he shouted back. 'Going into business is very risky and you must avoid this type of career.' Looking at me as though I was still a little boy, he continued, 'You should be looking for work in administration and earn a good salary. A job as a bank manager would be good for you.'

Though shocked and disappointed, I was adamant. After building up courage, I answered, 'I don't want to work for someone else. I want to run my own business. And furthermore, I hate working indoors, cooped up all day.'

But it was in vain. He wouldn't budge and still insisted that I forget about going into business.

One day, a few weeks later, I was with Dad at the farm where he was discussing some business with George, his insurance broker. George was always respectful towards Dad, probably because he wanted to sell him insurance policies. During their discussion my future career was brought up. I was quite close to the pair when I heard Dad say, 'I have a problem with this son, here. He's got it into his head that he wants a business career and I'm totally against the idea. He simply can't get it into his brain that business is always risky and that a well-paid job in administration is far better and safer.'

To my complete surprise, George calmly replied, 'Why don't you let him risk now while he's still young? If he fails at his age he'd still have time to recoup. But if he waits till he's settled and has a family he wouldn't dare take risks. The repercussions should he fail would be disastrous.'

I was enjoying this and continued listening to Dad's negative arguments to George's positive replies. In the heat of the argument, Dad seemed suddenly to realise that I was still at his side. He turned on me and asked me to leave so that he could continue with the argument. I obeyed, of course, but I was thrilled that there was somebody who supported my ambition. George didn't succeed in persuading Dad, however, which I found out when I brought the subject up with him again a few days later; he was still obsessed with the idea that I become a bank manager.

At sixteen, during the school summer holidays, I was still helping Dad harvest wheat and barley with a hand scythe. Mechanical ones had not yet been introduced in Malta. We would start very early in the morning, well before sunrise, to avoid the hot mid-morning sun which would turn the barley stem very brittle, causing painful bruises and scratches on the skin. In the afternoon we stayed in the coolness of the farm preparing short pieces of thin rope to tie the bunches of harvested wheat and barley we had left in the field. For this purpose we used wheat stems. Since these were very rigid and therefore hard to bend, we left them to soak in water for some hours. When they were pliable enough we would tie two or three together, end to end, to form them into short ropes, long enough to encircle bunches of wheat and barley. Then, late that same evening or very early the next morning, we would return to the field and tie the corn in manageable bundles. We then left everything on the ground where they would be picked up on the morrow by truck and formed into small heaps in the middle of the field.

What remained in the soil after we harvested the barley was very stiff with sharp stem ends. And as, like most, I went about bare-footed, the soles of my feet would be in constant pain as I moved around the field. But Dad never felt a thing. Decades of walking bare-foot over all kinds of terrain had rendered the soles of his feet as hard as shoe soles. He could even sustain a cigarette lighter flame for many seconds without flinching before pulling his foot back. He could have been the envy of most fakirs.

The long years of farm work had so thickened the palms of

my hands that I would sometimes use a razor blade to shave off the harder parts. I was embarrassed to show my hands at school and would keep them out of view as much as possible.

I became an expert at other things as well, like snake catching. Dad used to buy large quantities of bales of wheat and barley from other farmers. We had to collect these bales and deliver them to other farms as animal fodder or to stockpile them in readiness for the harvesting process as explained in the previous chapter. With the last few bunches of straws remaining, my friend and I would silently tiptoe around them and with the word 'go' he would shove one away while I jumped forward to catch a snake that might have sought a safe haven underneath. I would grab it by its tail and smash its head against the ground. The snakes weren't poisonous and were never longer than sixty centimetres. Sometimes I would also find mice, which I picked up with my bare hands and threw away. But sometimes I would come upon a large rat, which I would step on with my bare foot and crush with the full weight of my body. Young as I was, I never realised the risk I was taking had I been bitten by these rodents.

Throughout childhood and our teenage years, Mum was the one who made sure we carried out our religious duties. She was determined to give us the same Catholic upbringing she had. Thanks to her I never missed Mass on Sundays and public holidays. I would meet with my three closest friends at the same spot in church, and during Mass I would pray fervently to God to convince Dad to change his mind about my career. I would always recite the same prayer, week in week out, and it went something like this:

Our Lord and Our Holy Mother, I know that one day I shall make it and be successful in my business career, but I need your help in choosing the right way. I can feel in my heart that I shall make it, but I do not know how to solve this dilemma with Father. Lord, I do not have any money to start my own business and I would not even dare ask Father to lend me some. Lord and Holy Mary help me. Show me the path to success.

41

My performance at school was improving every year without any help from anyone at home. Nevertheless, I was surprised when I came first in physics and received very high marks in geography. My first-hand experience in farm work stood me in good stead because geography classes included practical lessons on rural areas and we had to deal with questions relating to the natural environment. Those of my classmates who were not familiar with the environment in which I was raised, or who just did not bother, would trade with me car magazines or rare stamps for my collection for helping them with their homework and sometimes for doing it for them.

During the last years at secondary school, students are asked to choose the subjects they would want to specialise in and which they think would help them in the career they would wish to follow. When given the choice I decided not to consult my parents because I did not want anyone to try to dissuade me from my ambition. I decided to choose commercial subjects like arithmetic, accounts, typing and geography.

Overall, although I gave much of my time to helping Dad, I managed to attain good results in practically all subjects except Italian. At the time, Italy wasn't one of my favourite countries, so I stupidly decided to give lessons in the language the least attention possible in class. The reason for this was as stupid as my decision; it was the result of a bad experience my brother and I had in Italy, together with our family friend Żeppu. We were involved in a minor traffic accident which could have been resolved in the simplest way possible. But we were treated so badly by the Italian police that I decided not to bother visiting Italy in the future. I decided to extend the boycott to the beautiful Italian language as well.

Accounts was the subject I took most seriously. My classmates found it very difficult and of the forty-one who started the weekly lessons, only four survived the first three months. This created a problem for the school because it couldn't afford a class of just four students with the remaining thirty-seven out of the classroom wasting their time doing nothing. The headmaster, therefore, decided to shift the lesson to after school hours. Though this decision was understandable and appreciated, as it allowed the four remaining students to continue with the course, it created a logistic problem for me because there was no school transport to take me home. There was also no direct public transport from Gżira to Naxxar. This meant that I would have had to take a bus to Valletta and another from Valletta to Naxxar – a journey that normally took about an hour.

I explained my situation to Dad, adding that I didn't wish to give up the studying of accounts and neither did I wish to give up helping him at his farm as arriving so late after school would barely allow me enough time to do my homework. So I risked proposing that, should I be allowed the use of one of his vehicles, I would arrive home early enough to do my homework and give him the usual helping hand. I was still sixteen at the time and had little hope of the wish being granted. To my complete surprise, however, he offered me the use of his brand new Toyota, which he normally reserved for relaxed and enjoyable Sunday drives.

I was already a fairly good driver. I had already been practising for two years driving pickups. But driving the 16HP Toyota hatchback in full view of my classmates would lift my pride sky high. This was an additional incentive to continue with my weekly accounts lessons. When I arrived home after each lesson I would park the Toyota somewhere where Dad wouldn't notice the heat radiating from its engine caused by my fast driving.

During our lunch breaks at school we had ample time for games, and the most popular game was football (although I wasn't very good at it). I remember once banging heads with an opponent, which ended up with me lying on the ground. I only remember feeling dizzy when I got up and we walked to the local shop to buy doughnuts. Back in class for our first lesson, I stood up and offered the teacher half of my part-eaten doughnut. The whole class erupted into laughter at my audacity; fortunately the teacher realised something was wrong. Dad was called and drove me straight to the hospital where I was diagnosed with concussion.

As a teenager I had a rather shy and withdrawn nature. This had its disadvantages, of course, but at school my character worked to my advantage as it helped me be more attentive in class. The very good results I obtained at the annual examinations, and the resultant certificates which I proudly hung in my room, prove the point.

My shyness, however, did not deter me from becoming an avid car enthusiast and I never failed to invent an excuse, however silly and childish, to drive Dad's new car. I remember one time, when driving fast down a main road and overtaking another car at a bend, I came face to face with an oncoming traffic policeman on his motorcycle. I was heading straight at him and a head on collision was a foregone conclusion. Somehow, I managed to swerve the car, barely avoiding a boundary wall, and avoided a serious accident with the traffic policeman. Looking sideways at the police officer while he rode by, I recognised him as one of Dad's close friends. He recognised me as Bertu's eldest son. I shook from head to foot, probably more from fear of Dad's wrath once he got to know about the close shave than from the close shave itself. I decided that if Dad should get to know about the accident it definitely wasn't going to be through me. Curiously enough, the police officer seemed to have had the same thought as, with the passing of days and with my relationship with Dad never getting any worse, I started to relax and to carry on with my fast driving. But I was far from relaxed whenever I encountered this police officer on the road after that. Then I would lower my head and drive very cautiously.

A few weeks later came the encounter I foolishly thought would never occur. While with Dad during his usual meeting with friends, I observed the same police officer making straight for us. I nearly died on the spot with fright and my first thought was to make myself scarce. But I stood where I was, trying to act as normal as my pale face and shaking body allowed. Every time the officer's gaze fell upon me, however, I tried to beg him with my eyes to keep mum about our unfortunate encounter of a few weeks back. When at last he acknowledged my presence, and with a mischievous look in his eyes, he said, as though as an aside, 'By the way, Bertu. Your son's quite a good driver. I saw him driving recently and I notice he can manoeuvre the machine very well indeed!'

I couldn't believe my ears. I felt the urge to hug and kiss him right there in front of everybody. But I just smiled sheepishly while giving Dad a sidelong glance to watch his reaction to the words. It seemed the officer's words not only got me off the hook, but persuaded Dad to let me use his car more often.

It was at about this time that the dreaded swine fever struck. There wasn't a swine herd in Malta and Gozo that wasn't affected and Dad lost all his. I remember the dejected look on his face each day as we stood together watching the burning of the infected carcasses. This sad operation continued every day until the once-healthy herd was burned among the billowing black smoke and the strong stench that seemed to hang in the air around us for days on end.

Dad took it badly and soon after this catastrophe he, in turn, contracted brucellosis fever. He was confined to bed for more than a month and we feared for his life on many occasions with a high fever never leaving him throughout.

This further compounded the difficulties the swine fever caused his farming business and his morale was at its lowest ever. When he was fully recovered he knew he had to make some very difficult decisions and take drastic action that could determine his future in this business. But fate seemed to deem otherwise. As I said in a previous chapter, the location of the farm and our bungalow commanded a breath-taking panorama. It had become a sought-after prime site by developers and an estate agent approached Dad with a very attractive offer to buy the entire area comprising the farm, bungalow and surrounding fields. Dad grabbed the opportunity with both hands and struck an excellent deal, which helped him cover his losses and make a large profit into the bargain. He immediately started looking for another location and settled for an area on the other side of Naxxar, which overlooked the opposite half of Malta.

Inside a year, he completed the whole development of a new and modern farm for his bulls, and a villa close by. The beautiful, new villa again attracted estate agents who talked to Dad about the possibility of renting it to foreigners at a good price. Not only did Dad accept, but a few months later he sold it, again at a good profit.

With his financial situation now better than ever, Dad seemed to have decided that his family's days of total isolation in the countryside should come to an end. It seems he wanted to go back to where he had started it all – in the very centre of his village. And he bought two large town houses right in the very centre of Naxxar. One was a stuffed-birds museum with ten large rooms, a large front garden and a larger one at the back, which also fronted on the back street. Dad decided this should be our home. The museum, which also boasted a large stuffed tiger as a star exhibit, was quite a popular tourist attraction back then. But in a few months, the artefacts were taken away by the former owner and we moved in.

We were now living in the very thick of village life with all the hustle and bustle that goes with it. Our free and wild living in the countryside was over. We now had to re-adapt to this new environment, away from the beauty of nature and the clean air we used to breathe.

But man is a master at adaptation. There are things, however, that take longer to adapt to. In our case, the tolling of church bells every quarter of an hour seemed an insurmountable problem. The church was only 100 metres away and the vibrating sound of the larger bells echoed throughout the large rooms of our big house, leaving us awake at night for weeks. But after a few months we became accustomed to their din and we started sleeping the whole night through, wondering what all the initial fuss was all about.

Since the days of our move from the alley to the farm and back, traffic had increased considerably. And since we were now living in the very centre of the village we couldn't help feeling

Mother and her brood.

My first bicycle.

The house where I was born in St Lucy Street, Naxxar.

Receiving the trophy from the American ambassador.

Going for an educational cruise with my colleagues from the college.

The shy boy!

Our bungalow close to our farm.

My three close friends – Emanuel, Alfred and Joe – with my first car. I was taking the photo.

Skinny at 16 years of age.

Naxxar church and crowd on Festa Day.

Courting with Jessie.

Jessie and me on our engagement.

Mosta petrol station.

Our wedding day.

Posing during our honeymoon,
carrying the 'cross' of married life.

My first construction van and new Fiat outside our 'Golden Home'.

Promoting my full name on my plant and equipment.

My first office.

it. The sound of traffic going up and down our busy street was a constant nuisance which took longer to get used to. The needless blaring of horns and screeching of tyres by youngsters showing off in the middle of the night would sometimes put our nerves on end. But, eventually, we were able to sleep even through this constant noise pollution.

Dad simply hated our annual village festa. He hated the noise of fireworks, the large crowds gathered in our street and the constant shouting of people and of hawkers trying to sell their wares. So he either took a few days' holiday abroad or spent the whole festa week evenings at our summer residence, which he had bought together with the two houses at Naxxar. But for Mum and her brood, festa day was the climax of the whole year. Living in such a large house with two gardens right in the centre of the village won us many friends and we would invite them to our house on festa day.

It was a tradition in most villages that on festa day the front doors of all the houses were kept wide open so that passers-by could admire and praise the decorations especially displayed for the occasion. We at Naxxar were no exception and Mum would sit with her friends on chairs near the doorstep and would graciously and proudly accept the compliments of the curious. Many would even open wide the front windows, most of which would frame a miniature statue of Our Lady of Victories (*il-Bambina*), surrounded by festoons of light and banners. Others would decorate the whole façade of their house with festoons of light and a flag on a long pole on the roof, also decorated with festoons of light.

Bars would expropriate a large area of the street in front with tables and chairs to cater for the thousands who flocked to our village from all around Malta to watch this very popular festa. Large profits were made by all around.

Three years following our move to the village centre, Dad thought up another profitable development. He removed our beautiful front garden, demolished the adjacent property and developed it into a block of apartments, a showroom and underground parking. The front garden was converted into a large, flat-tiled area. His reasoning being that it would be a better and safer place for my younger brothers, sisters and their friends to run around with their plastic baby carts and prams.

With everything changing around me, the one thing that remained was my love of cars. In fact, my enthusiasm increased as I got older. I felt relaxed and at leisure when I drove, but my enthusiasm for them did not stop there. I would spend Saturdays with Victor, a friend of mine, washing Dad's cars. We didn't just wash away the dust and grime accumulated during the week; we thoroughly washed the undersides, engines and the interiors as well. Finally, we polished them all until they gleamed. Victor, who later married my sister Grace, loved cars as much as I did and enjoyed this activity as much. Thanks to Victor's participation, Dad gave us LM1 for every car we cleaned. That was good money in those days.

Later, Dad decided he wanted a new 20HP Mercedes. It was a very elegant car and he wanted to collect it personally from the Mercedes factory in Sindelfingen, near Stuttgart in Germany. He wanted to drive it all the way through Italy and ferry it down to Malta. Since he knew he wouldn't make it on his own, he asked me to accompany him and act as his navigator. I jumped at the proposal. I had never been to Germany and with geography as one of my favourite subjects, I was certain of my abilities as a map reader. I had barely left his side when I started imagining myself behind the wheel, driving along those wide and smooth motorways – a complete contrast to Malta's uneven roads, full of potholes and inefficient patchwork.

I wasn't the only guest on this trip to Germany. Dad also took along Ninu (Anthony), a close friend of his, two builders whom he regularly employed in house building and my youngest brother Paul. Dad and I were the only ones who had ever been overseas. For the others, this once in a lifetime opportunity to visit Germany, Switzerland and Italy was too mouth-watering to refuse, and they couldn't thank Dad enough when he asked them to accompany him. It almost seemed out of character, but Dad, in a very generous gesture, paid for everyone to fly from Malta to Stuttgart via Rome.

It was winter and the six of us arrived in Stuttgart sometime in the evening to enjoy our first sight of snow. We had dinner and woke up for an early breakfast next morning so that we were the first people in the visitors' lounge at the Sindelfingen factory. After filling in the necessary forms and going through the usual formalities, we were given a tour of the factory while the car was being prepared for collection. It was an unforgettable experience for all of us. Never had we imagined such an assembly line with all parts being handled and mounted automatically.

Sometime before noon the car was ready. It was beautiful and we couldn't resist having our photo taken, posing beside the shining brand new yellow machine. Then we set off on our planned 1,500-km homeward journey. As the 'official' navigator, I sat up front with Dad while the other four made themselves as comfortable as possible in the back. Dad asked me to indicate the shortest route home, but having carefully planned a more enjoyable route weeks beforehand, I just said, 'Sure pa,' and pointed my finger at the road ahead. I had no intention of making any changes to 'my' route.

The drive to Malta was scheduled to last two days. This included an overnight stop in Rome, which was approximately halfway down. I wanted us to see different countries and enjoy beautiful scenery, but by the time we reached Geneva, Dad had realised that I was purposely taking longer routes which, to him, were unnecessary. He immediately ordered me to alter my route and plan the straightest and shortest journey home. I had to oblige. The generosity which Dad had displayed when paying for us all to accompany him had backfired; he hadn't allowed for the high prices in the hotels. We have to remember that we are talking about times before credit cards and Dad must have realised that he could not afford another night in a hotel, but, ultimately, he didn't appreciate it in the way that I did. Although all the beautiful mountains, rivers, snow and trees were there for us to enjoy, he would only stop for refuelling and to buy sweets from the petrol station. He simply drove on, insisting that stopping to enjoy sceneries was a complete waste of time.

As we continued our journey, he said he wanted to reach and cross the Alps as early as possible. I warned him that crossing the Alps could be more difficult and risky than he had imagined, but he just drove on, reaching Rome well before 6pm. Although I tried to persuade him to exit the motorway and enter Rome so that we could see the beautiful sites of this magnificent and historic city, he continued to drive fast towards Naples, the next big city. This entailed another two hours of hard driving.

We had already missed lunch and all of us, except Dad, were looking forward to reaching our hotel as it was already getting quite dark. I tried to persuade him to take the next exit into the city of Naples, telling him that it was another six or seven hours driving to Reggio Calabria, but he was adamant. He wanted to reach Calabria as soon as possible and catch the first ferry home. I remember him telling me that it couldn't possibly be true that Calabria was seven hours ahead and, pointing at some lights visible in the far distance, he continued, 'Look. That's our final stop. I've been to Calabria with your mother some years ago and can recognise its skyline and features anytime.'

It was already too dark to recognise anything, let alone a city's features from some dim light we could barely make out on the horizon. I disagreed about continuing on to Calabria that night, but Dad insisted. In hindsight it was probably because his cash was running out, but he would never admit that.

Eventually the inevitable happened; Dad became too tired to continue driving and none of the others would take the risk of taking his place behind the wheel. No one would dare drive on unfamiliar roads and in total darkness, and having a few hours rest on the side of the road in such alien surroundings was out of the question. We had no choice. Although I was still ineligible for a driving licence, I had to take over for a few hours. Should

I have been caught driving illegally there would be none of Dad's friends around to bale me out this time.

I kept carefully to the road I had mapped out on my chart and I knew that the next stop wasn't Reggio Calabria at all. Dad kept stubbornly insisting that he could recognise the area around the city anytime. This he kept repeating every time we drove over a hill, with the next one in the far distance on the horizon.

By now we were weak with hunger and close to exhaustion. Those in the back were dozing while Dad and I could barely keep our eyes open. The bright headlights from oncoming traffic rendered the situation worse; our eyes felt as though they were filled with sand and we kept them forcibly open wide with our fingers.

At last we reached Reggio Calabria in the early hours of the morning. The ferry to Malta was already berthed, but embarkation was scheduled for eight o'clock. Driving around the city to find a place to sleep for a few hours would have been a waste of time and money, so we had no option other than to make the best of the worst possible situation. We had to try to sleep in the same cramped position we had been in since we left Stuttgart. None of us could sleep properly; we were by now over-tired and very uncomfortable.

But at last it was eight o'clock and we were the first people aboard the ferry. Not one of us bothered about having coffee and something to eat at the canteen. We made straight for the most comfortable seats available and slept right through the whole eight-hour trip to Malta.

It was undoubtedly an unforgettable experience for all of us. The others had banked on the holiday of a lifetime, never imagining that their short trip abroad would consist of sitting for hours in a cramped position, suffering gnawing hunger and extreme fatigue as they sped along never-ending motorways and over pitch-black mountain tops.

It was around this period of time that Dad started thinking seriously about reducing his farming activities to concentrate more energy on the profitable, though risky, building industry, mostly by renovating town houses and building new ones. I still remember the days when I would dash straight from school at the end of the day, satchel and all, to a construction site close to home and put endless questions to builders in order to gauge the day to day progress of work. In fact, if Dad wanted any plans drawn he would ask me to do it. He would explain the layout he had in mind, together with the dimensions of the site, and I would transfer his ideas onto a plan drawn to scale. Then he would take the plan to his architect who would draw a more professional one to attach to the application for a building permit. This drafting of plans was something I very much enjoyed doing and served as part of my apprenticeship for the future. This apprenticeship extended to filing and bookkeeping, which I did at the office at home. When it came to filing away rolled plans, however, he always insisted that I keep them loose in cupboards or in bins so he could easily identify them when I wasn't around.

All this office work kept me inside the house during weekends when, as a seventeen-year-old I should have been enjoying myself with friends. When later I met my future wife and started dating her seriously, things didn't improve much. It always seemed that Dad had something very urgent for me to do every time I told him that my girlfriend and I were going out.

All these busy weekends notwithstanding, I still managed to find some time to spend with friends. Fredu (Alfred), Lelu (Emanuel), Joe ta' Klara, Joe Bellia and I would spend time chatting near a children's playground close to home. Then we would stroll all the way down to nearby Mosta and back – a 2-mile walk.

Some time later, Dad gave me a brand new bicycle. It was a racing bicycle, complete with multiple gears. As I was the only one among my group who owned a bicycle, I would find time to burn up my energy riding around my village and neighbouring Mosta. I became such an expert rider and physically fit that I would cycle hands-free all the way up the long hill from Mosta and control the machine round bends and corners with a slight lean of my torso.

My friends and I would sometimes go to watch a movie, which we called talkies at the time. We also rarely missed the annual festas in nearby villages. These were the ideal hunting grounds for girls who would be present in their hundreds. We would start out with bravado and eagerness, ogling all the pretty girls that passed by, some of whom would giggle and give us encouraging smiles. Then we'd just blush and stare open-mouthed, too shy to follow up on the obvious invitations. Altar boys would have done better.

In the meantime, I was totally absorbed observing Dad's method of closing business deals. I noted his tactics, his body language and the way he started the whole procedure of purchasing property to getting a building permit, construction and sale. The many years of continual exposure to Dad's business deals, especially when in later years the emphasis leaned more and more on the building industry, were a major influence on my decision to seek my career in the construction industry.

One day I built up enough courage to face up to Dad and make clear and final my decision to become a building contractor. I couldn't believe his strong reaction and refusal to accept the inevitable.

'Definitely not,' he said with finality. 'And you should have realised by now that the industry is a very tough and risky business. It's not made for the likes of you. And you're too young, anyway.'

He probably thought that this statement uttered with such finality would dampen my enthusiasm. In fact, he probably genuinely thought that my shy and retiring personality was completely unsuitable in a business that could either make or break one. He probably genuinely meant to give the best advice as a person who had seen it all and didn't want his first son to go through the heartaches and setbacks he went through over the decades.

'You should become a bank manager,' he continued in a softer voice, as though he could see the disappointment in my eyes his abrupt dismissal had caused. 'That's the most suitable job for an intelligent boy like you. And I'll go and have a word with my friends at the bank. You'll see. They'll surely appoint you manager.'

'Pa,' I replied in the strongest and most determined voice I could muster. 'In the first place, you have to understand that bank managers are not appointed the way you think. I would have to start at the very bottom. If I do well and work hard then, when I'm close to retirement, then maybe I'm appointed manager.' Before he could contradict me I continued, 'Secondly, I don't want to work in a confined office. I want to work outdoors, not tied up to a desk all day. Finally, I will never accept working under orders from anyone. I won't have anyone telling me what or what not to do. I want to be the one to decide what to do and what others have to do. I want to be the boss. And I know I can be one.'

Dad wouldn't listen and kept insisting on his bank manager myth. It was frustratingly useless to try and make him see reason. We could never ever see eye to eye on the subject and this started a rift between us that, alas, lasted the whole of the next nine years.

Malta's History

4

Meeting Jessie!

(1969–1972) 17–20 years

There I was, a shy seventeen-year-old gangling youth, more determined than ever to carve out a future I knew I was born to attain. But there was still a long way to go. I still had another year at school where, along with the commercial subjects I had chosen a couple of years back, I had to study shorthand. I had no choice. It was part of the school's curriculum. In the end I didn't regret it as, at the end of the year, I had another Pitman's certificate to hang on my bedroom wall. All this, however, was still some months in the future.

In the meantime things remained practically the same. I was still riding my bicycle around the streets of Naxxar and Mosta. I was still regularly meeting my friends near the playground and strolling to Mosta and back, all trying unsuccessfully to overcome our shyness when talking to the girls we met on the way. In a nut shell, I was still stuck with my old routine, but there were definite high points, like our neighbouring villages' festas, which were still our number one sources of entertainment. We would ogle all the pretty girls, eat hot dogs, sandwiches and ice cream, and rest at one of the many tables outside a village bar where we would have a couple of drinks and watch the hustle and bustle all around us. We never got drunk, however. We never overdid our drinking as some of the groups of young men around us seemed determined to do with their uncontrolled consumption of alcohol, which they thought would change them overnight into grown-ups. We always wanted to enjoy the whole evening of celebrations. We loved to hear the shouting of the people as they greeted one another amid the explosions of fireworks and the din of church bells. We loved to look at the dark sky and see it lit up with bursts of colour. We loved to listen to the giggling of young girls and envied the boys causing it. We loved to listen to the laughter of the children as they chased each other, throwing paper confetti at each other and hitting grown-ups instead, and watch them as they tugged at their mothers' skirts to make them buy an ice-cream, or a hot-dog, or a stick of candy floss, all sweet and sugary and sticky.

At last the procession would be approaching the end of its tour of the village's narrow streets, and the people would fall silent and strain their necks to catch a first glimpse of the statue of their patron saint. Mothers would call their scattered children to their sides, knowing that the large crowd would now move as one to occupy the most strategic places to watch the long procession make its way back into church. We would move with the crowd and get caught up in the enthusiasm, further supported by the cheering crowds as the statue approached the main door of the church amid the explosions of fireworks, the din of church bells and the band trying unsuccessfully to compete with all of the above.

All this was nothing compared to the celebrations at Naxxar for the feast of Our Lady of Victories on 8th September. This feast has been celebrated on this date for centuries. It celebrates Malta's victory over the Turks at the Great Siege of 1565, which is why it is so important and one of Malta's National Days. No wonder we *Naxxarin* (the Naxxar people) are so proud.

Celebrations started from the week leading to festa day and I, for one, always made it a point not to miss any of the celebrations that took place. I would always be accompanied by my friends and walk about the streets, watching people putting the final touches to decorations that took them a whole year to prepare.

We would visit the band clubs with the musicians going through their last rehearsals before going out to play their rousing marches along the narrow streets of the village. We would also go inside the church where the red damask was already hung on the walls and columns, and the enormous crystal chandeliers reflected even the faintest flicker of a lighted candle on a side altar. And we would be satisfied that the village would be having as successful a festa as ever.

For many centuries it has been a tradition that, during the festa, the churches are decorated with red damask hanging all along the inside church walls to represent the joyful spirit. During Good Friday, these walls were decorated with black damask to represent the sadness while, at Christmas time, some special areas would be decorated in white damask. Most of this damask was sewn by local women for free. If it was not available locally, the parish priest would have to order it from other villages at a low price.

The Maltese have always been very devout Christians, who have donated lots of their time to construct magnificent chapels, churches and cathedrals. There are over 600 of these scattered all over the small Maltese islands. This is proof of their devotion. Most of the larger parish churches and our cathedrals are impressively decorated and compete with other world-class churches.

At last, on the eve of the festa, the crowds would start to gather to follow the bands playing around the whole village. Other crowds would gather on the outskirts, unhindered by obstructing buildings, to watch the fireworks burst and fill the starlit sky. Later, they would flock to the church square where the bands would end their slow trudge and the ground fireworks would be ready to explode.

'Giggfogu' is a corruption of the Italian '*gioco di fuoco*', literally translated as 'game of fire'. These are fireworks burned on the ground. They are fixed to poles and, when set off, give a beautiful display of colour, with wheels turning within wheels accompanied by small explosions and the occasional rocket (nicknamed *il-mignuna* – the mad woman), which would propel itself straight up for hundreds of metres amidst shrieks of glee from the crowd, especially women and children. Hundreds of people looked on, and sometimes stood too close, many with sleeping children in their arms, cheering at the end of every display, impatiently waiting for the next. These fireworks were too beautiful to miss and no wonder people sat up till the early hours of the morning to witness them.

Following the fireworks, all is quiet and peaceful until very early the next morning when the shuffling walk of the elderly is heard making their way to church for the five o'clock Mass.

My friends and I would always start the day by attending high Mass on festa day. It is a beautiful liturgical celebration lasting two hours. I enjoyed the beautiful singing, the fragrance of frankincense, the long sermon in praise of Our Lady and the whole solemnity of the occasion. I have always had a strong devotion for Our Lady and I always felt that I could never celebrate and enjoy our festa unless I started it with prayers in church.

After Mass we would have coffee and *pastizzi* (cheesecakes) at a nearby bar already full of people offering rounds of beer and whisky. We would stick to coffee and, afterwards, squeeze our way out to join the crowd already gathered around the band, which had just started playing the first march. Young people would jump and dance in front of the band while the more sober and musically inclined would walk alongside the musicians, listening attentively and smiling at the well-executed simple notes, which collectively produced such melodic and rousing marches.

Most of the locals would venture out early. Those who formed part of the procession would be seen hurrying to church to have enough time for a chat with friends after a quick change into liturgical clothes. They would then be called to order and take their assigned places, where they would put a more devout expression on their faces. Young people, however, would have less devotional reasons for venturing out so early when the sun was still fairly hot. The girls, especially, would be eager to meet with their friends to have their opinion about the new dresses especially sewn for the occasion. Then, satisfied, they would smile and show off, and make certain that young men took notice and looked at least twice at them. My friends and I would be part of the 'noticing' group. We would definitely look once then blush and dare not look a second time.

In time, all the village inhabitants would start emerging from the side streets, the women in dresses made for the occasion, weighed down with all the gold and jewellery that their necks, ears and fingers could carry. Then, hundreds of people from towns and villages from all over Malta would make their way up the main street to merge with the locals and enjoy this very popular festa. Hawkers, in their mobile kiosks, would make the best of this opportunity and start shouting their wares until hoarse and out of stock.

The first sign that the procession would be emerging was when the bells started to ring. People would be asked to move back and let the procession through. Rows and rows of priests and monks, altar boys and confraternity members, would slowly walk past us before the beautiful statue of Our Lady appears at last on the parvis. The people would then explode in spontaneous cheering, clapping and shouts of 'Viva l-Madonna'. Some start crying unashamedly and I admit that, many a time, my sight would be blurred by stinging tears.

After this, my friends and I would start celebrating our way. We would visit all the bars and clubs, drinking sparingly, meeting other groups our age and all the time wishing they were of the opposite sex. Then it would be time for the procession to return to church, greeted by fireworks, music, cheering and sadness that it had all passed so quickly.

It wasn't completely over, however. There has always been an unwritten rule among the Maltese that nobody works on the morrow of festa day, whether farmers, employees or businessmen. Since time immemorial it has been the custom that on this day, all the villagers would decorate their carts and horses and take their families for a day at the seaside. In time, with the arrival of the automobile, groups of families and friends would pool their resources and hire a truck or bus for the day. They would tour Malta's beaches, making as much noise as possible and making sure that all who saw them knew which village they came from. Some would even hire a jazz band to accompany them throughout the day.

When more and more people could afford a car, buses and trucks were discarded and these celebrations took the form of carcades, which became longer and longer with each year that passed.

This celebration was called '*xalata*' (the 'x' pronounced 'sh'). Those taking part would congregate early in the village square to have enough time to decorate their cars with the coloured paper festoons taken from the street decorations. My friends and I would also be there in Dad's Toyota. Along with the festoons, we would all stick a picture of the statue of Our Lady on the car bonnet.

Dad's Toyota was a fast car, but we wanted it faster, so we would remove the air cleaner. This, apart from making it go faster, would also make the engine much noisier. After all, creating as much noise as possible was the principal aim of the *xalata*. To further add to the decibels, we would play the car radio at full volume and sound the horn all the way, even when there were no people around to wave at. How else could we make our presence felt? We usually made the rounds of Malta's favourite beaches, but sometimes we ventured to Gozo, which is much smaller, so it was easier to make sure that every Gozitan knew that the *Naxxarin* were invading their beautiful island.

Back in Malta in the evening, tired, sunburnt but happy, we would give Dad's car a really good clean up, reattach the air cleaner and put it back in the garage for Dad's scrutiny and satisfaction the next morning. Little did he suspect what his car had gone through.

During my final year at school Dad decided to go into another business venture. He bought a small petrol station right in the core of Mosta and asked me to take care of its accounts and finance. As I studied accounts at school, I was a natural choice. To avoid paying overtime to his employees he also asked me to man his petrol station after school hours. As usual I couldn't utter the word 'no', though I wanted to because I knew this would disrupt my homework routine.

A small cubicle served as an office, which had a desk just large enough to fit a typewriter. There, I was supposed to do all my writing and studying, which would be interrupted every time a customer stopped at the station for replenishment. As if this wasn't enough of a sacrifice, shortly after, Dad asked me to take over manning the station on Sundays and public holidays as well.

To be honest, I did enjoy the job. I liked serving customers, but not at the expense of my studies and summer holidays when I should have been swimming and playing with my friends. Sunday had now become the longest day of the week. I would start it with early Mass to enable me to be at the petrol station in time to catch most of the customers who wanted to start the day with an early morning swim. Mornings weren't too bad as I was kept very busy. Afternoons and evenings, however, were hell, with nothing to do but to sit and wish I were with my friends at our favourite sandy beach, watching all the girls and hiding our blushes under a well-suntanned skin. It was frustrating to watch cars drive by with their tanks still full, occupied by tired but happy families returning home from the beach. Then, at sundown, I would close shop and make for home, completely dejected and not a little angry that I was wasting my best summers.

There was a silver lining, however, and it had been there for quite some time, but with my natural shyness and withdrawn character it took me ages to notice it. My constant typing and writing at the minuscule desk had attracted the attention of a group of four or five young ladies. Unobserved by me, they would stroll past the petrol station, take a long sidelong glance at me (and probably giggle as well) and move on. They would repeat this pantomime many times in the course of the evening and Sunday mornings. I was probably too dejected to notice, but when at last I did, I became interested and started to keep a sharp lookout for them. I once noticed one of them look me straight in the eye and nearly topple over. It was love at first sight and on the following days I noticed that the girls' stroll past the station became more frequent and slower. They all smiled at me and I always managed to smile back. That's as far as my courage would go, however, because I still couldn't manage a simple 'hello'.

I was in love. I was madly in love, but however much I wished to share this feeling with somebody who understood, I was sitting at my typewriter, still grinning stupidly at the keys in front of me, not knowing how to react the next time the girls passed by. The first time I encountered my friends I opened my heart to them. Joe ta' Klara sympathised with my feelings and wanted to know which girl had turned my head so completely.

'How can I explain her to you?' I answered. 'All I can say is that she's the loveliest of the four.'

Since this explanation wasn't much help, my friends agreed to spend some time with me at the station and see the girls for themselves. I was then able to indicate the girl and my friends followed them discreetly all the way to the Mosta football ground. Later, Joe told me that the girl's friends kept calling her Guża or Jess. But he wasn't sure.

'I couldn't just stop and ask her, could I?' he continued.

I believed him. After all, he was a regular member of the shy quartet.

The next time I had some free time I accompanied them to the football ground. And there she was. She saw me at the same moment I saw her and I nearly stopped in my tracks. But my friends urged me on and I walked as leisurely as my trembling legs would allow me, past her and her group. She smiled at me and I smiled back as I passed by. I noticed that her smile was that little bit more knowing, but neither of us had enough courage to make the first move. From then onwards, every time she and her friends walked past the station, our smiles spoke volumes. But that's as far as it went between us, at least for the time being.

Sunday evening my friends and I went to the cinema, and so did my girl and her friends. They would always sit in the same row each Sunday and we would buy tickets for seats as close to theirs as possible. I remember one day (it was 19th March 1969, the feast of St Joseph and a public holiday) my friends and I were making our way to our usual seats at the cinema and I immediately realised that there was a vacant seat right beside the girl I fancied.

'It's now or never,' I said to myself.

I decided to pluck up courage and take up the vacant seat after the intermission. I honestly never knew what the film was all about; my concentration was focused solely on what I had to do after the intermission.

When the lights went on I made straight for the bar and bought two packets of Maltesers. Praying that courage wouldn't fail me at the last moment, I made my way straight to the empty seat beside her.

'May I take this seat?' I asked her.

'Yes. Yes, of course.'

It was the first time I had heard her voice and it was music to my ears. I offered her one of the packets of Maltesers.

'No thank you,' she answered.

At first I was taken aback at her abrupt reply, but I was there, sitting right beside her, and if I let my courage fail me now I would never forgive myself.

'What's your name?' I asked.

'Mary.'

Her answer surprised me. Mary had nothing to do with the names Joe mentioned.

'What's yours?' she asked.

'Ġolinu Xuereb,' I answered. I also told her my address and all about my family!

Some time passed, during which both of us said nothing, both pretending we were watching the film while the Maltesers were melting in my warm hands.

At last I asked, 'Shall we sit together again next week?'

'Yes.'

'Okay then. I'll buy tickets for the three of you and shall wait for you at the entrance.'

I could see her smile in the darkness of the hall. When the film was over we said our goodbyes.

'Her name's Mary not Ġuża or Jess,' I told Joe as soon as I met him outside the cinema.

Joe shrugged his shoulders. 'I don't know,' he replied. 'But that's what I heard them call her.'

'Anyway. I shall be meeting her again on Sunday. Then I'll know for sure.'

The days that followed were my longest ever. Sunday seemed so far away in the future that I wished I could sleep for six whole days and wake up just two hours before the show to have enough time to wash and shave. At last I was waiting for her at the entrance and saw her walking towards me, all smiling and happy. We found our seats and sat down.

'I want to tell you right away that my name's not Mary. My name's Jessie.'

'Jessie?' So Joe was right after all. 'Why didn't you tell me your real name last time?'

'Well...' she replied. 'You see, I'm a shy person and don't like to have boys chatting with me just to pass the time. I'm not the sort, if you know what I mean.'

I thought that maybe she had told her mother everything about me and she had decided that, since I was a well-behaved young man and came from a successful business family, her daughter should continue seeing me. Now that I could address her with her real name my confidence grew. I made a mental note to inform Joe that he was right after all. It would make him happy.

Jessie and I talked about many things while the film was going on and this time she accepted the sweets I offered. She told me that the girls she was always with were her sister Netta (Antoinette) and a friend whose name I have since forgotten. She even told me where she lived. She went on to tell me that being at the cinema on the previous occasion was a coincidence as she usually went to Rabat for the feast of St Joseph. It had been too windy, however, and would have disrupted her hair do. We talked and talked until the lights went on and we had to go our separate ways, but not before having fixed a date for the following Sunday.

Now that Jessie and I had decided to meet regularly, my time with my friends would be extremely limited. This was, however, something that was bound to happen to any one of us sooner or later. Now there was no looking back. Jessie and I would meet every Sunday evening and at some village festa. Yet, in spite of the fact that little by little we started to get to know each other better and conversation between us was becoming less formal, we held back from even holding hands, let alone giving each other an occasional kiss.

It seems, however, that while I was sweating it out at the petrol station and getting to know Jessie, Dad was planning big things for me.

One day he pulled me aside and said in a conspiratorial whisper, 'Gulin, my boy, I've just found the perfect girl for you. Very nice and hardworking just like your mother. And from a good local family as well.' Just like that! As if we were still living in the nineteenth century when parents decided who their children should or shouldn't marry. Before he could proceed with the number of grandchildren he expected from me I cut him short.

'Sorry, pa, but I have a girl already. She's a good girl from Mosta –'

'What?' This time it was his turn to cut me short. 'Who is she? Where does she live? Who are her parents?'

Before I had time to start answering the first question he was already on his way out of the house.

'Come. Show me where she lives.'

To tell the truth I was quite relieved with his reaction. He seemed to have already forgotten the nice hardworking local girl and we were soon driving down to Mosta with him behind the wheel. We drove slowly past Jessie's family's grocery shop two or three times (she had left school at fourteen to help her mother run it) with Dad literally putting his neck out of the car window to stare, hoping to catch a glimpse of my girl. I cringed in embarrassment at his unashamed antics and slid as far down in my seat as my long legs allowed. I did manage to see Jessie behind the counter, but thankfully she was totally oblivious to what was going on right outside her mother's shop.

'How come I don't know this family?' said Dad, very annoyed with himself. 'I know Mosta and everyone here like I know the back of my hand and yet...'

For some reason he failed to see Jessie and wanted to stop the car right in front of the shop and have me point her out to him.

'Don't you dare stop the car, pa, or I'll get out now and walk away. I'd die of shame if Jessie got to know what we're doing.'

He must have taken my warning seriously because after a couple of more attempts, and without looking at me, he said, 'She seems to be a good enough girl.'

I sighed with relief. His comment meant his endorsement of Jessie and, also, that we could now go home.

Soon, word that I had a girlfriend spread among the household and Sperry, my eldest sister, came up to me one day, all smiles, and asked, 'And who's this pretty girl of yours Gulinu, eh?' Although I knew that Sperry was happy for me I couldn't hide my blushes.

'Jessie,' I answered softly.

'Jessie,' she repeated as though to memorise the name. 'It's a very nice name – Jessie.' She smiled up at my face and held my gaze for a few seconds. Then she looked me critically up and down and continued, 'And this is what you wear when you're with her!'

I looked down at the shirt and trousers I had on and shrugged. I could see nothing wrong with them. They were what I always wore when I went out with my friends for our stroll to Mosta and to the cinema. They were what I always put on when I cycled around Naxxar and Mosta. I couldn't see what Sperry didn't like about them. When I looked up again, Sperry was still smiling while shaking her head.

'You poor village boy! This won't do. This won't do at all.' Then she assumed a serious look and said, 'Now listen to me. Tomorrow you're going with me to Valletta and I'll find you something better than those rags. You'll see. Jessie will love you more when she sees what a really attractive young man you are. No buts,' she added when she realised I was about to open my mouth. 'Not a word from you till I've finished with you.'

I was very thin then, so the wide, bell-bottom trousers and snake-skin patterned, tight shirt Sperry chose for me fitted well. Jessie must have shared Sperry's taste; I could see it in her wide eyes and smile of delight as soon as she saw me in my new outfit.

At last we did manage to hold hands, but it took us four months to build up the courage. Every time I now walk past the spot in Valletta where it happened I always smile to myself in happy recollection. And after that tentative first time, our hands wouldn't get unstuck until we got married.

With Dad's approval in place, he was free to concentrate once again on business, and his ideas were far from running out. He now went into the self-drive car hire business and bought two brand new Toyota Corollas, one of which he allowed me to use for my meetings with Jessie. She wouldn't ride with me, however, even though we were already in the 'hands-holding' level of intimacy. So we just took strolls.

By the following summer, her sister Antoinette, whom everyone called Netta, had found her own boyfriend and we would form two couples when we met at St Paul's Bay for a drink in one of the many outlets there. I had to be home by eight o'clock when the sun had not yet set and the streets of St Paul's Bay would still be practically deserted. It was the same for Jessie. This meant that Jessie and I had to meet at six o'clock, when it was even hotter and people inside would still be having an extended siesta while the rest would still be swimming and sunbathing.

Bars did not open for the public before half past six, so we would wait for one to open and we were always the first customers served. For me, to be home at the imposed time meant that we had to leave St Paul's Bay at quarter to eight because Jessie still refused to ride in the car with me, even though accompanied by Netta and her boyfriend Paul. Mosta was only 3 km away and I would easily have made the distance in five minutes by car had Jessie relented to my pleas. It would have meant another half hour of being together. I would drive with Paul beside me past the two sisters waiting at the bus stop in the hope that she had changed her mind, but it was wishful thinking. It took another five months of hand holding before she decided she could trust me enough to ride with me. And, at last, a further three months later we exchanged the first kiss.

In the meantime, we never saw the inside of a disco. How could we when both sets of parents were such sticklers for discipline and punctuality? I once was home ten minutes late and found Dad waiting for me in the hallway. I could see he was in a terrible rage and I had barely stepped inside the house when he started shouting at me.

'Don't you know what time it is? Don't you know it's already nine? Aren't you ashamed of yourself, staying out so late with a girl you barely know?'

For an instant I thought I must have made some mistake when I last looked at my watch before leaving St Paul's Bay. I looked at it in panic, but it was showing the correct time.

'But Pa, it's only ten past eight.'

'There you are. As I said, it's practically almost nine already.'

How could I argue against such logic? It would have been

useless because Dad couldn't suffer being proved wrong. So I just walked past him and made straight for my room, vowing that I would never again arrive home a second after eight. I wanted at all cost to avoid confrontation with Dad. The situation between us had already soured enough and I didn't want it to worsen. Jessie and I were, however, allowed more freedom on Christmas Day and New Year's Eve when we made the best of a rare occasion by hopping from one hotel to another, drinking non-alcoholic drinks and laughing our way full of hope into the New Year. But by one in the morning we were both home.

A year and a half into our relationship, Jessie wanted me to meet her parents. This wasn't an instantaneous inspiration on Jessie's part because I learned later that her brother, Salvu (Saviour), had spent a whole week doing the whole house in preparation for my first visit.

When the day arrived, Jessie walked ahead of me to the dining room where the whole family was sitting expectantly. The room was accessed through a very low doorway set in a metre-thick wall. Jessie and her father George warned me to keep my head low.

'Okay, thanks,' I muttered while ducking my head low enough to keep a full half metre between it and the low roof of the doorway. But I straightened up too early. 'Ouch!' I yelped.

Everyone laughed at my mishap and so did I, although I was certain that my head was already growing a sizeable lump. The incident, however, helped break the ice and the formality of a first visit, and I 'heroically' told them not to bother about the cold water they offered me for the bruise on my head.

After my introduction to Jessie's six brothers and sisters, her mother, Salvina, who possessed a very sweet nature, produced a welcoming cake on top of which she had place a large cherry. Instinctively I got out of my chair, picked up the cherry and put it in my mouth. This gesture from a usually withdrawn person produced further laughter all around and any leftover awkwardness soon dissipated.

George, Jessie's father, always sat at the head of the table and, when I got to know him better, I found him to be a very quiet, patient man, never given to panicking. He asked me many questions about my work and prospects for the future on that first visit. At one point during our conversation he surprised me when he turned on Jessie and exclaimed, 'Gulinu will grow up into a well-built man, and he's very intelligent.' Everyone in the room smiled at this compliment, but I could only blush, as usual.

This was my first of many visits. I would come to enjoy these visits, with the relaxed conversations with George and the traditional Maltese cooking of his wife, especially prepared for my benefit. She was an exceptionally good cook, in fact. Mum was also a good cook, but she was constrained to follow Dad's instructions to prepare the richest and most nutritious food in bulk, which didn't necessarily make for tasty dishes. Salvina's cooking, therefore, tasted that much better because the ingredients were meticulously measured for better results.

When I was nearing eighteen I finished my secondary education and never regretted attending Stella Maris College. Excellent teaching and discipline resulted in very good results, but I had no intention of going to university. I wanted to get down to setting myself up in business and, to be fair on Dad, he refrained from mentioning his 'bank manager' illusion, at least for a while. I didn't mention my business ambitions, though; I didn't want to resurrect the old argument although I knew that he was very angry that I wouldn't act on his suggestion.

While minding his petrol station and assisting him on his building sites, I thought of going into the import/export business; nothing big, just importing some small items that had nothing to do with Dad's business and reselling them locally at whatever profit. This was something I could manage now that I had finished school and had more free time. Dad didn't object when I told him what I was up to, but I could see from his expression that he was far from pleased.

My paid job with him consisted mostly of book keeping, correspondence, drawing of plans and other odd jobs. It paid a monthly salary of €140.00. This was roughly equivalent to an average worker's net earnings. In my case it was different, however; my job entailed much driving around in my car. I was responsible for its maintenance, insurance and fuel for which I didn't receive any allowance. These expenses eroded my monthly salary by €70.00, which meant that I ended up with half of what a worker took home. I tried to make up for these expenses by using the telephone more often when dealing with clients and by effecting payments by cheque, but Dad would have none of this. He insisted that I meet clients personally and even stand in long queues for paying bills in Valletta. I tried to explain that this was wasting time I could utilise better at the office, but he wouldn't budge and insisted that since I was his employee I had to obey his orders.

My father had, by now, drastically reduced his farming activities. It now seemed he also wanted to avoid the annual four-week hassle involving the exportation of potatoes to Holland. His trading licence was still valid, but it would become superfluous once he stopped the activity. However, since the government had not been issuing further licences for many years, Dad's was very valuable. One day he strode into the office and very matter-of-factly informed me that he was transferring his licence to Ninu (Anthony), one of his employees.

I couldn't believe my ears and it took me some time before I managed to find the words to express what I felt inside.

'But why, Pa? Why to Ninu and not to me?'

I knew I was capable of handling the process from beginning to end thanks to the experience I had accumulated over the years. I felt very hurt that Dad preferred a complete outsider to his own son.

'I'm your son, Pa,' I continued, on the brink of tears. 'I'm your flesh and blood and you know I can do the job. I'm eighteen now, Pa, and have enough experience. I know I can do it. Give me the chance and I'll prove it to you.'

We argued for a long time and shouted at one another until, at last, he began to waver. Not completely, however. He compromised on the condition that Ninu would still have a half share with me getting the other half. That was enough for me. It still gave me the chance to prove to Dad that I could deliver and I did not want to press him any further. Winning half of the deal was enough of a victory.

I had known Ninu since I was a boy. We worked together shoulder to shoulder and always enjoyed each other's company. He was a good and honest man, an ideal partner and I was overjoyed at the prospect of working with him. In fact, I couldn't sleep all night – at last I was in business. Admittedly, it was not the business I had planned – that would come later – but now, for the first time in my life, I was going to be my own boss.

The potato export business was seasonal, lasting four hectic weeks. In my enthusiasm I started analysing the costs and final projection well in advance. The whole work would involve only casual labour, as explained in a previous chapter, some of whom were housewives eager to augment their husbands' wages.

'Well,' I thought to myself. 'Since I'm going to be the one to fork out the expenses, why can't some of it remain in the household?'

So, I offered my sisters the normal daily rate of €2.33 if they cared to join me. It was good pay, but the work involved was very hard indeed. Two of my sisters took up my offer, while the others were too young anyway. The younger, however, including my brothers, would eventually carry out easy tasks which would be fun to do like printing the licence number on jute bags and the like.

Ninu was also very excited at the chance of proving himself, but it was going to be hard work, side by side for sixteen whole hours a day with little time for sleep. Our day began well before sunrise and sometimes extended until midnight. In the mornings we would drive around Naxxar to pick up our workers from outside their homes. By this time I was in possession of a driving licence and so I did the driving. The women and my sisters enjoyed this early morning ride. They wore tight jeans or the occasional pair of shorts, with hats and scarves to cover their hair. It looked more like the start of a picnic than a day's hard work in the fields.

I followed Dad's route to the various fields where my team would be doing the potato selection and packing in bags. I felt proud that it was me, now, who was doing all the directing and planning. I knew everything that had to be done, and also did my share of the hard work. I could also match Ninu at calculating the weight of a full bag just by lifting it a few centimetres from the ground. The farmer was always at hand to assist and confirm the weight while the official weigher was doing his job.

Before leaving each field we would hand out a voucher to the farmer, confirming the amount of bags collected. This voucher would be presented to us at payment time later on.

Ninu's brothers, Żeppu and Victor, were contracted to collect the bags from the fields in their Bedford J6. The process lasted till late evening each day and would have lasted longer had not Ninu and I done our bit of bag carrying. I was quite tall, so I could throw the 32 kilo bag higher and further on the truck than anyone else. This made Żeppu's job of stacking that little bit easier. I was, in fact, strong enough to lift and carry two bags at a time – a total of 64 kilos. When darkness started to fall and time was pressing, I would even ask somebody to add another bag on top of the two on my shoulder, to increase the weight to a total of 96 kilos and hasten the task. This was quite a heavy weight for a thin eighteen-year-old and I would literally wobble my way on the soft soil to the waiting truck. In the end, the truck would be stacked with bags as high as 4 metres.

At five o'clock the following morning, Żeppu would drive the bags slowly down to the harbour for the inspection, grading and loading procedure, as explained in a previous chapter.

By evening each day, I was totally exhausted with my bare feet and hands encrusted with dry soil, my hair all entangled and forming pointed edges, created by a combination of dried sweat and dust. But this was my first experience as a businessman and I was exhilarated. Some evenings I would forget my weariness and drive down to Mosta to share my happiness with Jessie. I would find her sitting outside her home chatting with her mother and some friends. I would remain behind the wheel and talk to her about the day's happenings and she would share my happiness.

Her house was just opposite a cycling club where many youths gathered for a drink and some fun. They would stare at me and wonder what this nondescript and scruffy bum was up to, talking to a nice, local girl like Jessie. She would notice and feel embarrassed, but I never bothered. She once asked me inside to have something to eat and when I got out of the car and she saw that I was barefoot, she tried to ignore the curious glances and whisperings from across the street.

'Why don't you come over one day and give us a hand,' I once asked her. 'You'll be working with my sisters and I'll pay you the same rate. What do you say?'

I knew she was interested in this kind of work because I had talked to her about it a number of times. I also wanted her to watch her future husband at work, and how well he managed his workers, especially the women.

'Okay,' she answered after some consideration. 'I'll give it a try. It'll be a new experience if nothing else.'

She joined us a few days later and it didn't take her long to realise how tough the job was.

When the process of selection and packing was halfway through, Dad came over to me and informed me that my sisters had complained that the €2.33 a day I was paying them wasn't fair for the hard work involved. He ordered me to increase it to €3.50.

'But, Pa, it would mean that we would increase our costs by fifty per cent and it could well result in a loss.'

He continued to insist and we gave in.

At the end of the four weeks of hard work, Ninu and I sat quietly at a desk and made our final calculations. After deducting all the expenses, we estimated a profit of €700.00 each. That was the equivalent of five months' salary – quite a handsome profit when one considers Dad's imposition of the extra cost. My next concern was to chase the Department of Agriculture to pay the amount due to us. Without that money we couldn't pay the workers and farmers and I couldn't wait to deposit my profit into a bank account. I was already envisaging the day when the €700.00 would start me in the business I was truly cut out for. However, since the trading licence was still in Dad's name, any payments by the Agricultural Department would be made out to him. So, when I found out that all payments had been made, I approached Dad and told him, 'You should have received the cheque by post yesterday. Did you, by any chance?'

'Yes, I did.'

'Thank God for that. Would you give it to me so I can start settling the accounts, please?'

'No, I won't.'

I was completely taken aback and for a moment I thought that this was one of his very rare jokes.

'Are you serious?' I asked tentatively, hoping against hope that that he would smile and hand me the cheque.

'Yes. I'm very serious and I'm not giving you any cheque.' I couldn't believe this was my father speaking.

'But why, Pa? You know half the money belongs to me.'

'Oh no it doesn't. And do you know why? Do you know how much it cost me to give you a good education?'

'What's that got to do with it? You know I've a lot of expenses and have to honour my obligations.'

'Of course you do. That's why I'm giving Ninu his money after deducting his share of the expenses. But I shall retain your share of the profit.'

I just couldn't believe it. I had been naïve enough to tell him about my share of the profit and he was now withholding it from me after the careful planning and hard work I had put into it. The basis of his argument was that he was still paying me for my normal work for him, even though he had agreed to transfer the licence to Ninu and myself. I was very angry about the way I was being singled out for this treatment.

'You cannot do this to me. I should at least be paid the rate you're giving the workers and my sisters.'

He just shook his head and made as if to turn from me, but I wouldn't let him go.

'Look. It was you who insisted that I increase the workers' hourly rate, and now you don't even want to pay me that rate after what I've gone through these past four weeks.'

'I've already told you. You're paying back what it cost me to educate you.'

'But you paid for my sisters' education as well and yet they're getting paid for their work. Why are you doing this to me?'

He just turned his back on me and walked away while I broke down crying my heart out. That same evening I went down to Mosta to meet with Jessie. It seemed that the expression on my face told it all because she greeted me with, 'What happened to you, Ġulin? What's the matter? You look as if –'

She didn't have time to finish the sentence because I broke down crying while between sobs I explained to her what had happened. It did me good to get it off my chest, especially with Jessie. She mothered me and sympathised with me, and when she thought I was calm enough she said, 'Don't let this thing get you down, Ġulin. You're still young enough to start all over again.'

'But how could he, Jessie?'

'No, don't take it out on him. Remember he's your father and he loves you in his own way. It's just that he's of the old school, that's all. He thinks he's doing it for your own good, so that you'll forget all about business and become a bank manager.'

She was laughing when she said the last sentence and I had to smile in spite of myself.

When she noticed the change in my expression, she continued, 'This should serve as a lesson to you. Don't go into this again unless the licence's in your name. You're always telling me what a tough businessman your father is. So if you want to become a good one yourself, you have to be as tough and more.'

I had to admire her common sense. 'You're right, Jess. But I won't ever give up. I just have to be more careful when dealing with Dad.'

'You see,' she joked. 'You've already learned your lesson.'

I was still very hurt, however, and I was already thinking about how difficult it was going to be to work for Dad as if nothing had happened. But this hard blow also taught me that business isn't the easiest of professions. I would have to be careful and shrewd in my dealings and this thought gave me courage. It was a lesson learnt the hard way, but I was now determined to be tougher in the future.

I need not emphasise that the incident continued to sour my relations with Dad, and from then onwards we practically never again saw eye to eye about anything. I still worked hard, however, and never shirked my responsibilities for which he was paying me a salary. I still took my turn at helping him with his laborious construction works if a worker reported sick, and still helped him in his wheat and barley harvesting, which was still being done by hand. I was also still packing hay for transportation to various farms as animal fodder, and continued with my full contribution in the potato export process.

One cold and wintry day, while working barefoot in Dad's field pushing soil with a hoe to form protective mounds around potato saplings, I asked myself, 'Why am I doing all this? How is all this helping me become the successful businessman I've been dreaming of since I can remember?' I shook my head in disgust at myself. 'I should be somewhere else. I should be spending more time doing things that would help me reach my goal. I'm just wasting my time here, slaving for Dad.'

From then onwards my work in the fields and in Dad's other farming activity was reduced to the barest minimum and I immediately applied for a correspondence course in accountancy with a university in the United Kingdom.

It was also around this time that, by coincidence, I came across a book entitled *The Human Machine* by Arnold Bennett. It wasn't much of a book – a little longer than a pamphlet and very easy to read, containing chapters not longer than a page or two – but its contents spoke volumes and completely changed my outlook on life. I have never been a reader of novels, reading only magazines and articles that dealt with business, but *The Human Machine* gives a powerful message to all those who want to overcome difficulties and take quick decisions in difficult situations. It absorbed me to such an extent that I reread it to make sure that I fully understood its message. It was exactly what I needed at that particular moment in my life. It told me exactly what I must do at that particular crossroads ahead of me. It made me realise that my shy and withdrawn character had always been a stumbling block when I wanted to express myself clearly to Dad and his friends. Now, any doubts that I may still have harboured about my future evaporated completely. The book strengthened further my determination to overcome all the obstacles that I could already foresee, and any that might confront me in the future.

Working for Dad was no picnic at all. I managed his office, supervised his development sites, carried out manual work including digging trenches using a pneumatic jackhammer, ran his errands and did everything that needed doing to help keep his business going. But even while doing all these jobs, my ambition to get out of it all and start on my own became almost an obsession.

I have already mentioned my intention of going into the importation business, as it was the only chance I had of making a little money to help launch myself in the construction business, so I made a start, importing chamois leather. I sold it at petrol stations and it wasn't easy because there were already some established brands in the market. One way that helped me make a few sales was by stopping at a petrol station for just 5 litres of fuel. I would then go to the cash point to settle the bill and show a sample of my wares to the owner. I would repeat this tactic at other petrol stations until my tank was full. I managed on occasion to persuade some owners to order a few, sometimes enough to cover the cost of the fuel. I didn't make much money but it was a start.

Those were the days when many Maltese were working in Libya and earning good money. Maltese businessmen were investing good money in that country and I began looking around for an opportunity that could open a window, however small, into that lucrative market. Then someone introduced me to a certain Jensen Lund, a Danish manager with an oil drilling company in Libya. He lived with his family in a luxurious villa in Mosta. He drove around in a self-drive hired car, always immaculately dressed and as jovial as one could imagine. His lifestyle resembled that of a millionaire. He turned out to be anything but a millionaire, however, as he was completely penniless and a chronic alcoholic. I wasn't aware of all this when I met him, and was still too young, eager and inexperienced to see through his smooth talking. I completely let my defences down. He agreed to give me all the advice I needed for a fee of €233.00. It was a lot of money to pay for one so young and with nobody around to consult, I paid the fee.

Later, he asked me for a loan of €700.00 to see him through until he received his pay cheque, which was held up in the post. Or so he said. To cut a long story short, he frisked me for a total of €1,400. This all but dried up my entire savings. Sometime later, when I tried to contact him, I found out that he had absconded together with his family. This was a shock and another blow to my ambitions. It meant that I had to start from scratch yet again.

This time, however, I wasn't sorry for myself. I was too angry to have the luxury of feeling sorry for myself. I was angry for letting myself be duped by a smooth-talking foreigner and angry at him for conning me so easily. I then remembered what Arnold Bennett said in his book and decided that now was as good a time as any to put into practice what I had learned.

I started asking around and discovered that Lund had cheated other people as well. He owed large amounts to the owner of the rented villa, the owner of the self-drive car and even to the owner of the bar he frequented every evening. So, I decided to somehow trace his footsteps all the way to Libya and make him give my money back.

Travelling alone to Libya at the time wasn't exactly what a mother would wish for her eighteen-year-old son, so I had to find somebody mature and responsible enough to take me under his wing. The opportunity arose when I met two local businessmen who were travelling to Libya to close some deals. I explained my predicament to them and they were more than willing to help me out. Luckily, I happened to have kept an envelope Lund had given me which contained the address and telephone number of his business in Libya. I, of course, never mentioned Lund in my parents' presence, least of all the way he conned me. I knew what a spectacle Dad would have made of me in front of the whole family. I just told them that I was visiting Libya with two others as tourists, and that was that. Mum, however, was still apprehensive about this adventure of mine; she made me wear my brand new suit and carry a smart briefcase. She wanted me to look impressive and business-like when I travelled with the other gentlemen. She even accompanied me to the airport and could not stop crying, even though I was in the constant company of the two businessmen who had made my trip possible.

Mum's apprehensions weren't totally unfounded. It wasn't the best time for a foreigner to be in Libya; self-styled, twenty-eight-year-old Colonel Gaddafi had taken over the country in September and was busy kicking out all western influences and workers. Currency regulations were very strict and anyone caught breaching them ended up in prison. A Libyan prison wasn't the best place to be and no diplomatic interventions could breach the thick walls.

Foreigners were looked upon with suspicion and sometimes with disgust. The revolution had put paid to the western nations' monopolies obtained at the expense of the ethnic population and its ripple effect could still be felt and seen all around. All past foreign influences were wiped out, sometimes rather comically. My hotel, for example, was originally named 'Welcome Hotel'. This 'western' name was now covered with an ordinary jute bag while its Arabic equivalent, 'Hotel Merhaba', was painted on a strip of plywood affixed over the main entrance.

I arrived in Libya in the evening and checked into my hotel. This left me no time to start upon my quest for the Danish crook. So, after I freshened up a little, I ventured out of the hotel to familiarise myself with the surroundings. I came across a cinema and, having nothing to do, I went inside. The hall was nearly full, but before the main feature the audience had to endure the screening of a few commercials, one of which featured an alcoholic drink. The shouting, whistling and commotion that greeted it were deafening. For a moment I had forgotten that alcoholic beverages were strictly forbidden in Islamic countries. The same reaction, however, greeted every beautiful woman that appeared on the screen throughout the main feature and I started wondering whether coming to Libya was such a good idea after all.

The following morning I hailed a taxi and instructed the driver to take me to the address on Jensen Lund's envelope. On enquiring about him, I was told that he was no longer an employee of the company and I was referred to another address a couple of miles away. When I arrived at the new address I found that it was just a shop selling car parts. The shop was situated in remote and forbidding surroundings, accessible only by non-asphalted roads. There were three men in the shop and as I approached them I could see them watching me suspiciously. This didn't put me at ease at all and for a moment I thought of walking back to the relative safety of the taxi, returning to the hotel and taking the first flight back to Malta. But I thought about Lund's self-confident smile whenever he sweet-talked me into giving him my money and the trouble I had already taken to try and wipe it off his face.

I asked them about Jensen Lund and their expression immediately turned into one of complete innocence and stupidity.

'Who?' asked one of them while looking at the other two.

'Jensen Lund,' I repeated. 'A tall, blond man. He worked...'

The three were already shaking their heads and looking at each other while I was trying to finish the sentence. The first man, who acted as spokesman, said that they had never heard of anyone by that name. Something in their innocent expression and concerned look assured me that they were lying.

'No. They must have given you the wrong address. You can see there are no foreigners here. Only Libyans in this shop, as you can see.'

I could see there wasn't anybody around, but I noticed a telephone on a desk in a corner.

'May I use your phone, then? Maybe I'll be able to get through to him.'

I didn't like the way they were looking at my brand new suit. I was sure they were sizing me up and wondering about the thickness of my wallet. It seemed that the waiting taxi was also making them feel uncomfortable, so they didn't object to my request. I took out the envelope from my pocket and dialled the number written on it. There was no reply.

The three men seemed to have realised that I wouldn't be shaken off so easily and one of them told me to return on the morrow.

'Maybe we'll be able to trace him for you. Who do we tell him came to look for him?'

So they knew Jensen Lund.

'Tell him it's Angelo Xuereb. He would know why I'm here.'

I returned to their shop the following morning without much hope of ever seeing my money again. This time, however, the reception that greeted me contrasted sharply with that of the day before. They were all smiles and handshakes.

'We made many telephone calls to friends and we traced your friend at an oil field very far away in the desert,' their usual spokesman told me. 'And he has instructed us to give you this envelope,' he continued while fishing a thick envelope from his back trouser pocket.

I didn't believe a word he said about Lund being at some far off oilfield, but I kept my mouth shut. Instead, I smiled and thanked them. I also shook their hands again before I turned to leave.

When I was halfway to the taxi, I heard the usual spokesman say, 'Young man.'

I turned and looked at him.

'Let me give you some advice before you leave, young man,' he continued. 'You are too young to run around collecting American dollars around here.' He looked around him to emphasise the bleakness of the surroundings. 'This place is very dangerous for foreigners with American dollars. You could be risking your life if some people were to know.'

He gave me a broad smile and I could only manage a feeble one. I was certain he meant what he said.

It was with great relief that I sat on the bed in my hotel room and slit open the envelope. When I counted the money I found $1,500 (equivalent to approximately €1,200 – €200.00 less than Lund owed me). The three Libyans must have taken their commission. They could have taken my life instead. I was satisfied with this success. The only problem now was how to smuggle the money out of the country. The best bet was to insert it between the sole of my feet and the socks and hope for the best.

At the airport I came across the two businessmen from Malta who asked me about the money.

'I'm walking on it,' I answered with a smile.

'You mean to tell us you managed to get your money back?' one of them asked, surprised.

I didn't answer, but continued to smile. Then both slapped my back heartily and laughed so much and for so long that they nearly choked.

In the safety of the plane, one of them said, 'Do you know

why we laughed so much down there? It's because of the irony of it all. You see, Anġlu, we are very experienced in business and yet we weren't able to close a single deal, while you, a mere eighteen-year-old, managed successfully what you came out here for.'

There were other occasions when I met these two gentlemen in later years and they would always mention this incident. Through them I also met another businessman who was planning to open a steel-wool manufacturing plant in Malta. This was a product that was widely used by Maltese housewives and when it was mentioned to me I expressed my interest in joining the venture. I had to admit the complete lack of funds, but the would-be shareholders accepted my offer to prepare the feasibility study and to procure various quotations for the whole plant in exchange for a minor shareholding in this new venture. I did all this in just six weeks and submitted the results in a neatly typed presentation.

A few days later, I was summoned to a meeting with the shareholders who expressed their surprise and satisfaction at the way I had managed to furnish them with all of the information required and in such a relatively short time. All of them congratulated me on the seriousness and professionalism of my report. After further meetings, the project was shelved for lack of funds, so I wasn't paid anything for my labour, but I didn't lose money either. In fact, I had gained much experience and learned many lessons, and had the satisfaction of knowing that I could perform well at any task I put my energy into.

On my eighteenth birthday, Dad bought me a brand new yellow Toyota Corolla Coupè SL. He had done the same for my elder sisters earlier. The Toyota was my dream car. Though not exactly a supercar, its 13HP engine made it a fast sports car. It was also more than I had expected for my birthday and I was so proud of it that I washed and cleaned it every chance I got. I even polished its aluminium cylinder head every weekend!

Saturday afternoons and Sunday mornings I would join other

young enthusiasts to race up and down the runway at the unused Ta' Qali airfield. Lookouts would sit in their cars at both ends of the runway to watch for traffic policemen. They would flash their headlights at the first sign of a white crash helmet and we would stop racing. Sometimes the police would leave after a few minutes and we would continue where we left off. At other times, however, they would linger as if they had nothing else to do but enjoy the wide open space, in which case we would leave slowly one by one like dogs with their tails between their legs.

This new car also meant more freedom for Jessie and me. Our relationship had, by now, grown deeper and we spent most evenings driving happily around. On Sunday afternoons we loved to drive to the countryside where we would take a stroll or just sit on the soft grass to enjoy the beautiful scenery around us. Eventually, my parents ordered me to start taking along my youngest brother Paul, and Jessie her younger sister Anna. Both were intended to act as chaperones, but they preferred to sit and play by themselves, and ignore Jessie and me huddling close by.

Sometimes a person becomes so absorbed in his work and thoughts that he is not conscious of other people's perception of him. This was happening to me. I was so absorbed in my work for Dad, the personal ambitions for my career and my future with Jessie that I never noticed what my younger brothers and sisters thought of me, their eldest brother. These pages, in fact, are full of my relationship with Dad. I had been his constant companion as his eldest son since I was able to take my first steps, and I have always been the son he leaned heavily on since I was thirteen. Willingly or grudgingly, I had always bowed my head to his demands, however unfair or illogical. And, in spite of our disagreements, especially during the previous three years, I never shirked from the duties placed upon my shoulders. I craved for just some simple reward, some sign of being appreciated for what I did, but Dad never responded in that way. In some ways, he was enormously generous (as in buying all his eleven children a new car on their eighteenth birthday), but I would have preferred to have been treated as an adult and allowed to earn my own money, and perhaps to have bought my own. As I reflect, I realise that bringing up children can be very difficult, each one is different, and to have eleven must have been a nightmare.

My younger brothers and sisters, completely unaware of the arguments and quarrels between Dad and me, which had become more frequent as time went by, interpreted my meekness and unquestionable loyalty as an endorsement of Dad's authority over everything that went on in the family. Dad was a strict disciplinarian (I have already written about his insistence that I must be home by eight o'clock during my first few weeks with Jessie); with my immediate younger sisters he was even worse.

They were now growing up and some of them were young teenagers. They had reached that age when boys became interesting beings and vice versa. Thinking that I was just an extension of Dad's authority, they did not dare be seen with boys when I was around. Dad, similarly, considered that my submission to his authority at work could be extended to family affairs, so he gave me strict orders to keep a close watch over my sisters during village festas and weekends, and to report directly to him any misdemeanours.

One evening, I saw my younger sister Doris with her boyfriend Salvu, who eventually became her husband. At first she did not notice me, but when she did, she went completely pale. Then she seemed to recover somewhat and whisper something to Salvu who turned his gaze towards me. She then pushed him along and he walked towards me.

'Ġulin, please,' he started saying as soon as he stopped in front of me. 'Doris has asked me to tell you not to tell your father anything.'

'Tell Dad what?' I answered, though I knew what he meant.

Salvu was taken aback as he didn't expect this reply. He looked back at Doris whose pleading eyes were urging him on from 10 yards back. Then he looked at me again and continued, 'You see, if he gets to know about us he won't let Doris go out and we won't be able to meet.'

'But how could he know about you?'

He couldn't believe what he was hearing. In his anxiety he wasn't able to realise that I was joking.

'Because Doris said that you'll tell your father.'

'Who? Me tell Dad? Why should I tell Dad?'

By now I was smiling at him.

'Well. She thought... You mean you won't tell your father about us?'

'Of course I won't tell Dad.'

Then I looked at Doris and smiled. She wasn't sure she should smile back until I called her over, and I wished both of them the best of luck for their future.

From then onwards my younger brothers and sisters started to treat me as their older brother, not as an extension of their father. I, for my part, became more conscious of the problems they were going through, which I could understand.

While I was working for Dad and planning my future, Jessie was working forty-four hours each week at a textile factory for which she was being paid only €6.00. Out of curiosity, I once asked her what she earned at her job and she could not bring herself to admit the measly wage she was getting, so she upped the figure to €7.00 a week.

'But Jessie,' I told her, 'that's too little for the long hours you're putting in. It's nothing less than daylight robbery. That's squeezing the workers dry and it's simply not fair.'

'I know, Gulin. But what can I do? All of us girls are paid less than the men.'

'What do you mean "what can you do"? Just leave. Soon I'll have my own business and you won't need to work.'

'It's all well and good, Gulinu, and you know I'm certain you'll make it in business. But what will my family do in the meantime? Mum needs all the help she can get with such a large family to feed. And Dad's not getting any younger, neither. Furthermore, I need to save something for when we get married.'

I had no argument against her logic. I could well understand the needs of a large family, but I did persuade her to quit her job when we became formally engaged.

It was around this time that the situation with Dad was becoming critical. I've already written about the various jobs I did for Dad, including digging trenches, but this was a new low; he ordered me to work as a helper with Jessie's brother, Salvu, in his plastering job. One can imagine how demeaning and frustrating it was for me, working for my future brother-in-law, doing work any unskilled labourer could do. As always, however, I obeyed. But one fine day, after just a few weeks, I couldn't take it any longer and confronted him.

'Look, Pa. Some time ago you deprived me of my hard earned €700.00 profit with the excuse that I should start paying back what you spent on my education. So, is this the reason you gave me a good education? To dig your trenches? To roam around your building sites and get as dirty as an ordinary labourer? Is this the future you planned for me when you sent me to college? I know I can be more useful to you in administrative supervisory work. It's what they trained me for at school, Pa.'

As always, it was to no avail. He could never be persuaded. I would protest and get angry at every order he gave me, but I would always carry it out to the full. So, I started thinking about other ways out of his clutches. I was facing a dilemma, however, because I couldn't yet start my own construction business as he would surely put all possible spokes in the wheel. He would do anything but give me the necessary push forward.

My chamois leather business wasn't generating the profit I had hoped and so I had to explore other avenues. I came up with the idea of exporting Maltese handmade crafts. It would not only generate the necessary profit I needed to start me off, but also increase the inflow of foreign currency into Malta. The snag was that I had first to buy the product with money I didn't have before I started exporting. I discussed the problem with Jessie one evening and told her about the money problem.

'I can't do anything while I'm still living at home, with Dad in control even of the air we breathe. But, in the meantime, I need to raise some cash to help me launch myself when the time comes.'

Jessie had never ever given me advice on business matters and my dream for the future. She always had complete faith in my abilities and knew that given the chance I would make a success of it. So, when I said that I needed some cash, she told me, 'Look, Ġulin, I have managed to save something from my wages. It's not much – a hundred Liri – and probably wouldn't make much of a difference, but you can have it if you wish. I'll lend it to you if you think it'll help you.'

I looked at her face. There was no doubt she was serious about it and I felt ashamed. She was offering me her savings to give me the chance to prove myself. She was offering me a chance to prove myself not just to me and her, but to my father and everyone else.

After long seconds of thinking about it, I shook my head. 'I can't, Jessie. I can't take your money.'

'But I want you to, Ġulin. I want you to have it because I know you'll give it back to me. Because I know you can do it, Ġulin. I know you can.'

In the end I took the money.

'But on one condition,' I said to her when she was handing me the amount. 'On condition that I'll pay you back in twelve months.'

Jessie informed her sweet mother about the deal.

'But what if he doesn't pay you back, Jessie, dear?'

'Who? Ġulinu? Just you wait and see, Mum. If I didn't believe in him and didn't trust him I wouldn't want to marry him, would I?'

I opened an account in her name in my journal. 'Jessie Abela' (her maiden name) The entries that I paid her in three instalments in less than a year are still legible in my records.

Sometime during this period I came across a newspaper advert offering part-time employment as a life insurance salesman. I applied, obviously to help raise the money I needed, and after a short course on life insurance policies I became a fully-fledged, part-time insurance salesman. My eagerness to earn money and my usual total commitment to a given task enabled me to become the bestselling salesman of the company and I was earning good commissions.

A few months into the job, a friend of mine, to whom I had sold a policy, needed to liquidate it because he urgently required all the cash he could lay his hands on even though he knew that he would be getting a small percentage of the premium he had paid. He asked for my assistance which I, of course, was only too pleased to extend. The insurance company, however, wouldn't honour the agreement. The directors of the company kept beating about the bush and did their best to parry every argument I raised in the client's favour. I thought this was downright dishonourable practice and didn't want to be part of it any longer. So, I resigned, giving up an income I sorely needed. But I didn't want to risk my credibility.

St John's Cathedral

5

The Turning Point

(1973–1975) 21–23 years

By now Dad had completely given up his farming activity. He closed down his farm to concentrate on the development of a small number of terraced houses and apartments, but was still not offering me a respectable position or the freedom to build my own business. In fact, his unbending attitude towards my requests for work more suitable to my qualifications further persuaded me to get married and leave home as soon as possible. This would allow me more freedom to follow my dream.

He had long been telling me that he would build a villa for Jessie and me.

'You're my eldest son, Gol, and have always worked hard for me. You well deserve a nice place to raise a family with Jessie and I'll certainly see that you get what you deserve.'

This he said a long time before I went up to him to inform him that Jessie and I had planned to marry in one and a half years' time.

'Pa,' I told him, 'now we have to talk really seriously about the place you promised us. Jessie and I have been talking a lot about it and we've decided we should be ready to get married in eighteen months.'

I wasn't banking on getting a villa. The one he had built had been rented out to foreigners who were paying high rent, which Dad would definitely not forfeit for the likes of me.

'Ok. Give me some time to think it over,' he answered. 'I'll probably build you a nice terraced house.'

'And goodbye to our villa,' I thought.

A couple of days later he asked me, 'How about a nice terraced house?'

I thought about it for a few moments and then replied, 'Why don't you give me the money you would spend on the terraced house so that I'll be able to start my own business? Jessie and I could live in a rented apartment until things improve and we could have our own house.'

He said he wanted some time to think it over and after a few days he told me, 'Let me tell you what we'll do. You can stay in that vacant apartment next to our home. In the meantime, I'll give you a vacant plot at Mosta for which I'll give you the cash to build a house in shell form. Then you can finish it with your own money. What do you say to that?'

What could I say? I had no choice. Later, however, when I had time to think clearly, I thought I could turn this to my advantage. If I could split the plot into three smaller ones I could then sell each at a good profit because smaller houses are much easier to sell. The plot had an awkward shape but a large frontage. This allowed me to come up with three compact but beautifully laid-out terraced houses.

I was really thrilled with this idea and, more so, because I was finally starting my own business. In the meantime, Jessie and I got down to the serious business of preparing detailed plans for our apartment and to discussing a date for our wedding. We decided on 10th August 1974.

This was probably the happiest period for Jessie and me since our first date. She was happy for me. My enthusiasm at the chance of starting my business was infectious and she went about making preparations for our future home. It was then that she finally decided to give up her job at the textile factory. She could now see that our future together was assured and could now dedicate her whole time to preparing for it. She even got her mother to teach her the method of cooking our much-flavoured traditional Maltese dishes, which I love so much. There was, however, too much work for me to do during the next eighteen months to allow me to dream about the tasty dishes Jessie would soon be preparing. There was the building permit to apply for and the engagement of a gang of builders and, soon enough, in less than two months to be precise, the first house was built in shell form and put up for sale. For some reason, which I could never understand, Dad had never advertised his properties in the newspapers. I think he assumed that would-be-buyers would just come knocking on his door as if he was the only person in Malta with property to sell. I advertised the first three-bedroom terraced house, having a built-up area of 160 square metres, in the newspapers, asking €15,000 freehold. When Dad heard about it he flew into a typical rage.

'You must be crazy' he shouted at me. 'Who is the crazy person to pay that amount for an unfinished building?'

In two weeks, however, I concluded a deal which would net me €14,000. I was so pleased that I went up to Dad and told him, 'Hey, Pa. I wasn't so crazy after all because I did manage to sell the house through the papers. And do you know what I'm getting? €14,000!'

I thought he would be pleased with the news, but he reacted as though I told him I had given the house away for free. He simply hated being proved wrong and he didn't like the potentially large profit I could make from the sale of the three houses if I managed to build them.

Unfortunately, when he gave me the plot of land, I made the mistake again of not transferring its title in my name. I seemed to have forgotten past mistakes and Arnold Bennett's *The Human Machine*. I paid dearly for the mistake because Dad made the most of it.

'I'll tell you what, Gol,' he told me. 'I'll sign the contract for this sale and from the proceeds I'll build a house on the next plot all ready for you and Jessie to move into, and the smallest one in shell form only.'

This last proposition would continue to guarantee him the income from the rent of the apartment which was earmarked for us.

I was aghast. After all the work, energy and money (the little I had managed to save) I had put into it, my father comes along and takes it all. My dream that at long last I would have enough money to start me off had again been shattered by my own father.

I couldn't believe that even then, practically on the eve of my marriage, he could still treat me like this. Not even Jessie could console me this time because even she broke down in sad tears. We just had to swallow this bitterest of pills and bow our heads. We had no means to alter what was legally binding and I had, once again, ended up penniless. To cap it all, Jessie's birthday on 17th March, the last one before our marriage, was too close for me to save enough money to buy her a special present. I had planned to give her something special with the profit I would have made from the sale of the house: something she would have remembered as my first expensive present to her. The only thing I could afford was a cheap woollen top for which I paid €2.33. I cannot forget the embarrassment I felt when I gave it to her.

'I'm really sorry, Jessie, but it's all I could afford.' And while she was carefully opening the wrapping, I continued, 'But I promise you, Jessie. I honestly and truly promise you that the next one will be much, much better than this. I really mean it because I know I'll be in a better financial situation when I start my own business after we get married.'

Jessie looked at me and smiled. 'Do you know, Gulin, that this reminds me of the parable in the Gospel? You spent everything you had to buy me a birthday present. I know you will be successful one day. That's why I shall appreciate this top all the better.'

She had a way of putting my heart and mind at ease. I don't know what I would have done without her backing me all the way.

* * *

With only two months to our wedding, the dream of living in a house of our own seemed likely to be shattered. Worse than this, however, the fact that Jessie and I would have to depend on Dad for a place to live was taking possession of my daily thoughts because I wanted a complete break from his dominance of my everyday life. It was this that led us to make a decision; we would scrap Dad's offer and I would build the second terraced house and have it ready for habitation in the two short remaining months. I decided I would go for it with all the energy I could muster. This was a personal challenge to prove to Jessie that her faith in my ability was not baseless.

During those last hectic days I had to admire Jessie's faith in my abilities. People who knew we were soon getting married would ask her where we were taking up residence after we were married and she would answer, 'Gulinu's just started building our house.'

'But until he finishes building your home where will you be staying?'

'In the house he's building,' she would reply. 'He said it'll be ready by the time we marry.'

She would, however, feel foolish when noticing the raised eyebrows her answer always produced.

'How I wish people would stop asking me these questions, Gulin,' she would tell me in exasperation. 'They seem to think I'm crazy to believe you can really finish the house in so short a time.'

'Let them believe what they wish, Jessie dear. You'll see. I'll finish it and that's where we'll go to live right after we're married.'

'I know Gulin. I know you can do it. But people don't have the same faith as I have in you.'

'I don't need them having faith in me. I need you to have faith in me, Jessie. It's your faith in me that keeps me going.'

I put my words into practice. I put my whole energy into the project and I would spend whole days on end working on the site. This time, I made sure that the property was transferred to my name.

When the house was completely built in shell form I immediately turned my full attention to the finishings. I was putting in a regular fourteen hours work a day on the house and I managed to construct my two-storey terraced house right from its very foundations all the way through to the smallest fitting in just seven weeks. I had always considered myself thin, but by the end of the seven weeks I could barely keep my pants up. I was just skin and bones, and it was a good thing that I was completely broke as the weight of a few coins in my pocket would have pulled my trousers down. When I now look at the wedding photos I still marvel at how thin I became during the last remaining hectic days leading up to my marriage.

However, notwithstanding my busy days throughout the few weeks before my marriage, I managed a few hours from my work, just a few days before the big day, to put a small classified notice in a local newspaper promoting myself as a contractor willing to carry out any minor construction works. I had done this in my eagerness to start on my own as early as possible, but not really expecting any immediate response. I was wrong because two days later, just three days before the wedding, I received a phone call. It was a man from Sliema wanting to erect a washroom on his three-storey residence. I was delighted with this prospect and told him I was willing to discuss the job with him.

'So, when can you come over to discuss it?' he asked me.

'Any day I suppose. I'll fix my schedule to suit yours,' I answered, trying to sound like an old hand at negotiations.

'Very well, then. How about Sunday?'

'Sunday suits me fine. Any particular time?'

'First thing in the morning, say, at around eight?'

'Eight is fine.'

I was due to get married in the evening of the day before and the reception wouldn't be over before two in the morning. So, on the first morning of our honeymoon, I would be working.

'Sure you don't mind?' I asked Jessie when I told her about this golden opportunity.

'Of course not, you fool. It's what we've always wanted, isn't it? And the first day of our married life is as good a day as any, I suppose.'

The day of our wedding arrived and Dad was so happy. He had issued hundreds of invitations and more than 500 guests filled the beautiful Palazzo Parisio and its ample gardens in Naxxar where the reception was held. An hour earlier, Jessie and I had clearly and solemnly uttered the binding words 'I do' in a packed church. With these words I suddenly felt a pleasant weightlessness, as if the famous words contained a magic formula. I suddenly felt that I had become my own man at last, with my wife beside me in perpetual support. I had not just married the woman I loved, but I had broken away from the yoke that had dominated my life since I was a small boy. Binding myself to Jessie gave me the freedom I had been yearning for since I was a mere thirteen-year-old when I had made the decision about the life I wanted to follow.

We walked down the aisle and out of the famous Mosta church in a trance, oblivious to the throng of people waiting outside and showering us with handfuls of rice. Photos were taken and a spacious American car drove us to the beautiful Palazzo Parisio where we suddenly became aware of the large crowd waiting for us. My mother hugged me and cried on my shoulder. Then Jessie's mother hugged me, calling me her son. Then it was my brothers' and sisters' turn before we confronted the hundreds of guests waiting to congratulate us on this special day. People I knew and many others I had never set eyes on congratulated me and kissed my wife as though they had known us all their lives.

There was enough food going round to feed the guests twice over and enough drink to cause a week-long hangover. Dad was feeling 6 feet tall; he was being congratulated all round for the sumptuous feast he had prepared for his son. It was the first reception Dad had given for one of his children and superlatives like 'fit for a prince' or 'fit for a king' were being thrown around like wedding confetti – he was in seventh heaven.

We didn't manage to have a bite of food during our wedding reception because, between trying to talk to all the guests and spending a lot of time posing for photographs, we never found the time to even pinch a sandwich from some passing waiter. So, we instructed the caterers to put aside some of the best food and place it in the car we were going away in.

Jessie and I, however, were living in a world of our own. We were living a dream come true, barely believing it was possible. We smiled and shook hands, and let people hug us and fete us all they wanted. Both of us knew that this was the day that had set us free. Now we belonged to each other and to no one else. Now we could plan and live the way we wanted, not the way anybody else decided for us. Now Pandora's Box was tightly shut, padlocked and the key thrown to the bottom of the sea.

Tired and completely exhausted after the reception, Jessie and I sped off to a local hotel and into a room without a view. It was the only room we could afford. At seven o'clock we were the only guests in the breakfast room and at eight sharp I was knocking on the door of my first would-be client in Sliema. Jessie had agreed to wait in the car until I closed the deal.

I was welcomed by a family of six and we all sat on comfortable sofas to discuss the project.

'You look quite young for a contractor,' the senior member of the family said after half an hour of business talk. 'How old are you?'

'Twenty-two. But I've had years of experience working for my father who has built extensively all over Naxxar and Mosta.'

'Are you married by any chance?' asked the wife, probably assuming that married men made better building contractors.

'Sure I'm married,' I proudly replied while fingering my wedding ring to make sure I hadn't left it in the view-less hotel room.

'Oh,' continued the wife, probably thinking that married men shouldn't be so thin. 'You didn't give me the impression of a married man, being so young. Been married long?'

'Since last night.'

Everybody's mouth, except mine, fell wide open. After a few seconds of stunned silence, the senior member seemed to get hold of himself and asked, 'And where's your wife, if I may ask?'

'Outside. Waiting in the car.'

The whole family stood up as one.

'You mean to tell us that you left your wife outside when you should both be on your honeymoon?' continued the man, just stopping short of telling me that I should be ashamed of myself.

It didn't take him a minute to escort me unceremoniously to the front door. I felt stupid and ashamed, standing there, on the pavement, with nothing to show Jessie for the patience she had shown. But I couldn't blame the family. They couldn't have understood my eagerness to start my own construction business.

Jessie felt completely let down and understandably disappointed. She had so much faith in my abilities that she was certain I wouldn't have had any trouble landing the job. She knew it would have been the right job to start us off in our married life. To further compound matters, we had to pay my life insurance premium amounting to €256.00, which was due on the morrow.

This life insurance policy scheme wasn't my idea at all. It was another of Dad's brainwaves. He had succumbed to the daily pestering of a persistent insurance salesman and taken out a policy in my name to get rid of him. This was all well and good, and I appreciated the thoughtful gesture. The snag was, however, that I had to pay the premium with money I didn't have. At twenty-two I considered myself too young to start thinking about life insurances.

Fortunately, our wedding presents included the amount of €466.00 in cash. That, at least, would take care of the premium and leave us with €210.00.

'But what can we do with €210.00, Ġulin? You know it won't last long. We're running expenses we can barely afford and by the time we settle them we're left with practically nothing. Why don't we skip our honeymoon in Gozo and go home instead?'

I looked at her and could see the worry in her eyes. After all, she would now be responsible for the running of our home and unless I started earning some money soon, she wouldn't be able to for long.

I smiled at her and said, 'No, Jess. We're still going to Gozo. We both deserve a honeymoon, however short. We're not different from other newlyweds.' And off to our sister island of Gozo we went. We spent three glorious days there and I showed Jessie the beautiful sights I used to speed through in the *xalata* days of my youth.

On arrival at Gozo we made straight for the beautiful sanctuary of Our Lady of Ta' Pinu where we attended Mass. Outside, I had Jessie take a picture of me posing beside a large cross as though I was lifting it.

'This is the burden I have to carry all my life, now that I'm married to you,' I told her jokingly.

Our trip to Gozo wasn't just honeymooning because I carried along with me a large number of my unsold chamois leather. I used the same tactics as in Malta of stopping at a number of petrol stations and managed to offload quite a few. It was, at least, enough to cover the cost of the fuel, and Jessie couldn't help admiring my salesmanship techniques.

After our three-day honeymoon on Gozo, we took up immediate residence in our new home at Mosta and were extremely happy.

Just four days after our wedding (15th August) was festa day at Mosta. Mosta celebrates the feast of the Assumption of Our Lady, popularly known in Malta as *Santa Marija*, celebrated in five other towns and villages in Malta and one in Gozo.

The feast is also synonymous with World War II because it was on 15th August 1942 that the most important convoy of the entire war, affectionately known as the Convoy of Santa Maria, triumphantly entered the Grand Harbour and saved Malta from surrendering to the Axis Powers. It is also a public holiday and Mosta, situated right in the centre of the island, with its church boasting the world's third largest dome, celebrates the feast in grand style.

'Gulinu, dear,' Jessie told me as I emerged from the shower. 'I've prepared your suit to wear for the feast. I think it merits the occasion.'

'Do you think so?'

'Of course, dear. Remember we're still honeymooners and everybody expects us to be elegantly dressed on this our first festa as a married couple.'

I wasn't relishing the idea of wearing a tie and jacket on such a hot day, the peak of our hot summer. I was already sweating even though still in my undershorts.

'Well, if you say so.'

I couldn't stand it for more than fifteen minutes, however. The crowd pressing around us and the high humidity were killing me. Furthermore, only a handful of people were wearing suits and, unlike me, they seemed as if they were born wearing one.

'Look, Jessie,' I said to my wife. 'Unless I take this suit off and wear something lighter I'm going to die here, right on the spot.'

Jessie looked at me and laughed. With the sweat pouring down my face and the sodden shirt stuck to my body I must have looked funny.

'Of course, my dear husband,' she answered with a cheeky smile. 'You look like you've just come out of a sauna.'

With the honeymoon over, I was desperate to start doing something that would launch my business career. I couldn't remain dependent on my job with Dad; the freedom won through marriage would be incomplete unless I started on my own. So, I started looking around for small construction works like redoing street pavements or building street boundary walls. These jobs never earned more than €1,200, but they would serve as foundations on which to build for the future.

Just a few days later, I submitted a bid for a small job worth €466.00 for the replacement of an existing street pavement. After three days, I received the award letter, probably because no other contractor bothered to bid for such a small and insignificant job.

'You see, Jess. I told you I could make it. Now I can quit my job with Dad, employ two workers and start on my own.'

'But, Gulin, it's just a small job. What if you're not given any other? Remember that the €210.00 won't last forever and your wages from Dad, at least... Why don't you wait just a little longer before you leave Dad?'

'Don't worry, Jess. Once I've started with the first job others will follow. You'll see. I'll keep my promise to you yet.'

As always, she believed in me, but Dad's reaction was the complete opposite. He couldn't believe that just two weeks into my marriage I was already leaving him.

'You must be completely mad,' he shouted at me. 'I told you a million times that the construction business is too risky and carries much responsibility. You know what I've been through these many years. You were with me all the time and yet you've never learned. And let me tell you another thing; you'll find out soon enough the truth I'm telling you and then you'll come crawling back to me to tell me I was right all along.'

I always knew what his reaction would be, but my mind was set. I simply bowed my head and said, 'Yes. Yes, Pa, I know. You've been telling me all this for years.'

I went out of his office and filled my lungs with real fresh air. I then recruited two workers, telling them I had a number of jobs to complete and that their employment was long-term. In truth I had only this one job of replacing pavements, but the week after I was awarded another tender for a minor construction job and this, together with the first one, kept us busy for two whole weeks.

The foremen at the Government Works Department were pleased with the work of a small contractor who could finish small jobs in time and to the required specifications. Therefore, each time I submitted bids they would recommend me highly. These jobs led to bigger ones and soon I was being contracted for works worth €6,000.

However, I kept holding back from submitting bids involving

construction of concrete roofing. I didn't want to go for works requiring experience and knowhow and, although I was now completely estranged from Dad, I didn't want him shouting his head off at my unwarranted risks. So, I limited myself to road-related works which were the least risky.

By this time I had taken on four additional workers and the profit I was making was encouraging.

Winning and carrying out government contracts guaranteed payments. Unfortunately, the government is notorious for the excessive length of time it takes to honour its debts. This always left me short of the cash flow required to pay wages and meet other expenses related to the works. It also meant that I had to resort to borrowing, at least until my financial situation improved somewhat. It always amazed me that when I started my business the attitude of the banks was that I was unproven, young and, therefore, they could not support me. However, when I had completed contracts and was winning more and larger contracts from the government, which should have been considered safe, the attitude of the bank was that I was overtrading so they could not support me. My only option was to approach Dad.

'Pa, you know how busy I am with government works. And you know, also, how slow government is to affect payments. Would you loan me a thousand Liri for just a few months?'

I was very pleased that Dad did agree to loan me the money.

More and bigger contracts came along and this required more and more cash to finance them. But this time I couldn't turn to Dad. Instead, I made the hard decision of parting with my beloved sports car and bought a second hand Ford Transit van. This left me with €1,400 to work with.

It still wasn't enough and three months later I was humbling myself yet again before Dad for another €2,300. I was then working a sixteen-hour day, taking Saturday afternoons off to keep up with my physical fitness unless I was too tired to move a muscle, and, of course, Sundays, which I spent with Jessie.

When Dad saw how hard I was working he told me, 'You're

killing yourself with all this hard work. You're overdoing it and it won't get you anywhere. But you won't listen, will you? I told you time and time again you're not cut out for this work. You should be working in a bank. You should be a bank manager.'

What could I tell him? We had been through all this so many times before that arguing with him was like talking to a brick wall.

A few months after I took the second loan from Dad, I had to approach him again with a similar request. This time he exploded and I let him vent his anger at me until he was nearly breathless. When at last he calmed down he said, 'Look. This is definitely the last time I'm baling you out. Next time it'll have to be the bank. I can arrange a loan of €11,650 for you if you wish. You can put your house as a guarantee.'

I went along with this suggestion and a month later we signed the necessary papers for the loan. What I didn't know was that Dad had approached his bank manager friend on the day the funds were available and instructed him to pay him the €6,900 he had loaned me from the €11,650 the bank was giving me. This meant that I was only getting €4,750 from the bank.

The bank manager was at fault as he had no right to affect this transaction without my approval or signature. His action was very unprofessional and completely contrary to the bank's code of ethics and procedure.

I sought out Dad and confronted him about it.

'Were you afraid I wouldn't honour my debt with you? You don't realise how much I respect you and how grateful I am for helping me out the way you did. It would have been a real pleasure and honour to make out my first cheque in your name.'

Two months into our marriage, Jessie informed me she was pregnant. It was a happy moment for both of us and I, at last, could look forward to having the family I always wanted. Jessie's parents and mine were overjoyed with the news and they started treating Jessie as if she was a priceless piece of china. The news spurred me on to work even harder.

On 3rd July 1975 Jessie gave birth to a boy, Richard. I had never before imagined that becoming a father could bring such joy. Richard wasn't just our new-born son, but also my parents' first grandchild.

I will always remember giving my old Transit van a really good clean-up, removing all the accumulated builders dust and rubbish, and driving Jessie and Richard home to our aptly named house, 'Golden Home'. It was a very proud moment when our little bundle of joy came home and I carried him inside.

Little by little, I was becoming quite efficient at dealing with my bank and managing my accounts and, slowly but surely, I became a frequent client and a familiar face at the bank's counter. It was there that I made friends with John, one of the cashiers. Making friends with him was easy because he was a likeable person and, also, he and his wife, Victoria, were neighbours of ours. Jessie and Victoria became constant companions, especially since we had children the same age. We would also spend Sunday afternoons together in the countryside. John and Victoria are still close friends and we still get together when our tight schedules allow us to.

Life was good, but my earlier decision to forego tertiary education was now weighing heavily down on me. As my business was getting bigger I regretted my lack of knowledge of economics, so vital to my activity. To remedy somewhat this deficiency I enrolled for a correspondence course in economics through a British educational agency. I started studying hard and was doing quite well for some months; but the continuous and ever-increasing demands of my activities and the resulting pressure made it practically impossible to carry out the assignments, without which I couldn't acquire the necessary qualifications and certificates. Reluctantly, I had to give up on a subject that I was finding very interesting and vital in my line of business.

The Maltese economy was passing through a bad patch during this time. Luckily, it wasn't affecting me too badly as I was still unburdened with excessive overhead expenses, unlike the big and established contractors. I was still doing my own paperwork, typing, payrolls, accounting and everything necessary to keep the business going. I kept increasing my activities in spite of the situation and some people thought me out of my mind to keep spending and investing when more seasoned businessmen were hanging on to their every penny. But it was my belief that business, like life itself, was a cycle; sometimes it's buoyant while at other times it's in the doldrums. I thought that it was better to risk when the going was bad and learn from my mistakes so that I would be better equipped when the going got better. I was proved right. I'll write more about this period in a later chapter.

I had never kept a diary and still didn't during my first five years in the construction business. I still, then, depended on my excellent memory and I don't recall having ever missed an appointment during those years. I would wake up early every morning and pick up those workers hailing from Mosta at six o'clock from their own doorsteps to drive them to the site we were working on at the time. I was so punctual that one of my men's neighbours once told me, 'Thanks to you I don't need an alarm clock to wake me up on time. The noise of your diesel engine tells me it's six o'clock. I hope it won't break down somewhere along the way as otherwise I would be late for work.'

I was also in no need of an alarm clock. I woke up punctually every morning no matter what time I went to bed the evening before.

Richard was four months old when Jessie told me she was expecting another child. We were happy with this news and looked forward to this new arrival.

I was, by now, very busy, and my makeshift office at home was overflowing with files, samples and what not. This, and Jessie's pregnancy, made me decide to move my office out of the building to create ample living space for a growing family. So, I converted the adjacent small and still-unfurnished terraced house into a garage/store at ground level and the first floor into a fair-sized office.

With my business picking up faster than anticipated, I had to delegate some of the paperwork to a new employee. I also appointed a foreman to supervise the various construction sites we were working on. These two new appointments left me with the time I needed to concentrate more on expanding my activities.

A typical day at the time ran as follows: I would give the new foreman his instructions for the day, which he would jot down in his diary. I would then tell him about the appointments for the whole week, which he also wrote in the diary. A week or so into his appointment, he asked me, 'Don't you carry along your diary with you, Mr Xuereb?'

'I'm afraid I don't keep one.'

He stared at me in amazement for a few moments, surprised at my ability to remember not just the appointments for the week, but also all the instructions I had given him since his first day on the job.

Eighteen months after I first started in business, busy with various construction works worth between €12,000 and €23,000, there was a trenching works tender that I knew would earn me a large profit should I be awarded the contract. The work, however, required an excavator, which I didn't yet own. So, I approached Ninu, my former partner in the potato business, to form another partnership with me in a joint public tender. He agreed and we got the contract on a fifty/fifty basis. Ninu was a good excavator operator and his daily rate on the excavator guaranteed us the profit I had forecast. I was also busy at other sites and I could not waste time laying drain pipes, which was essentially a labourer's job.

One day, Ninu accosted me and said, 'Look here, Ġulinu. This is not fair at all. I'm here all day working my guts out while you're always running around attending to your own business as well.'

I reminded him that he was being remunerated extra for his time. At that point I realised the difference between Ninu's attitude towards business and mine. While I, as an entrepreneur full of energy and vision wanted my business to grow, he just wanted to carry on as he had always done, with the occasional job that would earn him enough to last him until the next one.

Island of Gozo

6

The Beginning

(1976–1978) 24–26 years

This was a period when I considered my business had grown enough to merit setting up a limited company. Thus, Angelo Xuereb Limited was born. It remained the mother of my group of companies for a long time. In fact, it lasted a full decade and a half, after which I changed it to AX Holdings Limited.

The decision to name the company Angelo Xuereb Limited wasn't taken haphazardly. I spent some time pondering various options, some of which were easy on the tongue and to remember. But at the time I was practically unknown in the construction business world and, as I said in the first chapter, I was known by different names by different people, making me a man with different aliases. Furthermore, I wanted my name to become synonymous with the construction business. And what better way to kill these two birds with one stone than giving my full name to the company – a name given to me at baptism.

Suddenly, my name started to appear in bold capitals on large billboards, which I erected at every site I was involved in, no matter how small. I printed letterheads which, slowly but surely, started circulating in government departments, banks and other businesses. And, from then onwards, whenever my company was referred to by the above entities, my full name was being said aloud. It took some years, however, for my brothers and sisters to get used to calling me Anġlu (Maltese for Angelo), but Mum and Dad never gave up calling me by my pet names Ġolu and Ġulinu.

Contracts continued coming in at an increasing rate. From the construction of pavements and boundary walls, I moved up to the erection of small structures, but still shied away from going into concrete constructions. Dad's warnings still rang in my ears.

I was working a full eleven-hour day on site, from six o'clock in the morning till five in the afternoon. Back home, I would have a light snack and make my way to the office to continue dealing with the never-ending paperwork and the preparation of plans for the following day. I always planned meticulously, down to what every worker had to do and the tools and machinery he would require.

Two years after my first contract I submitted a tender for the construction of a large boundary wall. The job demanded extra care and responsibility as it was part of a much larger government project – the building of a large textile factory intended to employ a large number of unemployed workers.

My bid was accepted and its successful completion would have meant the biggest step so far for the company. The works, valued at €70,000, had to be completed in three months. I was initially hesitant to submit my bid, because I realised that as part of a policy with political ramifications the government would take a keen interest in it. So, I discussed the matter with two government works supervisors. Both felt confident that I could perform well and they mentioned my excellent performance at small contracts, which were a good indication that I could do just as well at bigger ones. So, I faced this new challenge, determined to make a success of the job.

It didn't take me long to work out a programme of works spread over a seven-day week, and the workers responded splendidly as there was good overtime pay involved. I considered this job so important for the company's future that I made it a point not to leave the site until the planned works for the day were carried

My first meeting with Minister of Public Works, Larry Sant, on site.

Proud parents of baby Richard.

Ta' Qali Football Stadium.

Villa Vistana under construction.

With my first slipforming concrete machine.

Supervising construction works.

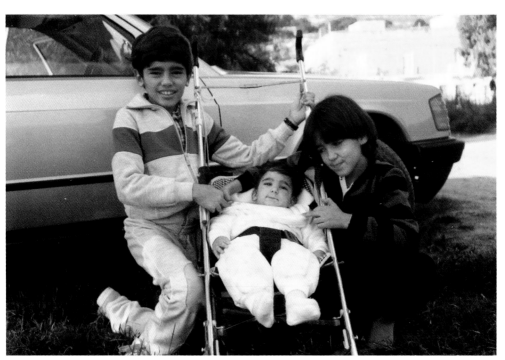

Richard and Claire proud of their baby sister, Denise.

Richard, Claire and Jessie with her first Mazda.

The inauguration of Sunny Coast Resort by Professor J J Cremona.

Road works.

Posing next to our first bulldozer.

Appreciating historical architecture at the Colosseum in Rome with Denise.

My family in 1988.

All brothers, sisters and in-laws at my head office.

Mum and Dad.

The first loadings at Hard Rocks quarry.

My first development - Sunny Coast Holiday Complex.

out. I wore my construction boots most of the time and worked alongside my men whenever and wherever required.

The works also included the fixing of a large number of steel railings, some 2 metres high, between stone pillars all along the boundary wall. To further speed up the process and not waste my men's time from the actual construction works, I recruited a number of youths, members of the local branch of the Christian Doctrine Society (M.U.S.E.U.M.), to paint the steel railings. This work was carried out during weekends when no government supervisors would be around. I offered these young men an attractive remuneration for their age and every weekend would see ten to fifteen of them flocking to be the first on the job, competing to be the fastest and most efficient. My youngest brother, Paul, was one of these competitors.

This huge factory was planned as six separate blocks. The tenders issued for their construction were, understandably, valued much higher than my boundary wall, and were awarded to a large and long-established construction company. After four weeks or so, the minister responsible for public works, Mr Lorry Sant, decided to carry out a site inspection to monitor the progress so far. Works on my boundary wall were well advanced. Much of the paintwork was finished and some of the railing already in place, and even an inexperienced eye could tell that the job would be finished well before the target date. The factory blocks, however, were still at foundation level and the minister was quick to notice this lack of progress. I wasn't close enough to him to overhear, but I was told later that he made quite a scene. He was surrounded by the Director of Public Works and his appointed project management team.

'What do you think you're doing?' he shouted at them. 'You must be the most incompetent team around. Don't you think it's completely illogical to finish the boundary wall while the really important structures are still at foundation level?'

The least scared member of the management team managed to whisper, 'But, Minister, a different contractor is building the boundary wall.'

The minister turned to the speaker and said, 'A different contractor? Who's he?'

'He's just a small contractor, Minister. But he's very efficient.'

'Yes. Yes. I can see that. But who is he?'

'Angelo Xuereb, Minister. He's already–'

'Never heard of him!' Then he turned from the lot and walked fast towards his waiting car, with his entourage doing their best to keep up.

Later the same day he called an urgent meeting with the top brass of the works department. Without any preamble, he asked for a detailed progress report on the project and also assurance that it would be completed in the stipulated period specified in the tender. It seems there was much beating about the bush, as nobody among those present wanted to end up the scapegoat if the project wasn't finished in time.

The minister wasn't too happy with what he was being told; he lost his patience and shouted, 'OK. OK. I get the message. The project won't be finished in time.'

Total silence followed this clear statement. Then he continued, 'Somebody go tell that small contractor, Angelo something – the one who's doing the boundary wall.'

'Angelo Xuereb,' someone volunteered.

'Whatever. Tell him I want to see him right now.'

'Here? Right now?'

'What are you? Deaf or what?'

No one disputed this possibility, but one of them sped out of the minister's office.

I was on site in my work clothes, helping my men, when a government supervisor came running towards me. Breathlessly, he told me, 'Angelo, go quickly to the ministry. The minister wants to talk to you.'

'Who? The minister?'

'Yes. And right now.'

'What about?'

'How should I know? They just told me to tell you, that's all.'

'Ok. I'll just pop home to change...'

'No!' he shouted as though I had just uttered an unforgivable swear word. 'When the minister says now, he means now.'

His hysterical utterance made me edgy. But, at least I managed to change my dirty shoes for a clean pair, which I always carried in my van.

I was at the ministry buildings in minutes and was instantly ushered into the minister's office. He was sitting at the head of a long table with the twenty or so senior technical and administrative personnel sitting two deep around it.

The minister looked hard at me and in a strong, loud voice said, 'What did you say your name was?'

Before I had time to reply, he continued, 'Angelo Xuereb? Excellent. Now, Angelo, come and sit right here, beside me.'

I was feeling conscious of my dirty clothes, hair and everything, while the crowd around the table seemed to be in their Sunday best. Everybody was staring at me but none seemed to notice my clean pair of shoes.

Somebody brought an extra chair and as soon as I sat down, the minister said, 'As from tomorrow I want you to ease a bit on the boundary wall and take over one of the blocks from another contractor.'

Before I realised that the minister was addressing me, Mr Godwin Drago, an architect by profession and the director of works, intervened. 'But, Minister, the other contractor has a contract on that block.'

These were the only words uttered by anybody but the minister during the short time I sat there. The minister slammed his hands hard on the table top and at one point I thought he was about to hit Mr Drago.

'You shut your mouth,' he shouted in Mr Drago's ears. 'What have they taught you at university, eh? Can't you see that the other contractor is far behind schedule? Didn't you see with your own eyes that he won't finish in time?'

I could see all the men around the table cringing and trying to reduce their size. I was as scared as them all, but I managed to ask, 'But, Minister, what if the other contractor sues me, or tries to stop me from taking over?'

'Listen to me, Angelo.' His voice became so soft, sounding as if it was coming from someone else. 'Should anything of the sort happen, or should you receive an official letter, don't you worry one little bit. Just forward it to me right away. Do you understand? And if somebody dares stop you, just tell him what I have just told you.'

'All right, Minister. I'll do whatever you say.'

The following day, I started work on the block indicated to me and, as was expected, a director from the other construction company came over and said, 'Don't you know that this is part of our contract?'

'Yes, I know. It's that the minister told me to continue where you left off.'

It seems that this particular contractor made the necessary enquiries and was told off in no uncertain manner because I was never approached again and didn't receive any legal letters.

I went into this new challenge – worth €70,000 – wholeheartedly and another ministerial inspection took place three weeks later. The minister, surrounded by a posse of works department advisors, noted that while my block was already taking shape, the adjacent block was lagging far behind.

He approached, shook my hand and said, 'I see you're making good progress. Now I want you to take over another block. What do you say?'

No one around him said anything and neither did I. I simply nodded and watched while he hurried to his car.

Two weeks later I was summoned to his office again.

'I've been monitoring your progress, Angelo, and I liked what I saw.'

'Thank you, Minister. I try to do my best.'

'I'm sure you do. And that's the reason I sent for you. I want you to consider taking over another block.'

I was tempted to say yes. An additional €70,000 doesn't fall from heaven every day, but, on the other hand, my workers were already stretched to their limit and I was barely sleeping at night. I shook my head.

'I think I'd better not Minister. I appreciate your trust in me and that's the reason I won't let you down on the jobs you've given me. But accepting another one would break the camel's back and I don't wish to accept a commitment that I know I cannot honour. I would be letting both of us down.'

In the end, while I managed to complete my three contracts in time, the other contractor, who was well established, had still not finished his. In three months I managed to complete three contracts worth €233,000 at good rates. My efficiency at these jobs impressed the minister, the director of works, director of contracts, the site supervisors, the officials and the other contractors. The name of my company was now on everybody's lips and I, at twenty-five became one of the promising contractors and, probably, the youngest of the lot. Moreover, I managed to build a reputation as a contractor who finishes a job on time and the highest quality.

A person's success in business is normally associated with long years of work. My young age, therefore, often surprised those who didn't know me personally. This was illustrated by a funny incident that started with a knock on our front door.

'In what may I help you?' asked Jessie of the man on our doorstep.

'May I speak to your father, please?'

'I'm sorry but my father doesn't live here.'

The man was disappointed. He was unemployed, had a family to support and was looking for work. 'But people directed me to this address. They told me this is where Angelo Xuereb lives.'

Jessie smiled. 'Angelo Xuereb is not my father. He's my husband.'

The poor man was totally embarrassed. He thought that Angelo Xuereb was a rich, elderly man who smoked long, expensive Havana cigars. At least that's the impression my name on the billboards gave him.

Claire was born on 20th August 1976. She was a beautiful baby. But what really stood out was her spiky hair. It just wouldn't be tamed no matter what Jessie did to it to keep it down. It would invariably spring out again like cactus spikes as they catch the first hot rays of a summer sun. It was rather funny, but Jessie didn't see it that way and she kept Claire's fuzzy head covered with a woollen cap in spite of the heat of summer. She wanted her friends to comment on Claire's beautiful face, not grimace at the spiky brush on top of it.

I was now so busy running around from one site to another, not to mention the many appointments I was obliged to keep, that it was virtually impossible to find time to drive Jessie on her frequent errands. I, therefore, encouraged her to start taking driving lessons. When she passed her driving test I bought her a new, small, blue Mazda 323 ... and an orange Fiat Mirafiore for myself.

My Fiat's shine didn't last long; I soon started using it the way I used my old Transit van. Its luggage boot was large enough to carry bags of cement and construction tools, while the back seat served as a mobile wardrobe for two complete outfits and two clean pairs of shoes. I needed to change clothes quite often during the day as I drove from building sites to office and to appointments. Often, I would park the car on the side of the road and quickly change clothes according to my destination. Life was so hectic that I very rarely went home for this purpose. I was so busy, in fact, that I often took to running down streets to arrive in time for an appointment. People staring and looking round at me on crowded streets didn't bother me as long as I was never late. Looking back now, after so many years, I wonder what people thought of a young man dressed in a smart suit running down the crowded main street of Valletta, our capital. Perhaps they expected a policeman sprinting after me.

In spite of this frenetic existence I always managed to eat five times a day. I started the day at half past five with a light breakfast. At around nine I would stop at some popular workers' snack bar and order two small Maltese loaves bulging with fried eggs and bacon, which I would consume while driving to an appointment. By lunchtime I would be home with Jessie to enjoy what she had prepared for me. Then, after five, I would eat half a large Maltese loaf spread with tomato paste, topped with ham and cheese. Back home in the evening, at around nine, I would eat a substantial dinner; usually roast meat or fish with sautéed potatoes. And yet, in spite of the thousands of calories consumed, my constant running kept me slim and physically fit.

Work didn't end with dinner; there would still be office work to be dealt with. I would record the day's expenses site by site then there would be the business letters to type. With computers still years in the future, I had to use Tippex to correct typing errors, thus rendering the end result not as neat as I would have wished. After I finished the letters I would move to plan the next day's activities, which included each worker's duties for the day, the tools each would require and, also, the expected output for the day. On weekends I would prepare each worker's payslip, which included the tax deductible. All this was done manually.

Dad was still calling me mad for trying to work myself to death. Unbelievably, he was still trying to persuade me to give it all up and go into banking instead. He was still not cured of his 'bank manager illusion'. One day, however, I decided to put an end to all this foolishness.

'Look, Pa. I've bought two brand new cars for me and another for Jessie, and they're all fully paid for. I have two ready-mix trucks, which are also fully paid. My business is doing well and I'm enjoying every minute of it.' Then I took out a bank deposit account statement from my pocket and handed it to him. It showed a balance of €114,000. 'And take a look at that.'

He took some moments to digest all the information I had given him and a further few to count the zeros in my bank book. At last he lifted his gaze at me and said, 'Ok then. Have it your own way and do whatever you like. I did my best. At the end of the day it's your life. I won't ever raise the subject again.'

And he kept his word. He never again tried to talk me out of my business. Nor did he ever again mention anything about a bank job.

Business continued to thrive and I needed to expand my operation. The store next door had become too small; half the space was taken up by stacks of cement bags, hardly leaving room for my construction tools and scaffolding. I also had to depend on a competitor of mine for the supply of ready mixed concrete for my trucks to enable me to continue with my projects. I was then still twenty-five and other contractors probably pitied me, seeing me running from place to place, working hard and asking for assistance. So, they always gave me a helping hand. Maybe this was because I was such a handsome young man, as Jessie used to tell me jokingly. But, whatever the reason for their assistance, the attitude towards me soon changed when I became one of their major competitors.

Progress begets problems and one of them was the urgent need of a new workshop. There were quite a few large garages around, waiting for someone like me to buy, but I always preferred to offer members of my family the 'right of first refusal' before approaching outsiders. So, I approached Dad about his old bulls' farm, which had been in disuse since he had given up the business two years previously. He sold it to me at market value. The bank, now happy to have a fast rising businessman as a client, was only too happy to extend my credit facilities for the purchase. The farm was built on two levels, comprising 500 square metres surrounded by an additional 5,000 square metres of open ground.

Dad was pleased with the deal and a few months later he came up to me and said, 'Since you will be requiring as much space as possible for your growing business why don't you also buy the remaining land adjacent to the farm?'

I took him up on his proposal and an additional area of 10,000 square metres became my property. I then had to think about the best way to utilise this vast area to its full potential. I opted for a batching plant and soon I was selling ready mixed concrete to other contractors. I equipped the plant with a proper workshop, stores and an office, and in four years I was considered one of the leading Maltese building contractors. My early idea of splashing my full name on large billboards and letterheads did the trick; my name had become synonymous with excellent performance, rapid progress and completion on time.

It's true that I had done without a diary during my first four years in business and I don't recall ever missing an appointment or being late for one. But, with the continuous rapid growth of my business, time management became of the utmost importance. Keeping a diary became imperative in the circumstances, although it took me two whole months to get used to jotting down daily notes, which I still, then, considered a waste of time. But one had to adapt, and I did. In the end I found that time was not wasted because I could now think about creating initiatives that would further benefit my business.

Even that sweet woman Salvina, my mother-in-law, kept track of my progress. Salvina had fallen in love with me the instant I had bumped my head on my first visit to her house.

'Jessie,' she would often ask my wife, 'how is Angelo's business doing? He is always buying trucks and cars and property. He must be doing well, isn't he?'

'Yes, Mum. Angelo is doing quite well.'

'Is he well, though? I don't see him that often nowadays.'

'Yes, Mum, I know. I don't see him as often myself. He works on weekends as well, as you know. But he knows what he's doing. I know, because I can see the results.'

As my business continued to grow, a fresh challenge, one I could really get my teeth into, appeared out of the blue. It came to my knowledge that a local company was successfully manufacturing pre-stressed concrete roofing. It was so successful, and was receiving so many orders, that new ones had to wait a whole year for delivery. This meant that there was room for a competitor, and I decided that the competitor would be me. Space to install the plant wasn't a problem thanks to the large tract of land I had bought from Dad. And so I started planning.

There were two major hurdles ahead of me before I could contemplate production. The first was the massive investment required for the installation of the necessary modern technology. The second was more difficult to get around because the other plant belonged to Prime Minister Dom Mintoff's brother.

To appreciate the enormity of the latter problem one has to understand the political climate of the time. Mintoff's socialist government had embarked on a vast nationalisation programme, which included the taking over of private banks, foreign fuel companies and also the importation of the most essential commodities through a scheme ominously called 'Bulk Buying'. Any businessman wanting to import even the simplest item had to go through a whole bureaucracy of form-filling and queuing just to obtain an import licence. So, the thought of importing large, heavy machinery to enable me to compete with the Prime Minister's own brother was next to an impossible dream. But, as a twenty-six-year-old I wanted my impossible dreams to come true and the problems facing me increased my determination to overcome them.

I knew what the risks were. If I went to the bank for a substantial loan, word would quickly leak out and my project would be hijacked. Even if I could have managed a loan without any mishaps, the moment I tried to buy the machinery necessary for the plant, all possible stumbling blocks would be put in my way and the import licence would not be granted. If then I were to be granted an import licence, as soon as I applied for a permit to build a factory for the purpose I had in mind it would have been offhandedly refused. Once my intention was known the government would put every spoke in my wheel and my project would become still-born.

In spite of all these politically created problems, or rather because of them, I was still determined to succeed and expand my business in that direction. The first thing I did was to engage a structural engineer, whom I took with me to the United Kingdom where we inspected the machinery used for the production of pre-stressed, hollow concrete slabs. What we saw was extremely expensive and would render the viability of my investment at risk.

Somehow, I had to find a solution to the problem. I had to find a solution that would save me from forking out such a huge investment, which would have required a bank loan that would definitely have been refused. A workable solution I came up with was that, instead of using heated steel beds (flat steel sheets as formwork), which was the standard system used by Mintoff's brother, I would use concrete beds finished with ground mosaic tiles. These surfaces would have to be perfectly level and smooth as they would become the exposed parts of the concrete roof slabs. The only disadvantage in this system was that while the concrete would take six to seven days to cure, those made on the heated metal beds would cure in twenty-four hours. This meant that I would have to utilise six times the floor space. But as I said before, floor area wasn't a problem and Malta's moderate climate would also help the concrete to dry faster

I also decided to do without a closed factory equipped with gantry cranes. Instead I would build my plant on open ground and use mobile cranes to handle the pouring of fresh concrete and to remove the finished product. Through this system I would be letting nature cure the concrete and, at the same time, saving myself from forking out a huge capital expenditure – thus, avoiding the need to apply for a building permit for the construction of a factory. It would also limit the importation to just the special cutting machine, the stressing equipment and the reinforcement stressing wire to place in the concrete – a far cry from the very expensive and sophisticated machinery used at other plants.

A further precaution I had taken when I ordered my requirements from abroad was to play a little with the technical wording. 'Hydraulic pumps for stressing equipment' was a general enough term and should I have been challenged for an explanation by customs officials, I could have got out of it quite easily. I couldn't do much about the cutting machine, so I used the term 'stone-cutting equipment'. And for the special pre-stressing wire I used the word 'reinforcement'. In reality, it was a concrete steel reinforcement, but I had counted on the probability that nobody at customs would have the technical knowledge to realise that this solid, 7-millimetre-thick, steel wire could be stressed. My competitor was using a seven-strand wire type for reinforcement, which is visually quite different from the choice I made. But, in spite of all these precautions, I still went through tense weeks until all the equipment was safely deposited on my property.

With the equipment now secure I could start preparing the plant I had in mind. I decided to lay eight production lines (beds), each measuring 100 metres long and 1.5 metres wide, so that each row would be able to produce a 100-metre-long slab, having a width of 1.2 metres. The finished product would, when ready, be cut into smaller slabs of various sizes, though the standard length was 6 metres. The cutting would be carried out with the 'stone' cutter using a special diamond cutter blade I had imported.

The next step would be to construct massive strong anchors on each side of the production beds – an engineering feat in itself. My structural engineer worked out his calculations in detail for heavy duty steel beams; they would have to be 5 metres long, 70 cm high and 25 cm wide. These anchor beams had to be cast in a massive reinforced concrete block buried in solid rock, leaving just the top 40 cm of the total 5 metres exposed above ground. Across these two anchors the engineer ordered us to place another massive, heavily reinforced steel beam that would have a number of holes to hold thirty or so of the pre-stressed, 7 mm wires. The beam would be 1.5 metres long and weigh more than a ton.

I passed on these details to my welders who immediately set about working on them. We started on the first two anchor sets and all of us looked forward to the casting of the first production line. When my experienced welder and his helpers saw these massive and heavily reinforced structures they convinced me that the excessive reinforcement was not really necessary for the work they were intending to perform. My welder was experienced and reliable, but, like me, he had no previous experience of the massive pull these anchors were meant to withstand. The following incident convinced us otherwise.

It happened when we started placing stressing wires over the first trial bed. Being the owner of the plant and the one who initiated the experiment, I asked all my workers to give me a wide berth while I carried out the dangerous part when the wires were being stressed. I insisted that they take cover behind something solid just in case one of the wires broke or slipped away. When everyone and everything was in place, I placed a steel net within a frame over the bed to protect me from any wire that might slip or break and roll with great force in my direction.

My intention was to pull 70 tons on each wire by means of a specially designed hydraulic jack. There were twenty of them for a total pull of 1,400 tons on this short steel beam. I knelt down at the end of the stressing bed and started by stressing 25% of the pull. After I had finished this initial operation I began giving each a full pull. I had managed seven or eight wires when suddenly the massive anchor began to twist and bend, and the short strong beam holding all the wires at the other end slipped away from its anchors and shot about 20 metres in the air. This released all twenty wires, which shot out like bullets from the holes at my end, entangling me completely like an animal in a trap. Three of the fully stressed wires went straight into my leg. The pain was so sudden, and my shout so loud, that my sister, living a full 100 metres away, ran out of her house to see what had occurred. One flat-ended wire went right through my shin bone, out of the calf muscle and continued its way a full 30 cm into a weak concrete joint behind me, where it stuck. Another stuck like an arrow in my knee, while a third impaled slightly my Achilles tendon.

Still in pain and shock, and restricted by the steel net entangling me, I pulled hard with both hands at the sharp missiles until my body was free of them. I will never forget the scraping sound of the long wire as I pulled it hard through my shin bone and out of my leg. The whole scene was so unreal that it seemed as though it happened in slow motion to somebody else. By the time my workers arrived at a run to give me assistance, my legs were already free, but I was still trapped.

The pain in my leg seemed suddenly to subside and all I felt was complete numbness. There was little loss of blood because the velocity with which the wires penetrated my body created so much heat that the wounds in my muscles were instantly cauterised. In fact, when my workers released me, I was feeling no pain at all and I thought of driving myself to hospital. But my workers would have none of it and one of them drove me fast to the hospital's emergency department while another sat beside me on the back seat.

It was there, at the emergency department, that the pain returned with a vengeance. It was an excruciating pain all along my leg, down to the tip of my toes. I had to endure it throughout what seemed to me to be the long time it took the medical staff to examine and x-ray my leg. The examining doctor couldn't believe how my shin bone wasn't shattered when he examined the x-ray and was told how the accident had happened. The wire had left a clean, perfectly rounded hole, seven mm in diameter, very much like a bullet hole, right through the middle of the shin bone.

The next few days were a continuous agony of excruciating pain. A feather dropping on my leg would have made me scream even though I was literally stuffed with pain killers. The doctor was very much afraid of a bone infection and didn't mince words to tell me that should this happen he would have to amputate. Thankfully, the pain began to ease and soon I could rest and relax. However, I found myself with nothing to do but think about the cause of the accident. Still in hospital and unable to move, I sent for my welder to instruct him how to correct the mistake and repair the damage. I also directed him to reinforce the beams and follow the engineer's design to the letter.

Three weeks later I was out of bed and on the job, albeit supported by crutches. The necessary alterations had been carried out and it was time again for the first production cast. I, again, insisted on doing the job myself with the workers well out of harm's way. I was now doubly aware of the danger I was facing and prayed fervently to God and Our Lady of Victories, while certain that my workers were doing the same from their safe positions.

I cast the crutches aside, went down slowly on my knees and began going through the same process as three weeks before, while muttering silent prayers and sweating with apprehension. But this time everything went well. The wires held and the first 100-metre stretch was ready for full production. My workers were as elated as I was. But there was no time for celebrations. We immediately cast the first bed and eight days later we cut this first cast into several pieces to honour the first order we had received.

I cannot describe the enthusiastic cheering of the workers as the first cast was being lifted, tested and found to be perfect. Spontaneous celebrations took place all around and we happily went about constructing the other seven beds according to the engineer's specifications.

News about another plant producing pre-stressed concrete spread like wildfire among contractors, architects and engineers all across the island. Although the finished product wasn't as neat as my competitor's, when tested it was found that its strength exceeded the required specifications.

A problem I now faced was that of mobility. These concrete slabs were very heavy and my cranes weren't efficient enough to move them from one site to the next. The only cranes existing in Malta at the time were the lattice jib type, which possessed very slow manoeuvrability. The only two hydraulic cranes belonged to Prime Minister Mintoff's family – my competitor. Customs duty at the time was at 55%, probably the reason for the lack of such cranes in Malta. It took me a whole month to convince the Comptroller of Customs that such machinery should not carry any duty. This was according to a detailed clarification in the importation clause of these cranes, which was not being correctly interpreted. Furthermore, I insisted that it was of the utmost importance for the construction industry to be equipped if the country really wanted to encourage this important job-generating industry. Thanks to me, the importation of cranes increased and the industry became more efficient.

After that orders started coming in fast, mostly for workshop and factory roofs. We were producing on a seven-days-a-week schedule, with overtime. We were working at maximum production.

This new successful venture gave me an advantage and competitive edge over the other contractors who, like me, were bidding for the construction of government factories. At the time, factory roofs with large open spans were still being constructed with heavy concrete roofs incorporating large sections of concrete beams in situ. The great height of these factories necessitated the extensive use of scaffolding and a total of a twenty-eight-day curing period before the supports could be safely removed. My system introduced a more efficient method, which required no scaffolding and, more importantly, could finish the construction of a factory roof measuring 1,000 square metres in less than two weeks. This system gave me room for manoeuvring prices. It gave me the luxury to work out my costing by the old traditional system, lowering the price by a good 25%, thereby eliminating any possible competitor as none could afford to go so low. Obviously, the government adjudicating committee couldn't afford not to recommend my company for the job as it offered many advantages other contractors couldn't guarantee. Furthermore, I was making a large profit and, more importantly, I was consolidating my reputation for completing jobs within the specified period.

Income and profits from normal construction works and from sales of pre-cast concrete were also very good. I remember the pleasure I felt every time I entered the bank to deposit large bundles of cash. Those were the days when the private sector still preferred to pay in cash rather than by cheque. My friend John Soler, the cashier at the small Naxxar branch of Scicluna's Bank, would beam with satisfaction every time he saw me approaching his window with an armful of cash. It was still a rarity in those days for a young businessman like me to be depositing such large amounts.

Then, tragedy hit my family. Jessie's mother, Salvina, was diagnosed with terminal cancer. It was hard for Jessie to reconcile herself to this cruel reality. She would spend most of her time with her mother and would frequently drive her mother to the specialised government clinic for the necessary treatment.

Great Siege of Malta

7

Determination

(1979–1981) 27–29 years

As I have previously explained, I've always been a car enthusiast and have loved driving at speed since well before I was old enough to qualify for a driving licence. Speed-mania is still in my veins, even at my age. So, imagine my delight when I was able to take this to the next level.

One day, a friend of mine was explaining to me his role as a navigator during car rallies. In fact, he'd had rally experience abroad and locally. This came as a surprise to me. I had been a keen follower of rallies on television but never knew that they were organised in Malta as well.

'So is there a chance I could participate in one?' I asked him after he explained in detail what goes on during a locally organised rally.

'Of course you could. In fact, we're organising one in two weeks' time. It's not actually a rally as we know it, but very similar. We call it a Wild Treasure Hunt and all driving is done around country lanes. So if you wish –'

'Really? And with you as navigator?'

It was settled. I would drive my relatively new Fiat and in my mind I was already seeing myself hurtling it along narrow and winding country roads. I was back in the days of my weekly accounts lessons at school when I eagerly waited six whole days until I could drive Dad's car as fast as I dared.

The activity was held in winter, Malta's rainy season, and the participants had to find some hidden item or text written on walls, or whatever the organisers thought interesting enough to make the treasure hunt more competitive. Fifteen minutes prior to the start, each participant was given a route drawn on a map and the winner would be the one who accumulated most points and covered the distance in the shortest time.

I was quite familiar with Malta's roads, but had never imagined we had so many country roads and paths crisscrossing such a small place. Malta must seem a veritable labyrinth from the sky. Some of these country roads were so narrow that my Fiat could only pass through them with a few centimetres to spare on either side.

We started this eight-hour rally at seven o'clock in the evening. As we progressed, the absence of tyre marks in front of us proved we were in the lead. In fact, a few miles into the race, my navigator asked me to slow down.

'I've served as navigator for quite a few top international drivers,' he told me. 'But you're something else. None could drive as fast on narrow, winding roads like these.'

Throughout the race we had to get out of the car to remove large stones blocking our way, which had fallen from rubble walls during heavy rainfall. At one particular difficult stretch along a valley, the path had been reduced to soft, sticky mud. We got out of the car to look for places where some traction was possible, but we found none.

'How on earth do we go through this?' asked the navigator.

'Don't worry. Get back in the car and I'll show you how.'

I drove the engine at maximum revs in first gear and it kept swinging from side to side as we drove slowly along the path. We could hardly see the way ahead; the wipers couldn't keep up with the mud splashing the windscreen and we couldn't afford to open the window. The mud would have ended up in our faces, but that was the least of our worries; the engine seemed about to explode with the pressure I was putting on it. Towards the end of the stretch, water must have seeped into the engine cables because we only managed to make it with the engine coughing its heart out, ready to die.

Safely out of this difficult stretch, and with the engine now running smoothly, we soon came face to face with another hazard – a stream of rain water speeding down the valley we had to cross. I knew the area like the back of my hand and, with the stream at least 60 cm deep, I knew that there was no way we could cross without flooding the whole engine.

'Quite a baptism of fire for a first-time rally driver,' I mused.

There was no chance of going back through the muddy stretch either. And so the navigator and I stood outside the car, contemplating a way out of this tight corner. Then, I noticed some accumulated debris, carried down the stream by the current and resting against something, probably a large stone, blocking its way. It gave me an idea. If I could direct my car so that one side hit the debris, the machine would tilt, thus keeping the engine out of the water. The stream wasn't too wide and with luck the momentum would be enough to carry us across, unless I tilted the car too far and overturned it.

'Let's go,' I said. 'But hold on really well.'

The navigator hesitated for a few seconds, not knowing what I had in mind, and then we were off. We just managed not to overturn. The navigator later told me that had he kept the window open he had a very good chance of getting his nose wet.

I learned later that the other participants had bypassed this difficult stretch, claiming that it was impassable. They wouldn't believe we had made it safely until our recordings were checked.

Further into the route we, at last, came upon the only asphalted part of the course. It consisted of a wide downhill stretch, part of a main road that bisected the many country roads we had to drive through. The recent heavy rains, however, had created numerous potholes which were patched by hand. I was driving fast down this stretch when, unexpectedly and too late as it turned out, I noticed a thick layer of gravel that had accumulated at a bend in the road after the potholes were patched. This gravel had been carried down by further rain and created a dangerous hazard. I was taken completely by surprise and I realised there was no way I could slow the car enough to avoid a potential disaster.

'Hold on for your life,' I shouted at my navigator above the din of the engine. 'I don't think I can make it.'

The car skidded out of control and spun twice before smashing into a wall, which completely reshaped its front and rear. In shock and dizzy with the spin and impact, we were still in one piece, but I was angry and disappointed; not because of the state of the car, which was fully insured, but because I couldn't now continue with the rally.

It was one o'clock in the morning and there was still a lot of ground to cover. I walked towards a reception hall close by, which still had its lights blazing. A wedding reception was in full swing and I went straight to the office to phone Dad and ask him whether he could ask one of my brothers or sisters for the loan of a car to help me finish the rally.

'What?!' he shouted in my ear. 'You smashed your car in a rally and now you expect your brothers and sisters to let you smash theirs? You must be out of your mind.'

'OK, OK, Pa. But at least have someone get my van over. I have to finish the rally.'

The van never arrived. Instead, it was my brother, Joe, who arrived in his new car.

'You can take mine,' he said. 'But be careful.'

'I will, Joe. And I won't forget this.'

I left my car at the side of the road and we were off again. In spite of the time lost, we still managed to win thanks to my knowledge of the country paths around Malta.

After all was over and I had time to reflect on the near fatal accident, I thought I needed to control this urge I had for excessive speed. I was no longer a youth, and had a family to take care of. So, I decided to buy a wide-bodied Mercedes 200, which ran on diesel (the Fiat was a total loss, of course). Now I had a heavy car with a strong protective body, better to protect me from similar incidents. Furthermore, diesel engines at the time couldn't generate as much speed as petrol-powered ones, so I was now doubly protected.

My workers at the plant and on sites would look at me in askance and pity at the car, and wonder at their crazy boss who drives his brand new Mercedes through mud and the roughest terrain. Then they would shake their heads when I opened the luggage booth and they saw it filled with cement bags and tools. Whenever one of them asked me why I was using such a luxury car like an ordinary van, I would reply, 'I wanted a car to protect me and to be at my service not the other way round.' A lesson well learned from the rally!

During weekends, however, I would give it a thorough clean-up and restore it to its former pristine, showroom condition for my family to enjoy on our regular Sunday drive. In this way I didn't have to buy another car for weekends' specific use. But it didn't remain 'brand new' for long as I was averaging 45,000 miles annually, which is a lot of mileage on an island like Malta where long distances are unheard of. After two years I sold it to a second-hand car dealer and bought another new Mercedes.

A few months after I had sold the first Mercedes I met the person who bought it from the second-hand dealer. He showed it to me, not knowing I was the original owner. I must confess that even I, an avid car enthusiast if ever there was one, could not have kept it in such a beautiful condition. He never even took it out of the garage when it rained. In fact, he took so much care of it that it seemed newer than my new Mercedes. He boasted about having made a fantastic bargain when he bought this 'new' Mercedes which had only 7,000 miles on the clock. I kept my mouth shut and just smiled and congratulated him on an excellent deal.

In the meantime, my construction business continued to flourish. I was constructing a number of factories concurrently in different industrial estates miles apart from each other. This necessitated the expansion of my administrative division. I, therefore, employed three other people to assist the one who was trying to cope with everything. This, in turn, compelled me to convert the terraced house adjacent to my home into offices. Two months later, I had to further enlarge my offices by opening an access through my personal garage, which I also converted into offices. Under the circumstances, it was better to park the family's two cars outside than lose precious office space.

Property was booming in Malta and the next logical step for me was to enter the real estate business. So, I started buying small plots and reselling them after just a few weeks. Later, I started buying larger sites and split them into smaller ones to sell directly to the purchasers. I very rarely made use of estate agencies' services.

First time buyers, mostly young couples aspiring to marry and raise a family, would have little or no experience and, sometimes, no ideas about converting a plot of land into a habitable place. So, I would prepare a sketch for them free of charge. I had always loved planning, and still do. I've loved it since, as a young boy, I would build my houses out of rouble stone all around the land surrounding our villa on the outskirts of Naxxar. Doing it for those young couples during weekends was more of a relaxation and a pleasure for me than a chore, especially when I later watched the expression of joy in their eyes when I showed them the end result.

Months later, I bought an extensive tract of land which could accommodate as many as three hundred plots for terraced houses. The land was located in a prime area and, shortly after I had acquired it, two well-known land developers offered to buy two-thirds at a very good price. I told them I would consider their offer while thinking to myself that, with the money from the sale, I would be able to buy other developable portions of land. These two individuals were very experienced and notorious for being tough negotiators, so I had to be very cautious in my dealings with them.

We met again and talked a couple more times, after which we agreed on a price and the terms of payment. It was a good deal for both sides and we shook hands on it. It was after all this that they told me they would be having their lawyer accompany them for the signing of the contract.

'I have no problem whatsoever,' I said. 'It's up to you who you wish to bring along. I have nothing to hide as you'll find out.'

But all this set me thinking. They were hardened negotiators, so why did they consider it necessary to have their lawyer present at the signing? I was not yet twenty-eight at the time and still considered myself a non-starter when it came to experience in this field. Dad, on the other hand, was one hell of a shrewd negotiator, at least on a par with the best of them (and I say this through personal, and sometimes painful, experience). So, I asked him to accompany me to the signing.

Dad and I made our way to the office of this very experienced and rather old notary at Siggiewi. We were the last to arrive and were ushered into the office where the other two, with their lawyer, were already seated around the room engaged in small talk. Every one stood up and we all shook hands, including the lawyer who was introduced as Dr Guido de Marco.

Dr de Marco was considered the best criminal lawyer in Malta. He was later to become Professor of Law, Minister for Justice, Minister for Foreign Affairs, Deputy Prime Minister, President of the United Nations General Assembly and finally President of Malta. Quite a handful to have on the opposite side, but he was just a 'renowned' lawyer at the time of our first encounter and I had only known him through news on television and the newspapers. It was the first time I was meeting him in the flesh and I was taken aback to say the least, having to deal with such a heavyweight.

Finally, with all the pleasantries over, we sat down to do business at three o'clock in the afternoon. The notary took his place behind the desk to start with the writing of the contract while the lawyer and I sat opposite him. I thought it was going to be a long, tiresome session because the notary, being of the old school, did not own a typewriter, let alone a computer.

The two developers sat quietly in a corner, leaving all the negotiations to their lawyer. Dad sat beside them and soon I could hear him talking jovially to the pair.

'Some assistance he's turning out to be,' I said to myself while trying to be as alert as possible to all the legal jargon the lawyer and notary were bandying about.

All was going smoothly, with both sides nodding in agreement and half-smiling suspiciously, until we arrived at a particular clause to which I objected. The lawyer insisted on its inclusion and this further convinced me to put my foot down and not to budge from my position. Arguments flew to and fro for at least an hour with both sides obstinately standing their ground. Then, at long last, Dad opened his mouth to suggest some form of compromise, but I simply told him that I wouldn't budge no matter what anyone said. We kept at it without moving one little bit towards an agreement. Then, at last, Dad couldn't take it any longer.

'My son,' he pleaded, 'we have been shut up in this office for three whole hours. There are people waiting patiently outside for their turn to speak to the notary and they must be as tired as we are. Please, Gol! ... I beg you to give in and accept their proposal. Let's get a move on and conclude this blessed deal.'

Then, to my surprise and consternation, he fell down on his knees in front of me and with the palm of his hands together in a praying position, he entreated me, 'Please, please give in and let's go home.'

I nodded my head while trying to pull him up from his humiliating position. 'Come on, Pa, and get up from there. Try to understand that I'm not giving in to their proposals. I know I'm in the right and that what they're asking me to accept could result in hefty taxes, which I would have to pay later on.'

Complete silence reigned for what seemed to me a long time. Dad stood up slowly, his face tired and suddenly aware of the tension his action had created all around him. Then the silence was suddenly broken by the sound of Dr de Marco's chair as it was pushed back with determination and force. Everybody's eyes followed him as he walked towards his clients, still in their corner. For a few minutes nothing could be heard except the murmuring of the three men in their corner, accompanied by the constant nodding and shaking of heads, shrugging of shoulders and movement of arms.

At last Dr de Marco turned towards Dad and me and walked over with long strides. He grabbed both my hands in his and with a strong voice that I came to know very well in the future, told me, 'We have decided to eliminate the contentious clause and accept your proposal.'

Still with my hands gripped in his, he continued, 'And I must grudgingly add something else. In my twenty-five years of practice I have had thousands of dealings with all kinds of people, and I have negotiated deals, most of which were beneficial to my clients. But I have never met a person as determined as you, Angelo. Well done! Well done indeed.'

Then, looking at Dad and still gripping my hands, he told him, 'Bert, you have an intelligent boy here. He's so hard-headed that you should have named him Testaferrata (Italian surname popular in Malta, literally translated as 'iron headed'), and people who would have the misfortune to negotiate with him should be named Tagliaferro (another Italian surname literally translated as 'iron cutter') if they wish to stand a chance of success.'

The contract was duly signed and during our drive back home, Dad told me, 'Don't you ever ask me to accompany you again for something of this sort. I have never been through such an ordeal... And for nothing.'

'If that's what you wish. But it wasn't for nothing. I was right and time will tell.'

We didn't have to wait long; in that year's Annual Financial Budget, the government succumbed to pressure and introduced an amendment to the law that dealt with sale and purchase of property. With this amendment I would have had to pay a large amount in tax as the seller of property had I given in to the two developers' insistence.

Months later, I was again with Dad, and Dr de Marco happened to be walking in our direction. He recognised me, smiled and made straight towards me.

'So how's our hard-headed Mr Testaferrata?' he asked jokingly while, again, grabbing both my hands in his and shaking them firmly. Turning to Dad he continued, 'Do you know, Bert, that he was right after all, that time at the notary's?'

From then on, every time Dr de Marco and I met, he would always address me as Mr Testaferrata, and would regale those around him about how my nickname came about. I was, naturally, proud of this compliment, coming from a man who would become world renowned, especially for the ground-breaking initiative he took to make the world aware of the Palestinians' plight during his tenure as President of the United Nations Assembly.

During the next two years I founded a development company, which I called Sunny Homes. Through this company I developed terraced houses on individual plots. I then designed a number of attractive plans and elevations for these plots. Soon, these designs were to become synonymous with the brand name of the company. I advertised these developments – plans, elevations and all – in the newspapers. This was still a new concept at the time. The aim behind this concept was to attract the readers' attention and arouse curiosity. Even now, driving around the island, one can still see terraced houses and semi-detached villas developed similar to my design and elevations.

With experience, I came to understand the development market quite well and became confident enough to introduce new concepts in the sale of property, especially to first-time buyers, mostly young couples. I would offer them a preliminary agreement for three months against a deposit of 10%. Then, should they, for some reason or other, decide not to go along with the final contract, I would refund them their deposit without any obligation or default. In some cases I was so confident of effecting a sale that along with the refund of the deposit, I would offer a further 10% interest thereon. This put the young couples' minds at rest and they would turn up three months later ready to sign the final contract. I would jokingly ask them whether they had come to retrieve their deposit plus interest, but they would smile and happily sign the contract.

The market was so buoyant that prices kept escalating from month to month. I knew that my prices were slightly lower than the current market price, but I had little, if any, overheads, thus enabling me to make bigger profits than the established development companies.

Cash flow was extremely good at the time. And it was about that time, also, that my brother, Joe, five years my junior, had opened a mini-market at one of Dad's properties. He needed an initial capital injection, which Dad provided for him with a loan. Joe had offered Dad rent for the place, but Dad was averse to accepting rent, fearing that his son would occupy the place for life. Rent laws, then, were very much biased in favour of tenants.

The mini-market was doing quite well, but – being in its initial stages – it didn't generate enough profit for Joe to pay Dad back the loan in a year or so. Dad started threatening him with eviction and Joe would come to me and cry his heart out at the way Dad was treating him, his own flesh and blood. I could very well sympathise with my brother as I had been through it for years on end, but I never told Joe about it.

One day I said to him, 'I'll tell you what you should do. Go to him and ask him whether he wants to sell you the place. If he does, come back here and I'll lend you the cash you need.'

He looked relieved. But then he knitted his brow and asked me, 'But what if he asks me where I'm getting the money from? What do I tell him?'

'Just say you'll make arrangements for a bank loan. But don't ever mention me.'

I understood Dad well enough to know that he preferred ready cash to the risk of losing the property to his son through the existing rent laws.

Joe approached Dad with the proposal and he agreed to sell

at market value. Two weeks later I handed Joe the money for which he signed a contract. He settled everything with Dad, following which he started paying me back the loan in monthly instalments as agreed. Joe kept his side of the bargain and Dad never got to know what had gone on between his two sons. Eventually, Joe became the sole owner of the business, went on to increase his stock substantially and is now a prosperous businessman.

Yet another brother was also destined to go through a similar bitter experience. Manuel had opened a bookshop and stationers in Dad's former car showroom next door to the family home. Dad gave Manuel the place rent free, obviously due to his inherent fear that his son would otherwise occupy it for life. He also loaned him the initial capital to stock the expansive premises.

One cannot expect to start making money overnight from a new business and pay back loans immediately, but it seems Dad wasn't of this general opinion. Living next door to Manuel's shop, it was easy for him to step right in each morning and berate his son for not repaying his loan. This, in itself, was already bad enough because Manuel wasn't a small boy to be shouted at for the least misdemeanours.

Manuel came to me and cried his heart out. It had become a familiar scene this coming and going of brothers, but my shoulders were wide enough for crying on and I gave Manuel the same advice I had given Joe. I knew Dad would rather sell than receive rent, and so he offered the place to Manuel at market price. I loaned the requested sum to Manuel who told me afterwards about the look of surprise on Dad's face when he saw his son with all that cash in his hands.

Then came Albert with almost the same experience. Albert was not short of ideas, and his suggestion of going into the laundry business was taken up by Dad, who made it his own. He loaned Albert premises close to the village centre and installed the necessary equipment at his own expense. Business, however, didn't exactly take off with a bang and Albert asked Dad to prop him up.

Dad's patience evaporated and he started threatening Albert with eviction and the rest. Albert came to me. I couldn't let him go through the same hell I went through at his age, so I loaned him the necessary cash to buy out my father. Eventually, he did make a success of his business, and paid back the loan.

As far as I know, Dad never found out where his sons were getting so much cash from, but following these nasty incidents, relations between father and sons improved considerably.

Jessie was still spending most of her days taking care of her terminally ill mother. Salvina, that sweet woman whom I came to like from the very first day I met her, put up a tremendously plucky fight for survival. But it was a battle she was destined to lose and she passed away on 18th June 1981. Jessie couldn't take it. Although she always knew that there was next to no hope her mother would survive the terrible illness, she always had faith in some kind of miracle. The blow was too hard to take and Jessie would spend hours on end crying. We all did our best to comfort her and make her understand that Salvina's suffering was now over, but it was of no use. She felt that half of her had been buried along with her mother and nothing could help her out of this deep depression. The situation didn't improve for weeks on end and it was affecting our two children who were still too young to understand.

One evening, Jessie and I sat down to discuss the problem and both agreed that a new baby in the family would compensate for the loss. Four months later, Jessie became pregnant with our third child and her mood improved with every day that passed. Mark was born on 26th July 1982. He was a real godsend. The whole family welcomed him with open arms and life returned to normal.

Our peace was not destined to last, however. Two months later we received a second hard body blow, which left us devastated. I found Mark dead in his cot. It was a tragedy that Jessie and I were not prepared to cope with. We couldn't even bear to live in the same house where Mark had lived during his short life.

Dad gave us his summer villa to live in until we decided what to do.

After this, Jessie and I would spend a long time together during the day, trying unsuccessfully to comfort one another. Members of our families would call every day in an effort to help us get over our loss. Fortunately, Richard and Claire were still too young to appreciate the sadness that had entered their parents' lives. And we thank God for that because their lives remained the same. They played and laughed together, and more than anything it was their cheerfulness that somewhat eased the grief that was dominating our days.

Days passed slowly and after a few weeks, when life was gradually returning to a semblance of normality, I began a slow process of trying to persuade Jessie that another child would fill the emptiness in her heart. She felt, however, that it was still too soon after Mark's death. It had come too soon after her mother's passing away fifteen months before. It took her the whole of two years to fully recover and on 3rd May 1985, Denise, the last of our brood, was born. She brought relief and much joy into our lives.

During this long interlude of heartbreaks and final bliss, I still had to find the time to cope with my business, which was still growing at a fast rate. The demand for pre-stressed concrete roofing slabs continued to grow and it became of paramount importance that I invest in modern equipment as the existing factory was becoming too basic. It couldn't produce slabs of certain thicknesses, which could be produced only through the introduction of modern technology. Furthermore, it could not cope with the ever-increasing demand.

The total overhaul of the plant required a huge capital outlay. More than that, it required courage on my part to decide whether to take the plunge or not because the change would also necessitate the upgrading of the transportation and crane fleet in order to better cope with the resulting increase in production.

After this total upheaval, and when we started with the new production plant, all local architects, engineers, and even we, acknowledged the outstanding quality and efficiency of its production. Everybody realised the huge savings that would be made through the use of my new pre-stressed concrete roofing slabs. Within months, there was nobody among the people involved in the construction sector who was not aware of the advantages I offered. The result was that we couldn't cope with the large orders that started flooding in. The waiting list became so long that clients had to wait a whole year for delivery. It was a long wait, but developers considered it worth their while when they estimated the savings involved and the superior characteristics of my end product. My workers were working long hours of overtime and some clients, those desperate for an early delivery, were willing to pay them double pay to work on Sundays and public holidays.

I took personal charge of the orders during the first two years of operations. It gave me the opportunity to meet clients who would show me the plans for their proposed buildings, mostly for terraced houses. Very often I would find that many architects produced very badly planned designs. My love for planning would make me wince at such amateurish and unimaginative efforts, and I could never allow myself to let a young couple's dream be tarnished by such an unprofessional lack of attention to simple logical details. So, I would offer them free advice, always on condition that the architect concerned wouldn't be told about who was carrying out the alterations because I never wanted them to take offence and refrain from referring further clients to me. I would normally do the sketching during weekends and the end result never failed to please my clients. In my designs I would try to include more open spaces and more comfortable living areas. I would try to turn a house into a family home.

I would draw the sketches very roughly as if done by someone who lacked experience, as my clients usually were. I always instructed them to insist with their architects that they had drawn the sketches themselves. This, of course, involved more work for me – something I could very well have done without, but I always enjoyed it, and it gave me great satisfaction to see the smiles of pleasure light up my clients' eyes.

143

Furthermore, this exercise gave me the opportunity to study and evaluate the planning qualities of a good number of architects – an opportunity that only the Planning Applications Permit Board enjoyed. I very much doubted how much this board bothered about the quality of design when assessing building permits applications. Years later, when the PAPB was replaced by the Planning Authority, this aspect was given more importance and it showed.

The large quantities of slabs we were producing and the equivalent quantities of ready-mixed concrete required in the process rendered urgent the need for an open hard-stone quarry. The ever-increasing demand for hard-stone gravel by the major contractors, coupled with the low production rate of quarry operators due to obsolete equipment, put at serious risk the high production rate at my concrete plant. I knew I had no problem regarding the financial requirement for such a new quarry project, but I could not spare any of my time to supervise such a big operation.

An opportunity to solve the problem came unexpectedly when my youngest brother, Paul, called on me one morning to discuss some problem he had been wrestling with for days.

'You see, Ġolin,' he continued after settling down on a chair and realising that his eldest brother was ready to listen, 'I think it's about time I started doing something. I'm eighteen now, you know, and out of school. But I don't want to work for somebody else. I would surely hate it. I want to be like you and my brothers, with a business of my own.'

I didn't answer immediately. I just looked at him, remembering the day Mum brought him in her arms straight from hospital to the new bungalow Dad had built on the outskirts of Naxxar. That was eighteen years ago and now, Paul, at eighteen, still baby faced, with that sing-song tonality in his voice that made him sound even younger...

'Tell me, Ġolin. What do you think I should do?'

I smiled. I realised that Paul must have thought I wasn't listening.

Then I looked him up and down, trying to size him up for what I had in mind for him.

'Let me tell you what I'm thinking, Paul. I have lately been toying with the idea of opening a hard-stone quarry. But you know how busy I am with other things and running it alone is impossible for me. So, what do you say if we open this quarry with you managing it?'

'Who? Me? Manage a quarry? I don't know anything about quarries, Golin. I've never even been down one, let alone know how it works. And I don't have the money, anyway.'

'I haven't mentioned money, have I? Your job would be to operate the plant, that's all.'

'To operate the plant? You make it seem as if it's just –'

'Look, Paul. You've just told me it's about time you started doing something. Now I'm giving you the chance to start with something big. I'll design the plant and in the meantime explain everything that needs explaining. I'll invest the required capital to start it off and give you a 49% share. Then you can pay me back your share of the capital from your profits. What do you say to that?'

To say he was delighted is putting it mildly. Paul, however, was the youngest of the family and Dad's pet from day one. Dad never refused him anything and the relationship between them was so close that Paul never held back any secrets from him. So, Paul went over to him for advice – something I had expected him to do.

'Don't you understand what your brother's proposing?' was Dad's immediate reaction. 'He's keeping 51% so he could keep full control and overrule any input from your end. That's what Golu's proposing.'

'Dad's right,' I told Paul when he came back with Dad's reaction. 'He's absolutely right because, in real terms, that's what our agreement would mean should you accept my proposal. On the other hand, you must appreciate the fact that you're still young and totally inexperienced, and don't even know the inside of a quarry, let alone how to run it. So, I don't know how much of a risk you'd be to the whole operation, do I? And giving you half the share would put the whole project in jeopardy. Imagine you don't deliver and the project goes bust. You could always shrug your shoulders and leave because you wouldn't have lost a single penny. But I would have poured thousands down the drain.'

In a way, Paul's continual shuttling between me and Dad served a good purpose because it saved me from going to Dad, and thus, we didn't ruin the mutual peaceful co-existence that reigned between us. He, however, still kept to his opinion regarding my offer to Paul.

Paul's going to and fro continued a couple of more times and I thought it was time he made up his mind once and for all. I repeated for the umpteenth time that I would always protect his shareholding once he took up my offer, while making it clear that should he fall short of expectations, I would find someone else who would jump at the opportunity.

'You either trust me or you don't,' I concluded. 'I'm already proving to you that I have trust in you, otherwise I wouldn't have made you this once in a lifetime offer. And, at the end of the day, it's you who has to decide. If I had let someone else make the decisions for me I wouldn't be where I am today.'

Paul must have understood this was a final offer and he spent a whole week trying to come to terms with having to make the decision of his life. At the end of the week he came to see me, his face tense and looking as though he had had a few sleepless nights.

'Dad is still against it, Golin.'

At these words my heart sank. I thought he had given up on a golden opportunity.

'But I trust you,' he continued, much to my relief. 'I know you won't let me down. So, I accept your offer.'

His sigh of relief was audible and the tension on his face disappeared, giving him back his youthful appearance. And at last he smiled.

Once the decision was made all went along smoothly between us and we were pleased. We immediately went about planning everything because the project had now become more urgent than ever. We bought a large area of barren land where we could blast the rock and another area close by where we could erect our plant. We made a tour of the other quarries still in operation after which we sat down to design a plant that would be more efficient and productive than our competitors.

Then we were off to the United Kingdom to find a second-hand plant and equipment suitable to what we had in mind. Since our design for the plant was made to fit our requirements, and therefore not the standard imported plant, we were constrained to contract local engineering firms to manufacture it section by section. As our design was rather revolutionary, certain sections were experimental and had to be tested when mounted in place. This involved much tension for Paul and me, and unplanned extra costs until the plant was built exactly according to our specifications. But, just nine months after the drawing of the first design, we started production. We named the company Hardrocks Limited and it is still very active today.

We did have some teething trouble until the sections we had designed began to function as efficiently as planned on the drawing board, but in a few months we managed to reach full production. I still recall the day we blasted the first section of rock in our quarry; Paul and I saw it all from behind a protective wall, watching amazed at the stones flying all around us.

We started production in winter. This meant that the raw material would be wet and more difficult to screed. During summer we were producing an average of 800 cubic metres of sand and gravel a day, but an extra two hours overtime raised the figure to 1,000 cubic metres. The quality of gravel we were producing was superior to everyone else's and we were selling all we could produce.

A few weeks after starting production we had a near fatal accident. Paul was still inexperienced and this, coupled with his enthusiasm and boundless energy, nearly cost him his life. It happened when he climbed up one of our large sand silos, located high above ground, to try to loosen sand stuck in the corners, thereby interrupting the flow of sand being poured into an idling lorry underneath. Suddenly, without the least warning whatsoever, the sand beneath Paul's feet caved in, engulfing my brother and carrying him right to the bottom of the silo. Paul was literally drowning in a sea of sand, unable to breathe and very close to suffocation, with his feet protruding through the small and narrow hopper. The lorry driver, who was looking up, waiting for the sand to resume its flow down, saw Paul's feet and instantly shouted the alarm while he reached up high enough to reach the opening. He pulled hard at both feet and singlehandedly got Paul completely out of the narrow opening. He came out shaken, breathing in big gulps and spitting sand from his mouth and nostrils, but he was alive. In fact it was his thinness that saved his life as he wouldn't have made it through the opening if he had been any bigger. Had he landed just a foot away from the opening, or if his feet hadn't made it through it, or if the driver hadn't been in the right place at the right time, Paul wouldn't have survived. And I wouldn't have forgiven myself, either. I wouldn't have been able to face my family and I doubt whether I could have lived with the sorrow.

The accident was a great shock for Paul and all the workers. They suddenly realised how dangerous this industry could be unless all the necessary safety precautions were taken and full concentration was maintained at all times. It was fortunate that this accident didn't claim any victims, but fatal accidents have happened in similar circumstances and still happen at other plants owing to lack of safety measures.

Paul was a quick learner and he soon became an expert at handling the whole operation singlehandedly. Thanks to him, and the lessons he learned, our operation became one of the leading plants in Malta and Gozo – a position it has held to date – and has maintained its profitability through the years.

In five years, Paul more than proved himself and I transferred my extra 1% shareholding to him so that we had equal shareholding.. Nearly three decades later, he is still responsible for the whole operation and he's still very proud of Hardrocks, and rightly so. He and I hold regular monthly meetings to go through the management accounts and every so often he asks me to visit the plant.

'Why don't you come down some afternoon this week, Angelo?' he would ask me. 'There's this new piece of equipment we just bought and which I'd like you to see. I'm sure you'll love seeing it in operation. It's so efficient, Angelo, you have to see it to believe.' Over the years he engaged himself in the property market on his own and has made another success story in this sector.

Although many years have passed since he started on the job as an eighteen-year-old, his enthusiasm and energy have not diminished one little bit. Over the years he has put on some weight and has a few white hairs near his temples, but his face still carries that youthful expression. I have never regretted bringing him on board.

'Come over some time and see this piece of land we've just bought, Angelo. You'll like it because it has potential.'

I would smile and he would smile back, both thinking about our father's initial objection, and both pleased with the decision we made.

AX Construction

8

Decisively Into Tourism

(1981–1985) 29–33 years

The December 1981 general election gave the Malta Labour Party a further five years' tenure in government. It was a closely contested election with the Nationalist Party, in opposition since 1971, garnering more than 50% of the popular vote but winning a minority of seats in Parliament. It was the first time in Malta's constitutional history that the party enjoying the majority's support ended up on the opposition benches.

The result plunged the country into general confusion which negatively affected the general economy of the island.

Dad was a staunch Nationalist Party supporter and he was very disappointed and disgusted with the result, especially since he had harboured very high hopes that his party would make it this time round. He took it so badly that he simply lost his will to continue working and decided to retire from every activity. He was still fifty-six at the time and as strong as an ox.

His early retirement was a major worry for the whole family, especially for me who knew him better than anybody else. Everyone tried to talk him out of it, but he wouldn't listen, his reason being that he had worked hard throughout his life, his sons were settled in their own business activities, his daughters settled in marriages and with a Labour Government for another five-year period there was nothing else left for him to do but to enjoy life.

With my eldest sister, Speranza, the only one still at home

after all my brothers and sisters were married, Mum and Dad had plenty of free time on their hands, so they took to travelling abroad. But, while Mum preferred going to Australia where many of her brothers, sisters and other relatives had emigrated during the early 1960s, Dad preferred mainland Europe.

I thought that at fifty-six it was too early for him to retire completely from work when he still had so much energy and was as healthy as I had ever known him. I was afraid that once he got bored with the constant travelling he would fall into apathy and end up aging prematurely. I couldn't picture him driving idly around between Mosta and Naxxar, sitting all morning on a bench in the village square, idling his time gossiping with old timers about how times change and how today's young people have no shame and no respect for their elders, and waiting for the church bells to sound noon, the time for them to disperse, each to his own lunch, followed by a long afternoon siesta, which one day might not end. No! Not my father! But I couldn't think of anything that would rouse him from the self-destructing life he had chosen.

A year or so later, I thought I had found the solution. It was thanks to a good piece of land I found, situated in a central position in Naxxar. It was already covered by the necessary building permits and just large enough to fit a few terraced houses. Naxxar and its surroundings had always been Dad's favourite areas for development and the piece of land was small enough to keep him fairly busy without occupying most of his time. I thought it was the perfect bait.

I approached the owners, but the price they asked for it was far too high for Dad to even tickle his business instincts. I couldn't let this deflect me from my intentions, however, so I agreed on the price on the condition that I pay half of it while the other half would be paid by Dad. I also bound the owners never to divulge the real price to Dad and to never mention my involvement. The owners were delighted with the deal and accepted my conditions wholeheartedly.

The first time I mentioned this piece of land to Dad, and told him that the owners were giving it away for peanuts, he showed not the least interest. He told me that his decision was final and there was no going back on his word. I kept at him for a few days until I could again notice the old, familiar look in his eyes. From then onwards it was all plain sailing. He went into it with his typical frenzy of energy and the houses he built were immediately sold for a very good profit (naturally).

He still isn't aware of my involvement in the whole scheme, but the whole family breathed a long sigh of relief. He continued with some small developments to keep himself busy and at the same time he had more time to relax with his friends and his ever-growing family.

In the meantime, my construction business continued to do extremely well. The high quality of my finished product was not being achieved at the expense of my reputation for meeting deadlines, and this was soon to be tested to its limits in the challenge I chose to face.

Accessibility to water had always been one of Malta's major problems. Our numerous valleys, formed by rivers during the last Ice Age thousands of years ago, had slowly dried up over a period of many centuries. When the Order of St John was given full sovereignty of Malta by Emperor Charles V in 1530, it sent over a forward party to investigate and report on the state of the island. One of the major problems mentioned in the report was the acute lack of water and this was the reason that, when the Knights built the fortified capital city Valletta, they made sure that it was well supplied with water by excavating enormous underground cisterns, which were fed by the monumental aqueducts that extended from Rabat located on the higher part of the island. This is the reason that these aqueducts were so strongly guarded throughout the Knights' reign.

With the ever-growing population, coupled with the drying up of a number of natural springs, the supply of water remained a major headache for whoever administered the island since the Knights. Industrialisation and tourism continued to add more pressure and, although most of the potable water was being brought up from the underground water table, unchecked abuse of this important source was slowly and steadily rendering the water salty owing to the seeping of sea water into the source.

The situation became so bad that the government decided to issue a call for tenders for the construction of a reverse osmosis plant, which was intended to be the world's largest at the time, capable of supplying 3 million gallons daily.

To further compound the problem and render the construction of the reverse osmosis plant even more urgent, we had a very dry winter and the government-run reservoirs were at their lowest level ever. So, one could imagine the situation the country was in.

Government had already awarded the contract for the purchase of the plant from the international firm, Du Pont, a leading group specialising in this field, and government workers had already started on the construction of the enormous building to house the plant. But, as always, the going was extremely slow and Du Pont was certain that the construction phase wouldn't be completed in time to start production during summer as planned. So, the government decided to issue an urgent call for tenders specifically for the completion of the works in under three months.

My company's bid was the cheapest, but the adjudicating committee had serious doubts about whether I could finish the work on time. I was thirty years old and still referred to as 'the young building contractor'. Since mine was the cheapest bid, however, I was invited for a meeting with the adjudicating committee. This was very unusual, but owing to the importance and urgency of the project, the committee broke away from standard practice and decided to convey directly to me its preoccupation about the whole thing and, also, to listen to my opinions. It was also an ideal opportunity for the members to meet face to face with this young contractor who had managed to establish such a good reputation.

The twenty people sitting around a large table looked me up and down as soon as I was ushered in. The chairman indicated a vacant chair beside him at the head of the table and, as I made my way towards it, I could feel twenty pairs of eyes watching my every step. Looking at all the heads turned in my direction, I felt I was about to be interrogated for a crime I didn't know I had committed.

'Look here, Mr Xuereb,' began the chairman in a voice very much like a police interrogator. 'It's true that your bid is the most competitive for this major project. But, to tell you the truth, and here I speak for all the members,' I noticed that the members' heads began nodding simultaneously, 'we're not at all convinced that you have the ability to finish it within three months. So, we're suggesting that the contract be shared with another big contractor, thereby ensuring completion in time.'

Just like that! Guilty without given the chance to prove my innocence!

It was the last thing I had expected to hear. I could feel anger building up inside me, but I made an effort to control it and not let it show. I considered it all an insult to my capabilities because it had always been my belief and pride that I could meet any challenge once I knew I had the ability to meet it. And this was one such instance.

With all the calmness I could muster, I said, 'I'm sorry, Mr Chairman, but I don't agree with the committee's decision and, therefore, won't accept it. I know I can finish the works in time. Otherwise, I wouldn't have submitted a bid for it. My track record speaks for itself and I'm sure you have done your own homework. So, I don't have to prove anything.'

I could see that my words had softened up some of the members, but the chairman spoke again.

'We all know your past performance is highly commendable, Mr Xuereb. We have no doubt about that and there's no arguing about it. But this time it's different. This time it's the survival of the people that's at stake, Mr Xuereb. We shall all face extreme hardships, God forbid, should the works not be completed in time.'

'Mr Chairman, I appreciate and understand your concern, and let me assure you that the wellbeing of the people is my concern as well. But let me also assure you that I am capable of finishing the works in time enough for the plant to start functioning as planned.'

My words were greeted with complete silence. The members looked at one another but none spoke. It was clear that my strong words had taken them by complete surprise and they were totally unprepared. The thought that their meeting with me was just to confirm a *fait accompli* had completely evaporated.

At last the chairman broke the embarrassing silence. 'Would you wait outside while we discuss it please, Mr Xuereb?'

I walked out of the room without saying another word, but a quarter of an hour later I was back, sitting beside the chairman.

'Mr Xuereb,' he said without any preamble, 'we have all expressed our views regarding your assurances. You have to appreciate our situation, Mr Xuereb. Our decision today is probably the toughest each one of us has ever had to make because on it hinges the very lives of our people. You may be confident about your abilities and we all appreciate and recognise them because your record speaks for itself. But you must appreciate, also, that in this exceptional case we have to have safeguards. And so we have decided to include a clause in the contract that stipulates that should you fail to finish the works in time, your company would be blacklisted from all future government tenders.'

All my works at the time were dependent on government contracts, but I didn't hesitate to reply, 'You go ahead, Mr Chairman.'

'You mean you'd risk being blacklisted?'

'I have no problem with that because I shall not be blacklisted. You may go ahead and include the clause in the contract.'

I was awarded the contract with the insertion of this clause but I was confident I could prove myself once more and immediately embarked on a long-working-hour schedule spread over a seven-day week.

When the work had already started and was moving at a fast rate, an American representative of Du Pont walked up to me and said, 'Mr Xuereb, are you aware you have created a major problem for us?'

'A problem for you? How's that?'

'Well,' he replied, looking a bit lost for words. 'You see, we were assuming that the construction phase wouldn't be completed in time. But at the rate you're going...'

'That's the very reason we're working at this rate, isn't it? To finish it in time.'

'That's just it. It'll cost us heavy penalties if you do.'

'And it'll cost me if I don't!'

I did finish it in time and, eventually, Du Pont came to an agreement with the government to have part of the plant in operation before the start of the hottest summer months and to complete the rest during the subsequent months.

My ability to meet this widely considered impossible deadline was declared a great feat around official circles. I earned much new respect and recognition from the members of the Government Contracts Committee, whose necks I probably saved in the process, and from all government ministers and other high officials.

It was just a year later that I was again asked to rise to the occasion and prove yet again my determination when faced with what would seem an insurmountable challenge. This time it was the construction of the grandstand of our national football stadium at Ta' Qali. It was scheduled to be completed within four months, a condition stipulated in the contract.

This time I enjoyed a competitive edge over rival bidders thanks to my own precast and pre-stressed concrete plants. This project was different in that it involved multi-discipline construction-related activities, which included, among others, a large cantilevered steel canopy, a post-tensioned reinforced concrete anchor and the placing of large precast concrete steps. The above works were enough to render this project breathtakingly challenging, but the limited number of mobile cranes I could use on this six-storey structure made it seem daunting.

The minister responsible, Mr Lorry Sant, was the one who had given me the first big push forward years before. His portfolio now also included sport in addition to public works. He was, therefore, the minister totally responsible for the success or otherwise of the project. He was well aware of my reputation for taking risks and facing difficult challenges, but this time he wanted strong assurances that there wouldn't be any reckless risks on my part. The political implications were too high for the minister to risk being let down by a contractor, however efficient.

So, he sent for me to go to his office. This time I was given ample forward notice and had all the time in the world to dress as smartly as possible. He sat at the head of the long table while I occupied the chair next to him and opposite his private secretary.

'Listen, Angelo,' he began, barely giving me time to sit down. 'I'm told yours is the best bid. I haven't brought you here to congratulate you, OK? I'm not one to beat about the bush. So, I'll lay it out to you simply and bluntly because it's one hell of a big and important project. I want an honest answer from you. So you either assure me you can finish it in time or that you're not able to. That's all I want from you and I won't hold it against you if you back out now.'

'Minister, you've had ample proof of my capabilities. So, what can I say? If you want my solemn word that I'll finish it in time, then I'll give you my word.'

'Okay, Angelo. That's all I wanted to hear.' He stood up and shook my hand. 'I'll take your word on this.'

Back home that evening, I sat comfortably and relaxed watching the news on the national television channel, but not really absorbing what was being said as my mind was occupied by business-related matters. Suddenly, Minister Sant's face appeared on the screen and my attention shifted completely. I realised that he was giving a press conference and what really made me sit up straight was his solemn declaration that the government would be constructing a grandstand at the new national stadium and that the minister himself would be inaugurating it on 13th December, Republic Day, less than four months away.

I was completely dumbfounded and for a few seconds I just stared at the television screen, oblivious to what was being said.

I realised that the success of this national event rested solely on my shoulders. I realised that should I fail in this enterprise, whether through any fault of mine, bad weather or anything, I would be held responsible and my name would become dirt nationwide. I was suddenly scared and started to shiver. The minister had a reputation for stamina and drive, and letting him down was tantamount to crossing him. It would spell complete disaster for me and my company. I would be blacklisted for life.

This was 14th August, the eve of the feast of The Assumption of Our Lady, a public holiday and the titular feast of Mosta. Most of my workers came from Mosta, which meant that they would be taking the 16th August off, as is the custom in Malta. This meant two working days lost, and the minister had just been stating on television that the project would be ready for inauguration on 13th December. For the first time in my life I was feeling overcome by panic. Every lost working day was a day closer to doomsday.

With an effort, I managed to calm down and started looking at the problem like any problem I had to deal with. I asked myself, 'When have I ever let anyone down once I gave my word?'

'Never!' I answered myself loudly. And saying it aloud gave me the confidence I sorely needed.

All the workers were back at work on 17th August and in two weeks we were working in full swing, but the terrain we had to work on was difficult. It contained a high percentage of clay and this made it difficult for us to manoeuvre our heavily loaded trailers. But, again, we managed to complete the works on time, and the minister inaugurated the new national stadium on 13th December as promised.

I was invited for the occasion and the President of the Malta Football Association was one of the speakers. Among other things, he said, 'Four months ago the minister made a public statement. He said he would finish this magnificent stadium by 13th December. Everybody, then, shook his head. Everybody thought it preposterous of the minister to be so reckless in his public announcements. But, here we all are today, December 13th, sitting under this magnificent grandstand, and asking ourselves how it was possible that just four months ago this was a complete void.'

I couldn't have received higher praise, even though my name was never mentioned in the speeches. This gave me much pride in my work and the courage, optimism and enthusiasm to continue to face all challenges that came my way.

With business booming, I had ample cash flow and I thought it was the right time to start diversifying my business interests. There were a number of options I could juggle before making a final decision, but it wasn't so easy because I wanted to be certain of its long-term sustainability before plunging into something that would look attractive at first glance.

One such option, and one that was uppermost on my list, was the manufacturing industry. It was a very attractive option because our wages were very low when compared to those paid on mainland Europe, partly due to a wage freeze imposed by the government. It was a time of austerity resulting from the government's botched policies when even to acquire a simple telephone line one had to be in the ruling party's good books, and when people flocked in their thousands to nearby Sicily for such 'luxuries' as toothpaste and chocolate, since the locally manufactured alternative was simply inedible.

Thinking deeply about it, I decided against this venture. Should there be a change of government, wages were bound to increase and our competitiveness would not remain so clear cut. Added to this were the extra costs involving the importation of all the raw material required – costs that for other countries were minimal. I had to consider, also, the high costs for haulage and shipping the finished product and I decided that all this would put me out of business in a few short years. Time proved me right because not many years passed before Chinese and Indian products started flooding the world markets, while in the process putting well-established industries out of business.

After considering various other options I decided to invest in the hospitality sector. I didn't arrive at this decision haphazardly. On the contrary, I spent a long time weighing the pros and cons, especially since tourism is such a fragile industry that depends on factors one could never hope to control. But, I strongly believe in the Maltese product. With such a long and unique history and rich architecture, which includes the world's oldest free-standing structure, the hospitable instincts of the population (the majority of whom are bilingual) and the moderate climate, Malta is the proverbial gem of the Mediterranean.

Once I had made up my mind I began to act with the usual enthusiasm. I identified one of Malta's prime sites situated at Tignè Point in Sliema overlooking the capital Valletta across Marsamxetto Harbour. It consisted of a number of ex-British Army barracks surrounded by a large tract of open land. My idea was to convert the whole area into a large tourist complex and I immediately set about drawing the plans.

There was a snag, however; the whole complex was government owned. So, I had to face two options. I could either give up the whole thing and let the place become a slum or I could try to find a way to turn it into something beautiful and useful. I thought that the only way forward was to persuade the Prime Minister himself that the project I had in mind was feasible and beneficial to the country. A friend of mine, Effie Mamo, was quite close to Prime Minister Dom Mintoff and he managed to fix a meeting with him.

The Prime Minister agreed to meet me in his office at midnight. The time wasn't as unearthly as one may imagine. Mr Mintoff had the habit of taking a longish afternoon break from work to enable him to take a swim in the open sea in a secluded bay in the south of Malta, whatever the season, after which he would return fully refreshed to his office and continue working long hours, sometimes until after one in the morning.

My friend Effie and I were ushered into the Prime Minister's office and while both of us were in our best suits, Mr Mintoff was comfortable in an open-necked shirt. I was feeling very nervous and shy, but while the Prime Minister was pumping my hand vigorously up and down in an iron grip, I noticed that his trousers were being held up by a wide belt decorated with his trademark enormous buckle.

Then we went straight to business. I opened my plans and Mr Mintoff, an architect by profession, took immediate interest. We talked for more than half an hour, he asking me to explain and I tried to be as clear as possible. I noticed that every time he wanted to take a closer look at something he would take off his glasses and poke his face very close to the plans, nearly touching them with his nose.

At one point, while I was explaining what I had in mind for a particular building, Effie, almost embarrassed by how long this meeting was taking and considering the time of night, intervened. 'Angelo, don't you think you should stop now? We've taken up too much of the Prime Minister's time already and he's a very busy person.'

Then I saw the Prime Minister in action and it wasn't the pleasantest of sights. He turned abruptly from me to face Effie. 'Who asked you to open your mouth?' he shouted. 'Shut up and don't say a word unless spoken to. Can't you see this young man knows what he's talking about? Haven't you realised what an excellent proposal this is? Or aren't you interested in what's good for the country?'

I stood open-mouthed, watching Effie literally trying to make himself smaller during the Prime Minister's outburst and for a moment I thought he was going to faint. But the Prime Minister's next words diverted my attention.

'Go on, young man. What did you say you wanted to do here?' he calmly continued while pointing to a particular building on the plans spread on the table.

For the remaining time with the Prime Minister I became so absorbed that I completely forgot Effie's presence and predicament. I talked and talked with the scale ruler in my hand, sometimes pointing with it at particular parts on the plans as though lecturing to a student while the Prime Minister followed attentively every detail I explained.

A few weeks later the government passed a resolution in Parliament for the lease of this prominent site at Tignè Point for sixteen years. It was to be developed as a joint venture between government subsidiary companies, which would own 75% of the shareholding, and my company, which would own the remaining 25%. We named the company Sliema Point Co. Ltd. with a capital outlay of €233,000. It was a lot of money at the time.

When other leading and prominent businessmen became aware of the project through the media all hell broke loose. Jealous at being left out of the reckoning, they started an intensive and destructive campaign through high-profile intermediaries to force me into giving up my shares in their favour. I stood my ground and refused, but they managed to force the other board directors of the company to resign *en bloc*, leaving me as the only remaining director and unable to manage on my own.

I realised I was up against the establishment and this very thought angered me and hardened my determination to resist. The people involved in the plot against me were big wigs with long tentacles that penetrated every nook and cranny, and influenced every government decision. They wanted to force me down on my knees to beg for my money back. But, I could afford to wait even though my share of €58,200 was quite substantial at the time.

When months passed and I hadn't budged from my position, Air Malta's chairman, representing one of the government subsidiary companies, tried to force me to wind up the company so that the airline could use its dormant initial investment. But, as the only remaining director, I just sat back and dug my heels in.

Though my investment was substantial, I could still carry on with my business without it. I preferred to stick to my guns and keep the company in a dormant state even at the risk of losing my investment, and it soon became clear that those involved had never expected such a strong reaction from such a young entrepreneur.

The times weren't ideal for private investors. The Socialist Government's declared policy of nationalising banks and large companies didn't encourage private investment. The government played a dormant role in all this, leaving everything in the hands of a few top and trusted executives to control all parastatal subsidiaries. I was too naïve at the time to understand all the underhand manoeuvres going on. I was not a political person and hated all dirty underhand games. Later, I realised that each government-related board member, especially the chairman, were politically appointed puppets to see that government objectives were adhered to. These boards would act as a front for the ministers' or cabinet decisions. Unless there was the politician's blessing, it was almost impossible to acquire what seemed to be a legitimate right of any citizen.

This experience left me with a bitter taste in my mouth and I decided that, from then onwards, I would go it alone, whatever the business circumstances. I soon set about buying a 1,000-square-metre piece of land right in the centre of the popular tourist resort of St Paul's Bay. I started planning a hundred-room, four star hotel with myself as the sole owner. Its construction and works on furniture and fittings started simultaneously and I wanted all to be finished inside a year. Works on the hotel were still at first-floor level when I started marketing it with tour operators for the coming summer. During one such meeting with a particular operator, the manager started asking me interesting questions.

'So, Mr Xuereb, how much do you intend to invest in your hotel?' he asked.

'Well,' I replied. 'I expect half a million would cover everything.' (Half a million Maltese Liri, equivalent to €1,165,000, was a lot of money at the time.)

'That's a lot of money, isn't it? Especially when it's quite a distance from the seashore. How much would the same hotel cost if located on the seafront?'

'I don't think it would cost more than an extra ten thousand. It's the price of the land that would make the difference.'

'So don't you think that for such a relatively paltry sum your investment would generate higher occupancy and higher room rates?'

I looked at him for a few seconds, wondering why on earth I hadn't thought this in the first place.

'You're absolutely right,' I said at last. 'Tomorrow I shall stop all works and you'll be seeing me again soon. I shall have a hotel with a sea view for you!'

At seven o'clock the following morning I was already on site, giving orders that all construction works must stop. I could see the look of consternation on the workers' faces, all wondering what could have happened overnight. The furniture maker had already purchased all the required material and a third of my order was already completed. I instructed him to continue with my order as I intended using the same furniture in the new hotel on another site.

Two months later a middleman approached me with a proposal. He told me about a site at nearby Qawra, already making a name as a popular tourist resort, measuring approximately 1,000 square metres and located right on the coast, which meant an uninterrupted sea view. I drove to the place with the middleman and as soon as I saw the site, I said to myself, 'This is exactly what I'm looking for.'

I fixed a meeting with the owners for the following day and signed the preliminary contract. A month later we signed the final one and as soon as I had the necessary building permit I decided to name the new hotel Sunny Coast Holiday Complex.

On 20th December 1981, when work on the construction of the hotel was in full swing, my hardworking foreman, Karmenu, fell from a height of 17 metres through an internal shaft while working on the half-finished sixth floor. It happened at half past seven in the morning and I was on the ground floor giving instructions to some workers when the cry went up that Karmenu had fallen down a shaft, but none seemed to know which.

We were all stunned, but frantically went to his rescue. He was still conscious when we located him, but later in the hospital, we were informed that he had various fractures and that his lungs and other internal organs had been severely damaged. This was bad news indeed and when he was transferred to the intensive care unit, we were further informed that his chances of survival were very slim.

I joined his wife, children and relatives in a long vigil lasting days and nights. The waiting room became our temporary living quarters where we prayed and hoped for the least sign of improvement in Karmenu's condition. I was really sad and worried. Karmenu wasn't just a good and loyal worker; I considered him a friend. I was completely distraught and I remember pestering the head nurse of the ITU every time I saw her, begging her to do her best to save Karmenu's life. It was Christmas time and I distributed presents to all the ITU staff and, as always during the festive season, to all my workers. I was depressed but didn't want my staff to realise what a sad Christmas it was for me. It was the worst of my life. However, it seems God was listening to our prayers because Karmenu was discharged from the ITU two weeks after Christmas.

Work on the hotel continued at the same fast rate after this and we kept to our schedule to finish it in less than twelve months to open it officially on 2nd April 1982. That same week I had a meeting with a Dutch tour operator. I wanted to negotiate a package deal for the coming summer season.

'But, Mr Xuereb, you don't even have a swimming pool,' he told me.

'Why? Does that make a difference to you?'

'Does it make a difference to me? Of course it makes a difference to me. It makes all the difference. My clients opt for hotels with swimming pools.'

'Oh. So that's it. OK then. So if I had a swimming pool would you sign a contract?'

'If you had a swimming pool, yes, I would sign a contract. But you don't. So, we have no contract.'

'But you would if I had one?'

'Well, next year if you –'

'No, this year. I mean this year.'

'Come on, Mr Xuereb. Be serious. We're talking business, you know.'

'Of course we're talking business. That's why I'm asking.'

'You mean to tell me –'

'You said you'd sign a contract if I had a swimming pool. So I'll give you a swimming pool.'

We shook hands on the deal, both smiling, but for different reasons.

I had already bought the additional adjacent land right at the water's edge specifically to construct a large swimming pool and ancillary facilities. So, I immediately started on their construction and all was completed in less than a month.

True to his word, the Dutch operator was back in Malta during the second week in May specifically to see whether I was true to my word. And he was astounded.

'Let me tell you honestly, Mr Xuereb. I never believed it could be done in a month. Well done. You really surprised me.'

The contract was signed and his company continued to be our main supplier of Dutch tourists for many years. Fifteen years later, I bumped into him at the Berlin Hotels Fair. We enjoyed each other's company and joked while recalling the unforgettable experience of the construction of the swimming pool.

A year after I had finished the swimming pool I set about the construction of a health and leisure club. This project was carried out simultaneously with the construction of a restaurant, which I named The Coral Reef. I planned it to compete with the classiest restaurants in Malta and both projects, from the laying of the foundations to the beautifully prepared fine dining tables, were completed in just three months.

It was around this time that the concept of time share was introduced in Malta, when the Sunny Coast Holiday Complex was a year old. It was an initiative of a local hotelier. In my case, it would involve the complete upgrading of all my holiday complex apartments to luxury level, including all related facilities.

My holiday complex was practically new and it required a courageous decision on my part to scrap everything and replace it all with something more luxurious. I decided to take the risk and planned to split the operation into three phases. In the meantime, I engaged a marketing team to sell my newly refurbished units, while my company controlled the whole operation. The first phase was completed in two months and the immediate resulting cash flow was really good. The location of my complex right on the water's edge, enjoying fantastic views and offering an extensive number of leisure facilities, produced a most attractive package to prospective buyers. Others soon picked it up when they learned it was generating ten times more cash flow than the normal tour operation business.

At the time I was still personally managing most of my business activities in the construction and development sectors and, also, in the tourism sector. I had able assistance from a young and promising hotel manager, three construction foremen and four administrative officers, but this wasn't enough, as one cannot run a hotel and operate a construction company singlehandedly because a day is only twenty-four hours long. I was still trying to oversee the organisation of barbecues for tourists at the lido and these normally lasted till one in the morning. Then I had to wake up at five thirty later the same morning to start work on my other construction business. I would wake up so tired and disoriented that sometimes I would just stare at the bedroom ceiling, wondering whether it was already morning and time to get up, or whether I had just gone to bed for a night's sleep.

'I can't go on like this,' I thought. 'At this rate I'll either work myself to death or force my family to institutionalise me.'

So, I employed a junior construction manager to lessen part of the load I was still carrying from day one of my business career. I also gave up picking up my workers from their doorstep at six o'clock each morning. Believe it or not, this was another chore I was still carrying out so many years into my business.

The change gave me an extra hour of sleep and made a lot of difference both mentally and physically. But it also left me with a slight feeling of guilt. I wasn't used to starting work in the morning when the sun was already up. It made me feel lazy, but it also left me with more time to concentrate on business deals while leaving other not-so-important activities to adequately qualified members of my staff.

The continual expansion of my business activities brought with it bigger challenges and experiences in managerial skills where the advantage of a tertiary education would have stood me in good stead. To make up for this I attended a number of short courses on the relevant subjects during which I realised that my attitude to and perception of the business world were not off the mark. I realised, in fact, that what I lacked in formal education I made up for with my long and wide experience, starting from the days when, as a child, I accompanied Dad during his business deals. I also had the advantage of being very self-disciplined and, also, a workaholic. Although I could, perhaps, not match the other participants at these courses where it came to academic theory, I excelled when it came to practical exercises. I also attended various conferences and seminars which I considered relevant to my chosen vocation, and these gave me further exposure to new knowledge and techniques.

In the meantime, my holiday complex didn't take long to start doing as well as my other business interests in construction and real estate. All were now doing better than ever. But my office space did not expand at the same rate. In fact, it did not expand at all and I had to make the bold decision of moving house in order to give my office space more elbow room. Jessie and I loved our home where we experienced all the joys of raising a family and, also, shared the troubles and tragedies that helped cement our marriage bond. So, we were understandably sad at having to leave so many memories behind, but, as always, Jessie – pregnant with our third child, Denise – was practical and mature enough to understand the necessities of my ever-growing business interests. Considering the urgency of the situation we had no option other than to take up temporary residence in one of our hotel's better apartments which, although beautifully furnished, was very compact compared to home. It was, therefore, imperative that I find the right piece of land as soon as possible where I could build a spacious villa for my growing family.

It didn't take me long to find the perfect site. It was in Mosta, not far from our home, but commanding panoramic views. I designed the villa myself and immediately applied for a building permit. It was obvious from the very outset that the processing of my application was going to take a long time (in fact, it took a whole year). This meant that my family's temporary stay at the hotel's two bedroom apartment would be longer than anticipated and waking up each morning surrounded by my staff was not something I relished. Neither did my staff!

Luckily, I was informed that a maisonette adjacent to the hotel was up for sale and I went for it right away. It would mean more space for my family and, with the sea view it commanded and the moderately sized back garden, it was ideal for the children. So, I immediately started out upgrading it to have it ready in time for our next child.

Our stay at the hotel lasted six months and it was with a sigh of relief that we moved next door. The smiles on the faces of my staff as they bid us goodbye told it all.

The house was a convenient place to live in during the summer, owing to its proximity to the hotel swimming pool and facilities, and to the open sea. I made the best of it during weekends when I practically tried every available amenity. I even practised wind surfing and water skiing, and also bought a 24-foot boat, which I conveniently berthed next to my hotel complex. When water sport was not possible in winter I availed myself of the facilities offered at the hotel gymnasium, including the squash court. During this period I learned that while I could still work as hard as ever, I could still manage to find time to enjoy my free time with my family and keep myself fit in the process.

One day a few months later, a middleman I had often done business with approached me. He told me that a large tract of land close to my hotel was up for sale. I knew the area and it was perfect for a large hotel and extensive facilities as it extended right to the water's edge and was served by roads on all four sides. The price the owners were asking for it was very high, but I knew it would turn out to be a good investment for whoever bought it.

I was very low on cash at the time and since I had known this middleman for quite some time I told him, 'I would have been interested to go for it, but you've found me at the worst time possible. I've invested a lot of money in my hotel, as you can see for yourself. I simply can't afford such a huge investment at this point in time.'

'Oh come on, Angelo. I've never known you to get discouraged by such a small problem.'

I laughed at the sincere way he spoke the words. 'You call raising hundreds of thousands of liri a small problem?'

'I didn't mean it that way, Angelo. What I meant is that you always somehow manage to find ways to solve problems.'

I didn't answer as these words set me thinking. I was wondering whether there was some way I could acquire this ideal piece of land.

The middleman knew me well enough to realise that his words had struck a chord.

'I'll tell you what, Angelo. Why don't you meet the owners? You have nothing to lose. But who knows? Maybe you could come to some sort of agreement.'

'What agreement? An agreement that I won't be able to pay?'

This time it was his turn to laugh. 'You disappoint me, Angelo. I've known you for years and it's the first time I'm seeing you unsure of yourself.'

He was right. I looked at him and I could see from his eyes that he was challenging me to take some action. I shrugged my shoulders. What was there to lose if I met the owners?

'Okay, then. Fix a meeting and waste some more of my time.'

He laughed and walked away. I met the owners the next day. They confirmed the price the middleman mentioned the day before and although I tried my best to force it down, they wouldn't budge.

'Listen,' one of the owners told me at last, 'we have almost concluded a deal with another investor whom we know very well. He's the chairman of the largest group of companies and I'm expecting a confirmation from him any moment.' He stopped to see what effect his words had on me then he continued, 'So, as you can see, if you don't go for it now someone else definitely will. Give us 10% deposit and the deal is yours.'

I thought for a few moments, wondering whether he was bluffing. But I couldn't risk waiting to find out. 'Okay,' I said. 'It's a deal. But on the condition that the preliminary agreement is signed today.'

We shook hands and agreed to meet at the notary's at six o'clock that evening.

When we were out on the street, the middleman told me, 'Well done, Angelo. That was more like you. You're a sharp businessman and I wish you all the luck.'

After we had walked a little further towards our cars he stopped, looked back once and turned to me. 'I think there's something else you should know, now that you've clinched it. You remember they mentioned another investor who's interested in this piece of land. He wishes to develop it into a hotel. Negotiations have been going on for six months because he wants to bring the price down. But the owners wouldn't budge as you well know. So...' He nodded a few times before he concluded. 'So I'm sure you made a good deal.'

I was at the notary's with my deposit money at six o'clock sharp and the owners arrived a few minutes later. The agreement was signed in no time at all. It was my largest investment to date.

The following day another person came up to me. He told me he had heard that I had just signed the agreement.

'I know the owners very well. They're hard nuts to crack, Angelo. So it's a good deal you've just made and I congratulate you for it. But there's an interesting story you should know.'

I was wondering what this interesting story had to do with

the deal when he continued, 'When yesterday you agreed on the price and shook hands on it, one of the owners tried to contact the other person. You know, the one who is chairman of something or other. He wanted to tell him about your offer and ask him whether he was prepared to up the price. He tried and tried but couldn't get hold of him. He even left a message with the secretary stating that the matter was of utmost urgency.'

There were no mobile phones at the time and the importation of VHF radios was banned by the Socialist Government.

'But even she didn't know her boss's whereabouts,' he concluded. He laughed and patted me on the shoulder. 'Then, after you signed the agreement yesterday, this chairman at last got back to the owners and demanded to know what all this urgency was about. The owners didn't mince their words. They told him that it was now too late as they had sold the land to you. He was livid with anger. He said he had spent the day on his yacht with his business partner and nobody knew his whereabouts.'

Two days later I received a phone call from this chairman. I was surprised because I never expected a call from him.

'Can we meet for a talk, Mr Xuereb?' he asked.

'I suppose we can. Any particular day you have in mind?'

'How about today?'

'Yes. Why not?'

We met in his large and tastefully decorated office. After a few minutes of pleasantries and small talk we got down to business.

'I know you've just bought that piece of land at Qawra, Mr Xuereb,' he said at last. 'Did you know we were in the middle of negotiations for its purchase?'

'Yes. I got to know about it after I signed the agreement.'

He looked sharply at me, not sure whether to believe me or not. 'Look, Mr Xuereb,' he continued, still not completely sure about the truth of my answer. 'Let me make you a good offer. We'll give you €117,000 in cash as your profit, wholly tax free, and you'll transfer your rights to the property to us. It's a good offer, Mr Xuereb, and I'd take it if I were you. What do you say?'

'I say thank you, but no. It's a very attractive offer but I have my own plans on how to develop the property.'

His face reflected his displeasure at my answer, but he still tried to take his chances. 'Then how about developing it together on a fifty/fifty basis? Together we can turn out a really quality project. We have the necessary cash, which you can't produce for the potential of the site.'

His patronising tone of voice angered me. He was much older than me as I was still thirty-three at the time. So, I answered in the same tone of voice. 'I must again thank you for your offer, but I intend to develop this project my own way as you shall soon see for yourself.'

My answer seemed to deflate him completely. He realised there was no chance of my letting go and in fifteen minutes I was out of his office building. The anger I felt at his patronising attitude made me more determined to start on this project as soon as possible to prove to this chairman that there was more to me than met the eye.

But it wasn't the best of times to start on a project of this magnitude. The political situation was worsening with every day that passed and I never imagined the political harassment and commercial setbacks I would soon have to overcome to bring to fruition the plans I had for this piece of property.

Tourism in Malta

One month into construction of the Suncrest Hotel.

Six months later.

Directing works at Suncrest Hotel.

Proudly posing in front of the Suncrest Hotel completed 13 months from commencement.

The lobby of the Suncrest.

The inauguration of the Suncrest Hotel by Prime Minister Dr Eddie Fenech Adami.

Constructing the 150 metre concrete chimney on 24/7.

Chimney and other works at the power station.

With some of the workers during the construction of the chimney.

Interior of GPC factory.

GPC concrete factory.

Old Palazzo Capua, when purchased.

The stolen sculpture of the lion.

My investiture as a Knight of St. John of Jerusalem with Grandmaster Chev. Victor Xuereb.

Testing my courage.

Our proposed project for Albania.

MIDI'S Proposal For
Tigne Point.

Our Proposals For Tigne Point,
and Manoel Island.

Manoel Island

9

Baptism of Fire

(1985–1987) 32–35 years

I wasted no time after I had signed the formal contract for the purchase of the large piece of land at Qawra. I set about planning to convert the 10,000 square metres of barren land into a large hotel and extensive facilities.

I have already had occasion in previous chapters to mention my interest in design and planning, and as time went by I became even more adept. But, building a large hotel extending right to the water's edge, facing the picturesque and quaint Salina Bay, stretched my planning talents to the limit. I wanted to maximise the number of guestrooms enjoying a direct sea view and I juggled with various options before deciding that the most advantageous would be to erect a structure in the shape of a capital E with its fingers facing the sea. I managed to design a four hundred and fifty-eight room four-star hotel, including a number of suites and leisure facilities. When ready, it would be, by far, the largest hotel in the Maltese islands.

Once I had finished my plans, I appointed a draughtsman to draw them up neatly to accompany my application to the Planning Applications Processing Board. I also engaged an architectural firm to present the formal building permit application. As the plans had already been drawn to scale I saved a huge amount in architectural fees.

I was well aware that I would be facing difficulties to obtain the necessary financial backing and the political situation was worse than ever. The party in government was set on continuing with its declared policy of nationalising the major industries and banks, in spite of having lost the majority of votes in the last general election, while the opposition party's demand for constitutional changes were being stubbornly rejected, resulting in quasi stagnation of all economic activity. This did not augur well for my dream of building the largest hotel in Malta, which I had already decided to name The Suncrest Hotel.

I needed bank financing very badly, but I knew it wouldn't be very easy. In fact, I was fairly certain that it would be refused, so I decided to tread softly, be as cautious as possible and not create too many waves that could topple the whole ambitious project. I therefore went for just 40% financing and the first thing the bank manager asked was whether I could offer any collateral as the bank's security. I told him that the freehold land costs of the future Suncrest Hotel were already settled and that I could place my other hotel complex, The Sunny Coast, including its leisure centre and the excellent Coral Reef Restaurant as collateral. Since these properties were developed without any bank's financial assistance, the bank manager's face couldn't hide his surprise.

'In my opinion this would make all the difference, Mr Xuereb. I don't think you should have any problem for the approval of the Board of Directors as your application is sound enough.'

Then he sat forward, looked me straight in the eye and, in a lower voice, as though his office was bugged, he continued, 'Let me put it straight to you, Mr Xuereb. I'm sure you're aware of how things have changed these last couple of years. The board's approval is not enough. You'd need government's approval now, as well. And it could be quite difficult unless, of course, you happen to know certain people...'

'So that's it,' I said to myself. 'It's my time to go through the baptism of fire. I have the biggest investment of my career and I have to depend on politicians to make it happen.'

The government's ideological drive to nationalise major industries and banks was still going on and the two major banks had been the first victims. This was going to be the largest private investment ever in Malta and I didn't want to succumb to the politicians' diktat. I was determined, however, to treat all this as simply another obstacle I had to overcome. I was determined to make this dream come true, politicians and all. So, I decided to take the initiative and take action to make it more difficult for the authorities to create pitfalls in my path. As soon as the building permit application was submitted and being processed I had a meeting with my brother, Paul. He was now well settled at Hardrocks and had learned all the ropes. We decided to buy a second-hand bulldozer equipped with a ripper that could excavate the whole site, made up of solid limestone, down to 10 metres below street level. Work was started forthwith and during weekends our quarry trucks were utilised to dispose of the excavation waste. It turned out to be a long procedure because of the equipment's limited efficiency, and the whole operation lasted a full year. Buying the bulldozer reduced the total cost to just the drivers' wages, replacing worn out parts of the bulldozer and the maintenance of the trucks.

While all this was taking place, Jessie gave birth to our last child. Denise was born on 3rd May 1985. She brought relief and much joy into our lives. A few days later Jessie brought her proudly in her arms to the house, which we named after her. And she deserved it because she brought me luck when a few days after her birth I received the building permit for our new villa. I had to postpone its construction for a few months owing to financial constraints, but Jessie didn't mind. She was well aware of the situation and our extended stay at Qawra turned out to be enjoyable indeed. The house was just 200 metres from the future Suncrest Hotel site and this was an added advantage because I wanted to be personally responsible for the management of the project. Moreover, Richard and Claire were still very young, so the small back garden and facilities at the Sunny Coast Holiday Complex were the perfect playgrounds for the pair.

It was towards the end of that year that I was financially secure enough to engage three builders to start work on our villa. I planned it to be a slow-moving construction so that I could afford the cost without having to turn to the bank for assistance. I was too busy with the Suncrest and other works to find the time to supervise the villa's construction. I found myself in a situation perfectly described by an old Maltese proverb which translates as 'the cobbler always wears torn shoes,' which means that some people are so busy with other people's problems that they forget their own.

Finally, what I had been dreading started happening. I received a letter from the bank informing me that my request for financing the Suncrest Hotel couldn't be met. I was further informed that 'a commercial bank' cannot finance long-term investments, and I was referred to the newly set-up, government-controlled, Investment Finance Bank (IFB). So I had to start everything from scratch and apply to the IFB.

I duly filed in my application, stating that the whole project would cost around €12,800,000, and asked for 40% financing, amounting to €5,125,000 – much less than the standard 60% to 70%.

'Well, Mr Xuereb,' began the manager after the usual niceties, and after his offer of a drink was graciously refused, 'I see you have quite a project here.'

'Thank you.'

'And it'll cost you quite a lot,' he continued while glancing up and down the sheet of paper in front of him.'

'Yes, it will.'

'Yes.' At last he looked up at me. 'Yes, Mr Xuereb. You certainly have quite a project. But, you see, much as we would like to accede to your request...' He looked down again at the sheet of paper on his desk. 'We're a small bank, Mr Xuereb, and our licence from the Central Bank does not allow us to lend more than 25% of our registered capital to any one company or individual.'

He continued talking, but I wasn't listening. His words struck me dumb. It was the second blow in as many weeks and I was wondering why the government had seen fit to name its bank Investment Finance when it wasn't allowed to do any proper financing. I noticed that the manager had stopped talking and was looking at me.

'I'm sorry. I didn't get your last bit.'

'It's all right, Mr Xuereb. I asked you whether you're willing to accept the maximum we can offer. That'll be €3,260,000.'

There was nothing I could do. I had no other option and shrugged my shoulders. 'I accept, of course. I shall develop two sections of the hotel and hope that your bank would, by then, increase its capital so that it'll be in a position to lend me the necessary funds to complete the project.'

And we left it at that. But, a few days later the bank 'regrettably' informed me that financing would only come as an end financing, meaning that first I had to produce all receipts of my share of expenses following which the bank would issue payments directly to my subcontractors. My back was against the wall. Again, I had no choice but to accept and the bank sent me the sanction letter, which included these rigid conditions.

The manager called me in again to inform me that the minister could still overturn the bank's decision. This was a huge risk indeed because, in spite of my producing the receipts from my subcontractors, the minister could still give orders to the bank to withhold payments. Dad's open support for the party in opposition was causing a rippling effect.

'You could have informed me about all this by post,' I said, unable to hide the anger from my voice.

'Yes, we could have. But it's not nice to put all this on paper, is it?'

'I agree because what you've told me is not nice at all.'

All this, however, made me more determined to turn the tables on this misnomer that went by the name of Investment Finance Bank. I immediately prepared a programme of works to ensure that this nine-storey hotel would be open for guests in less than twelve months. On 2nd May 1986, I put the planned construction programme on the fast track, totally ignoring the possibility that the Minister of Finance might refuse to endorse the bank's approval. I set up a small mobile office on-site and moved into it together with Mario, my secretary, to assist with the numerous phone calls. I also appointed an interior designer to help out with the finishes. We met at his office to review and modify designs as we went along. I usually called at his office after eight o'clock at night for meetings that sometimes lasted till midnight.

Another priority was preparing a hotel brochure, which I intended to launch at the ITB Tourism Fair in Berlin. This fair is considered the best for the European tourism industry and I decided to set up my own stand, which I personally manned with the help of an assistant. The interest shown by tour operators was very encouraging but most doubted I could complete the hotel in time. However, we still managed to get some bookings.

The construction of the hotel was progressing at a very fast pace. In fact, we were averaging one floor every ten days. I designed my own fast formwork system as well as some precast concrete elements to further speed up the works. But then there was another problem which, somehow, I had to overcome; plant and equipment such as elevators, air-conditioning and boilers could only be ordered from abroad. The manufacturers, however, could not deliver according to the timeframe I had set. Somehow, we managed to find suppliers who required full payment cover by letters of credit. I was too tight for the cash necessary for this huge upfront outlay, but we managed to arrive at an agreement whereby I would place a 30% deposit upon order with the balance to be settled prior to dispatch from the factories.

Concurrent with the construction of the Suncrest, the government was close to finishing its own hotel – a five-star complex that had taken years to construct. The size of the building wasn't even a third of the Suncrest, but its cost for the exchequer was astronomical. Most of the leading Maltese services sub-contractors were fully committed in this government project and, therefore, unavailable for mine. Some of them wouldn't have given me a quotation had they been free to do so, anyway, as they were sceptical about my claiming I had the financial backing and the ability to see it through in the timeframe I had set. Rumour was rapidly circulating around the business communities that I wouldn't be able to make it happen. This caused much uncertainty among sub-contractors, services contractors, banks and politicians and it made me very angry and anxious at the same time. It also, however, helped strengthen my determination to prove everyone wrong. But then difficulties started cropping up with the furniture and fitting supplies. The interior designer insisted that he wanted to view three sample rooms before giving the go ahead for the placing of orders and almost all nine floors were finished by the time we did. Apart from this, however, the construction of the hotel was still progressing at a fast pace.

Many people around the island had heard about the new and large hotel that was being constructed at Qawra, and families would include the site during their Sunday drives just to have a look and note the progress from week to week! In the meantime I had managed to accumulate enough receipts from my sub-contractors to cover 60% of the total investment. These I immediately passed on to the bank so that payments could be effected as early as possible. But it wasn't as easy as I thought or believed. The bank informed me that each and every receipt had first to be carefully checked and scrutinised, and the supplies and services would have to be inspected on site and found to tally before any payments could be made.

'And these things take time, Mr Xuereb,' continued the bank official delegated to deal with me because the manager was too busy with more important business. 'What with all those receipts to check and verify... And then we have to find a day agreeable to both of us for the inspection on site of—'

'But the opening of the hotel is only six months away,' I interrupted angrily. 'What about the bookings I already have from various operators?'

The official remained poker-faced while informing me that there were procedures that must be adhered to.

'And anyway, Mr Xuereb,' he concluded. 'We still can't start with the checking procedure before we receive ministerial approval.'

Any lingering doubts that the government wasn't doing its utmost to put all available spokes in my wheels evaporated with the last sentence. I felt the anger welling up inside me and it was with great effort that I curbed the urge to topple the desk in front of me and bury the bank official beneath it. But that would have been playing into the government's hands. It was the hasty action that they wanted to force me into. It would have completely compromised the hotel's completion and forced me into some panicky action that would have crippled all my business interests. I was now in a situation where I had hardly enough cash to pay my workers' wages. This made me nervous and I could hardly sleep a wink at night.

The regime's long, slimy, blood-sucking, constricting and all-consuming tentacles were awaiting me around every corner, and it was now my regular bank's turn to start making unpleasant noises. The manager formally demanded that I pay back all excesses within forty-eight hours. The funny thing is that these excesses were normally approved over the phone with no questions asked and this sudden decision bewildered me, although I suspected its origin. I just couldn't honour the forty-eight-hour ultimatum and the bank started dishonouring my cheques, which were boldly stamped 'refer to drawer'. The situation became so farcical that the bank even stooped so low as refusing to cash a cheque for €11.65!

Word about my situation spread like quicksilver and a number of suppliers and sub-contractors became very concerned. My local bank manager was sympathetic and understanding, but he was under very strict orders. I tried to call the chief executive of the bank but his secretary was under instructions not to pass my calls through. This unattainable CEO was the same person who very often praised my entrepreneurship and abilities during functions and when surrounded by a receptive audience; the same person who accepted my calls any time during the day when I needed approval for any excess on my account.

I decided to call on him one morning unannounced to protest about his uncalled for change of attitude, but it was to no avail as he wouldn't see me. Not prepared to take this insult lying down, I sat patiently for two whole hours in the waiting room, hoping I would button-hole him for five minutes between appointments. It was useless. He was obviously obeying strict government instructions to make it impossible for me to continue operating. This useless waiting, away from my hotel building site, was a sacrifice I could ill afford to prolong. Mobile phones were still a long time in the future and there were no means of contacting my workers at this very crucial time of construction. I was the sole project manager and, although I was ably assisted by Joe Camilleri (then still a junior student of architecture who would follow me around wherever I went, eager to learn all the ropes), Lorry (Lawrence) was the only foreman on site with instructions to supervise the workers. My absence from the site for two whole hours was too long and I had to leave the bank, angry and frustrated.

Eager to solve my problems, I moved out of the small mobile site office and took over a large room on the second floor of the unfinished hotel. It was situated at the front of the building and in it I installed five telephone lines, which Mario, my secretary, handled with unparalleled efficiency. He was blessed with a strong and mature voice which soothed the more agitated callers. After the hotel was finished he left my employment to join the police force where he was assigned duties with its elite section. I can still visualise him now, handling five simultaneous calls with the five telephone sets precariously balanced on both shoulders, or spread on his desk, all awaiting my personal attention.

'This one's first, Mr Xuereb,' he would say while handing me a phone. 'This one's next and...'

It was an extremely hectic time trying to cope with all those calls and knowing that people were waiting outside my office in a long queue, itching for a few words with me. Looking back in disbelief at those times, I still wonder how I managed to fit in the supervision of the works on all floors. I remember running

along corridors, climbing stairs two steps at a time and bounding
down them four or five at one go, risking sprained ankles and
broken bones. I hate to imagine what could have happened had
I missed a step in that mad rush. I couldn't risk being immobile
for weeks with a leg in a plaster cast, but I had to stay a step
(excuse the pun) ahead of the regime, which was set on my total
annihilation. It was a matter of survival and I wanted to prove
myself the fittest.

One morning, I was on the top floor, nine floors up, and
Mario espied me from his office window.

'Mr Xuereb! Mr Xuereb!' he shouted. 'You have an urgent call.'

I bounded down the stairs all the way down to the second
level, sprinted down the corridor like an Olympian and, completely
breathless, picked up the phone.

'Good morning, Mr Xuereb.' I instantly recognised the voice
of a middleman. 'There's this piece of land going at a bargain
price. Would you be interes –'

I slammed the telephone on its cradle and shouted at Mario,
'Do you call this urgent? Goodness, Mario, you know how busy
I am. You should have told him to come after hours when all
the workers have left.'

It was the only time I had raised my voice at Mario and I felt
ashamed. But I couldn't help it at the time. The pressure and
exasperation were taking their toll on me.

Another time there was an Italian supplier waiting to see me.
He had travelled to Malta for just one day, specifically to negotiate
a package for some kitchen equipment. His local supplier's agent
brought him over, completely unannounced, on a day when I
couldn't spare even one single moment. He eventually had to
leave empty-handed after six hours waiting outside my office and
after I had offered my apologies and an appointment for another
day. That's how hectic it was. Even my accountant had to keep
up with this frenetic pace. He used to drive down from head
office and run around with me while I signed cheques. I barely
even had time to eat, with lunch consisting of two slices of a

crunchy Maltese loaf spread with tomato paste and topped with ham or tuna, gobbled hurriedly while running from floor to floor, supervising works.

Nine months into the project I was literally out of pocket. All income from construction, pre-cast concrete sales as well as that coming in from the other hotel and timeshare sales, was being siphoned off to pay wages and settle the more urgent bills in order to keep going at the fast momentum I had set at the very start. This left me with no money with which to pay sub-contractors and suppliers, and I decided to talk to each one of them honestly and openly about the situation.

'Look,' I would tell each of them. 'The honest truth is that I have absolutely no money with which to pay for your services. I have the bank's sanction letter here, as you can see, but for some reason I can't fathom, this money is not yet available. If you have trust in me and are in a position to sustain your cash flow until I have the necessary funds, you can continue working. If you're not in a position to accept these terms you are free to stop and I won't hold it against you. I won't even impose a penalty and I shall pay you all your dues as soon as I have the cash which, I'm sure, will be soon.'

Most of them accepted my terms and continued with their work, much to my pleasure and satisfaction. I have never forgotten their loyalty and have continued to show my gratitude up to this very day.

In the meantime, I managed to convince the main mechanical plant manufacturers to ship the goods to Malta on condition that I pay them before the cargo's release from the docks. The goods arrived in good time, but I still couldn't settle the bills and have them released by customs because the minister hadn't yet given his approval for the release of funds by the bank. To make matters worse, custom's daily demurrage rates were exorbitant and prohibitive for my tight financial situation. I became desperate and decided there and then to speak personally to the Minister of Finance, Mr Wistin Abela, who was still adamant at withholding his approval. I phoned his ministry a number of times, asking to be put through to his private secretary, Joe Cassar, but each time I was kept on hold by the telephone operator for long minutes on end, after which he would hang up. This pantomime was repeated so many times that, at last, I hung up on him, changed into a suit and drove straight to the ministry. I was determined not to leave the ministry building until Joe Cassar saw me and listened to what I had to say.

When I arrived, the ministry corridor was packed with more than twenty unemployed men, all shabbily dressed. I stood out like a sore thumb in a suit among those poor men. They looked desperate and talked in high voices, all complaining about the high cost of living, the long months they'd been on the unemployment register and complaints from wives who couldn't make ends meet. With the general elections scheduled for 9th May 1987, less than two months away, this was their last chance to beg for a job – any kind of job – in exchange for their families' numerous votes for the minister.

I had to wait a full hour before I was ushered into the presence of Joe Cassar, where he indicated a chair with a nod of his head as both hands were holding telephones to both ears, reminiscent of the situation in my office.

'Yes, that's right,' I heard him say to somebody at the end of one of the lines. 'I'm speaking on behalf of the minister...'

There was a short pause, which I correctly assumed was caused by an intervention at the other end.

'Of course I'll tell him about your eternal gratitude Mr ****. That's why he asked me to call you today...' Pause. 'Yes, it's about another job...' Pause. 'Of course he knows you've already employed nine men, but he told me to assure you that this'll be the last...' Pause.

'Yes Mr ****. He appreciates your sacrifices more than you think. But it's only two months to go now and once he's minister again...' Pause. 'No, no, Mr ****. Definitely he'll be a minister again, and I know what I'm saying. The Nationalists don't stand a chance as long as people like you continue to help the minister in . . .' Pause. 'Of course I'll tell him and rest assured that you'll be the first one he'll show his gratitude to. Now, here's the name of the person he wants you to employ . . .'

As soon as he put down the receiver he spoke into the other one. 'Hello. Sorry to have kept you waiting. Joe Cassar here, from the ministry . . .'

After minutes of listening to assurances and names and addresses of people from the minister's constituency, I interrupted him.

'I'm Angelo Xuereb and you know why I'm here. You're spending hours on the phone begging for jobs for the minister's constituents when I can employ one hundred and fifty outright if he accedes to my request. That would solve you some telephone bills, wouldn't it?'

He looked me up and down as though I was some kind of a nut to offer so many new jobs when the rate of unemployment was at a record high and industry was shedding workers like dandruff from shoulders. He thought I was bluffing and continued to talk into the telephone. I shrugged my shoulders. After all, I had no election to win.

After another five minutes of more of the same and I interrupted him again. 'Look, Mr Cassar. I'm here because I need to talk to the minister. I want to talk to him about the approval of the bank's sanction letter which I have here.'

I had to wait until he ended another call.

'Okay,' he said at last. 'Just give me your name and a number where I can contact you. I'll try to arrange an appointment as soon as possible.'

Joe Cassar's idea of 'as soon as possible' was anything longer than two weeks, by the end of which I decided to take the matter up personally with the Prime Minister. Mr Mintoff, however, was no longer the man to talk to. He had abdicated the post some months earlier in favour of Dr Karmenu Mifsud Bonnici, a lawyer by profession who had never contested an election, and Mintoff's personal choice. I went to seek him in his office at Parliament with no appointment, but the police officer at the entrance, seeing me elegantly dressed, wrongly assumed that I was expected and allowed me in without as much as a word.

Fifteen minutes of kicking my heels in the corridor outside the Prime Minister's office were rewarded when a secretary ushered me in and Dr Mifsud Bonnici listened to me for fifteen full minutes without uttering one single word. In fact, he sat immobile in his chair, looking at me through half-closed eyes, giving the impression that he was completely bored with what I was telling him.

'Thank you, Mr Xuereb,' he said pleasantly, but in a toneless voice. 'I shall definitely take this up with the Minister of Finance and you'll be hearing from me soon.'

At last, I said to myself, I had found a man of immediate action. And he was the Prime Minister, no less. He'd soon put the Minister of Finance in his place and I'd be able to pay the sub-contractors, and suppliers, and wages, and release my goods from customs...

Two weeks passed without one word from the office of the Prime Minister and the situation had now become untenable. Every minute lost could cost me everything I had managed to build over the years. I tried calling Joe Cassar again and I never got through. His minister was determined to bring me down on my knees even with the general elections so close.

Two months earlier, I had engaged a financial consultant to help me with the interviews of prospective staff for the Suncrest. I had also asked him to do me a favour and write to the Governor of the Central Bank for an appointment. A week later, the governor wrote back to inform me that '...we do not meet with private companies or individuals, but only with civil servants'. The government had used every means at its disposal to close down my business as it had done to other big companies in order to create an excuse to nationalise it.

Time was pressing because the Suncrest's official opening was planned for 1st May 1987, just eight days before voting day. We had an encouraging number of bookings, but the hotel was not ready to receive them. The newly appointed hotel management team and I tried to find them alternative accommodation in other hotels, but all were fully booked. Meanwhile, the government's long-awaited hotel was newly completed, but there were problems. The Holiday Inn Management Company was not happy with some of the works hurriedly undertaken to finish in time for the elections and refused to take over the hotel's management unless they were rectified. This five-star hotel, however, was our only option as relocating our tourists to Spain or some other Mediterranean country wasn't practical owing to the financial burden it would entail.

When we approached the Holiday Inn's new hotel manager he said he would only be too happy to accommodate us. When he noticed our sigh of relief, he continued, 'At our rack rates [full rates with no discounts] of course, and with payment in advance.'

The rates he quoted, the highest rates of their hotel, were five times higher than what we were charging our first tourists at the four-star Suncrest and we had absolutely no cash with which to settle the advance payment. I could feel the Minister of Finance's long shadow in all of this as he was the minister responsible for the Holiday Inn as well. Somehow, however, I did manage to collect enough cash and my tourists were happily accommodated at this much trumpeted five-star hotel. One can imagine, therefore, our surprise when a few tourists complained about the high price for beverages when compared to that charged at a four-star hotel.

I decided to take another chance with the Prime Minister and drove to Valletta dressed in my smartest suit and carrying a brief case. I wanted to impress the police security at Parliament well enough to let me in without the least trouble. This was during the last week of April 1987, a few days before the general elections, and quite warm for the season. In fact, most of the government Members of Parliament had taken to doing away with jackets even during sittings. So, the police officer and a member of the armed forces doing sentry duty at the entrance to the Palace must have been impressed with my attire and they both gave me a stiff salute, just in case I was some foreign dignitary.

189

Once inside, I climbed the beautiful circular staircase that leads right into the wide, historic corridor, beautifully decorated by the finest artists the Order of St John's ample coffers could commission. I walked along it, flanked by portraits of past grandmasters, until I arrived outside the Prime Minister's office and took a position where I could easily be seen by anyone opening the door. While I stood impatiently waiting, I saw the Minister of Finance walking towards me, practically obscured by a crowd of canvassers and bodyguards, a few of whom were conspicuous by the abnormally bulging trouser pockets and self-confident stride as if the palace belonged to them. I had never had any previous meetings with the minister, but apparently he knew me because when he got to within 2 metres of where I was standing, he stopped abruptly and his crowd followed suit.

'What are you doing here?'

Although he shouted his question at me, I could detect some apprehension in his voice. So, I thought I would make the best of it.

'Waiting for the Prime Minister to summon me so I can tell him everything about you.'

'Is that so?' he said in a sarcastic tone.

I could feel his men closing in on me, but I forced myself to ignore them and concentrate on the minister.

'And what will you be telling him about me if I may ask?' he continued in the same sarcastic tone, which prompted some of his men to laugh derisively.

From the corner of my eye, I could see that two or three police officers started walking towards us, presumably because they suspected trouble.

'Nothing much, really,' I said, doing my best to sound flippant. I think I even shrugged my shoulders when I said these words. 'I'm just going to tell him that you are purposely refusing to approve the bank's sanction letter. I'll also tell him that if by noon tomorrow I don't get your approval, I shall stop all works and lay off all workers, including the ones I have taken on for the new hotel operation, and put them on the unemployment register. I shall, of course, tell the workers the reason for their unexpected dismissal. I owe them that, at least. Wouldn't look good for you on the eve of the elections, would it?'

I could see that his face had changed colour, but he recovered very quickly and, although he was the smallest man in the crowd, he still wanted to prove he had enormous powers.

'You do just that because it suits me exactly fine,' he said in a confident tone probably for the benefit of his cronies around us. 'We'll take over and continue where you leave off.'

These last arrogant words made me very angry and, completely ignoring all those thugs around me, I moved forward, pointed a finger close to his bespectacled face and said, 'Let me tell you something, Minister. The property is mine and no one else's since I don't yet have a bank loan. Nobody can stop me from boarding the whole place up and sending the workers to the labour office – not you and not even the Prime Minister. If you think I'm bluffing just wait till noon tomorrow and you'll get your answer. Am I clear enough or do I have to spell it out for you?'

As soon as I finished speaking I realised the danger I was in. The minister's thugs were so close to me that I could smell the horrible stench of their unwashed bodies. They were not used to having their protector spoken to in that manner and were itching for the least sign from him to give me a good beating, for which they were notorious. But the minister was unsure of himself. He stood there in front of me, straining his neck to gaze straight into my eyes through thick lenses, trying to read my real intentions.

At last he said, 'Okay. Tomorrow, phone my private secretary for an appointment with me at my office.'

I realised that I had him at last. He was playing his last card in the hope of gaining some time so that I would have to postpone my ultimatum.

'Your private secretary? You must be joking, Minister. It's easier to get through to the Pope than to Joe Cassar.'

He wasn't pleased with my reply. It put him in a desperate

situation, not certain what I would do should he shun me one more time.

'And anyway,' I continued as nonchalantly as I could manage, 'I'm here to talk to the Prime Minister. It'll then be up to him to solve the problem, not you.'

That seemed to have settled it.

'All right. Be at my office tomorrow at eleven and I'll see you.'

'I'll be there at eleven, Minister. All these men here are witnesses to everything that's been said. If by noon tomorrow I don't have your approval you know what will happen. Now I don't need to talk to the Prime Minister, so I'm leaving. But we'll meet again tomorrow.'

Walking along the corridor, I could feel a dozen pairs of eyes boring into my back and I forced myself to continue walking briskly and purposefully even though my legs felt like jelly.

The next morning at eleven, I was sitting in the ministry's waiting room. The optimism I felt as soon as I entered the building began to dissolve with every minute that passed. I kept checking my watch every few seconds and when more than ten minutes had passed, I began to prepare myself for the inevitable. The minister must have had second thoughts and decided to call my bluff. I started thinking about the men in my employ, most of whom had been with me since the early days of my business, and who were now married and had children to support. I thought about my investment in the new hotel, which was so near completion and felt angry at this, my first failure of my business career. I also felt bad and very sad about what I had to do in three quarters of an hour's time. Dismissing loyal workers felt like separating them from my family, but I had to go through with it. I never went back on my word, least of all this time when I had no other options.

I didn't notice a messenger entering the room and he jolted me out of my thoughts when he asked, 'Are you Mr Xuereb?'

I stood up, hoping that I was going to be saved from a most horrible noontime deed at, literally, the eleventh hour after all.

'I'm sorry, Mr Xuereb, but the Minister can't see you.'

I felt the blood draining out of my face. All my last minute hopes were completely dashed.

'He's busy at some meeting outside this office,' continued the messenger as if I didn't know that this was a standard lie which messengers are made to memorise. 'But he's just phoned in with instructions to tell you that you are to go straight away to the Central Bank where you have an appointment with the governor. He also asked me to tell you that everything's OK. He said you'd understand.'

I couldn't believe my ears. I still stood there, staring at the messenger with my mouth open to form the words 'thank you', but they never came out. When I came to, I ran down the stairs and was entering the Central Bank building less than five minutes later. It seems the governor was thoroughly informed about the urgency of the matter because his secretary ushered me in the second she saw me. I found myself entering a large office with a large desk behind which stood the governor with his right arm stretched towards me.

'Sit down, Mr Xuereb. Sit down,' he said in a most pleasant voice. 'You will have coffee, won't you, while we go through the papers?'

'I certainly will. I think I deserve one after nine months of torture.'

He laughed nervously at what he decided to consider a joke. This was the same person who, a few weeks earlier, had written to tell me that he only met with civil servants.

After his secretary had brought in the coffee, he continued, 'It was just a mistake, Mr Xuereb. You might call it a misunderstanding. But now everything's been ironed out and you can start withdrawing funds from your bank loan from tomorrow if you wish.'

I didn't need to hear anymore. I just wanted to drive back to my hotel site as quickly as I could. But the coffee was still too hot. On my way back to Qawra, my mind was already at work deciding which of the payments were the most urgent to enable work on the hotel to continue at the fastest rate possible. On arrival, I made straight for my site office, but I didn't say a word. I didn't have to. My smile said it all and everybody understood. I could feel the tension among my workers melt fast like ice cream at noon in August. Jessie was over the moon and hugged me and I felt great satisfaction as I signed the first cheque at the beginning of May, exactly one year after the start of the hotel project.

One of the first calls I received when back at the site office was from the bank's CEO's secretary. She told me that her boss wanted to see me at his office the following day. This was the same person who was refusing to take my calls and requests for appointments. I was surprised at his sudden shift of 'policy', but agreed to meet him. The moment I entered his office he was all joviality and camaraderie as if under an acute attack of amnesia.

'You've lost me a bet, you know,' he said still laughing. 'I was more than certain you'd never manage to win back the bank's support. But, my God, you did!'

I did not dare answer. I was afraid that nine months of frustration would force me into doing something that would put me behind bars. I was there strictly on business and nothing else. The most important thing was that I had managed to break through the thick walls that the regime had built all around me. Now I was free to finish what I had started a year earlier the way I intended to.

The CEO noticed my reticence and, to break the ice, said, 'I'm sure this calls for a small celebration. Let's have a scotch together.' While pouring whisky into two glasses, he continued, 'I must admit you're a determined person, Mr Xuereb. You have a strong character and I admire your vision and guts. It's men like you that make my bank proud to assist.'

I let him drone on until my business with him was finished and I walked out. I went on to settle all my outstanding dues on the project and breathed a long sigh of relief.

On Saturday 9th May 1987, 97% of the Maltese cast their votes. One could feel the tension all around Malta and Gozo as it was evident that whichever of the two major parties won, the margin of victory would be slight. After two whole days of prayers and nail biting, the results were out. The Nationalist Party had won by a margin of just over 5,000 votes. At last, after sixteen years of Socialist domination, we had a government whose democratic record was historically proven.

Less than a month later, on 7th June 1987, a public holiday and a date synonymous with Malta's constitutional history (and only thirteen months after the first day of construction), the Suncrest welcomed its first guests. I can still visualise the first foreign guests checking in and being presented with a beautiful bouquet of flowers.

The hotel building structure was completed, but was only two-thirds finished for occupation. But now I could continue with the finishing touches of the other third with an easy mind, knowing that the new regime was the 'natural' enemy of nationalisation and a strong stimulator for private initiative and entrepreneurship.

At the same time as my struggle to complete the hotel was taking place, Taylor Woodrow, the renowned British company, was working on the Freeport project at Birzebbuga. One of the company's representatives used to visit Malta regularly to supervise progress and I happened to bump into him years later at some function or other.

'Do you know something, Mr Xuereb?' he told me after washing down a miniscule sandwich with a sip of champagne. 'When you were constructing your beautiful Suncrest I used to come to Malta often to check on the Freeport works. On landing, I would instruct the taxi driver to take a detour through Qawra before dropping me at my hotel. I did this to monitor the progress on your hotel, and let me tell you, Mr Xuereb, that not even we, at Taylor Woodrow, could match your speed, even with our efficiency.'

He would have been even more surprised had he known the immense financial difficulties I was going through at the time!

More than a year earlier, a retired English friend of mine, Tony Scopes, had taken up residence close to the hotel. He was a keen amateur photographer and carried his camera wherever he went. On 2nd May 1986, he noticed some unusually fast construction activity taking place on the derelict site, which would later become the Suncrest. Tony decided to take a few snapshots over the whole duration of the construction period during his daily walk along the seafront. He continued taking regular pictures of my project every week, with the last one taken on 7th June 1987. Later, he presented me with a thick album full of photographs as a memento on the occasion of the soft opening of the Suncrest. It shows clearly and undeniably the fast momentum of the construction rate, which was maintained throughout. I still cherish it and it holds its own pride of place among my mementoes.

The celebrations and pride, however, could not detract from the fact that the last wing of the hotel was not yet completed with all the internal finishes and fittings. I knew that the IFB could not finance the cost of the additional €1,865,000 required because of the restrictions on its capital imposed by the Central Bank by the previous government's legislation. So, I decided to try my luck with the new Finance Minister, Notary George Bonello Dupuis, and my request for an appointment was immediately granted – a far cry from the delaying tactics employed by his predecessor. To tell the truth, I didn't expect too much from this meeting, not when the new minister was trying to find his feet after so many years in opposition. The best I was hoping for was a promise from him that the threshold imposed by his predecessor would be removed by some parliamentary something or other, and that it would take some weeks. I was prepared for that. What I wasn't prepared for was the minister's quick understanding of the situation I was in.

'It just doesn't make sense at all,' I remember him telling me. 'How is it possible for anyone in his right senses to create hurdles and barriers for anyone wishing to bring into Malta the foreign currency we sorely need and make it impossible for the banks to help? It's completely illogical.'

Then he did something that astonished me. He issued instructions there and then to the Governor of the Central Bank to allow a commercial bank to issue the remaining loan I required. I couldn't find enough words to thank him for this very courageous act, and for the tangible proof of his government's support of private investment. Thanks to this loan we carried out the remaining works on the last wing, which was ready to receive guests before the summer of 1988.

The construction of our villa was now completed and Jessie asked me to do the choosing of wall tiles and other fittings.

I answered, 'You know how busy I am trying to get my business running smoothly again.'

As there was no way I could afford the time, I recruited a professional interior designer to do the job for me. I did not regret this decision because he came up with a modern design for furniture and fittings that was in harmony with the villa design. The irony of it all was that while the four hundred and fifty-eight-roomed four-star Suncrest took just thirteen months to finish, our villa took twenty-two.

Meanwhile, I had moved back to head office where I could better oversee all my business operations. My long absence from base had caused business to slacken considerably, but this was a situation I was prepared to face. However, the overall expansion of my business demanded more office space. Our former terraced house had done its job as my head office, but it couldn't cope with the pressure we were putting on its limited space. After all, it was built as a home for a family with children, with just enough space for sleeping, eating and relaxation. It was never meant to house clerks and desks, and files piled up to the ceiling. I had to have a place built specifically as a modern office where workers would have enough space and a healthy working environment.

In three months, I constructed and finished the beautiful office block, which I still occupy. Six weeks before its official opening we ordered all our modern furniture from an Italian supplier. The delivery date was dangerously close to the opening day. In fact, a mere fortnight from D-Day, the furniture had still not left the factory in Italy and, since the date had been publicised weeks before and the invitations already printed, my staff at the office started having the jitters.

'What shall we do, Mr Xuereb? Do we still issue the invitations? We're all worried that the furniture might not arrive in time. We can't bear to imagine all those people in an empty building.'

'Go ahead and issue the invitations. Don't worry. This is a challenge we'll have to face together.'

The invitations were posted and the furniture arrived in Malta on the eve of the official opening. I somehow managed to persuade the people at customs to bypass superfluous bureaucratic procedures and this allowed us time enough to unload the containers during the night. All my office staff stayed on to help unpack the furniture and place it where it fitted according to plans. The next morning, we gave the place a thorough clean-up and by evening it was ready to proudly welcome the invited guests who couldn't help expressing their astonishment at the beauty of it all.

I then appointed Tonio Farrugia as administrative manager to take care of all the office work. He was very professional in his approach and organised my office to reflect the size and importance of my group of companies. He recruited the necessary new office staff and introduced certain modern office procedures, which I had lacked until then. He even managed to persuade me that I needed a personal secretary who would take over most of the less-important administrative chores. Tonio was supportive throughout the twenty-one years he spent in my service until retiring in 2008.

The Suncrest Hotel

The Sunny Coast
Holiday Resort

10

A Public Figure and a Miracle

(1988–1990) 36–38 years

At long last we moved into our villa in the summer of 1988. It was situated right on the border of Mosta and extremely modern, surrounded by extensive gardens and panoramic views. We named it Villa Vistana.

After two years living in cooped up quarters at Qawra, roaming around the open space of the villa, we felt like freed cage birds, and we definitely deserved this new luxury after fourteen years of much hard work. The children also loved it; they now had enough space to roam and play, and they could invite their friends for a swim in the pool, or to play indoor games during the cold weather.

The situation with the hotel was now equally harmonious. With the Suncrest now fully completed and efficiently run for a whole year, the management and I began preparations for its official opening. Dr Edward Fenech Adami, the Prime Minister, acceded to our wish to officially inaugurate it and we set about promoting this special day with energy and the utmost attention for detail. Our public relations agency, which we had recently appointed, took over the preparation of the formalities for media coverage. This included a four-page, A3, colour supplement to be distributed with all local newspapers.

I prepared the first draft of my speech, which my secretary Caroline typed before forwarding it to the PR agency to check for any deficiencies and make suggestions for changes where required. The next day the agency's general manager phoned me.

'You don't seriously intend reading this speech in the presence of the Prime Minister, do you?' he asked. 'I hope you realise there would be 1,500 people listening.'

'Don't you think I know all this?' I retorted. 'I wouldn't have written it if I didn't mean to read it, would I?'

What worried the general manager was the recounting of the saga I was made to endure, thanks to the former Minister of Finance's dirty tactics through the banks. I ended the speech on a positive note, however.

'*My approach is that no problem is insurmountable and, in spite of these difficulties, my strong determination never failed and we kept moving forward. The greater the difficulty which presented itself, the stronger was my determination. So, I consider the opening of this hotel as my baptism of fire.*' I was here intimating that this event was just a prelude to more daring and interesting projects.

The PR agency informed me that they had finished editing my draft, which they forwarded to me. I was surprised to note that they had completely left out my reference to the previous government's tactics at the hands of the Minister of Finance and replaced it with a eulogy to every government department and ministry, without which the Suncrest wouldn't have been possible. I could well appreciate the agency's rationale because nobody knew about the hassle the previous administration had forced me to endure. It was also general practice to laud government ministers and high officials whether deserving or not during occasions of this kind.

'I'm sorry but I'm sticking to my draft,' I told the agency representative. 'My guests have the right to know the facts as they truly happened.'

The official opening was set for 16th June 1988, the day following my thirty-sixth birthday. It would be my very first attempt at public speaking and the tension that gripped me at the thought of reading such a strongly worded and rather long speech in front of so many people and TV cameras weakened me physically for days before the event. I would spend hours practising in front of a full-length mirror to acquaint myself with standing on a podium and, after twenty tries, by the end of which I had almost memorised the speech, I felt confident enough that my posture and facial expressions would pass the test.

During my speech there was complete silence. I had the crowd listening, spellbound and in complete surprise about what had gone on behind the scenes in the building of the Suncrest. I could see it all in the wide open eyes in front of me and nearly as many mouths as well. When I had finished, it was the Prime Minister's turn to say a few words. As the able speaker he was, Dr Fenech Adami emphasised the turbulent years we had all survived and reminded those present that to construct such an edifice as the Suncrest during normal times was already a feat in itself. Managing to do so, however, during a time when private initiative was not only discouraged, but officially and openly undermined was nothing less than heroic determination.

When the formalities were over everyone was treated to a lavish reception, which many described as the best in decades. I found myself surrounded by hundreds of people, all waiting their turn to compliment me on my courage at being so blunt and honest in my strongly worded speech.

The PR agency had made arrangements with the local media to carry out interviews with me the following day. My natural shyness resurfaced at the thought of having to face a TV camera. So, I had somebody stand beside the cameraman, holding a board with the main points written in large capitals. I can still recall one of the questions put to me by the interviewer.

'Don't you think, Mr Xuereb, that the hotel is too big for our islands and that you're going to negatively affect the other existing ones?'.

'Absolutely not,' I answered. 'In fact, I believe in the complete opposite. I believe that if we really want to strengthen our tourism industry we have to have at least four quality hotels like the Suncrest. And we need to have them during the next three years.'

The people in the room looked at me as though I was a false messiah. But, following the success of the Suncrest, other investors started putting their money in the construction of a number of four- and five-star hotels. Within three years, Malta boasted a number of beautifully constructed luxury hotels. Again, I was proved right and people started noticing me. I was becoming a public figure.

A year after the Suncrest, I was contacted by Godfrey Grima, a renowned journalist, who informed me that Television Malta, the state TV station, had commissioned him to carry out a series of interviews of successful local businessmen and other personalities.

'Would you be interested in being my first guest?' he asked.

'I'm not sure, Mr Grima. I'm a very shy person and have never been on TV.'

'There's a first time for everything, Mr Xuereb, and now, in your position, you can't escape media attention whether you like it or not. But seriously, Mr Xuereb, you've nothing to be afraid of. The questions won't be difficult and I won't put you in any embarrassing situations, believe me.'

Two weeks before the programme was scheduled for airing, Mr Grima came to my office after hours in order to learn more about me and my business, so that he would be better prepared for the live interview. At the time I wasn't aware that he was a professional in his field and that he had conducted numerous interviews of famous people throughout his long career as a journalist. We talked informally for hours over drinks and I didn't realise it was already eleven at night until Jessie phoned, worried that something must have happened to me. She wouldn't believe that I wasn't sick or something similar and I tried for minutes to persuade her that I wasn't surrounded by a crowd of doctors and nurses. Then, Godfrey snatched the telephone from my hand and spoke to Jessie himself.

'Hello, Mrs Xuereb. I'm Godfrey Grima from Malta Television. You don't have to worry about your husband. We've just had an interesting talk and you've caught us just as we're about to finish.'

After he hung up I asked him about the title of the programme. '*Darek mal-Hajt*,' he replied. (Translated as 'Your back to the wall').

An ominous title, I thought. It was similar to *Cross Fire* which was, at the time, being screened in the UK, Godfrey informed me.

'So you would be grilling me in front of thousands of viewers for... How long's the programme anyway?'

Godfrey laughed. 'Don't worry too much about the questions. You'll do fine, I'm sure. It only lasts ninety minutes...'

'Ninety...!'

'...Which include phone-ins and breaks for commercials. But you're worrying too much. You'll do fine and I know what I'm saying.'

Two days later, he phoned to ask whether I would mind if he interviewed the Chief Justice on the first programme. I certainly didn't. In fact, I was relieved. It would give me the chance to watch the programme and get to know how it was run. So, I settled in to watch the first episode, which afforded me the chance to be better prepared. The phone-ins were few. Who would dare ask the Chief Justice embarrassing questions?

Before closing the programme, Godfrey told his viewers, 'I'm sure you wouldn't want to miss next week's edition. Sitting beside me I shall have a millionaire – none other than Mr Angelo Xuereb. You'll learn how he made it to the top... And maybe learn from him how you too can become a millionaire.'

I was flabbergasted. These last few words put paid to the optimism of a few minutes before. At the time, Television Malta was the only local TV station. Therefore, many tens of thousands must have listened to Godfrey's parting shot during peak viewing time. I felt shivers running down my spine. In a week's time I would be sitting in front of a TV camera with only Godfrey for company, and I would be bombarded with God knows how many questions to which I would have no answer.

The week passed quickly and a few minutes before the start of the programme I was nervous with fright. In fact, I even asked

Godfrey to tell me what the first question was, so that I would have time to prepare an answer, which would put me at ease for what came after.

'We'll soon be starting and there's no time for that, but don't worry; you'll know your first question soon enough.'

I swallowed hard. I didn't like it at all. I thought that that was it. I thought that he didn't want to oblige because he wanted to start with some really tricky question which would put me on the defensive for the whole ninety minutes. Journalists were notorious for this sort of stratagem.

Once we started, and Godfrey introduced me to his viewers, he turned to me and asked, 'Now, Angelo. What can you tell me about your background?'

I tried to make my sigh of relief as inaudible as possible. It was familiar ground and I could have taken the whole programme, and possibly a sequel as well, recounting my background. Then the questions started getting tougher and tougher. But that first question had put me at ease and I was able to answer in a most relaxed manner, and very truthfully.

After this, the phone-ins started coming in, and so fast that we couldn't take them all. I wondered whether the Chief Justice was feeling envious! A particular viewer asked why I had demolished a small building without the necessary permit and wanted to know what I had to say about it. I was aware that tens of thousands of viewers were at that moment wondering how I would get out of that, but I stayed calm and relaxed.

'I'm sure that as a good Christian you know the Scriptures and must surely remember what Jesus said to the mob that was about to stone the adulterous woman. He said that whoever was without sin should cast the first stone. But nobody did and the mob melted away.'

Godfrey congratulated me on my answer. There were many other questions. But none were really hard to deal with and the interview was a success. Over the next days I had many phone calls from people wanting to congratulate me. I was even stopped

204

in the street by people wanting to shake my hand. One must keep in mind that this was the first programme after sixteen years of Socialist rule where one could speak one's mind on the national TV channel without risking being censored or ostracised.

Among the many congratulatory letters I received there was one from a nun who referred to my quotation from the Scriptures. It seemed that half the people of Malta and Gozo had watched the programme and wherever I went people would smile at me and pass favourable comments. The Suncrest saga had put my name on everybody's lips, but it was this interview that had made my face familiar to the population. I had now become a public figure.

With the success of the Suncrest firmly established, I then turned my attention to tendering for major redevelopment projects. My first bid was for the redevelopment of the former Sheraton Hotel. The Sheraton was situated in a prime tourist area at Dragonara Point in St Julian's, surrounded by extensive grounds and commanding a beautiful coastal panorama. It was also one of the many properties taken over by the former government through its Socialist nationalisation ideology.

Although Dad was a staunch and notorious Nationalist Party supporter, I never inherited any of his political zeal. My life, at least until then, had been a continuous struggle to build up my business and to be successful. My only involvement, or rather clash, with politics was my year-long struggle with the Socialist regime to hang on to my rights. Otherwise, I was politically naïve, and that's putting it mildly. It had never entered my head, for example, that big political parties depended on the input of millions by capitalists who don't necessarily embrace any political ideology for their survival, so much so that many invested in both political parties just in case. All this created obligations that a political party, once in power, had a 'moral duty' to fulfil.

The Nationalist Party had been in opposition for sixteen years and, over such a long period of time, it was only natural that it had to depend on strong financial backing to survive. So, although my proposal for the Sheraton was good, there existed no clear criteria to determine which of the offers was the most advantageous. Needless to say, I lost it to a rival group of companies.

Soon after this episode, a letter of intent, which had been issued years before to an Italian businessman for the development of Manoel Island, had elapsed and, therefore, it was cancelled by the government. I wasted no time and wrote to the minister responsible to inform him that my group, together with a large company from Hong Kong, was willing to develop the small island of 0.5 square km. The island bisects Marsamxetto Harbour, a few hundred metres across the water from Valletta on one side and approximately the same distance from Sliema on the other.

Things soon got moving and we even signed a letter of intent, after which we were instructed to liaise with the Planning Services Division (later the Planning Authority) to come up with an acceptable design. This initiated a number of meetings during which various design proposals were discussed and dismissed. At last we came up with acceptable plans and these were referred to the minister to attach to his memorandum to the cabinet.

The prospects looked good, but to our complete amazement and disappointment, the cabinet decided to expand the development to include the Tignè Point peninsula. In due course, they issued an international call for tenders about which I shall write extensively in a subsequent chapter.

With this project out of reach, I concentrated my energy on one of the largest real estate developments in central Sliema. When it was eventually completed it was described as one of the elite developments in the best part of this popular and sought after town. The name I chose for the development was Falcon House and the building permit application was duly completed and submitted. I presumed that the process of this application shouldn't encounter complications. What I had failed to make allowances for, however, was the composition of the planning decision board. Some members who sat on it were survivors of the Socialist era, used to ignoring regulations and procedures, and acting as they

With Claire on her graduation.

My family at Jessie's
birthday celebration.

The Xuereb extended family.

With Prime Minister Fenech Adami.

With Prince Andrew.

With President of Malta Dr Censu Tabone.

With Dr Edward Debono.

With the President of Albania, Dr Sali Berishia.

With the President of Malta, Dr
Ugo Mifsud Bonnici (centre) and
Prime Minister
Dr Alfred Sant.

At one of the campaign parties for the local council elections.

As Mayor.

A typical local council election campaign activity.

As Mayor unveiling the 3rd Millennium Monument.

Presented with a memento in my home village of Naxxar.

Receiving the trophy for the best managed local council from Minister Charles Mangion.

President Professor Guido De Marco, presenting me with an honour for my outstanding dedication to Naxxar village in the presence of the new Mayor, Dr Maria Deguara.

Father chatting with Prime Minister Eddie Fenech Adami.

With President Arafat and my friend Stewart Eliott.

With the Italian President, Dr Luigi Scalfaro.

pleased as long as the all-powerful Socialist minister's whims were considered directives. But, as presumed, since my application was strictly according to policy, its processing didn't take long and as soon as the building permit was issued, work on the project began.

This being a large-scale development, the engineers were extra cautious in the design of its structure and they came up with a heavy concrete sub-structure. Although, as experienced building contractors we considered it over designed, we didn't argue and constructed this sub-structure concrete frame as designed. After we had reached ground-floor level, and without any prior notice whatsoever, or without our having filed an application to alter the original overall design, we received a revised building permit eliminating one of the five blocks which had already been approved in the original permit.

I considered this highly suspicious and irregular, and drove straight to the planning office to enquire about this unilateral decision. Every person I approached came up with the same answer: 'I'm sorry, Angelo, but I'm not part of this decision. I only follow orders.'

Continuing with my ferreting, I at last discovered the reason behind it: the Chairman of the planning board was a close friend of a neighbour of Falcon House. This neighbour considered the development objectionable even though it abided by all existing policies. But he also had strong and influential political connections, and the chairman took it upon himself, without consulting any other board member, to order a set of copies of all approved plans and, without anyone's knowledge, delete the 'offending' block and some other floors from the adjacent three blocks of apartments. After rubber-stamping these 'revised' plans and adding his signature on each, while bypassing all the other departments, he posted them to us as 'official documents'.

I had to stop all works because, for all intents and purposes, these were legally binding official documents. I then immediately initiated a constitutional court case against the government who, unbelievably, instead of taking criminal action against the chairman for fraudulently altering already approved documents, chose to apply delaying tactics, thereby forcing me to refer the case to the European Court. The case is still pending, but I'm positive that I acted in the correct manner.

Not wishing to waste my time and energy on litigation, I turned my attention to the newly planned power station at Delimara. The construction included a 150-metre-high chimney for which I tendered together with my Hong Kong partner. We won the award and decided to adopt the 'slipform' system, which meant that we had to work on a twenty-four-hour-a-day, seven-days-a-week schedule in order to finish it in time. It was a big new challenge for me, and also for the workers I needed to recruit for the job, because no one had ever worked at anything higher than 30 metres.

This slipform system entails formwork (making a mould) made out of steel panels, leaving the void in between to take the reinforced concrete. This 5-metre-high formwork would be continuously lifted by a number of hydraulic jacks, while some of the workers would be tying the reinforcement, some would place the concrete, whilst others would mix the concrete at ground level and hoist it through a lift within the void of the chimney. By the time the formwork is lifted by about 3 metres, the high quality concrete would have already cured and achieved its strength to be exposed and finished.

Once the construction has started, the operation cannot stop, as otherwise the concrete solidifies and the formwork would get stuck. This forced us to duplicate all the machinery, in case one item became unserviceable.

The whole operation is spectacular and works like clockwork, but it necessitates a team of fifty specialised, skilled workers, which I didn't have. Therefore, a construction company with the government as the major shareholder, set up by the previous administration, was the ideal recruiting ground. Most of the workers at this company were skilled enough but, working under government 'discipline' rendered them lazy and apathetic, and working against the clock wasn't exactly their idea of spending a day away from home. I only required fifty of the thousand on the company's books and when I approached the company management it was agreed that a written call for volunteers would be posted on the notice board for all workers to see. Not one worker responded to my call and, not wanting to call it a day after just this one try, I asked for and was granted permission to address the workers myself.

A hundred or so assembled in a hall, more out of curiosity than for any other reason. From where I was standing, I could see the cynical looks of men who had attended to break the daily monotony of doing next to nothing and, maybe, enjoy a laugh in the bargain. But this didn't put me off. A few years back I was one of them, getting as dirty and speaking the same language.

I was comfortably explaining what I had in mind, while watching the change in their faces as they stared up at me, absorbing every word I was uttering, when, suddenly, one of them, apparently some sort of leader, interrupted me with, 'No, no. This is not acceptable for us.'

All the others stood up as one and made to turn away from me. But I somehow stood my ground and many sat down again to, at least, listen to what I had to say. It took me a whole hour of coaxing and cajoling to convince fifty of them to take up my offer of five weeks at very good pay. We started work, aiming at constructing 4 metres a day.

Every week, families on their Sunday drive would park their cars along the perimeter road to gauge the progress from week to week – reminiscent of the Suncrest days. They would note the 30 metres' difference on the previous week and I could see the looks of surprise, satisfaction and pride that Maltese workers were as good as any.

We completed the chimney in the planned five weeks and the result was of the highest quality, with the temporary workers from the government company working on a twelve-hour shift over a seven-day week. They had decided not to shave for the duration and, at the end of it all, they all laughed at each other and at how scruffy everybody was. They all celebrated sumptuously and came over to me to thank me for the opportunity I afforded them. Most begged me to look out for them again should I have a similar project.

It was in 1989 that the government announced it had engaged the world famous architect, Renzo Piano, to design and rebuild the former Royal Opera House, which had been in ruins since it was bombed by the Germans in World War II. Piano's brief also included a new design for City Gate to replace the unpopular one constructed during the 1960s which, in turn, replaced the beautiful, but impractical, one constructed by the British in the nineteenth century. All hell broke loose when Piano's scale model was put on display. Everybody seemed to hate the concept, including myself. But, while newspapers were inundated with letters from everybody who had something to say about it, I held back. I was still too shy to write, even though my ideas were now being listened to, although not necessarily taken up. I had to be away for a few days on a business trip, anyway, so I thought I had better concentrate on the important meetings I had scheduled for the trip. After Jessie had dropped me at the airport, however, and as soon as I had checked in, it was announced that my flight would be delayed by two hours.

So, there I was, resigned to sit for two whole hours with nothing to do. Jessie left as soon as she had dropped me off and taking a taxi back to the office for an hour of catching up with my paperwork wasn't worth the risk of getting stuck in some traffic jam on my way back to the airport. I just sat there, thinking about the Piano project which, in my opinion, could be much improved upon because Valletta's problems weren't confined to just the Opera House and City Gate.

'It's no use thinking about the problems unless I come up with solutions,' I said to myself. 'I owe it to the people if to no one else.'

There and then I decided to put my thoughts to paper and publish. Planning is, after all, my specialisation and I felt it my duty as a Maltese citizen to put forward my valid contribution. I thought that, while I was at it, I should design a master plan for the whole capital city instead of limiting myself to City Gate and the Opera House. I got up from my chair, searched for a public phone and instructed my secretary to fax me the maps of Valletta and its suburb Floriana at the hotel where I would be staying.

During my wait at the airport, and at every opportunity that availed itself on the trip, I worked on a draft plan, which would incorporate not just City Gate and the Opera House, but also traffic management, transportation across both harbours, parking areas, pedestrianisation and new tourist attractions.

When back in Malta, I made a tour of all the areas indicated in my draft to confirm the feasibility of my plan. But I wanted to go further and learn more about the city, so I paid a visit to the National Library where I scrutinised the original plans for Valletta, drawn up over 400 years ago. I was impressed by what I found; the details of the plans were fantastic and I discovered a whole underground city. What intrigued me most was the labyrinth of tunnels connecting palaces and auberges, all crying out to be restored and opened as tourist attractions.

These latter plans were known only by the higher hierarchy of the Order of St John. All the tunnels had escape routes leading to various innocuous and well-hidden openings to the sea. They would have saved the Grand Master and his knights should Valletta have been besieged again and overpowered by the powers of Islam. Thankfully, Valletta never again had to withstand another attack after the Great Siege of 1565. It was, however, heavily bombed by the Italians and especially the Germans during World War II.

One entrance to the tunnels was situated beneath Palazzo Castellana, which housed the Health Ministry. Dr George Hyzler, the minister, happened to be a friend of the family and I contacted him to grant me permission to inspect the tunnels located about 30 metres below street level.

'Of course you may, Angelo,' he said in his usual jovial manner.

'I didn't even know I was sitting on one of them. In fact, I'd like to go down with you if you don't mind carrying me on the way up.'

'Of course, Minister,' I replied while listening to his chuckling at the other end of the line.

'Now, then,' he continued. 'What do you say if we meet on Saturday? There would be nobody around to disturb us.'

All my brothers wanted to join me on this once-in-a-lifetime adventure and they all came equipped, like me, with torches, lengths of light rope, boots, and even raincoats in order to face any eventuality down in the dark unknown.

The entrance to the tunnels was blocked by many cardboard boxes packed with archived files, which we patiently moved aside to disclose a trapdoor which, when lifted, revealed a steep flight of stairs, at the bottom of which there was nothing but a long, narrow passage many metres below street level. It was unexpectedly clean, free of rats and other vermin, but very humid (though not enough for raincoats). It was 1.7 metres wide and 1.8 high, and, as we walked with our torches showing the way, we noticed other tunnels on both sides, undoubtedly leading to other large houses and palaces, with their exits all walled up for security reasons. We could, however, only explore 300 metres because we ran out of rope.

This, together with the information I had gathered from the National Library, confirmed the feasibility of my proposed master plan and I was now ready to edit and finalise it. I then showed the draft of my article to the editor of the Sunday Times. It was a long article and I watched him reading it through with the utmost attention until at last he looked up at me and smiled.

'I must tell you that this is an excellent article, well researched and very well written. Congratulations!'

'Thank you.'

'You brought it to me at the right time because the cabinet will be making a final decision on the Piano plans in the next few days. So, if we publish it on Sunday...'

'But I still need to do some editing. And I haven't yet included the colour codes on the plans so that everyone understands.'

It was published in its entirety and in full colour on four whole pages on Sunday 29th October 1989. It also included my photo. I was lucky; the Sunday Times had just turned to colour two weeks before and my article was all the more attractive and interesting to read.

This very first newspaper article was well received and quite a few people phoned and wrote to congratulate me. In the end, the government shelved Piano's proposal and at the time of writing, twenty-one years later, this world famous and respected architect admitted that his plans had not taken full consideration of our capital's rich history throughout the centuries. He has now been re-appointed by the government to come up with another proposal to make up for the oversight of twenty-one years before.

Over the past twenty years since I published my article, the government adopted a number of my proposals. Many other valid ideas are still pending, but should be implemented over the next few years.

At the time of the Piano controversy, the government was also in the process of preparing a draft structure plan for the Maltese islands for the next twenty years. It was, in addition, preparing legislation aimed at setting up a Planning Authority to replace the notorious Planning Board. The Planning Authority would also have the brief to draft a number of local plans for approval by Parliament. The government had contracted a foreign consultancy firm during the preparation of the structure plan and one of the consultants, Peter Anderson, a chief town planner in the UK, asked for a meeting with me soon after his arrival in Malta. He told me that he wanted my reactions as a developer and planner to some of the proposals being suggested for inclusion in the structure plan.

The first introduction led to regular two- or three- hour meetings during which we discussed various points and ideas that were eventually included in the plan. Little did I then imagine that the Planning Authority would turn out to become the major tool in the hands of bureaucrats to stifle development.

In 1990, I made the decision to expand my pre-cast and pre-stressed concrete plant yard and equip it with the latest technology available on the market. My plant at Naxxar was now fully committed and completely surrounded by residential development, so its expansion was out of the question. Furthermore, it was next to impossible to identify a suitable site for the required 40,000 square metres at a reasonable price in an industrial area and covered by a building permit. The only available areas were situated in government-owned industrial estates. The major problem, however, was the financing of such a big project and the lack of local knowhow about large pre-cast elements, such as pre-stressed bridge beams, pre-cast industrial beams, columns and wall panels.

Thankfully, I managed to rope in an Italian partner who was already producing these elements. I also managed to secure the support of an equity shareholding by a leading local bank. With this backing, my partner and I could plan the first full-scale and largest pre-cast and pre-stressed concrete factory in Malta. It would be equipped with the most modern plant using steam curing for the utmost efficiency. It went into full operation in less than nine months and on 1st September 1991, it was officially inaugurated as the General Precast Concrete Factory (GPC). Even before the factory was officially opened we won a contract worth €2.5 million for the construction of twelve warehouses, each measuring 1,000 square metres, for the Malta Freeport. Once the company was in full operation we managed to erect one warehouse every two weeks. The demand for our superb quality, pre-stressed roofing slabs was so high that we started producing a staggering 700 square metres of pre-stressed roofing slabs a day, apart from other pre-cast elements.

Rumour spread among stone quarry owners, however, that my factory was built specifically so that I would be in direct competition with them. They wrongfully assumed that I would be constructing completed pre-cast concrete housing units, which would render their product obsolete. In truth, the reality was the complete opposite because I would be building more concrete frame structures, thereby requiring more stone or bricks with which to enclose them. This would, in fact, render brickwork in direct competition with the stone. But the quarry owners, without deigning to clarify matters, went on a total strike and took to the streets for three weeks in their huge trucks, causing traffic jams along main thoroughfares while sounding their ear-splitting air horns to the annoyance of everybody. They made it a point to make their massive presence felt in front of Auberge de Castile, the Prime Minister's office, where they would stop for long minutes and disrupt any important meeting going on inside with their relentless sounding of their hateful horns. They would repeat these tactics in front of Parliament in the very centre of Valletta and in the centre of villages and towns.

After three weeks of this mayhem, the government gave in, cancelled a very large tender I had won and re-published it. This tender was for the construction of a new Technological Park, which would incorporate a number of high-tech industrial buildings. In the end, the final cost of this project rose by more than 50% of the estimate while the duration of the construction was three years instead of our projected ten months.

Throughout this hullabaloo, my company was being constantly mentioned in the news as the 'cause' of the industrial action. Thanks to this constant media coverage, it was not just the architects, engineers and developers that got to know about my revolutionary product, but every Tom, Dick and Harry who read the newspapers or watched TV news. This 'free' advertising campaign resulted in an overwhelming amount of orders for my product for large projects and regular orders for the manufacture and delivery of pre-stressed concrete roofing slabs for private individuals. GPC also undertook several major construction works including bridges, and industrial and commercial buildings. Practically overnight, it became the leading producer of pre-cast concrete structures and fast construction.

Dad became so proud of my achievements that he would look forward to watching the news on TV in the hope that my name would be mentioned, or better still, he could watch me being interviewed about some project or other. It would tickle him pink to hear my name mentioned in public. It made him feel proud that he had fathered me. After every news bulletin where some reference was made to me, he would phone me to give me the 'news'.

'I've just seen you on TV, Ġol.'

I had at last proved myself to him and I consider this my greatest achievement, whatever else could possibly come later.

In the midst of all this activity and the success of GPC, my family was struck a blow that could have ended in tragedy. One day Jessie was busy at home, as usual, when the phone rang. She left aside whatever she was doing and answered it.

'It's Mrs Xuereb, isn't it?'

Jessie recognised the voice of Claire's school administrator. Our elder daughter was thirteen at the time. A quiet and keen student, she had never given us cause to worry about her performance and behaviour at school.

'Yes. This is Mrs Xuereb,' answered Jessie, wondering what could have prompted the school administrator to call at such an odd time in mid-morning.

'It's about Claire, Mrs Xuereb. Nothing to worry about, but she's not feeling well and we thought it would be better if you pick her up.'

Jessie was somewhat relieved that it wasn't anything to do with Claire's behaviour. Not that she was ever a troublesome student, but at thirteen, when girls grow up suddenly and start to rebel, a cold or, at worst, influenza was a relief.

'Do you know what's wrong with her?'

The school administrator didn't reply right away. 'Well... We don't really know for certain. But I'm sure it's nothing serious.'

Within minutes, Jessie was driving fast to the school and parked right in front of the main door, leaving the engine running because it was only then that she realised she was still in her housework clothes and wearing indoor slippers. It wouldn't do to be seen walking along the school corridors in that attire. So, she hovered near the front door hoping to find somebody who could carry a message to Claire. She did; it was one of the school staff.

'Excuse me, Miss. Would you do me a favour and tell my daughter Claire that her mother is waiting for her outside. She's in reception.'

'Of course, Madam.'

And the young lady hurried towards the reception room while Jessie waited, expecting any minute to see Claire walking towards her. But, instead of Claire, Jessie saw the same young lady walking hurriedly back to where she was waiting.

'I'm sorry, Mrs Xuereb. The Head thinks it's better if you park the car and come with me to reception. Claire can't come by herself. I'm afraid you will have to help her.'

Jessie just stared at the girl, unable to understand what these words meant. Even if Claire had influenza, she couldn't be so weak.

'Please, Mrs Xuereb. I think you'd better hurry.'

These words jolted Jessie into action. She parked the car somewhere out of the way and ran all the way down the corridor to the reception room. Claire was lying face up on a narrow bench.

'My God, Claire. Whatever is the matter with you?'

'I don't know, Ma. All of a sudden I can't walk.'

'What do you mean, you can't walk? Let me see. Try to stand up.'

But Claire couldn't make it by herself and Jessie had to help her. Jessie just couldn't understand. Claire was in great pain and could only manage two steps in as many minutes. Jessie couldn't believe what she was witnessing; her daughter, full of health and energy a few hours earlier, was now reduced to horrible pain and unable to put one foot forward. She had to help Claire to the car with the help of two of the school staff and drive her home immediately. She phoned me as soon as she arrived and I drove

217

recklessly home, praying that Jessie was grossly exaggerating. She wasn't, and the doctor arrived very soon after I phoned him.

He carried out a thorough examination of every inch of Claire's body with special attention to her feet and leg muscles, after which he stood up scratching his head.

'I can't understand,' he told Jessie and me. 'I'm completely baffled. There's absolutely nothing wrong with her and yet...' He stopped and turned towards Claire as if to start his examination all over. Then he stopped and, still looking at Claire but addressing me, he asked, 'May I use your phone, Angelo?'

We listened to him talking for five minutes to a consultant friend of his, explaining Claire's symptoms and his examination in minute detail. When he stopped talking, Jessie and I watched him listening attentively for a few more minutes, very often nodding his head and saying an occasional 'yes', until at last he hung up, turned towards us and said, 'He has consented to see you this evening. I'll write down the address of his clinic.'

The consultant had Claire's feet and legs x-rayed, examined all her muscles, carried out innumerable blood tests and I don't remember what else. Jessie and I were too dazed to keep track of what he was doing. We just prayed that Claire would come out of it as whole as ever.

'Nothing,' he said after he finished studying the x-rays and his notes for the umpteenth time. 'Just nothing.'

'What do you mean nothing, doctor?' asked Jessie.

'I mean there's nothing wrong with her – her muscles, her bones and all else. Everything's in perfect condition. She should be up and running, and yet ... and yet I can't understand why she can't stand up by herself and walk. I've never come across such a case before.'

We felt completely shattered. If the consultant couldn't find out what was wrong with her, what else could we do?

The consultant must have been reading our thoughts because he continued, 'Let me tell you what we'll do. I'll refer you personally to a colleague of mine. He's a specialist in the same field and maybe he'll discover something I may have missed.'

Even the second specialist was baffled. 'Could it be something psychological? I wonder.' And he referred us to a psychologist.

Jessie and I were shocked. We couldn't believe there could be anything psychologically wrong with our daughter. We just told Claire that we were taking her to another doctor for yet another opinion. We never mentioned the word 'psychologist' in her presence. But Claire was no fool. She soon realised from questions put to her that she was being probed for any possible mental disability and midway through the examination, she broke down crying. The doctor pulled Jessie and me out of the room to inform us that she could find nothing wrong with Claire.

We consulted all known children's specialists, but they all arrived at the same conclusion – there was absolutely nothing wrong with Claire. In the meantime, life had to go on as normally as possible in the circumstances. We would carry Claire in our arms wherever she needed to go, including school. Every morning Jessie would dress her and I would carry her in my arms to the car and drive her to school. The school authorities had granted us permission to carry Claire to her classroom ten minutes before classes began in order to avoid the rush and bustle of crowds of students hurrying to their classes. I would sit her down at the desk at the back of the class to make it easier for school staff to bring her down to the front door in a wheelchair fifteen minutes before end of classes. Jessie or I would then drive her straight home, thus avoiding the many cars and mini-buses which usually clogged the area around the school entrance.

This unexpected blow had taken us completely by surprise, and more so because no doctor was able to solve this mystery. None would dare take the responsibility of suggesting any treatment or medicine. But something *had* to be done. We couldn't go on living a seemingly normal life without at least having an inkling of what could be wrong with our daughter.

'Look,' I told Jessie one morning, 'we can't go on like this. Every time I look at Claire my heart bleeds for her. Not just because she's immobile – though that's bad enough – but not knowing what's wrong with her and being unable to do anything for her is driving me up the wall. She's suffering, Jessie. And everybody else here is suffering with her.'

This was a short time after we had taken her to watch the carnival, dressed in a carnival costume, from the car, and I remember the sad look on her face as she watched the revelry, which she couldn't take part in.

'I know, Angelo. I can't bear to look at her sometimes, knowing that just a few weeks ago she was a bundle of energy. But what more can we do?'

'There is something we can do, Jessie. I'll take her to London – to Harley Street, where people say there are the best doctors.'

On landing at Heathrow, we had to wait for everybody to disembark. Then a wheelchair was produced and I could see from Claire's expression that she was forcing herself to hold back her tears. This treatment was reserved for disabled persons and my heart went out to her. I could well imagine what was going through her mind. We were then driven to the terminal in a battery operated carrier (buggy), also normally reserved for the disabled, sick and elderly.

We visited the first specialist on our list but, after a very thorough examination, he confirmed what all the doctors in Malta had told us. We made a 'pilgrimage' of Harley Street and, after each visit, Claire and I were becoming as perplexed and frustrated as the doctors examining her. One of them ended up so frustrated and at a loss that he couldn't find the words to describe the shame he felt at his inability to find the cause for Claire's condition.

'I simply don't know what's wrong,' he told me apologetically, 'because I can find nothing wrong with her. It belies all my medical knowledge and experience.'

Then, as if an afterthought, he continued, 'What I suggest she should do, and maybe it'll help...' He stopped as if unsure of himself. 'Mr Xuereb, make her try to unroll a toilet paper roll, one with each foot, using only her first two toes. It's difficult, I know, but it could slowly force her muscles to do their job and, in a few years' time, she'll be able to walk again.'

As soon as we were back at the hotel, Claire wanted to start with the exercise right away with renewed hope. But it was useless. She couldn't even move her toes, let alone unroll a toilet paper roll. It was then that I realised that there was no medical solution, and I think Claire arrived at the same conclusion because she just sighed and gave up on the exercise. I knew that she was mentally resigned to a life in a wheelchair and I moved away from her. I couldn't bear to look at her young face and her weak body. Neither could I bring myself to phone Jessie with the bad news. At the airport in Malta, before Claire and I left for London, she was all optimism and hope. So, I had to be there with her, to support her when breaking the news. We needed each other's support.

It was with a trembling voice that I told her, 'There's no cure, Jessie. Let's go home. I don't want her to overhear.'

Late in the evening, with the children asleep, Jessie and I had a heart to heart talk in the living room.

'Listen, Jessie. There isn't a specialist in Malta who hasn't examined her and they all ended up baffled, not knowing what to say. At Harley Street it was no different. So, for all intents and purposes, there exists no cause for this phenomenon and, therefore, no cure. I was doing some thinking during the flight, Jessie. I said to myself that it is useless to try and find a medical explanation. So, we have to turn to something else and I thought about Doctor John.' (Doctor John was a local doctor renowned for his faith healing powers.)

'I'm told that wherever he goes, the churches are packed,' I continued. 'He heals people there and then, in front of everybody's eyes, as if by a miracle.'

'Yes,' said Jessie. 'In fact, I was thinking on the same lines and I'm glad you brought it up. You remember Victoria, Claire's nanny? I spoke to her and she told me about similar cases which Doctor John has cured. She offered to talk to his sister because she knows her very well.'

We phoned Victoria right away and, a day later, she phone back with her answer. We were to go to Doctor John's clinic on Saturday evening when I was due to meet some foreign representatives over dinner.

'Don't worry, Jessie. You go ahead. We can't miss this opportunity. He's our last resort.'

She agreed and spent the remaining days to Saturday praying that this visit to Doctor John would be the last. She later told me that Claire's appointment with the doctor was his last before closing the clinic for the night, and she and Claire sat in the waiting room, watching other patients go in and out until they were the only ones left. And when the clinic door opened for the last time, Doctor John accompanied the patient to the front door which he, then, locked from the inside.

'Okay. You may come in now.'

And when Jessie had settled Claire on the couch, he continued, 'All right. What seems to be the trouble?'

Jessie recounted everything from the morning she was summoned to Claire's school to our recent 'door to door' campaign in Harley Street.

After a few minutes in deep thought, Doctor John said, 'This is what we're going to do now. We shall pray together to Almighty God and He will listen.'

After fifteen minutes of praying, Doctor John asked Claire, 'Do you feel any improvement in your condition? Let's see you try standing up by yourself.'

Claire tried to move her legs, but couldn't. 'It's no good. I can't.'

Doctor John was not flustered in any way. His face did not betray any frustration whatsoever. Instead, he remained as calm as ever and in a gentle voice he continued, 'Don't worry, Claire. Now you both go home and by midnight you'll be cured.'

'*Minn fommok 'l Alla, Tabib*' (literally, may God listen to your words, Doctor), said Jessie, 'and He'll sure cure her.'

Jessie opened her purse. 'How much do I owe you, Doctor?'

'One Maltese Lira. It's a normal medical visit.'

'You must be joking.' She pulled out an LM10 note. 'Here, Doctor. Take it. You deserve it.'

'No, Mrs Xuereb. Just one Lira please. I'm only God's servant and don't get paid for doing His work. Go home and may God be with you. Phone me tomorrow and let me know how Claire has fared.'

Back home, Jessie and Claire continued to pray. At eleven o'clock, while Jessie was preparing Claire for bed, Claire said, 'Ma, I'm feeling intense heat in my left leg. I don't know what it is, but maybe Doctor John was right. I think I'm cured.'

Jessie couldn't believe her eyes when she saw Claire already trying to stand up by herself.

'Are you sure, Claire? Do you need any help?'

Claire waived her away and to Jessie's amazement, she stood up by herself and was moving her left leg. Even Claire could hardly believe it, and she laughed and cried at the same time. Then she started to hop on her left leg all around the room while shouting and laughing.

'Look, Ma. I'm cured. At last I'm cured.'

She didn't want to wait till the morrow to tell everybody the good news even though it was so late. She, therefore, started phoning all her friends, explaining what had happened through laughter and tears. But she didn't want to phone me. She wanted to surprise me on my arrival from the business dinner.

'Claire, you have to rest now. With all that hopping around you're risking breaking your leg and it'll be two surprises for your father.'

Jessie helped her get into bed and left the room. After half an hour, she was jolted out of her chair by Claire's shouting.

'Ma! Ma! Come quickly. It's my right leg now. It's become quite hot. I think it's healing as well.'

Jessie ran to Claire. 'Let me see. Stand up and try to walk.'

And that's exactly what Claire did. She started walking normally as if the last three months had never been.

'Ma! I'm cured! Completely cured!'

Jessie sat down on the bed in complete disbelief while Claire danced around the room, hysterical with joy. Then she made another round of phone calls, after which she went out of the house to run round and round the pool, shouting and singing for everyone to hear right in the middle of the night.

I arrived home at midnight, parked the car and walked towards the front door, key in hand as usual. But I didn't have the chance to insert it in the lock as the door opened seemingly of its own accord. Claire was standing right in front of me, all smiles and looking me straight in the eyes.

'Look, Pa. I'm completely cured.'

For a few short seconds I wasn't sure it wasn't just a dream. Maybe it was the long day I had, culminating in that confounded business dinner at a time when I should have been with my daughter at Doctor John's. Or maybe it was just wishful thinking, and I would come out of it as soon as my head cleared. I did come to. It was Claire hugging me close to her that cleared my head. I embraced her and pressed her hard against me while my glazy eyes dimly saw Jessie standing a few metres back with her hand to her mouth, trying to hold back her tears.

At last I disengaged myself from Claire and asked, 'What happened? How is it that you're –'

'It was Doctor John, Pa. It was him, Pa, with his prayers and our prayers. And it happened exactly as he said it would. He said I'd be able to walk before midnight. And look. I can even jump and dance and even run.'

I cannot describe the happiness that enveloped my whole being. I must surely have been the happiest man alive at that moment. And we stayed up all night talking and laughing, and hugging again and again. I wanted to be certain it wasn't all a dream.

Next morning – it was Sunday – I phoned Doctor John.

'You don't have to thank me, Mr Xuereb. It wasn't me who cured Claire. Thank God. It was He who cured her.'

Claire spent the whole Sunday phoning and re-phoning her many friends, recounting again and again her unique experience. Monday happened to be her school's annual sports day and she decided to take part. At school, fully equipped with her sports gear, she was joyously welcomed by her mates and staff. The headmistress allowed her to take part in various events, knowing full well that she had no chance of success after three months of complete immobility, during which her muscles would have weakened drastically and joints become stiff, but at least it would boost her morale. She surprised everybody, however. She came first or second in all the races she competed in. We couldn't believe our eyes when she returned home with six medals hanging around her neck.

Her complete recovery was the most moving experience my family had ever gone through. It was surely a miracle. How else could one explain this phenomenon? The following Monday, I called personally at Doctor John's clinic. He was surprised to see me.

'Come in, Mr Xuereb. Come in. How's Claire? Is she still doing well?'

'She's doing fine. Everybody at home is doing fine. All thanks to you. I'm here to thank you personally for what you've done for my family. I want to repay you. The €2.33 you charged my wife is ridiculous.'

But he wouldn't accept any money and I couldn't break his resistance.

'I'm just God's messenger, you see. I haven't done anything. I don't perform miracles.'

I had to respect his wish.

'But at least, Doctor John, let me know when I can be of service to you. If there's anything that you need... I have no words to thank you enough. So please...'

He just smiled and nodded his head.

After that, I attended a number of his healing services, which were always attended by hundreds of people from all walks of life. I was witness to the healing of disabled people on various occasions and I was always highly impressed. He and I have remained good friends and I would assist him when he required adequate premises to conduct his services.

I had always tried to give assistance to people with special needs, but after this impressive episode I increased my assistance both to individuals and organisations. I try to give financial assistance where required, but I also give other means of support and whenever I do so, I always feel better. I feel pride and satisfaction, knowing that in a small way I'm sharing my success with people who haven't been as lucky. I have learned that the little I give could make life that little bit better to live.

The Maltese Islands from the air

11

Establishing AX Holdings

(1991–1993) 39–41 years

By this time my group was well established and had become one of the leading companies in Malta. I, therefore, thought it was the right time to create a suitable name and logo. We opted for AX HOLDINGS – a name which sounded right and was very easy to remember. It is still the name we carry today.

The motto, which we chose to run concurrently with the name and reflects the Company's philosophy for success, was 'CREATIVITY – EFFICIENCY – CHALLENGE'. A few years later we added 'DETERMINATION' because it was through sheer determination against all odds that I had started my business and kept it going through thick and thin.

I presented each of our top managers with this logo framed to be hung on their walls to serve as a reminder of their group's objectives, and also as an encouragement to be more innovative in their approach to solving problems. Experience has taught me that progress can be achieved only through new and innovative ideas. Only in this way could one stay a step ahead of one's competitors. Should I have, at some point in time, decided to rest on my laurels and let my business run itself, within a short time, I would have found myself lagging far behind, with a stiff hill to climb in order to catch up, and with an even stiffer one to overtake my competitors.

Every new idea creates its own challenges, which have to be

faced head on and solved. New ideas create changes, and changes sometimes create difficulties. This is the reason for so much resistance to change and the reason why a creative person with vision is so misunderstood, and therefore resisted by those less creative and lacking in vision. I say this through experience because I have never come up with an idea or a concept that wasn't resisted and obstructed all the way to its fruition.

As I have already said, 'DETERMINATION' was added to the logo a few years after its inception. Anyone who has enjoyed any kind of success would know that no achievement is possible without determination. Even getting out of bed for work on a cold wintry Monday morning requires a certain amount of determination. The higher the aim, the greater the determination required. Life is full of ups and downs, and it is during the 'down' period that determination has to be at its strongest. In my case, life is 'down' when I come up with a feasible idea that makes sense and all possible obstacles are put in my way. But this is the time when sheer determination to succeed wins the day. My advice through experience is that one must never give up and should persist with determination to see one's dream to the end. If one's ideas are financially feasible, or do not wholly depend on government approval, one should see them through to fruition. This has led me to accept the fact that not all of my ideas could be implemented. But I always aim to implement 50% at the very least.

The first time I attended a conference about Lateral Thinking by compatriot Dr Edward de Bono, who is a leading advocate, I was introduced to him as another Maltese with vision. Dr de Bono has written eighty-six books on the subject and they have been translated into forty-three languages. He prides himself on having written a complete book during a flight from London to the Far East. After one such conference, we sat down for two whole hours discussing and exchanging ideas and I showed him one of my latest articles for the newspapers. He went through it, after which he told me, 'Angelo, this is a well-structured article and readers will realise that you're talking from practical experience. Congratulations!' We have remained good friends and he is often my family guest. Although he spends most of his time travelling around the globe delivering lectures on lateral thinking to top-brass company executives and at educational institutions, he still finds time to visit Malta where we meet over a drink or a day's trip with my family on my boat.

I have written about resistance to innovative ideas; the following is a classic example.

In 1991, I prepared and presented a master plan for a reform of our public transportation for the Maltese Islands. The biggest problem centred round the public bus service. To call it inefficient was charitable. Most of the buses were old relics seemingly held together with string. Most towns and villages had their own bus terminus situated in the main square – the centre of town and village life. In time, these were relegated to side streets.

The service had degenerated so much that people preferred to use their own transport to work and spend time stuck in traffic jams after which they had to look and fight for a parking space rather than risking life and limb on a public transport bus. No wonder Malta's roads leading to Valletta are congested for most hours of the day. Malta is a small place with hardly enough space for its 400,000-plus inhabitants, let alone for over 300,000 vehicles that are let loose daily on its roads.

My proposal included an underground monorail service system to run around the inner and outer harbour areas, which include the most densely populated towns that surround Valletta, where traffic congestion has become a part of life. The service would have included a limited number of interchange stations with access from large car parks. In my opinion this was, and still is, the most logical solution to this chronic problem. It would have given efficient, round-the-clock transportation and considerably eased the load on our roads.

The idea was rejected not only by the sceptics, but by the central government, questioning the possibility of having an underwater tunnel spanning the 300-metre stretch across the harbour. Maybe the doubters had never visited the places I'd been to when abroad. I had seen similar projects working efficiently around densely populated cities all around the world. So why couldn't it work for Valletta?

I published my master plan in a leading local newspaper and among the negative comments that it generated, I also received many favourable ones. It was an impressive scheme and so avant-garde at the time that many people got to know about me through it. It is only now, twenty years later, in 2011, that the government has at last decided to do something about public transport without proper research of the actual need. New air-conditioned buses replaced the old (in many cases, vintage) buses. Though more comfortable, they still have to compete with other traffic on our overcrowded roads. Some of these new buses are so large that they can hardly pass through the narrow streets. The routes are badly designed by foreigners who probably never lived or experienced the local needs and this has resulted in many more delays with some journeys taking as long as 90 minutes for a relatively short distance. This has created frustration amongst the commuters and has led to a vote of no confidence in the minister responsible. The vote did not pass thanks to the Speaker's casting vote. Still, the government continues to shy away from introducing the underground, mass transportation, circular route, which I'm certain will have to be introduced in the future.

Any new form of public transportation system must aim at more efficiency to encourage more people to make use of this public service, rather than use their private vehicles, which are choking our roads.

It was around this time that the government decided to issue an international call for tenders for the development of Manoel Island and Tignè Point. It was, then, being considered the largest development of the century. In a previous chapter I have stated that I already had a letter of intent for Manoel Island and a Parliamentary Resolution for my consortium for Tignè Point. I knew the area earmarked for development like the back of my hand and decided to form a joint venture with Hopewell Holdings of Hong Kong, headed by Stewart Elliott, to renew the partnership that had presented the plans for Manoel Island and for which it had a letter of intent. We immediately recruited respectable local and foreign architects and engineers to assist us in the preparation of our bid, ensuring that we strictly adhere to the government development brief.

Apart from our bid there were two others. One was from a consortium and the other from a company which was closely related to this other consortium. This relationship was obvious because some of the latter company's shareholders were also partners in companies forming the consortium. This was further confirmed a few months later when the company withdrew from the race soon after the offers were made public, leaving just the two consortia still in the running. We knew that the rival bid had many flaws and that it did not stick completely to the development brief conditions, but the members forming the consortium had close connections with some members of the government.

While all this was going on, we received a message proposing joining forces with the other consortium. This was followed by discussions in which we proposed a fifty/fifty split. The other side offered us just 35% and further included certain conditions, thereby leaving us with no say in the final decisions. With these conditions, the offer was definitely unacceptable.

During the negotiating talks, Stewart Elliot, then a partner of Hopewell Holdings, who was sitting beside me, asked, 'Tell me, Angelo, would you trust any one of these gentlemen here with your wallet?'

'Not on your life! You see, it's the easiest thing in the world to spend other people's money. Even a child can do it.'

Needless to say, the negotiations fell through. We knew where we stood. The last thing we expected was for the government to split these two separate and distinct large developments to the only two consortia in the running. In fact, a couple of months later, we received the only communication on the subject from the government. It stated simply that 'your offer has not been accepted'. Not even an explanation or reason, or simply some recognition of the voluminous studies and documentation laboriously prepared by a very professionally assembled team. Shortly afterwards, the government issued a letter of intent for the two developments to the other consortium.

It should have been a plain sailing agreement, since the tender document clearly spelt out the details, but it took nine years of discussions between the government and the consortium. The plans finally approved for both projects were a far cry from the original tender development brief:

- Instead of a four-storey building, the government approved fourteen floors.
- Instead of a tourism and office-related development, the government approved a speculation real estate development.
- Instead of a number of hotels, the government approved a high-rise, luxury apartment block.
- In the original specification for a development of four storeys high, 50% of all infrastructure costs (i.e. roads, drains and other services) would have to be met by the developers. In the now, much bigger, fourteen floors proposal, the government did not require any input from the developers and were quite happy for the tax payer to pick up the bill for it all.
- Instead of restoring five scheduled old barracks as specified in the brief, the government was happy to approve their demolition and replace them with fourteen-storey real estate blocks of apartments.

However, it seems this decision caused some sleepless nights for members of the government, as it insisted that the two-storey-high façades of two of these old barracks should be reconstructed. Part of the brief called for the construction of a breakwater to protect Sliema Creek. To date, after twenty years, there's still no sign of it and the project is still far from completed.

The general public is, of course, unaware of these variances from the original brief and, therefore, does not complain except for the odd letter in the newspapers complaining about the ugly concrete jungle, which completely spoils the view of our historic capital a short distance across the harbour. I still cannot believe that these banana republic antics can happen in a democratic country and member of the European Union. We have lost a unique opportunity to build two substantial developments that respect and complement the surrounding architecture and, at the same time, create a pleasant neighbourhood for the long-suffering residents of the area.

With all of this going on, I had completely lost all track of time – suddenly, I was forty! Forty years old and I was completely caught unawares. How was that possible? How long ago was it when I was running in the fields of my village with my friends? Or building those rooms with rubble walls in the field close to my family's villa? I looked closely at my face in the mirror while shaving and I noticed that I had less hair on my head and that some had changed colour if one could qualify white as a colour.

Jessie and the children wished me a happy birthday before I left for my office and reminded me to be home early as we had some friends coming over for the occasion. At the office, everybody made sure I didn't forget what day it was and I had to smile my thanks for every present I received.

At the reception, everybody was slapping me on the back and telling me that it's all in the mind. That it's just another day, like yesterday and tomorrow. When everybody had left and I sat down in a quiet corner, however, I started thinking; thinking about what my friends had told me; it *was* just another day, another working day as far as I was concerned, like all the thousands of working days of the past decades when it was just work, work and more work. I had never before given any thought about the long hours I was still putting in to run my business as intensively as when I had just started it so many years before. So what was there to impede me now from continuing to work relatively hard and at the same time enjoy life as much as possible?

Once I had made this decision I felt better. I bought a new 33-foot power cabin cruiser and told Jessie and the children that from then onwards, every summer we would be taking a week-long holiday cruising around nearby Sicily. I also decided that Jessie and I would take a regular winter holiday as well. I have always loved speed. So, what better than trying my hand at skiing down some mountain slope? Jessie was all for it and on our first holiday in the Alps we both got the hang of it in a matter of four lessons. I even managed to ski fast down a 'Red' slope without mishap and afterwards jokingly challenged my instructor to a race down a path of a red slope. Funnily enough, she took me seriously and after lunch she left us to fetch her racing skis. She well and truly beat me, of course, but I was satisfied that she considered me already good enough to let me race her after only four days of skiing. We now go regularly to different places in the Alps where we meet friends with whom we spend a most enjoyable annual holiday.

In 1992, we had another general election, won once again by the Nationalist Party, led again by Dr Eddie Fenech Adami with a massive majority. The Prime Minister reshuffled his cabinet and Prof. Demarco was given responsibility for justice and the police. Prof. Demarco was the same lawyer who, years before, had given me the nickname Testaferrata for my unbending determination. A few weeks into his new appointment, he gave me a pleasant surprise; he found out that the government was illegally withholding the keys to a large and prominent historical building which belonged to me. It didn't take long for the Commissioner of Police to write to me with instructions to collect the keys and I didn't waste time in driving straight to Palazzo Capua in Sliema to see the inside of this magnificent building once again. But I was in for a shock; I found that a number of heavy and unique stone artefacts had disappeared. One particular missing item was an enormous stone sculpture of a lion, together with its base, which used to adorn the wide main staircase. I tried to comprehend how burglars could have accessed the building, which was completely enclosed behind a solid 4–metre-high wall, and when the place had only one entrance, the keys to which had always been in the possession of the police. Furthermore, the stone lion alone was so heavy that it would have required at least eight strong men to carry, let alone to lift it over the high wall. It was obvious that the burglar must have entered by the main door.

I went straight to the police, but they were no help at all. They didn't know where the keys had been locked for safe keeping. They couldn't find any written records. When, a few years later, I was in the process of restoring the palace to its former splendour, a person spoke to me in confidence. He told me he had seen the large base of the sculpture in an antiques shop. I thought this was worth investigating, so I sent someone with instructions to pretend he was a collector of antiques to verify the base's authenticity. I also gave him a picture of the whole sculpture to make sure he made no mistake. He came back to say that the base was the original and that the shop owner was asking only €233.00 for it.

Again, I made straight for the police station, certain that this time I had enough proof for them to take action.

'But, Mr Xuereb,' the duty sergeant said after I had finished telling him the above story, 'he could have bought the item in good faith from someone else.'

'That's fair enough,' I said. 'But couldn't you ask him where he got it from? He would surely remember. The thing is so big...'

'Maybe it's not the same base that you said went missing. Maybe it's just a copy.'

'It can't be because it was sculptured on site with... Oh what's the use!'

I turned from him and walked out. What was the use of trying to explain anything to a police officer who was more interested in covering up for his colleagues than justice? There was no other way than to take the matter in my own hands. I phoned the antiques shop and told the owner that I knew the sculpture was mine and that I wanted it back.

'Certainly, you can have it back. Give me €233.00 and it's yours.'

His attitude irked me and I became really angry. Why should I pay for something which rightfully belonged to me?

'Listen, my friend,' I shouted into the phone. 'If you think I'm enjoying your joke you have another thing coming. I want that base back where it belongs by noon tomorrow. If not, I shall go straight to the police and tell them that there's a strong possibility you're dealing in stolen goods. Just try me if you think I'm bluffing.'

He didn't like my threat at all and after some more heated words from both sides, he agreed to bring my property back to where it belonged.

With the matter settled, I immediately started working on the most intense and intricate restoration of the two-hundred-year-old palazzo. It took two years of hard work to restore it to its former glory at a cost of €5 million. In the end, only one important thing was missing – the massive stone lion. But Malta is a small place and a piece of that size is not so easy to hide forever. Furthermore, I had some very good photos of the sculpture and I was certain that someday I would come across it and place it in its rightful prominent place.

The prestigious Palazzo Capua was built in 1830 by Biagio Tagliaferro, a wealthy Russian banker for his residence, but when it was almost completed, he rented it to the exiled Italian Prince of Capua, brother of King Ferdinand of Naples. Over the years this palace was used as a residence for ambassadors and later on, during world War II, as a school run by nuns. It was then left in a neglected state, until I recognised its potential value. I felt proud of the way I had given it new life and, today, it forms an integrated part of our five-star hotel – 'The Palace'.

The palazzo was surrounded by some 4,500 square metres of ground in the most prestigious and expensive location in Sliema.

The land was crying out for development, but I didn't want to develop it into a run-of-the-mill block of apartments. The beautiful palazzo deserved much better and I spent a lot of time weighing the possibilities between a luxurious hotel and a private hospital.

In the early nineties, the only hospital in Malta belonged to the state. It was a general hospital, giving free treatment and surgery to all. It also dispensed free medicine to all sufferers of chronic illnesses. Apart from a few private clinics, which did not cater for emergencies, there was nothing that one could consider a hospital. This was what persuaded me to go for the more challenging option – building a state of the art, one hundred and twenty bed private hospital, which would compete with other modern and prestigious international ones.

Malta enjoys an excellent reputation for its excellent doctors and surgeons. It goes back a long way, to the time of the Knights of St John, an order which was founded during the Crusades as the Order Hospitalier of St John of Jerusalem, specifically to give medical assistance to the wounded during the long battles for the Holy Land. Although in time it also became a military and naval power, it never lost its original vocation and when it settled in Malta in 1530, and soon after the foundation stone of Valletta was laid a year after the Great Siege of 1565, the building of the magnificent Sacra Infermeria (converted into the Mediterranean Conference Centre in 1984) was one of the first buildings planned for the capital. The Sacra Infermeria soon became the best hospital in Europe and men of means from all over Europe came to Malta for medical treatment. The Knights weren't just healers, however; during a time when practically every illness could prove fatal, and when there were no cures for most infectious deceases, the order built a large quarantine hospital isolated on Manoel Island. This hospital was still in use during the second half of the twentieth century. In fact, it was referred to as the Isolation Hospital.

The more I thought about it, the more I liked the idea of developing a private hospital for acute surgery, which would serve not only the Maltese but patients from mainland Europe.

What further helped decide the issue was the ideal location of Malta, right in the centre of the Mediterranean, within easy reach of countries in the Mediterranean basin, our excellent doctors and surgeons and, most of all, the opportunity to create a new tourism niche. I figured that healthcare tourism would be more beneficial to the economy owing to its value-added element of being an all-year-round industry rather than seasonal. I, therefore, designed the hospital with five operating theatres for more efficiency and as a further attraction for foreign patients.

I spent the next few months searching for and engaging top British hospital planners and consultants. When the plans were ready I applied for a 120-bed private hospital. After a further three years of discussions with the Planning Authority, I had to accept downsizing to eighty single-bed rooms, retaining five operating theatres and including an eight-bed intensive therapy unit (ITU), which would enable the hospital to perform all kinds of acute operations, including heart surgery. All this taught me that developing an efficient hospital was five times more difficult than developing a hotel. Every single item had to be in perfect condition before the first patient could be admitted and operated on. We were made to follow the most stringent supervision and when the hospital was ready, we were first made to run it for two months on full services before we were finally given the operating licence. The conditions were so strict that, on inauguration day, not even the Prime Minister was allowed to enter the operating theatre floor corridor for fear of possible contamination. I had never imagined that every cubic centimetre of air had to be purified over and over again with special ultra-clean equipment before surgery could be undertaken.

The first few years of operation were very difficult financially. The Maltese were used to a free hospital service provided by the government and, therefore, very few were covered by a private health insurance policy. As a consequence, very few had the opportunity to compare the service provided by a privately run hospital with that run by the state. Furthermore, we had overrun the budgeted capital expenditure quite substantially. During the first year of operation the hospital lost about €2,330,000. But every subsequent year the loss was reduced until the sixth year when we registered a profit. This, however, did not justify the huge capital outlay.

To aggravate matters even further, the government, for some unknown reason, was reluctant to issue us with a licence to operate the Intensive Care Unit. We couldn't understand this reluctance because our ITU was equipped with state of the art technology and was to be run by some of the country's top surgeons, supported by well trained paramedics. The result was that we couldn't carry out major operations, including open heart surgery, for which the hospital was more than sufficiently equipped. This seriously affected our management plans and, hence, our financial projections. My hospital was especially built to attract foreign patients requiring major operations in Malta's ideal climatic conditions. The government's reluctance to issue the licence forced us to shelve these plans indefinitely.

The only ITU on the island was housed in the government-owned St Luke's Hospital. A few years after we had opened our hospital, this unit was very much in the news when a particular bacteria started creating havoc with mass infections and the government had no option but to close it down for a thorough disinfection. Ours was the only available alternative and all cardiac patients were immediately transferred from St Luke's. The licence was issued in less than a day and twenty open heart operations were successfully carried out in one short week. The government propaganda machine was quick to join the bandwagon and began publicising this as proof of its constant support of private health care.

Our satisfaction was short-lived however. As soon as the government's ITU was certified bacteria free, the Health Ministry had the nerve and unashamed gall to withdraw our ITU operational licence immediately!

Four years into the hospital operation I was approached by Dr Josie Muscat. Dr Muscat owned and ran his own private clinic and was very keen to extend his operations by buying my hospital. He found me at a time of disillusionment with this latest investment, it not being the profession I was trained for and therefore having to rely completely on my medical consultant's advice, and I was open to negotiations. The government's total lack of support and open hostility to this private initiative in such an important sector, and Dr Muscat's eagerness persuaded me to go on with the sale, retaining the old Palazzo Capua. It was too historic and important to give away. The hospital business didn't generate any profits, but neither did I suffer any losses because I managed to negotiate a good deal. It wasn't a highly profitable experience, however, and I learned that I must be extra careful before going into something which I knew next to nothing about. Incidentally, this sale was the very first of my developments, the proceeds of which I invested in other developments. These will be dealt with in subsequent chapters.

While the hospital saga was in full swing, my construction company was entrusted with the construction of a four hundred and forty room, five-star hotel, all in in-situ concrete walls and ceilings. The owners had appointed a top international engineering company and interior designers. The local construction industry was still not geared up for the high specifications required to achieve the best concrete structure and finishes. I felt that this was a challenge I would love to bury my teeth into, but we did not have the local skilled formwork erectors capable of doing the job and the supervisors to go with them. So, I decided to adopt special formwork which was totally new to Malta, and also very expensive. Since I knew I wouldn't have been able to find the required skilled labour locally, I decided to take on specialised skilled workers from the former Yugoslavia, which was then still plagued by a long and bloody internal conflict. My main problem was that foreign workers would not be allowed employment in Malta unless it could be proven that no Maltese workers could be found for the job. I knew I wouldn't be able to find Maltese workers for this job, because it required technical skills never practiced here, but government officials couldn't understand this and I was forced to issue a call for applications in all the media to prove that no Maltese was qualified enough to apply. Only then was I issued with work permits for sixty foreign workers so I could start on these specialised concrete construction works.

When the hotel was completed to the satisfaction of all the technical professionals and the owners, other architects began applying this type of formwork. In five years, this system was being adopted in 90% of large structures. This meant that more skilled foreign workers had to be recruited, but these served to train local workers in this still unfamiliar technique.

I have always considered myself a patriot. I love my country and am proud to declare it publicly. My business gives me the opportunity to travel often and widely, and wherever I go I make the best of my stay to see how other countries manage to be so successful in sustainable development. Every time I return to Malta, however, I feel a sense of deep frustration. I compare our way of doing things with what's happening in Northern European countries and ask myself what could be the reason that Malta does not yet manage to have quality infrastructure. Then I answer myself with John F. Kennedy's dictum, 'Do not ask what your country can do for you, but what you can do for your country.' Because, after all, it's so easy for me, and for everybody else for that matter, to criticise while it's so much harder to act and make things happen. So, I decided to take a leaf out of Kennedy's famous saying and adopt one that suited me personally. It says, 'I love my country. God, help me to give my share to develop our country into the Jewel of the Mediterranean.' I carry this statement in my briefcase and take it with me to every country I visit on business and holiday.

This dictum encouraged me to set up an environmental group way back in 1992, among some of my old friends from Naxxar, my childhood village. The scope for this group was to embellish the locality, thereby improving its environment. It was non-profit making and a branch of an Environmental Committee of which

I was chairman and which operated within the Chamber of Commerce. Eventually, the group became a committee, which met once every two weeks. My job as its chairman was to request the main business entities to sponsor particular areas indicated for embellishment. In return we would fix a small commemorative plaque on the sponsored items and would also include a write up about the sponsorship together with a photo in the committee's bi-monthly newsletter, which was distributed to every household in the locality. I enjoyed this personal initiative because I could see that the people in the village gave their full support. In time, this work was taken over by the local councils, which were established in 1993. After a few initial hiccups, mainly caused for partisan political reasons, all political parties recognised the advantages of local governments in all localities and, today, one can notice the improvement to the environment that has taken place in all our towns and villages since 1993.

As an entrepreneur always on the lookout for possibilities for original projects I once took a close look at the demographic survey of the Maltese islands and realised that what was happening in Malta was no different from what was happening in Western Europe. The baby boom triggered by the end of the Second World War was having its effect now – 50 years later. The young couples responsible for the phenomenon were now old people seeking a decent place to end their days.

This wasn't a problem up to the sixties and seventies, when elderly parents unable to take care of themselves took refuge with their married daughters or sons. Few were the old people who resided in old people's homes mostly run by the government and the Church. In time, however, married couples decided on smaller families and consequently, smaller homes and apartments. Furthermore, many married women decided to join the workforce, usually to help pay for house loans. To further compound matters, life expectancy was becoming longer and longer until we arrived at a situation where families had no space to accommodate their ageing parents as there would be nobody at home to care for them. Therefore the demand for beds in old people's homes multiplied to such an extent that a long waiting list was created.

I visited these homes and what I witnessed was shocking and disconcerting. To ease somewhat the long waiting lists, more beds were installed and this resulted in overcrowding. Furthermore, there existed no segregation between healthy and active inmates, and the bedridden. Some of the inmates were sufferers of Alzheimer's and other mental disorders. These were the very same people who half a century earlier had endured untold hardships and privations during the onslaught of non-stop aerial bombing by the Germans. These were the same people who were awarded the George Cross for their *'heroism and devotion that will long be famous in history'*. Looking at them I felt ashamed. Ashamed to watch them sitting quietly, looking at nothing and waiting patiently for the end.

'Is this their reward for a lifetime of hard work and sacrifices?' I asked myself. 'Is this the gratitude they deserve from my generation?'

Back in my office I couldn't forget the misery I witnessed and I became determined to do my bit to alleviate the suffering. I thought about the empty space that once housed my first concrete factory. The very first piece of land I had bought from my father way back in 1976. It was now surrounded by residential units and I thought that something similar for the elderly wouldn't be amiss in such surroundings. My idea gained momentum and very soon I was designing this new project. I designed three blocks, each accommodating the elderly according to their state of health, thus ensuring segregation. The concept ensured that healthy inmates would have their own small apartment, but spacious enough to entertain members of their families. Each apartment would have a decent sized terrace enjoying a pleasant panorama. The complex would include a spa, a crafts centre, food and beverage outlets, children's play area for visiting families, a specially designed chapel, a large underground car park and a system of a shuttle bus service to the village centre. This was an ideal development which would give the elderly the opportunity to invite their families to their 'new' home rather than having to wait to be picked up for a once weekly release from the claustrophobic atmosphere I had witnessed. We named the development 'Simblija Gardens' to represent the large open spaces around the area and the relaxed atmosphere that the development would offer.

The first development application was submitted to the Planning Authority in 1991. I thought that the Authority would jump at this opportunity of converting a polluting industrial plant in the midst of a residential area into such a pleasant and useful development. But no! To my total disbelief and consternation, all imaginable excuses and reasons were brought up by the Authority not to approve this unique concept for the Maltese islands. One silly – if not tragic – objection was that there was no policy under which our application could be analysed!

'What if you take ten years to draft a policy?' I asked. 'Would I have to wait that long with a dead asset on my lap?'

Another objection put forward was that the development goes against their policy of encouraging married couples to accommodate their elderly parents in their home.

'That would be ideal,' I answered, 'but you don't seem to know what's happening out there. You don't seem to know that many married women are now part of the workforce. So who's to take care of these elderly during the day?'

But, as always, it was like talking to blank walls and I realised that this was the beginning of another long saga to which I shall return in a later chapter.

AX Holdings

12

The Challenging Years

(1994–1996) 42–44 years

These were the three most active years yet, both where business was concerned and my social activities. It was, therefore, a good decision I had taken when reaching forty that I take two holidays each year; otherwise I would have worked myself into the ground.

It was also around this time that I received a jolting shock when Mum was diagnosed as suffering from dementia at the relatively young age of sixty-nine. In later years, this developed into Alzheimer's. Since no one at home knew much about dementia, nobody recognised the early signs. But when Mum started repeating questions that had already been answered and even completely forgetting phrases and actions she was familiar with, we brought in a doctor who did not take long to recognise the symptoms. He even gave her just a year or two to live and we could hardly believe that our seemingly healthy mother would die on us in such a short time.

Dad was simply destroyed. He became a complete recluse, never moving from her side and seeing to all her needs. Contrary to the doctor's prediction, however, Mum lived for another fifteen years, during which time her condition continued to worsen progressively and she passed away on 14th January 2011.

In the meantime, Parliament had passed legislation for the introduction of local councils in all localities in Malta and Gozo. The Nationalist Party, the party in government, had been in favour of local government for years and it was included in its electoral manifesto for the first time in 1981. They were also in favour of political parties presenting their candidates for these elections, while the Labour Party, in opposition, was totally against this as it would extend the polarisation to the localities. So, while the Nationalist Party presented its candidates, the Labour Party encouraged its activists to contest as 'independent' candidates.

I did not care what the political parties wanted to do with the local councils. I was only interested in making Naxxar, my beloved hometown, a better place for the inhabitants. I didn't need any organisation to push me forward. I decided for myself. I, therefore, decided to contest as an independent candidate, even though my political leanings were hardly a state secret.

The people of Naxxar welcomed the news of my decision. They had already seen what I had done through the Environmental Committee and they all knew I could make things happen. I became the talk of the whole village. People talked about me on street corners and shops.

'I remember him with his father after Sunday Mass. He was only this high, then.'

'You should have seen him riding that infernal *karru* (cart) down steep and winding alleys with his friends. He always returned home bruised and bleeding all over and he'd be back on the morrow with a knee or both bandaged.'

'I remember him the first time he brought that beautiful wife to his home to meet his family. And look at him now, what he's become.'

I had become the local boy everybody was proud of. I had become the person who could give something back to the village that turned a boy into a man.

While I was eagerly and openly planning how I could further my good work for my village of origin, other plans were being hatched behind closed doors. Unknown to me, the two major political parties were separately thinking of the best way to pull the rug from under my feet and thereby derail my plans to contest the local council election. It seems that political parties, like fundamental religious groups, think they have the prerogative of knowing what's best for each and every one of us. They probably also assumed that this election would serve as a first stepping stone in my ambition to form a political party to contest the general elections. Both were aware of the popularity I enjoyed in Naxxar, where I was the honorary president of the two rival band clubs and the football club and chairman of the local environmental committee, which I had set up and which was still very active. Finally, I was well known and appreciated for my generosity towards people in need and charitable institutions. So, in order to reduce my chances of becoming mayor, the political parties sought as many of their activists who were deemed popular in the locality to stand as candidates in the hope that I wouldn't garner enough votes. In fact, twenty others applied to contest seven seats. This was three times the national average.

As if this wasn't quite enough, the Nationalist Party initiated a court case to contest my eligibility to vote on the pretext that my residence was outside Naxxar's boundaries. Thanks to what I had learned from my experience in business (that to be successful one had to stay a step ahead of one's rivals), I took the necessary precautions beforehand so that I wouldn't be caught on the wrong foot. I had studied the local council legislation quite well and immediately changed the address on my identity card well before the time allowed for objectors to file their complaints.

What really baffled me, however, was the war declared on me by the party I supported. My family had a long tradition of support for the Nationalist Party and nobody should have had any doubts about my loyalty. I couldn't understand this persecution from the party I had supported throughout my life, so I decided to seek an appointment with Prime Minister Fenech Adami at his residence. I explained to him my dilemma. I tried to show him that I had no hidden political agenda, and that all I wanted was to do the best for my locality and its inhabitants.

'I don't know why my own party's doing this to me, Prime

Minister. I'm sure your intention in enacting this legislation was for the benefit of the localities and I know I can do a lot of good if elected. This court action against me is superfluous because I'm going to win the case even though I'm small fry compared to the Nationalist Party. It'll be a repeat of David and Goliath.'

The Prime Minister shook his head and told me that that's not what his advisors were telling him.

'Some advisors,' I said to myself. 'I hope he won't have the same advisors for the next general elections.'

The meeting with the Prime Minister made me more adamant and I left more determined to win this landmark court case, more so in order to prove the 'advisors' incompetent.

I immediately addressed a formal objection to the Chief Electoral Commissioner against the Nationalist Party's contestation. Ironically, this tiff with 'my' party favoured the Labour party, which reasoned that an enemy of its enemy was its friend. The Labour Party hierarchy, therefore, refrained from creating further obstacles to my candidature and started showing sympathy for my case against the Nationalist Party. This served to further convince the Nationalist Party of my ulterior motives, but it wasn't I who created this problem. I had others issues to contend with and solve – the first one being when I was summoned to present my case to the Electoral Commission.

The commission was composed of four representatives from each of the two main political parties and a chairman appointed by the government. When I entered the boardroom, however, I noticed that one of the Nationalist Party representatives was absent, which I hoped would work in my favour. I presented my case and when the vote was taken, Labour voted in my favour and the Nationalists against. The chairman then intervened and said that the law gave him the power to vote and, as expected, he voted against me. So it was a tie.

The chairman didn't seem at all happy with the result and, for a few seconds, he lost his composure. Pulling himself together, he stood up, said something about consulting some legal advisor and left the room. When he returned he seemed his old confident self again.

'Well, gentlemen,' he said as soon as he sat down. 'The law states that in cases of a tie, I, as chairman, have the right of a casting vote.'

I couldn't believe my ears. It meant that the chairman could vote twice. And so he did – against me, of course.

I left the room completely disgusted at the manoeuvrings in a supposedly democratic country, and decided there and then to file a court case. Maltese courts are not exactly renowned for jumping the gun, with court cases often taking forever, but, in my case, I had less than three weeks to wait.

The media weren't heavy footed, and soon I was headline news. Since I had changed the address on my identity card to that of my office situated within the boundary of Naxxar, and since I didn't want to take any chances with inquisitive journalists, I converted my office staff canteen into a small apartment where I could spend my nights until the local council election saga was over. The office cleaner had an extra chore each morning to clean my 'apartment'.

This whole thing took place during the cold of winter and it was hard for me to spend my nights away from my family, even though the 'apartment' was fairly comfortable. It was harder still after some dinner or reception, which always lasted till well after midnight, to drop my wife home and drive to the office to try and catch a few hours of sleep. My short nights, however, were regularly being interrupted by anonymous phone calls. Every time I would lift the receiver and say hello, the coward at the other end would hang up. I had a good guess where the calls were originating and the reason behind them and, although I couldn't care less, they still spoilt my few hours of sleep because I still stuck to my old routine of always waking up at five o'clock. Then I would drive home, take a quick shower and breakfast with my family, and rush off again to take my place behind my desk promptly at the office at seven thirty sharp, this time as chairman of the group. I was practically spending twenty-four hours in my office building.

Some people, however, seemed to want to have it their own way by hook or by crook. The Secretary General of the Nationalist Party, a lawyer by profession, is not renowned for his subtlety and his comments, as reported by the media at the time, couldn't have been less subtle. He said that he could never believe that a big businessman like Angelo Xuereb was giving up the comfort of his villa to spend his nights in his office. At first I took this comment very badly because my whole family was making a big sacrifice to enable me to comply with the law. But after some consideration, I decided to dismiss the Secretary General's comments as indicative of first sign of panic in a person used to having everything his own way. Luckily for me, but not for him, my rough and non-cosseted upbringing, together with two decades of tough confrontations under my belt, stood me in good stead for the trials that loomed ahead.

When the court hearing arrived, I recognised the presiding magistrate as a former legal advisor to the Nationalist Party. This didn't augur well for me. I was also concerned about the fact that Jessie had to give evidence; she was extremely jittery as it was her first ever visit to this imposing edifice. As a witness, she had to remain outside the courtroom until summoned, in a totally alien atmosphere, surrounded by gossiping members of the media (my case had made headline news and was a talking point in prominent features in all the media) and a crowd of a mixture of Nationalist Party hangers-on and a group of unsavoury court regulars. While waiting anxiously for her name to be called, she had to listen to the gossip and innuendo based on downright lies designed to test her love and loyalty to me.

As she walked slowly towards the witness box, I could tell from her expression that she was making an effort to talk. And the way the magistrate put his first question didn't help to put her at ease.

'Is it true, Mrs Xuereb, that your husband is sleeping in his office?'

'Yes,' she answered in a tremulous voice.

The magistrate didn't bother to put further questions to her. 'I don't believe you're telling the truth.' And he decided the case against me.

I had never before heard of a court hearing that was decided during the first sitting, and so abruptly.

Upon leaving the court and being reunited with Jessie, I was shocked to hear about the way she had been treated and spoken to whilst waiting to give evidence. In court I had been protected, but it was Jessie who had been subjected to the vilest of lies and mischief making. Those people who had done such things had evaporated into thin air as soon as the case was over, so Jessie was unable to identify them. They were probably trying to tempt me into retaliating, which would have excluded me from standing for the council. Having experienced this unfair hearing of my case at the Magistrates Court, I then decided to open an appeal in the High Court.

Chief Justice Prof. Giuseppe Mifsud Bonnici, flanked by two other judges, began listening to the arguments from both sides in the case. A rare sight in court this time was the participation of the Secretary General of the Nationalist Party himself. In fact, he was leading a team of three lawyers for the Nationalist Party. After the first hearing everybody expected a decision three weeks before the elections at the latest. But, surprisingly, the court decided to leave the decision till just one week before polling day. This caused a lot of head scratching in government circles. They had two options; they could either postpone all elections in twenty-three localities or print two sets of ballot papers for my locality – one with my name included and another without. They opted for the latter option. It was less expensive.

In the meantime I continued with my election campaign, although officially I was not a candidate. I distributed thousands of leaflets and personalised letters by name to each household in the locality. I spent long hours signing those thousands of letters and by the end I had discovered what writer's cramp meant. All the other candidates were conducting house visits, but I decided against knocking on doors to beg for votes. I considered it an intrusion into the privacy of people's personal lives.

My last election campaign activity consisted of a big event. My friends organised a large party for all the residents of Naxxar in one of the church-owned halls in the centre of the village. This was just eight days before voting and one day before the decision by the Constitutional Court. I couldn't blame my campaign helpers for feeling uncertain and confused because they couldn't foretell what would happen on the morrow. I still wasn't a candidate and it all depended on what would happen during the following day's court sitting.

'What are we to do, Angelo?' they asked a day before the big party. 'What if the court decides against you? It'll be money and effort down the drain and, what's more, you won't be able to face the people.'

'Just carry on with the preparations and don't think about what could happen tomorrow. I'm going to win this case because I'm in the right, and I want you to believe this as well.'

We distributed invitations to all the residents of Naxxar and my friends prepared a number of campaign billboards and a short promotional DVD for screening during the party. As if the past months' court hearings and the major political parties' underhand manoeuvrings were not enough, I came face to face with another problem with catastrophic results if not solved inside minutes. It would have undone me right on the eve of the election.

As usual I went early to the venue of the activity. I had made all the necessary arrangements with the parish priest who gave me his permission to use the large hall at the back of the church. It was generally referred to as the Oratory where most of the parish indoor activities take place, including the teaching of catechism. When I arrived at the place I found the door shut. Some of my friends were already there and we decided to wait for half an hour. Then guests started to arrive and still no one from the church had turned up to open the door. A passerby who happened to be a regular church helper told me that all the parish priests had been given strict instructions by the Archbishop that no political activities could be held inside Church property. This news nearly panicked me. I imagined the hundreds of people who would soon be coming out of side streets to attend this last activity, the climax to my campaign.

'Don't let anyone leave,' I instructed my helpers. 'I'm going to talk to the parish priest.'

I walked hurriedly to the front of the church and entered. To my dismay the parish priest had just started saying Mass to a packed church. I felt the blood drain from my face. By my calculations the Mass would last at least half an hour and it was unthinkable that I walk up to the altar and interrupt the most important liturgical service of the Catholic faith. I had no option but to kick my heels and bite my fingernails in the sacristy.

I cornered the parish priest as soon as he came in and, without letting him remove his liturgical vestments, I asked him the reason for the prohibition when he had already given his permission for the Oratory's use. He repeated what I already knew from the church helper.

'But this has nothing to do with general elections,' I argued. 'This is a local thing and most of your parishioners are already gathering outside the place. What do I tell them? That their parish priest has gone back on his word?'

'Sorry, Angelo, but I have to obey superior orders,' he replied in a subdued voice.

'Yes. I understand all this. But we had a commitment and you know it. You should have told the Archbishop that you had already given your word.'

He shook his head. I could see that he was of two minds. As a priest he was obliged to obey the Archbishop's orders, whatever the consequences. But on the other hand, once he had given his word...

'Look, Angelo, I'm sure you understand my position. I'm a priest first and foremost. So it's not that I don't wish to help in the circumstances. But the use of the Oratory is out of the question.'

I could see that he was thinking about some compromise.

'But I don't think I would be going against the Archbishop's directive if I let you use an open space.'

I heaved a sigh of relief and resisted the temptation to kiss his forehead. I immediately called my friends to transfer everything to this new venue. I also instructed the catering team to start serving right away and the musicians to start playing while all the other equipment was being moved to the alternative venue nearby. Many of the guests gave a helping hand and things got going without further mishaps. Luckily it didn't rain and my speech was received with roaring applause. In the end it was an overwhelming success and this small incident helped to gain me more sympathy with the voters.

The following day, a Saturday, we were in court for the final decision and the hall was packed with lawyers and journalists. Jessie and I stood right in front of the judges and while the Chief Justice was reading his forty-five-minute-long deliberation, it gradually started becoming obvious that he was leading towards a decision in my favour. His concluding paragraphs were a non-stop censure and condemnation of the Nationalist Party's ruthless, unfair and unjust opposition to my candidature.

At the end of this long monologue, Jessie and I couldn't remove the wide smiles dominating our faces. The decision fully vindicated my constitutional rights. But now the Chief Justice was speaking directly to me.

'And now, Mr Xuereb, you don't have to worry any longer. You don't have to sleep in your office any longer. Your place, now, is with your family because you're free to contest the election.'

Jessie and I couldn't believe our ears. Our ordeal was over at last. I always knew I would win the case and was prepared to face whatever sacrifice to make it happen, but the Chief Justice's last sentence sent me over the moon. It was the cherry on the cake. At last I could join my family after those lonely and interrupted wintry nights, and I couldn't hold back my tears. All present stood up as one and exploded in tumultuous applause. Many came over to congratulate me unashamedly in front of the judges, who hadn't yet left the hall. Things took some time to quieten down and, at last, Jessie and I could exit the hall.

As we walked slowly towards the door, one of the Nationalist Party lawyers came over to me and whispered in my ear, 'You're celebrating a week too early, Mr Xuereb. It's not quite over yet. We shall file another case against you.'

Unfortunately for him, he hadn't enough time to carry out his threat. One week was too short and no macho talk was stopping me contesting the election. So, I ignored this legal genius and walked arm in arm with Jessie out of the court building.

A month later, however, I was accused (again by the Nationalist Party) of spending more than the allowable €1,400 on my election campaign (must have been the legal genius at work). It was really sad to see the political party I supported stoop so low and clutch at sodden last straws. The Nationalist Party I knew had always been one to do its homework properly before taking the plunge. What the Party's trio of esteemed lawyers failed to take into consideration was that I had only been a candidate from the moment the Chief Justice declared so. And since then, the only expenses I incurred were my lawyer's fees, which weren't much, considering the licking he gave his 'learned colleagues'.

But I had to admire other people's determination because after this last puerile attempt, the Nationalist Party went one further, as if to be consistent to the last. It requested the court to interdict me. That meant that should I have lost the case, I would not have been able to sign contracts and would also lose the right to vote in all elections. When the case was called, the presiding judge simply dismissed the case and formally instructed his clerk to record in writing that 'the court does not have any time to waste'.

It goes without saying that the people of Naxxar were elated when news reached them of the Constitutional Court decision. On election day, Saturday 22nd January 1994, Dad wanted to be the very first to cast his vote for Angelo Xuereb. He was the first to arrive outside the polling station at five o'clock on that cold morning when voting didn't start until seven o'clock.

When the votes were counted, I polled 40% of the total votes cast – the equivalent of three seats out of the contested seven. The other genuine independents totalled 18% between them, while the remaining candidates representing the political parties had to be content with 42%. When one considers the number of candidates – twenty-one in all – the success I achieved was tremendous. I received one of the highest totals of votes from among the four hundred odd candidates contesting the local elections in Malta and Gozo.

At the first meeting of the council, held less than a month after the election, I was unanimously elected the first Mayor of Naxxar. A week later, the two local band clubs got together to put up a programme of marches along the streets of the locality to celebrate this landmark occasion.

The first council meeting was held at the local council's own office, made available by the government. It wasn't anything much as far as equipment and staff were concerned. In fact, the whole staff consisted of the council Executive Secretary and his assistant together with their desks, another desk for the mayor, a larger table around which the council could conduct its meetings, one computer, two telephones, one fax machine, one calculator and two ballpoint pens. Admittedly, it wasn't much, but it was enough to start us off as a fully-fledged local council.

This first meeting was also characterised by the presence of a large number of locals and members of the media, all eager to witness my election as their first mayor. All these, especially the members of the media, were expecting a word or two from me as mayor after all the media coverage leading up to the election, and I stood up to thank all those present for the support they had given me throughout the ordeal.

'As I promised throughout my campaign, I am committed to turning our locality into a role model for all other local councils.

It is not an easy task and it never will be. We can never be wholly satisfied with what we manage to achieve. Every achievement is a stepping stone to the next as we continually aim to effect improvements in our locality and, thereby, improve the standard of living of its residents. But we, the councillors, must work together as a team. And we can work as a team if we first and foremost keep in mind that we all form part of the locality of Naxxar and, as such, our first loyalty is towards our native village and its people. Political alliances must be put aside when the general good of the locality is at stake, and now that the election campaign is over and done with, we need to sit down around this table and work out how best to work for the people who put their trust in us. So let's not waste time and get down to business right away. I suggest that for the first few months the council meets regularly every week.'

I gave an example of not wasting time and immediately prepared an action plan to present at the next meeting. I divided the locality into thirteen areas, each administered by a sub-committee led by a chairperson appointed by the council. Each area would be allocated funds in proportion to the number of residents. Each sub-committee would have separate meetings with the council every month, during which it would present and discuss a progress report.

Early into my tenure as mayor, just a month after my appointment, I had my first problem with the staff. Two incidents involving the secretary led to his dismissal. The first one involved an elderly lady. Unbeknown to me, the secretary had set his own office hours during which he would be available to the public. He had decided that his office would open for three hours only, ending at ten thirty in the morning. This elderly lady happened to arrive at the council office just five minutes late and the secretary had the gall to send her back, telling her to call on the morrow. The second incident started when a cabinet minister asked to pay us a formal visit. This was to be the first by a cabinet minister and we were not yet stocked with drinks for such occasions. So, I asked the secretary to buy a bottle of whisky. All well and good! A week later, however, when another cabinet minister wanted to visit us, I offered him a drink and found an empty cocktail cabinet. The secretary had downed the whisky himself in just a week. This humiliating experience left me with no option but to dismiss him on the spot.

Shortly afterwards I recruited two secretaries, but they could not cope with my regimen and they left soon after. Then a godsend appeared in the person of Noel Toledo. He called on me one day to tell me he was interested in the post of Executive Secretary.

'I have been observing you going about your duties as mayor these past three months and I was intrigued,' he told me. 'I have been taking note of the progress so far and I can see you're a man of vision by the way you've managed to make your council look ahead. The way you divided Naxxar into different areas was a good idea and makes for more progress. I can tell because I have been regularly doing the rounds and noting the progress week by week. I would like to work for a man like you and I feel confident I would give my fair share should you accept me.'

'That's great because I need a really committed person to do the job,' I answered. 'I'll take you on, but on one condition; you must be prepared to work long hours. If you do, you'll be part of a winning team.'

He took the job and his contribution was instrumental for the local council to gain the reputation of being the best among the sixty-seven around Malta and Gozo. This was further confirmed during the first College of Mayors' Assembly when a small group of 'colleagues' came up to me.

'Did you know, Angelo, that you're creating one heap of a problem for us?' one of them told me.

'Me? Creating problems for you?'

'That's right. You're making your council work too hard and now the people in our localities are complaining that we're not doing enough for them. They're telling us that we should take a look at Naxxar and at the improvements that have already taken place.'

I was relieved that this was all the trouble I was causing.

'The people don't realise that it's because you're forking money out of your own pocket,' the other continued.

So that was it. They thought I was using my own money to make things happen.

'You've got it all wrong,' I answered. 'I'm not paying for anything that's happening at Naxxar. The difference between us is that I enjoy improving infrastructure and don't need to appoint architects and consultants to slow me down through long bureaucratic procedures, which sometimes cost more than the actual works.'

The council worked very hard during the first year. The councillors and sub-committees soon got used to my way of getting things done and they gave their full share. Our work wasn't only appreciated by the residents, but by the Government as well when it awarded us the prize for the best kept locality.

I took my responsibilities as mayor very seriously. Every morning at seven o'clock, before going to my own office, I would do the rounds of all the on-going works around Naxxar. I was also committed to continual improvement, which is how I came to propose the removal of a dangerous central strip along a main road during a routine council meeting. Although the proposal was vehemently opposed by two councillors, it was approved by the majority, but this wasn't to be the end of the matter.

In the meantime, I had to leave for a business trip to the Middle East. Between the many business engagements on my agenda, I was due to make a short trip to Bahrain to meet with a Sheikh I had befriended during a cruise. Midway through a meeting, however, I was summoned to answer an urgent call from Malta. It was Noel Toledo who told me in a flustered voice that the two councillors who had objected to the removal of the central strip had called an extraordinary meeting to pass a motion that would cancel the decision already taken.

'But how could they, Noel, when I'm not able to attend?'

'Yes, they can, Mr Xuereb. And the meeting has been called for the day after tomorrow.'

'For such a minor thing?'

'Yes, Mr Xuereb. Even for such a minor thing.'

I nearly laughed at the incongruity of the situation. On the other hand, I was angry that these two councillors acted so deviously while I was abroad. I couldn't let anybody drive a wedge that could cause divisiveness among the council members.

'Okay, Noel,' I said after some thought. 'Thanks for alerting me. I'll be there to chair the meeting myself. But keep it to yourself. I enjoy giving pleasant surprises.'

Noel laughed and hung up. I then called the Sheikh to inform him that I had been called back home for an urgent meeting and apologised for cancelling my meeting with him.

On the day of the meeting, I went to the council offices earlier than usual and took my place at the council table. I had to do my utmost to repress a smile when I saw the looks of surprise on the faces of the councillors as they entered the room. Inevitably, the motion was defeated and my action proved to them that I meant business and wasn't so easily fooled. The two councillors who had moved the motion apologised and we were back in business. I continued to introduce various innovative ideas in the locality and every resident started feeling proud of forming part of the community of Naxxar.

As my tenure as mayor progressed, I had to deal with a rather delicate situation involving Prof. Guido Demarco, then Minister for Justice with responsibilities for the police force. He was also Deputy Prime Minister and had recently moved his residence to a new area in Naxxar. Prof. Demarco was the same lawyer who nicknamed me Testaferrata and we both had great respect for one another.

The matter started during a routine council meeting when a councillor brought a new case to my attention. He informed me that a resident had planted trees right in the middle of the narrow pavement in front of his villa, thus making it difficult for people to squeeze their way past and impossible for anybody with a wheelchair, pram or pushchair. I thanked the councillor for bringing up the matter and told the secretary to write to the offender to instruct him to remove the trees forthwith.

The councillor who supplied the information smiled and said, 'This is a rather hot potato, Mr Mayor.'

'What do you mean a hot potato?' I asked.

The councillor was still smiling rather mischievously. 'The thing is that this particular resident won't remove his trees unless Minister Demarco removes his.'

This was something I knew nothing about and I could see that the councillor was enjoying the situation, thinking that I would waver and somehow find some compromise whereby the minister would be able to keep his trees.

'So?' I said. 'So, instead of one letter the secretary will write two.'

The councillors shook their heads in unison.

'Easier said than done, Mr Mayor,' said one of them.

'Do you think so?' I said. 'What's so special about a minister after all? Isn't he a citizen like everybody else? And isn't he also a member of our community? So, he should be treated as such.'

All the councillors kept staring at me with their mouths wide open and their minds full of doubts, wondering whether I would succeed in my actions against such a powerful, intelligent and popular minister.

The following weekend I happened to be at a reception to which the minister's family was also invited. At one point, the whole family group, minus the minister, came over to where I was standing and spent half an hour trying to persuade me that I could not treat Prof. Demarco as a common citizen. I told them that I was sorry to have to take such a decision and I did my best to make them see reason and at last, when I couldn't make headway, I gave them an ultimatum that if the trees were not removed in a week's time, the council would do it instead. We agreed to disagree and left. The trees were still there a week later, but only until seven o'clock the next morning when the council had them uprooted and the pavement restored. As expected, members of the minister's family called me in the morning, irritated by the council's action. I patiently explained that I had written to them and warned them that as mayor of the locality I could not treat one citizen differently from others. This would amount to discrimination which, I'm sure, the minister would hardly condone.

'As you know, I have great respect for the minister and for his immense contribution to the wellbeing of our people. I'm sure he'll continue to work as hard as ever for the benefit of our country. But I also have duties to carry out as mayor for the benefit of the people of Naxxar.'

Prof. Demarco knew well through personal experience how determined I could be when I know I'm in the right, and he was mature and intelligent enough never to call me about the incident or mention it on the many occasions we had the pleasure to meet. Thanks to this action, the other resident immediately followed suit and replanted the trees in his garden.

It took me just a few months as mayor to learn first-hand how government departments tie themselves up in red tape so tightly and efficiently, while cutting themselves free, Houdini-style, when pressure is put upon them. A typical example, early in my tenure, was the Works Department's non-response to my council's request to repair the main sewage pumping station, which was causing an unbearable stench for the residents in the area, not to mention the potential health hazard. When weeks dragged on and the department failed to act, I organised a protest march around the streets in the vicinity of the pumping station. I, as mayor, and carrying a placard, marched in the front row of a fairly large procession of residents, all with our mouths and nostrils covered. Happily, though belatedly, the damage was seen to soon after. I also organised competitions among the residents for the best decorated house façades, balconies, trees, alleys, streets and the rest, all carrying prizes consisting of sponsored holiday trips and other attractive awards. The residents responded with enthusiasm and supported them with pride.

Dad was my biggest fan and the proudest person in Naxxar. He wouldn't stop boasting about my achievements with whoever he would meet, even complete strangers, sometimes to my embarrassment. As I said earlier, he wouldn't miss the evening news in the hope that I would be featured or mentioned so that he would have more to boast about the next morning. Being a mayor and a businessman among other things increased my appearances on TV, which regularly covered conferences and discussion programmes in which I took part. So, Dad was never short of topics to talk about with his cronies. His pride would inflate further every time some friend would accost him with, 'Bert, I saw your son, Anġlu, on TV last night.'

Although I was enjoying the success of my tenure and separate business enterprises, my days had become too short. I could have done with a thirty-hour day as my duties as mayor, my activities in various entities and my business were keeping me busy every minute of the twenty-four hours available. I had always had a good memory, but with the many daily meetings I had to attend, the countless telephone calls and the many unexpected and unwelcome problems that cropped up regularly, I was left with very little time to stop and do some thinking. It was only while relaxing at home in the evening and during weekends, or when driving, that I had the luxury of thinking and planning. The problem was that by the next morning it would take me some time to recall a few of the many thoughts of the night before. It became very frustrating until I came across a small voice recorder that fitted snuggly in my pocket. I soon made very good use of it because every time I had a new idea I immediately recorded it no matter where I happened to be. I now record thoughts and simple messages even while shaving, breakfasting, watching TV and during dinners. Sunday Mass was sometimes inspirational, especially during an occasionally long homily during which only the monotonous voice is heard droning. At the end of Mass I would record my thoughts as soon as I was out of the front door and before people started stopping their mayor in his tracks with their many simple requests. Then, on Monday, I would hand over the recorder to my secretary who would transcribe and type everything, word for word. This helped me take whatever action was necessary in the shortest time possible. The recorder became so much a part of my set-up that I would prefer to be without my wallet than without it.

Business was flourishing and I was contributing about 1% of the country's National Gross Domestic Product (GDP) with direct employment of around 1,000, and this not counting the numerous sub-contractors and service providers I very often employed. With this success firmly established, I shifted my attention towards overseas investment; Albania, just out of the Stalinist dictatorship of Enver Hoxha, seemed the most suitable source to tap. On my first visit I was introduced to the country's first democratically elected president Sali Berisha. He allowed me and my economist consultant, Prof. Edward Scicluna (later to become a member of the European Parliament), the use of the only helicopter in the country, which was restricted for his personal use. We wanted to view the country from the air to allow us to take a good look at Butrinti, near Saranda, which I had already identified as a possible site for a large tourist development. We took the opportunity to tour the whole country and took various pictures of other potential locations. In the end, however, we confirmed our initial choice, because Butrinti was very close to a beautiful and important archaeological site, which included a safe harbour built by the Romans. The place was surrounded by very picturesque terrain and a narrow river fed by eight natural springs up a neighbouring mountain, encouraging some of the richest flora and fauna in the country to flourish.

During the flight, when at a short distance from Korca, I asked the pilot whether we could make a brief stop in the village where a small Maltese community had established itself, with the aim of giving an adequate education to the poor children of this mountain settlement. The pilot was happy to oblige and in ten minutes, we could see the few thousand villagers and their children hurrying towards the landing spot to get a close look at this rare mechanical contraption falling from the sky. A police car could be seen making its way from behind a cluster of buildings and speeding towards the general direction of the populace, probably because its occupants thought that their president was honouring the place with a surprise visit. Realising that the people below were expecting someone important to emerge from the hovering machine, I hastily put on my tie and jacket prior to my cramped disembarkation. We explained the scope of our visit to the surprised police who, somewhat relieved that they didn't have to stand stiffly to attention, gave us a lift in their car. I then knocked on the door of the Maltese compound, which was opened by my old friend Charles from my village. He was so surprised that he stood there, gaping in front of me, still with his hand on the door knob, probably wondering whether working too hard at such high altitudes was causing hallucinations.

To further add to his confusion, I put on the most serious expression I could muster and in a pompous, 'mayoral' voice, I said, 'Charles, I, as Mayor of Naxxar, have been entrusted by the local council which I lead, and the people of the locality which I represent, and on behalf of same, as entrusted by same on their behalf, do hereby by special delivery using the Republic of Albania's official helicopter, consign to you this package from Malta.'

For a few long moments it looked as if he believed what I had just said. But I couldn't keep a straight face any longer and burst out laughing. A wide smile relaxed his face and he pulled us in for some coffee. I went on to update him on the goings on in Malta while he recounted his experiences among the poor people of the village. Then, we left him for a scheduled meeting with President Sali Berisha and his minister responsible for tourism to discuss the way forward.

I left Albania with a clearer idea about the country's tourism potential to return two weeks later accompanied by the renowned

British architect David Walton, and David Camilleri, a structural engineer from my own group. This time we made it by ferry from Corfu and our arrival in Albania was greeted by an interpreter appointed by the government to accompany us throughout and smooth our way through the primitive bureaucratic practice still prevailing. Our interpreter was Dolores Dhima, an Albanian with an excellent command of English. She and her husband Michael taught the language to Albanians and were both well versed in their country's history. She loved her country and was staunchly patriotic.

Entry visa procedures were very strict, though less so than during the Communist era. As soon as we berthed at Saranda we were directed to Customs and Immigration Control to have our passports stamped. The office was nothing more than a small shed on a slope a hundred metres away, overlooking Saranda Bay. The winter evening was extremely cold and our entry into the hut must have awoken the solitary duty officer who was sitting comfortably in an armchair with his legs stretched close to an electrical heater, which had its elements completely and dangerously exposed. Even the electrical connections, including that leading to the power point, were exposed and I thought that should the sleepy officer accidentally trip he would end up fried in a split second.

Following some routine questions, translated for us by Dolores, the officer stamped an entry visa on a small piece of brown paper, very much resembling recycled toilet paper. David Walton couldn't help bursting out laughing as soon as we were safely out of earshot outside the shed.

It was a short drive to our hotel, the only one in the area, classified as a five-star. But it wouldn't have made it to one star in any other country. There were no blankets in our bedrooms. There was only a thin, stuffy, bed cover under which we were expected to get a good night's rest. There was no way I could stay warm with the ice cold wind blowing through the flaps of the door leading to the balcony and the bathroom window, which was determined to remain open no matter how hard I tried to slam it shut. Unfortunately, we were not prepared for such extreme weather conditions and there was no warm water in the shower, so I thought to, at least, wipe my body clean with a wet towel. As soon as I opened the tap of the wash basin, my legs froze. I looked under the basin. It had no drain connection and the icy water splashed all over my legs and feet. Nevertheless, I managed, somehow, to wipe my body clean.

The temperature must have gone down to sub-zero during the night as I could see snow close to the hotel when I looked out of the balcony. No wonder I had to wear two pairs of woollen socks, two pairs of trousers and wrap myself in my thick coat to stay relatively warm under the flimsy bed cover. The next morning, I learned that my colleagues had done the same and the three of us woke up checking whether any toes had fallen off during the night. It was the coldest night of my entire life.

The evening before, on our arrival, we had dinner at the hotel. Only hunger and the sheer cold forced us to eat the inedible food on our plates. The meat was so heavily spiced that we couldn't tell what it was. To help wash down the non-chewable lumps of meat, we decided to order a bottle of wine from the list in front of us. Every item on the list I indicated was received by the waiter with a shake of his head and a repetitive, 'Sorry, but we don't have'. He kept doing his best to look and sound like as a waiter in a five-star hotel. He was even wearing dark trousers, white shirt and a flimsy bow tie, standing stiffly at my elbow, patiently waiting for my finger to exhaust the long list of wines so that he could escape to the warmth of the kitchen.

'Okay,' I said when I was through the wine list. 'Can you bring us a bottle of whatever wine you have?'

He smiled and sped towards the kitchen. For a moment I expected Basil Fawlty to appear out of nowhere holding his waiter by the scruff of the neck. But it was just wishful thinking because the waiter wasn't from Barcelona and he was walking hurriedly towards us. Proud as a peacock, he presented the label of the bottle for my inspection, although I could not understand what was written in Albanian. At my nod he applied the corkscrew with professional dexterity, but as soon as the cork was released, the wine was so sour that it gushed out like champagne. David and I burst out laughing.

'That's not good,' David tried to explain to the waiter.

'No, no. This good wine. Very best good wine,' he answered. And to further reassure us, he tasted it. 'See? Very good wine.'

But we wouldn't accept it and he had to go back to replace it. He returned with the same bottle after having forced the cork back in place, and he went through the motions of struggling with the corkscrew. We tasted it just to make sure and it was horrible, just like harsh vinegar. The waiter couldn't understand what was wrong with the wine. According to him, the liquid had the colour of wine. So it must be wine!

The next day we made a tour of the coastal area, which further confirmed Butrinti's ideal location. Back in Butrinti, we expressed our desire to visit the archaeological remains preserved behind a high wall all around. It seemed that Dolores was held in high esteem by everyone because the gate was instantly opened by the watchman manning it and she gave us a thorough guided tour of the place. She explained how only 10% of the site was exposed, a result of a strong earthquake a long time ago, which covered the area with debris. This was further compounded by large trees, which had taken root many years ago.

Later, we hired a small rowing boat for an hour's tour of a vast and beautiful lake, which fed a natural canal delivering fresh water into the Ionian Sea. We noticed that the owner of the boat, who was rowing us around, was casting for fish without bait. At first I was puzzled and impressed by this strong faith in Divine providence. But, when at last I asked him the reason, he explained that since the lake had not been properly exploited, it was teeming with fish. As if to prove his point, he landed a real beauty just fifteen minutes later. Back on shore I asked him how much we owed him.

'Two hundred American dollars,' he answered. And when he saw the astonishment in my face, he added, 'And you can have the fish as well.'

The amount was probably equivalent to what he earned in three or more months. He probably assumed that anybody who wasn't Albanian must be loaded and that $200 was nothing. I didn't argue. I thought that maybe he had a large family to support and the money would be well spent. We then made straight for a hut where a man was serving freshly grilled mussels. I asked whether he would fry our fish and he did so splendidly. It was well cooked and we enjoyed it very much. It couldn't have been otherwise, considering the high price we paid for it, but we laughed all the way to the hotel, boasting that we had eaten the most expensive fish ever.

We had a dinner appointment in the country's capital, Tirana, the following day with the minister responsible for tourism. This entailed a car journey all the way from Saranda in the south to the capital, situated in the northern part of Albania. The roads were narrow and the long drive would take us over a high mountain as tunnels were non-existent. When we were close to the peak, however, we encountered a major problem. The road was snow-bound and the car tyres couldn't find any traction. There was no way we could get through without tyre-chains – amenities unheard of in Albania. Our driver reversed and tried again to no avail. After his second attempt, however, I urged him to try harder, reminding him that we had an urgent appointment to keep. I could see he was scared and I understood the reason. There were no safety barriers at the edge of the road and one mistake could see us hurtling down the steep precipice, so he was reluctant to press the accelerator enough.

'You need to press it all the way down,' I shouted at him. 'Unless you do so the car will go back downhill every time. So you either do it yourself or let me take the wheel. We don't want to be stuck up here all night where no one would find us.'

There were no mobile phones back then, nor a VHF system,

and if the car had broken down we could easily have frozen to death.

It took some time for the driver to understand my reasoning, but at last he built up courage and, with the engine at full revs, we made it to the top of the mountain.

The long drive down was a long sigh of relief and we arrived at our hotel in Tirana at eight o'clock in the evening. The minister and his delegation were already waiting in the dining room, and so I instructed my colleagues to just dump their luggage in their rooms and hurry down as fast as possible. We formed a shabby trio, dressed in winter casual wear for our drive through the mountains. David, the English architect, was the worst off because he hadn't shaved for two days. They followed my instructions to the letter, but when I entered my room, and after placing my luggage in the bedroom, I went into the bathroom to splash some water on my face. As soon as I felt that beautiful hot water cascading through my fingers, however, I said, 'That's it. I'm having a warm shower whatever the consequences.'

Ten minutes later, I was entering the dining room, freshly shaved and dressed in a smart suit. My colleagues looked a miserable couple and from the corner of my eye I could see the smile on my architect's face. With his two-day-old beard, he looked like a chimney sweep.

'Angelo, you really screwed me tonight,' he told me jokingly after the ministerial delegation had left. 'I was dying to freshen up. And when I saw you walking in like some prince charming... My God, I could have killed you.'

Back in Malta, we immediately started discussing the project and making draft concept drawings for a fully-fledged tourist resort containing a number of villas and town houses similar to those at Port Grimaud, opposite St Tropez in the South of France. We had an area of 22 square km to develop and we made it clear from the outset that the project would respect the sensitivity of the archaeological and natural heritage of the whole area. We, therefore, decided to restrict development to outside a very wide

Delivering my speech on our group's 30th anniversary.

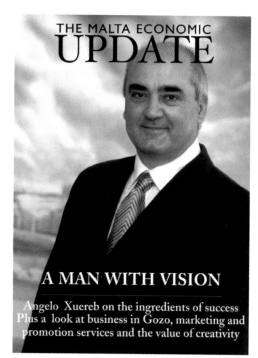

THE MALTA ECONOMIC
UPDATE

A MAN WITH VISION

Angelo Xuereb on the ingredients of success
Plus a look at business in Gozo, marketing and
promotion services and the value of creativity

Front page of *The Malta Economic Update.*

With the President of Malta Dr George Abela.

Some of the Billboards promoting AN's vision.

With my leader of the new political party, Dr Josie Muscat.

At the AX 35th anniversary with Prime Minister Dr Lawrence Gonzi.

A selection of press cuttings.

With Denise in Paris.

With Claire at
The Palace.

With Richard.

Sketching new projects.

With my brother Paul in our quarry.

My family.

Inspecting works in progress with Richard.

With Denise joint project managing in the new Parliament building.

Artist's impression of a section of the new Parliament building.

Yachting against the outstanding backdrop of our capital city, Valletta.

My Aston Martin DB9, the 'beauty and the beast'.

Battling a Ferrari on the circuit.

buffer zone and we spent a long time poring over the hundreds of pictures we had taken of the site to make certain that our master plan would be carefully designed with this in mind while, at the same time, blending beautifully with this pristine part of the country.

A month later, I was in David Walton's London office to see the first draft of the master plan he had prepared. We discussed it and when I suggested a number of changes, he was surprised at my attention to details.

'I never imagined you to be so good at this sort of thing,' he told me. 'I always imagined you as a big developer out to make money.'

'I don't blame you, David. But I've been doing this sort of thing since I was a boy playing in the fields.'

He laughed, thinking I was pulling his leg.

'Don't tell me you were already planning tourist resorts back then.'

'No, David. Not hotels and villas — just small rooms out of rubble stones.'

We both laughed at this.

'Ah, Angelo,' he said at last. 'But this is much, much different from those primitive rooms.'

'Do you think so? We could easily find out, couldn't we? Let me tell you what we'll do. You prepare a revised master plan and I'll prepare another. Then we'll meet in a month's time, compare them and decide which one to adopt.'

I phoned him three months later. 'My plans are ready, David. When can we meet?'

It took him a few seconds to reply. 'Can you send them to me to give them a quick glance over?'

I laughed. 'No, I won't. That wasn't the deal. I want to know what you've come up with.'

We agreed to meet over the weekend at a hotel in Port Grimaud. Jessie accompanied me on this short break and David and I spread our plans on a large table. I let David go over mine, while I took a good look at the revisions he had made to his. It didn't take me long to confirm that he had taken up some of my suggestions. At last he straightened up, rounded the table to where his plans were spread and tore them up into small pieces.

'I concede defeat,' he said at last, standing amid what remained of his painstaking effort. 'Your concept makes more sense. Now, you and your lovely wife can go out to enjoy some sightseeing while I remain locked up in this room to work on your plans. I promise you I won't go out until I have them ready. By tomorrow I shall have applied some cosmetic improvements to your master plan.'

Although he took it all with typical English sporting spirit, I could see that he wasn't exactly euphoric that a renowned architect like himself could be outsmarted by an 'amateur'. The next day we met again and he was in much better spirits. He was extremely pleased with the improvements he had made to my plans, which were the basis on which the final drawings would be prepared. His touches were outstanding and I could well understand the good humour he was in. He based his ideas on those of the famous French architect François Sperry for Port Grimaud. This proved that our approach to our master plan was excellent. Fully satisfied with my positive reaction, he later joined Jessie and me for an enjoyable stroll on the waterfront.

'My dear Jessie,' he said at one point. 'I can't imagine how you manage to put up with this man. You need to have the patience of a saint to live with this man. He always wants to be the best, and in the shortest possible timeframe.'

Over the course of this period, we had to travel to Albania practically every fortnight to make sure that we were adhering to the country's building regulations and that whatever we were planning would respect the environment. But eventually, after nine months of hard work, involving Albanian architects to help translate all our titles and documentation in their language, we prepared a number of brochures, presentation boards and a power-point presentation. We asked the Prime Minister, Alexandër Meksi, whether he would accept a formal presentation to his cabinet.

So, I invited some of the local architects and archaeologists, together with Dolores Dhima and her husband Michael to Malta to help us prepare for this important and detailed presentation.

A few days later, I chartered a ten-seat private jet to fly me and my delegation for a day's visit to Tirana in order to give the two-hour presentation to the Albanian Cabinet of Ministers. The delegation included my architects, financial consultants and Professor Edward Scicluna, and we were determined to show them how we could make a difference to Albania, which was still the poorest country in Europe, just out of decades of extreme Communist rule under the dictator Enver Hoxha. He had managed to completely isolate his beautiful, mountainous country from the rest of the world. In fact, he was so obsessed with making the country inaccessible to foreigners for fear of an armed invasion that detailed maps of Albania were impossible to obtain from outside its borders.

It was a beautiful, clear day and when approaching Albania, the pilot tried many times – always unsuccessfully – to contact the air control tower for clearance to land. Since I had a previous opportunity to fly over the whole country by helicopter, I knew the whereabouts of the airport, and when it became apparent that no response would be forthcoming from below, I had to direct the pilot to the airport and its short runway.

After we landed safely, with a collective sigh of relief, we were informed by the stern-faced security officers that landing in Albania required clearance from the control tower at least forty-eight hours beforehand. We then realised that we had landed ourselves into a difficult situation. We could see from the way they looked at us, and the way they formed a semi-circle around us, that they suspected us of being spies (I wouldn't imagine that they considered us as illegal immigrants) and wholesale arrests seemed a high possibility. Thankfully, at the eleventh hour, a government car sped towards us and out jumped one of the President's officials. He shook us all by the hand and welcomed us to Albania. Then he explained to the security officials that we were the honoured guests of the Prime Minister and led us into the terminal where he asked us to fill in an application for permission to land (but dating it two days previously). That got us and the people responsible for the control tower out of trouble. One couldn't blame the reaction of the security officers at our arrival; at the time, very few commercial planes ever landed at their old airport, let alone a private jet.

Jessie formed part of the delegation and when, while walking outside the air terminal, she saw a number of children begging from every passer-by, she gave them some American dollars. She immediately realised her mistake because the children started fighting over the dollar bills, which ended up torn and worthless. One particular small boy came over to where she stood, crying his heart out and holding up half of a one-dollar bill. She took pity on him and surreptitiously gave him some more money to take home to his poor family.

Taking a taxi from the airport to the conference hall, where we were scheduled to give our presentation, we had another interesting and unforgettable experience. The driver took a roundabout route over rough roads and along narrow side streets, intent on avoiding as much as possible the main thoroughfares. We later learned that taxi drivers who failed to pay their car's licence took these longer routes on purpose in order to avoid detection by the police and a resulting hefty fine – such was the situation in Albania shortly after its liberation from the iron-fisted Communist rule.

We were welcomed on our arrival outside the conference hall by the Prime Minister and numerous TV cameramen and photographers. We went on to give an excellent power-point presentation of our concept and every one of my consultants gave his input. The indispensable Dolores Dhima gave a simultaneous translation throughout the two hours. When it was over, we paid a courtesy visit to President Sali Berisha, who hosted us to an excellent lunch in the beautiful ambience of his palace. During lunch, we had the opportunity of watching the news on TV; our meeting with the Prime Minister and presentation to his cabinet was the first item covered. Later, we made our way to the airport, satisfied with the outcome of the day's work.

We followed this up with several other meetings with various Albanian Government departments, all of which practiced a complicated bureaucracy to the limit. Finally, we signed a preliminary agreement for the lease of the site for ninety-nine years. As soon as we signed, we were asked to deposit the first year's rent, which amounted to the equivalent of $300,000 before we could proceed any further. This we did before the week was out, but since the government officials we had to deal with were not used to processing building applications for such huge projects – their only experience being mainly with small residential developments – they created many problems for us, resulting in unnecessary delays and frequent shuttling between the two countries.

At last we could see the light at the end of the tunnel. All problems had been solved and a date was fixed for the signing of the final version of the contract. However, other, more dramatic events were taking place in Albania. During the long months of our constant travelling to Albania and back, trying to find ways around the country's bureaucratic practices, the effects of a countrywide scam were being felt by the poor populace. Unscrupulous foreigners from the West had introduced a pyramid scheme whereby all those joining it were supposed to become rich overnight. The people were promised a 10% cash return per month on all the capital invested. The people of Albania had, for decades, no contact whatsoever with the outside world. They were as naïve as small children where money matters were concerned. All they knew was that they were very poor while anyone coming from the West was filthy rich. They probably thought, or were made to believe, that people from Western countries made big money through pyramid schemes like the one introduced in their country. People started selling all their assets to raise as much cash as possible to put into the scheme. Those who joined it at the very beginning, and who had received the monthly interest, were over the moon and started selling whatever was left to further increase their capital investment. Farmers sold their animals, others sold family heirlooms and millions poured into the pockets of the foreign conmen.

Even Dolores was duped and expressed surprising enthusiasm about the project. 'I know for certain, Angelo, about people who are already receiving large sums of money which they're putting back in the scheme so that they will receive more every month. Isn't it a good thing to receive 10% each month on what you put in?'

I shook my head. 'I'm not convinced, Dolores. Money isn't come by so easily. The whole thing stinks. No clean business yields 10% per month. Something is definitely wrong about it.'

'But people are becoming rich overnight. How can you say that the system is flawed when people are already receiving monthly returns on their capital? They're so satisfied that they're putting it practically all back so that the next month they'll get more. They can watch foreign TV channels now, and they are able to see for themselves people, who they suppose, have become rich in this manner.'

As much as she respected me and believed in my judgment, she couldn't believe that the scheme was a scam and, two months later, the bubble burst. The scheme failed and millions became destitute. People took to rioting in the streets. They burned houses, factories and even government buildings. The Government fell and new elections saw another party taking power.

Much to my sorrow, this led me to abandon the project. The country wasn't yet ready for such a development. It was only five years later, and after countless requests to the Albanian authorities, that I was refunded my rent deposit. It was a hard decision to make after all the time and energy I had spent to turn out a feasible project and then see everything run down the drain. But the episode taught me a bitter lesson, and I used the experience to face the next projects with more determination and caution.

Other opportunities to invest overseas presented themselves, among them in Palestine, and I was soon meeting with President

Arafat to explain our plans to develop a complex of 1,100 housing units. The meeting, which took place in his office, lasted twenty minutes. We even had the backing of the International Finance Corporation (IFC). But when the war with Israel resumed I thought it would be too risky to invest in so volatile an area and I abandoned my plans for this project.

In November 1994, back in Malta, I submitted a tender for the purchase of a government-owned hotel. This hotel had been nationalised by the Socialist administration during the Mintoff era. When the Nationalist Party took over in 1987 it found itself lumped with a white elephant of extreme proportions. This was just one of many Socialist actions to take over large properties that the new government could ill afford the necessary funds to refurbish. There was a whole herd of white elephants requiring the urgent attention of the vet, with the consequence that the hotel was left to rot for years.

The Grand Hotel Verdala was, in its heyday, one of Malta's finest five-stars, commanding one of the most beautiful panoramas overlooking two-thirds of the whole island. When the Socialists had taken it over, tens of diehard supporters were recruited and given positions for which they were ill suited, with the consequence that the five-star tag became a misnomer. To add insult to injury, the Socialist blue-eyed boys were paid the highest salaries, out of the taxpayers' pockets. In 1987, the Nationalists realised that they couldn't flog a dead horse and immediately took action to offload it at the earliest. But every time investors came forward they were immediately put off by the fact that they would be obliged to retain the inefficient staff 'running' the hotel. Nobody was mad enough to go for a thing that guaranteed a loss. To entice investors, the government had even prepared a prospectus, which included the promise that it would help the buyer acquire the adjacent public-owned land to develop into an eighteen-hole golf course with the possibility that it could be expanded into a twenty-seven-hole.

The government issued a tender for the lease of the hotel and my group submitted two offers: one, on a fifty-year leasehold and another for a freehold property. Naturally, the freehold offer was much higher. In fact, when the government realised the potential loss in revenue if it pursued a leasehold title, it reissued the tender on a freehold basis as we had proposed. We were disappointed about this move after divulging our offer to prospective bidders and, because of the burden of the large number of politically appointed hotel staff, there were only three offers. To prove that our previous offer was correct and advantageous, we submitted the same sum again. The purposely appointed adjudicating team had decided that our offer was still the most advantageous and asked us to proceed with the discussion on the details.

During my negotiations with the government over details, I made it amply clear that I was taking over the property on a freehold title without any burdens or service rights with the exception of the responsibility for the welfare of the employees. When asked how I intended to develop the hotel, I said that my plans were to build a five-star hotel with adjacent apartments intended for sale. The government, however, wanted my assurances that the shedding of employees wouldn't take immediate effect, as a general election was looming and the ruling party couldn't afford to lose votes and, to be certain about my intentions, suggested a clause in the contract that I would retain a hotel complex of at least a four-star standard. I accepted this on condition that it would not deprive me of my rights as a freehold owner without any burdens except those of the employees. On this commitment, the government-appointed committee, which included two high officials from the Planning Authority, promised it would make sure that my building permit application would be processed in less than three months.

Just two weeks after signing the preliminary agreement, we submitted an application for permission for the necessary works, put the staff on an intensive training programme related to their duties, engaged a new general manager, a marketing team and interior designers and negotiated a 20% partnership with

Intercontinental Hotels and Resorts. The agreement included a management contract.

As I had intended to make the new hotel a major local player in the conference and incentive segment of tourism, I didn't waste time in agreeing on a financing package with a local bank. I also prepared five different sample rooms and a high-quality marketing brochure. And since the government had declared itself positively on an adjacent golf course, I submitted a separate application for an initial eighteen-hole course.

It is said that man proposes and God disposes. In this particular case, the saying should change to 'the government proposes and a bureaucrat disposes'. The government-appointed negotiating committee had promised me that the processing of my application would take less than three months. Unfortunately, the 'authority' benignly bestowed on the Planning Authority was so total that the government's wishes could be completely ignored, shunned and forgotten. The people who controlled it were in a position to not only delay or hasten an application according to whims, but also to hinder government projects without anybody able to lift a finger. It was the same in my case. Some people in the authority, either through jealousy or sheer spite, managed to hold back my application for months on end, thus hindering me from starting any works. When six months had elapsed without a permit being issued, I wrote to the minister responsible who promised 'to try' to expedite matters. I was really anxious and very worried because I was incurring huge daily expenses, not to mention the embarrassment caused with Intercontinental Hotels, banks and tour operators.

Three months later, I wrote to the Prime Minister whose reply said a lot without saying anything – typical of a politician. Two years passed and still I had no permit, and was left with no option but to release Intercontinental Hotels from the agreement.

In 1996 we had a change of government, with Dr Alfred Sant as Prime Minister of a new Labour administration. Dr Sant was a Harvard man and supportive of private initiative – the complete opposite of the two Labour Prime Ministers before him. I requested and was accorded a meeting with him in less than one week, during which I told him about the Verdala Hotel saga and my dilemma caused by the Planning Authority's delaying tactics. I told him about the group that was lobbying against the development of a golf course and that I could live with the fact that this would delay its development permission. But, the least I would have expected was that the hotel application would be processed because I was incurring huge, unnecessary costs. Dr Sant listened attentively and, at the end, promised that he would personally see that the application would be processed without further delays. I was happy and much relieved with the outcome of this meeting. I was now certain that the Prime Minister's prodding would force the Planning Authority into action and the early issue of the permit was now a foregone conclusion.

We shut down the hotel, transferred all staff to my other hotels for hands-on experience, stripped down all fittings and removed all the furniture, most of which went to charitable institutions. The Planning Authority's go ahead was now just a formality.

Eighteen months later, however, I was still without a permit and a further four months later the government fell when Dom Mintoff, now a backbencher and in direct confrontation with Dr Sant, voted with the opposition. A few weeks later, we had a government led again by Dr Eddie Fenech Adami.

My case, however, could wait no longer and I requested a meeting with the Prime Minister, during which he promised he would take action to expedite matters. It was clear that the Planning Authority was totally against the golf course whatever any minister or Prime Minister might say, and was out to make it as difficult as possible for me. In fact, during the application's processing, I was asked to submit ninety-six reports, all accompanied by voluminous back-up documentation prepared by golf experts of international renown. All these professional consultants had to be verified and approved by the Planning Authority and paid by us. In fact, some of them I never met or had any contact with other than to pay their fees.

The full report by these independent English golf consultants concluded with the words, 'Considering all aspects, there are more positive impacts than negative impacts' in the project and that the application should be 'favourably considered'.

But the Planning Authority didn't like these conclusions. It objected vehemently to the words 'favourably considered' and demanded their deletion. The experts who had written the reports were understandably offended by the authority's arrogance and flatly refused to remove one single comma from the report, arguing that it wouldn't make sense to commission a report from professionals to have it refused because they weren't to some people's liking. The Planning Authority was adamant, however, and was in a position to use strong arm-twisting tactics it had become notorious for. So, the consultants deleted the 'offending' words much to our disgust at the arrogance manifested by people in absolute power. We had prepared thousands of leaflets in colour to present to the general public at various localities to explain the benefits of a golf course to the country's economy and to the environment of the area. We were convinced about the positive impact of the development and our environmental experts had covered all aspects, but I shall write more about all this in a later chapter.

Meanwhile, my application for the redevelopment of the hotel was put on the agenda of the Planning Authority Board for a decision in July 2001. This was seven years from the date of my application, when I was promised it would be processed within three months. Three months, my foot! The Authority's Director General had an inkling of the board members' positive view about my application and it was becoming clear that both his and his directorate's recommendations for refusal would be overturned. He, therefore, decided he would have to do something about it.

During the public hearing, at which he was present, not one objector was present to put forward any representations; the disappointment on his face was apparent. At one point he objected to the front elevation; he said it could be improved upon and suggested that 'the elevation is still a reserved matter' with the full building permit application. Although I had always been proud of the high quality of the design in my developments I said that I had no problem with the suggestion.

'Even I want the best elevation possible,' I continued. 'If needs be, I'll appoint the best architects in Europe to come up with the ideal design.'

But the Director General was a shrewd fox and as devious. His intention was that whatever elevation I submitted would be objected to even if it was the best in the world. In fact, the top-class architects commissioned to make the design had to withstand three whole years of meetings with the Director General and other top Planning Authority officials who went into all kinds of nit-picking over every minor detail, including colour schemes. At last, when he had exhausted his voluminous dictionary of objections, he reluctantly gave his verbal approval. But, again, months passed without it being brought to the attention of the board and, therefore, no decision could be taken, no permit was issued and we were powerless. Legislation to establish the office of the ombudsman had not yet been discussed in Parliament, so we had no overriding authority to turn to. In other words, the Director General was playing God and there was nothing anyone, not even the Prime Minister, could do about it.

On the plus side, we still had the permit issued in 2001 for the redevelopment minus the elevation. At least we could start with the internal construction works and carry out all the modifications as well as demolishing and excavating areas which were intended to be developed as extensions. However, without approved elevations, the architects, structural engineers and my construction company could not embark on works that would be affected by the pending permit. Since we had originally planned a very fast construction rate where all my construction workers would be committed round the clock, we had to reject other third party contracts. After six months we had to halt all construction activity. All internal works together with a huge underground car park topped by an extensive garden were completed. What was still missing was the approval of the elevation.

Yet again, as if to prove that you have to be resilient and persistent to get anything built in Malta, my plans for Simblija Gardens were just lying dormant. But, as I was now Mayor of Naxxar and as an advocate for creating a better neighbourhood, I felt I needed to lead by example, to convert this industrial site into a residential neighbourhood as the old factory was now surrounded by houses. My fellow councillors, as well as all the residents of the area, unanimously supported this project. We even carried out various studies to prove the many advantages. However, all my efforts were useless and after seven years my application was refused. It was then that I decided to make an appeal to the Appeals Board. After another two years, against the wish of the main board, they approved an outline permit. It was a great relief and I thought that now it should be just a formality to put forward our detailed plans for the Main Board's consideration to get a full permission. But I was wrong, as I was never expecting to spend another thirteen years to get this full permit. It was obvious that the top executives within the Planning Authority were irritated that the Appeals Board had decided in favour of the project and against their recommendation for refusal.

I said, 'I will continue to pursue my way, irrespective of all odds and will not allow such unethical behaviour of those in power to diminish my determination to succeed.'

We went on to present numerous reports, letters, presentations and appeals to the appropriate minister, Prime Minister and cabinet ministers and I even invited all the main board members of the Planning Authority for an on-site inspection. They accepted my invitation and when they visited the site, they realised that my proposed project was ideal for the site, but, just to make a remark, they said that instead of a height of four floors, similar to all the surrounding buildings, they recommended a reduction to just one floor. Even though the surrounding buildings were maximizing every square metre of land with building, my development had 50% of its footprint in open landscaped areas. The protracted negotiations continued.

In order not to waste more time, and with the hope of getting this saga over after eighteen years, I instructed my architects to change the plans once again to reflect the board's wish. It is only now, after twenty years of constant battling and harassment, that my project has finally been approved!

This is yet more proof that, with persistence and determination to succeed, anything can be accomplished. It will be another challenging project, but I am committed to establishing a higher standard of living for the elderly who have worked hard all their life and would now like to enjoy the rest of their lives with more dignity. I am sure that, following the success of this project, other developers will turn their attention to similar projects which are ideal to attract foreign retired residents to enjoy our beautiful islands and our culture.

 Malta Enterprise

13

Involving My Children
(1997–1998) 45–46 years

The next development after my state-of-the-art, eighty-bed Capua Hospital was a hotel on the adjacent site, situated right in the centre of Sliema, the most popular town in Malta. We immediately started on a project management exercise for the new 140–room, four-star establishment, which necessitated advanced skills in project management so that we would minimise inconvenience to neighbours. Works involved cutting rock down to four floors below street level and the construction of eight floors above.

We decided to name the hotel The Victoria, on a style reminiscent of the great empress' era. The development of two major projects practically concurrently put further pressure on our cash flow. The introduction of the first private hospital in Malta was already a great feat on its own, even though we lost over €2 million during its first year of operation, and this loss was noted by my bank. When I asked for another loan I wasn't greeted with the usual effusiveness on the part of the manager. My problem was that should the hotel not be completed in time, irreparable damage would be caused to the administration of the hospital next door. So, I went to another bank and settled for only a 33% loan on the capital required. We had no alternative but to accept the loan, which was subject to a drawdown to run concurrently with our equity increase. It caused a strain on my whole group of companies' cash flow, but we still managed to complete the hotel in time, creating an outstanding business hotel right in the city centre.

Its construction, however, was dogged by hitches and sabotages. During the construction phase, a politician approached a Planning Authority official, telling him that I had infringed permit conditions. Without bothering to verify the allegation, this planning official issued a stop order notice, which grounded us to a complete halt. This put my project in jeopardy as it left me with a large number of workers, sub-contractors and plant and equipment idle on site. I drove straight to the Planning Authority to complain about this planning officer's unilateral action. The person I talked to, however, told me that he couldn't lift the stop order notice unless the whole issue was discussed by the main deciding board, which was not scheduled to meet for another month. I couldn't wait that long, so I filed a court case, claiming abuse of power by the Planning Authority. This action caused ripples and the media picked them up and splashed them as headline news. The government had no option but to intervene. I was called to a meeting with the official responsible for the stop order notice and his crony and saw that some Planning Authority officials treated government intervention the same way as a duck treats water on its back.

'And from now on,' the official continued after exhausting his anger at my 'arrogance' for taking court action, 'all your applications will be blacklisted. They will be placed in the black cupboard and left to rot.'

'What did you say?' I answered angrily. 'I thought I was brought here to talk things over not to be blackmailed. I'm here to be told what I've done wrong so I can remedy the mistake.'

'Oh. So you don't know what you've done wrong,' continued the same officer in a sarcastic vein. 'Then how about all those construction vehicles parked in the vacant site next to yours? That's not covered by a permit.'

I became angry and pointed a finger at him. 'Is this all you can bring up? Is this the reason for the persecution? It's the most pathetic and puerile excuse ever. I thought you could do better than this.'

Both officers were stunned into silence.

'Is this why the taxpayers pay you good money?' I continued angrily. 'You sit warming your bums all day while other developers block whole streets with their heavy equipment, causing nuisance to the neighbourhood and creating mile-long traffic jams. Why don't you get out of here and see what's really happening out there instead of picking on me for buying a vacant site specifically to park my equipment instead of leaving it on the street? You should have thanked me not punished me for giving others a good example.'

Both realised that they had made a gross mistake and didn't answer back.

'Because of you, my project has been at a standstill for three whole weeks. Now I'm going back on site to continue with the works as of right now.' And I stomped out of the meeting.

The works continued at my typical fast tempo and, when completed, we filed the usual application to the Planning Authority for the issue of the compliance certificate, without which no water and electricity would be provided to the hotel. In the meantime, we went about recruiting our hotel management and other staff who had to undergo pre-opening training before taking up their posts. We even set the date for the official opening of The Victoria and issued invitations. Tour operators and agents were looking forward to see this new, charming hotel in operation.

To our complete disgust and utter disappointment, however, I learned that the same high official who had threatened to blacklist me was vindictively refusing to issue the important compliance certificate. Following my urgent request for an explanatory meeting, I received a cold, formal letter informing me that a small part of the façade was painted in a colour not so clearly explained in our original application submitted some eighteen months before. It was unbelievable how low and petty the Planning Authority could reduce itself to and I became really furious, and not solely for this reason. I simply couldn't take this lying down and made straight for this official's office.

'How can you state such stupid things when you were present for the presentation?' I shouted at him. 'The colour scheme was all there, explained on the presentation board for all to see and comment on, and you didn't utter one single syllable.'

'But they were not in the file,' he answered. 'So I couldn't check.'

'Oh. I never knew you now have files as big as this room to fit presentation boards,' I said sarcastically. 'Furthermore, the colours are clearly indicated on each plan. What did you expect us to do? Go through the hundreds of shades of yellow that exist?'

'No, but—'

'And why didn't you bring this up three months ago? Building inspectors have been coming and going throughout all these months and not one commented unfavourably about the colour texture. Everybody except you, here, from behind your desk, commented favourably.'

It was another clear case of abuse of power, and when he couldn't find words to rebut mine he requested me to file a fresh application for the approval of the colour scheme, which he promised he would have processed in a week. First thing by post, the next day, he had our application. Unbelievably, however, two days later, we were served with a refusal. I just couldn't believe my eyes. I couldn't believe that such a cold, irrational and ruthless person could really exist. I thought about inauguration day with all the guests arriving to be greeted by me in total darkness. I imagined them fumbling their way about, trying to see the inside of the hotel by the flickering light of a few candles. I thought about the tourists that had already booked their sojourn at the hotel. What excuse could I cough up? How could I tell them that the Planning Authority is run at the whim of one single person?

All of this was going on a few months following the general election, which saw Dr Alfred Sant swept to power with his New Labour. I decided there and then to ask him for an appointment. Two days later, I was sitting in his office telling him about the threats of 'blacklistings' and 'black cupboards', and also that the Minister for Tourism had already accepted to officially inaugurate the hotel.

'We have also sent you an official invitation, Prime Minister,' I concluded and I could see that he was getting angrier with every bit of information I was feeding him. When I finished, he promised to take up the matter right away and that he'd come back to me during the next twenty-four hours.

On my way out of his office I received a call on my mobile phone. It was the Chairman of the Planning Authority asking me to call on him as soon as possible. His office was only a five-minute drive away and, upon my arrival, I was instantly ushered into his presence where I found that the mean official was also present. I nearly turned round and walked out because I couldn't stand being on the same planet with him, let alone a small room. I hated his cowardly and vindictive actions in my regard. But the Chairman stopped me.

'I'm sorry, Mr Xuereb,' he said in the other's presence. 'I want him to be present because I don't want my words misinterpreted. I want him to understand clearly what I have to say.'

At these words I sat down on the chair he indicated.

'I want you to know, Mr Xuereb, that the Planning Authority had nothing to do with the actions taken against you. The board and I knew absolutely nothing about them. They were all taken on the initiative of this one person, here. Even this last application you were asked to submit about the colour scheme; it was all his doing and it was never brought up for the board's decision.'

He further promised me that he would bring the issue before the board on the morrow and, as expected, the application was approved.

Within the week, we received the compliance certificate. It was good to see the hotel connected to the water and electricity supply.

In spite of these obstacles and political sabotage, we still managed to complete this beautiful Victorian-style hotel in time. It was inaugurated on 18th June 1997 and was well received by the tourism industry. It is a success story and very popular up to this day.

On 8th March 1997, I sought re-election to the Naxxar Local Council, but I didn't have time for campaigning this time; business was keeping me too busy. Neither did I have to spend cold nights in my office and waste my time in court litigation. The performance of the outgoing council under my leadership was enough to ensure my election with the same majority of votes and the same landslide victory of three years earlier. This was another feather in my cap and confirmation of how my performance as mayor was viewed by the electorate. Once again, none of the newly elected members contested me and I was elected mayor unanimously. Some members were replaced by new ones, but they were able to recognise and appreciate the harmony I had managed to create, and they continued where the others before them had left off. The residents also continued to give us their full support, proud of the fact that their local council was unique in veering away from partisan politics, which obstructed progress due to blinkered party interests. It is with great pride that Naxxar Local Council further confirmed its number one position throughout the next three years.

It is with this pride and unity in mind that, when I inaugurated a monument to usher in the third millennium, I insisted that both the local rival band clubs, all non-government organisations (NGOs), together with names of the councillors should be included on the commemorative plaque. The monument carried the inscription, 'United we can go further.'

Throughout my six years at the helm, I did my utmost to sustain this unity among the councillors, and it is thanks to their maturity that Naxxar became the benchmark for all the other localities. I was so proud of this unity that during my last speech at the Annual Congress for Mayors, coincidentally held at Naxxar, and in the presence of the Prime Minister, I stressed the fact that in order to maintain unity, the mayor sometimes has to close one eye, or one ear, and often bite his tongue, but must never close both eyes, or ears. This was the maxim I followed throughout my six years' tenure as mayor, and what made my council the best of the lot. All the mayors present were very well aware of this fact.

At the conclusion of my speech, I declared my intention not to contest for another term, and closed by wishing the mayors present success in their endeavours. I was given a deafening standing ovation and, later, Prime Minister Fenech Adami showed genuine surprise at my decision and asked me to reconsider, promising his party's support given the huge popularity I enjoyed all over Naxxar. I appreciated his comments, which I treated as a compliment (and which contrasted sharply with the hassle his party's General Secretary had given me six years earlier), but I told him that I still intended not to contest the election. I stressed the fact that I had done my utmost and I was happy and satisfied to see all the residents proud of my council's performance. It was time that I concentrated more on my businesses.

As well as my involvement in the local NGOs, I was also a very active council member of the Federation of Industries (FOI) and the Chamber of Commerce, the two main representatives of the local business sector. My activity also extended to the BICC (Building Industry Consultative Council), where I was an active council member, and to the Federation of Building Contractors (FOBC), where I held the post of Deputy President and later President. On top of all this, I wrote regular articles for the local newspapers about subjects on which I had gained experience throughout my active life. Furthermore, I regularly gave interviews and participated in prime time TV and radio discussion programmes. I was recognised as a man of vision – a man who very often came up with creative and revolutionary ideas. When, for some reason, I didn't produce one of my regular articles, or didn't appear on some discussion programme on which I featured regularly, I would be pleasantly surprised when people told me that they had missed my article or my comments on TV. They would tell me that my comments always contained interesting ideas that set people thinking and that the way I expressed myself showed that

I wrote from practical experience, unlike others who wrote without knowing what real business life was all about.

Sometimes I was also invited by groups of university students to deliver talks about entrepreneurship and leadership. My first experience of this was when I was invited by the Dean of the Faculty of Commerce at the University of Malta to participate in a discussion with his students about business life and entrepreneurship from a practical point of view.

'I would find no problem taking part,' I told him, 'and it would certainly be a pleasure to meet your students. But I've never been a university student myself and I'm afraid I would be out of my depth among them.'

The Dean smiled. 'No, Angelo. Absolutely not. You see, Angelo, you have managed to learn on your own what we at university cannot teach our students. Your attitude towards business is different from what we normally teach here. We teach them the theory while you have taught yourself the practice. Our students leave here full of themselves, thinking that they know it all and sometimes look down on others who never had the opportunity of a university education. They think that the degree attached to their names will make people flock to them. Many of them end up coming a cropper when they try to practice what they learned here. And do you know why, Angelo? Because they have never tasted the bitterness and difficulties that form a man's character and make him whole. You haven't been to university and yet you have made a success of your career, while students who finished tertiary education with the highest degrees are still struggling to justify the years they have spent here. My students need to learn, and they want to learn. What better man to teach them than you?'

I wasn't prepared for this eulogy from a university Dean and it took me some moments to come up with an answer. 'Okay. I accept. But what format would the discussion take?'

'There's nothing to worry about. You start with a thirty minute presentation about your views on the subject of business after

292

which you'll answer questions from the floor.'

When the day arrived, I was overwhelmed when I looked up at the auditorium from the stage with only the mediator for company. There were at least 150 students looking curiously at me, many with writing pads on their laps and all eagerly waiting in silence to listen to what I had to say. The warmth of their welcome soon put me at ease, however, and I thoroughly enjoyed this first experience, knowing that I was sharing some of my hard-earned knowledge with young people who wanted to listen and learn.

Eventually, I was invited to give a regular annual lecture to final-year students in the Faculty of Architecture and Engineering. I always spent a long time preparing for these lectures, but always enjoyed myself sharing my experience in the construction sector. Sometimes, I was surprised by the fact that some of the final year students had never been on a construction site, or never held concrete in the palms of their hands and felt its texture with their fingers, let alone other critical areas that are a must for an aspiring architect or engineer.

It was around the time of my association with this new generation that I took an inevitable step – I learned how to use a computer, which was a source of much excitement. As soon as we installed the system I couldn't wait to run my fingers along the keyboard to check whether my touch-typing skills had diminished with time. It was satisfying to discover that they had lost none of their nimbleness. I guess it's like swimming or riding a bicycle; once you acquire the skill, you have it for life.

It was, however, the introduction of email that fired my enthusiasm to use the computer. This breakthrough in technology enabled me to draft and send letters by pressing a few keys. It also gave my personal assistant breathing space from keeping up with my demanding regime. The whole office became more efficient and we soon wondered how on earth we used to manage before the invention.

My son, Richard, obtained a degree in Construction Management from the University of Manchester around about this period. He was followed by Claire, who graduated with a distinction in Hotel Management from Glion International School in Switzerland. Jessie and I were understandably very proud of our children's efforts and success. This also meant that two of my core businesses would be carried through to the next generation; Richard was given responsibility in the management of my construction company while Claire was appointed assistant general manager at The Victoria. Two years later, the general manager decided to change careers and created a vacancy for the post. Claire was only twenty-five at the time and I summoned her to my office.

'Claire, I have been keeping a close watch on your performance. You have done well at your job and have worked hard to improve the hotel standards and increase profitability. What would you say if I offered you the job of general manager?'

'Who? Me? General Manager?'

I laughed at her reaction. 'Yes you. Why not you? I know you can do it. Don't be afraid to take up the challenge. I shall always support you if you're in difficulties.'

She still couldn't believe her ears. 'Wow, Pa! It's a big challenge for me.'

'I know enough about challenges. And I know you can make it.'

'Thanks, Pa. And thanks for the encouragement.'

Thus, she became the youngest Hotel General Manager in the Maltese Islands and, soon after taking up her post, she started introducing new procedures and created a supportive team around her. Profits improved and The Victoria became the envy of its competitors. A few years later, she was appointed council member of the Malta Hotels and Restaurants Association (MHRA), which is the most important NGO in the sector. Noting the success she achieved as general manager and the respect she enjoyed in the tourism sector, I then appointed her the group's hospitality director, responsible for the management of our four hotels, which she later grouped as AX Hotels. By the age of thirty-four, she managed to make a name for herself and became recognised as a major contributor in the hotel sector of the tourism industry. The government went on to appoint her as Chairperson of the Institute of Tourism Studies (ITS), an educational institution especially set up to train and educate young people for the tourism industry. I am convinced that, with her energy and ability, together with the enterprising spirit inherited from her parents, she will achieve yet more successes in her career.

With two of the children now out of the house all day, Jessie suddenly found herself with more free time on her hands – free time which she had always yearned for in order to realise her own dream. She contacted a number of like-minded friends and organised them into a philanthropic group called The Charitable Welfare Committee. The scope behind this initiative was to support large families in need of assistance and also individuals with special needs.

The committee did not shy away from making use of the various amenities available in the many properties belonging to the Group and these were readily made available whenever required and, sometimes, I also ended up giving a helping hand. In fact, the Group ended up being one of the main sponsors for the committee's many activities because, apart from making locations available, we even offered the free service of our food and personnel.

Eventually, the committee extended its services to various charitable homes in the same line of assistance to the community. In time, their activities widened further and the work was well recognised and appreciated. The organisation improved to such an extent that the committee changed its name to the AX Foundation and amended the statute accordingly, thus guaranteeing that the good work would continue long after we're gone. I became very impressed with the dedication of its members and their effort to alleviate the suffering of so many people with special needs.

With our children (now young adults) taking their responsibilities seriously and giving a good account of themselves in the work they carried out within the Group, I was able to ease back a little and let them take over some of the administrative problems that usually landed on my desk. This meant that Jessie and I had more time together, and we bought a new power boat, which I christened 'Saranda' after the town in Albania where I had planned to develop a large tourist village. We managed to enjoy whole weekends together in summer thanks to this boat and twice every season we made trips to Sicily. Unfortunately, however, other commitments (mostly invitations to special functions) restricted somewhat my idyllic weekends with Jessie.

Skiing holidays became my favourite winter pastime and I would let no function spoil this regular annual appointment with the mountain slopes. Whenever possible our three children would accompany us. With practice, I managed to become a moderately good skier, definitely above average, especially when speeding down straight runs. I find these holidays relaxing and rejuvenating. The snow, mountains, rivers, clean air, low temperatures, woods, and the blue skies peeking between mountain, away from traffic noise and other man-made pollutants contrasted deeply with the environment of overpopulated and tiny Malta.

These holidays also encourage us to completely let go among long-time friends, with whom we share jokes while stuffing ourselves with calorie-laden lunches inside quaint taverns on steep, snowy mountain slopes. No wonder Jessie and I make it a point never to miss this annual appointment.

Helmut and Ingeborg Wittman are two of the friends we spend our skiing holiday with. They're German and often invite us to their chalet in Königsleiten in Austria. Helmut and I became acquainted when I was Mayor of Naxxar and he was a member of the local council of Neuburg an der Danube in Germany. We had formed a twinning agreement between the two towns, and Helmut and I immediately hit it off. Helmut speaks very little English, but Ingeborg manages a little better – enough to translate for us when we get stuck. Their daughters Ulrike and Christine, however, are always around to help out their mother when she stumbles on difficult words.

I also became a close friend of Mayor Gunter Hunier and his wife Christle. The three families have remained close friends and this annual holiday has become a must for each of us. Nothing beats a week in the Bavarian Alps, eating the never-ending local dishes and washing them down with litres of their famous beer.

Jessie's enthusiasm for skiing, however, is not something to shout about. But she loves to ski around at her own moderate pace assuring everyone that she has no intention of starting an avalanche. One day, while still sitting on a chairlift taking me up a mild slope, I espied her below, skiing at her usual sedate pace. I smiled to myself and thought that as soon as I was up the mild slope I'd show off my skills for her to admire. So, as soon as we men stepped off the chairlift, I went straight down towards her at speed with the intention of braking abruptly a few metres from her and showering her with the resulting flying snow. But my calculation was off the mark because my speed was excessive and when I tried to slow down, I lost balance and ended up the last few metres face down and arms fully extended forward. I couldn't stop laughing at the ridiculous posture I ended up in. Neither could Jessie and our German friends, especially after I stood up covered in snow from head to foot, very much like a snowman.

I also enjoy taking holidays driving overland and have retained my love of fast driving, much to Jessie's annoyance. In fact, she hates excessive speed and when I decided to bring down a new Mercedes with a powerful V8 AMG engine overland, Jessie gladly opted out. But I wanted to do it because I still recalled the fun I had driving Dad's Mercedes part of the way down from Sindelfingen in Germany to Sicily to catch the ferry to Malta. My plan was to renew the experience and drive through places I missed exploring properly owing to Dad's determination to make it to Malta in record time.

When I arrived in Italy, I phoned my Italian minority partners in my General Pre-Cast Concrete (GPC) factory and invited them to dinner. They accepted and welcomed me most heartily. They also suggested that I spend the night at an old castle which had been converted into a boutique hotel. I accepted and followed one of them for twenty minutes along a narrow road, which passed through a thick wood, until we came in sight of the castle perched on the very top of a hill. The place was clean and well kept, but rather spooky, reminding me of *The Addams Family*. In fact, I half expected Lurch to materialise from some hidden door to take my hand luggage up to my room. But, I was alone going up the wide wooden staircase, every step of which squeaked loudly as I progressed. Bookcases lined the corridor and a quick glimpse at the book titles confirmed that they dated back to the early nineteenth century.

My room was on the first floor. It was large, with a high ceiling and spread over two levels. The double bed was right in the centre of a round corner that formed part of the old watch tower. I left my luggage on the bed and hurried down to my friends.

After dinner in the old town of Perugia, we drove back to the castle. We said our goodnights at the castle door and I went straight to the reception desk. While the receptionist was handing me the key to my room I noticed that mine was the only one occupied in the whole castle. I went up to my room, undressed and slid under the blankets, but I couldn't sleep. The room was freezing cold even though the windows were tightly shut. I couldn't understand why this was so and, although I covered myself, including my head, with extra blankets, I couldn't get any warmer. Then, at exactly midnight, a grandfather clock I had noticed on my way up started striking the hour. Simultaneously, I heard the screams of young children running down the short corridor outside my room.

'How come all this noise all of a sudden when I'm the only guest here?' I pondered.

The screaming and sounds of running wouldn't cease and I thought that the corridor was too short for the length of time the children were taking to run all the way along it. It was very disturbing and I thought I'd get out of bed and put an end to it. As soon as I lifted the small, old latch of the ancient door, however, the noise outside suddenly stopped completely.

'That's funny,' I said to myself while opening the door to take a look outside with the intention of telling the children to go to play someplace else. But the corridor was as silent as a tomb and not a single child was around.

'That's even funnier,' I mused while still looking up and down the corridor to make sure I wasn't mistaken and wondering whether I should go down and tell the receptionist about it.

'The receptionist probably fell asleep and didn't hear a thing,' I concluded while closing the door, and walked towards the bed. I tucked myself under the blankets, buried my head and tried to force myself to get warm.

I came to the conclusion that the children outside were ghosts, but I knew that I had nothing to worry about; according to what I've read about ghosts, they wouldn't have been able to lift the bed and carry me along with it.

After that, however, I realised that the room wasn't cold any longer and that I didn't have to bury myself under tons of blankets. I slept soundly all night and, on my way out next morning, I didn't mention anything to the receptionist. But when I met my Italian friend Piero Calderini, I recounted the whole experience. When I finished he started laughing and couldn't stop. All he could do was to nod his head up and down as if to confirm something he already knew.

I couldn't help smile at his funny antics, but still asked, 'Would you tell me why all this laughter?'

He still took his time laughing his heart out and wiping tears from his eyes. At last, and between giggles, he said, 'You see, Angelo, I'm laughing because you're not the only one to have had this experience at the castle. Those you heard were truly ghosts and no one has yet found out why these children start screaming and running right on the stroke of midnight.'

'You should at least have warned me beforehand, Piero. It's not that I'm afraid of ghosts because I'm not. But I would have been prepared. I wouldn't have got out of bed if I had known.' Then I stopped and thought about all the ghost stories I had heard and never believed.

'Do you know, Piero, that I've met many people who believed

in ghosts and I always laughed and scoffed at them? But now I known better. Last night's experience has completely changed my mind.'

Back home, I found out that Mum's condition had started to deteriorate rapidly. She had now developed severe Alzheimer's and my family had no option but to place her in a special home. The best place was at the hospital, which I had just sold, where part of it was reserved specifically for fully dependent elderly people. The best we could now do for her was to give her the best room and visit her as frequently as possible. Dad was never away from her side for long. In fact, all of us, her eleven offspring, managed to visit her very often and her thirty-five grandchildren always found time to pop in her room at all times during the day. So she was never alone. She was given the best treatment possible, thanks to which she survived until 14th January 2011.

The Victoria Hotel

14

Challenging Projects

(1999–2001) 47–49 years

During the twenty-two months of Dr Alfred Sant's Labour administration of 1996–1998, the government had announced its intention to upgrade the cruise liner and ferry terminals at Pinto Wharf at the magnificent and natural Grand Harbour. These had been reduced to a sorry state over years of neglect and apathy by previous administrations. The environment that greeted cruise liner passengers did nothing to enhance our reputation as a tourist destination. In fact, the whole area was characterised by industrial activity with containers haphazardly scattered with all kinds of loose cargo and fork-lift trucks speeding dangerously all over the place. This was the first impression of Malta that welcomed the tourist walking down the gangplank.

The subject of the government's plans for the cruise liner terminal cropped up during conversation when I was having a meeting with my friend, Stewart Elliot, managing director of a Hong Kong-based group diversified in various sectors (for which I was constructing the 440-room, five-star Excelsior in Floriana). Stewart was very familiar with the BOT (Build, Operate and Transfer) concept in the Far East in the building of power stations and toll roads.

'I think you should go to see the Prime Minister about a possible joint venture,' I told him. 'You're the best man to do it, with your experience.'

'I like your idea and it wouldn't be difficult to explain it all to him,' he answered. 'But I have to leave for Hong Kong in two days.'

'That's a pity because by the time you're back... Hold it though! Though it's true that Dr Sant's new at the job, I understand he's a strong supporter of private initiative and quite approachable. Why don't I try and fix an early appointment with him? Who knows? Maybe he'll find time to see us before you leave. We'll soon find out if what they say about him is true.'

'Sure, Angelo. Go ahead. I'm game if you are.'

I called the Prime Minister's personal assistant who listened to all I had to say and was very appreciative about the urgency of my request.

'Can't promise you anything, Mr Xuereb,' he told me over the phone. 'It doesn't depend on me as you may well appreciate. But I promise I'll do my best. If you give me your mobile number I'll get back to you as soon as I can.'

I thanked him, but I wasn't very hopeful. I had had enough experiences with civil servants to know better than to hope. But, to my complete amazement and pleasure, he phoned back less than two hours later to inform me that the Prime Minister would see us the next morning. I thanked him effusively and the next morning Stewart and I were sitting in Dr Sant's office. I introduced Stewart who went on to explain the concept of BOT. In a nutshell, the concept called for the lease of government property at an agreed annual rate of rent or terms for sixty-five years or any length of time agreed upon. I explained the developer's responsibility for all the necessary investment to upgrade the infrastructure and the present facilities. At the termination of the contract, the project would revert to the government without the developer receiving anything in compensation.

The whole thing took half an hour to go through, with the Prime Minister listening attentively and interrupting on occasions to ask for clarifications. When we were finished, he asked, 'Are you really serious about this?'

'You bet we are, Prime Minister!' I answered enthusiastically. 'We truly believe in this concept and that our magnificent harbour deserves nothing less.'

The Prime Minister thanked us, shook our hands and we walked out. We spent the next two months on tenterhooks, eagerly awaiting some contact from the Prime Minister's office. Instead, I was stunned one morning when, unexpectedly, I saw a full page government advert in the papers stating that it was issuing an international call for tenders on the BOT principles for a period of sixty-five years for the upgrading of the cruise liner and ferry terminals, and for the upgrading and restoration of the 250-year-old Pinto Stores, a few metres from the shore line. These stores were built during the reign of Grandmaster Manuel Pinto de Fonseca, a Portuguese knight who ruled over Malta between 1742 and 1773. They were now in a very derelict condition and, for decades, had been used by the Customs Department to store seized goods and as bonded stores for spirits and tobacco.

I was utterly shocked and disappointed by this revelation. 'Oh God,' I thought. 'So the Prime Minister has used our ideas so others can benefit from them. He didn't even bother to offer us the right of first refusal.'

I phoned Stewart in Hong Kong.

'Don't take it so badly, Angelo. These things happen all the time and I'm used to them. We're dealing with politicians, you know. We'll make sure to put forward a well-prepared and solid offer and hope for the best.'

'Thanks. I needed your reassurance. Would you mind if I try to rope in some local and other foreign investors... And consultants as well? I need them to prepare a really good and credible offer that would make ours the best.'

'Why should I mind? Go ahead and keep me informed about what's going on. You know I have complete faith in you, Angelo.'

I engaged American consultants experienced in designing cruise liner terminals the world over and we immediately set about working with local architects and engineers. In the meantime, I had discussions with Malta's leading bank, Air Malta and other local and foreign reputable companies to join my group to form a formidable consortium. In the end, we were a total of nine shareholders forming a consortium named Valletta International Sea Passenger Terminals, better known as VISET, to bid for this major project.

One of the senior technical managers appointed was Chris Paris. Chris was passionately in love with our magnificent Grand Harbour and from an early age kept detailed records of every vessel that entered it. He was born and bred in Floriana, a suburb of Valletta, enjoying a panoramic view of the harbour and overlooking Pinto Wharf, the location of this project. To top it all, he was blessed with the gifts of freehand sketching, honesty, intelligence and a natural knack for coming up with original ideas. He and I had one other thing in common; we both had a passion for original and quality planning, and together we formed a formidable pair – a combination of knowledge and experience. I immediately singled him out and, even before I asked him to take over the design team, he was already smiling.

'And why were you smiling in the first place, Chris?'

'Because I guessed what you had in store for me, Mr Xuereb, and it's a big challenge for both of us. But it would have been a pity to bypass it and let other bidders steal the show.'

My Pakistani construction manager, Tariq Qureshy, was also as enthusiastic about the project. He considered it a challenge to his abilities and, all in all, including our specialised consultants, we formed a team that was hard to beat. With the backing of the other reputable shareholders I was highly optimistic about our chances. Never had a more professional team been assembled for a project of this magnitude and national importance.

All of us would spend long hours sketching and throwing ideas around, and I had converted my boardroom to suit our purpose. I can still picture the members of the American team walking and nearly tripping on discarded large plans and sketches; with the quay projected to reach a length of nearly a kilometre, we required large tracing paper on which to sketch our original ideas.

I recall one time when, at some point during our thinking aloud sessions, Chris inserted a small opening in the large open space up to sea level. It was a good idea, and it immediately triggered my imagination. I snatched the pencil from him.

'This is one hell of an idea, Chris,' I said. 'How about having more and larger openings here and here,' I continued, doing rough drawings with the pencil. 'And we can connect all with small bridges like this, look.' I kept sketching roughly and with enthusiasm for the idea I had in mind. 'You know what I mean. Just like those small bridges across the canals in Venice.'

Chris instantly caught on and, the next morning, he came back with an artist's impression of exactly what I had in mind. We sat down to study the plans of the original quay and discovered that two centuries earlier the Knights had constructed it in large stone blocks. These were now buried under tons of material, topped with a concrete ground slab. I looked up at Chris.

'Do you know what I'm thinking?' I asked. 'What if we expose this sea wall and restore it to its original state?'

His eyes shone. We must have been on the same wavelength. So, we acquired some old plans and copies of old paintings and started finalising this improved concept, which would include a large lagoon and the conversion of the restored, nineteen historic stores named after Grandmaster Pinto into catering outlets. We shifted the road to the back of the buildings, thus allowing us to create a magnificent wide promenade.

When the whole team was assembled for the finishing touches, I said, 'Gentlemen, together we have managed to definitely create a winning design.'

It took us long hours to prepare the offer and, in the end, we submitted everything in a voluminous professional package that required a number of large cardboard boxes to contain it. We were later to find out that there were a total of thirteen submissions from as many consortia composed of leading local groups of companies and renowned international companies.

When the proposal was complete, each member of the team went about his business day after day, trying to act as if nothing was out of the ordinary. But each one of us was biting his finger nails, wondering whether tomorrow would be the day that the government would publish the shortlisted bids.

The days stretched into weeks, and the weeks into months, and we had no more finger nails left to chew on. At last, at the end of the third month, we were informed by post that our bid was one of the three shortlisted. Although it was still premature to celebrate, the tension eased somewhat and there was a lot of backslapping among us. As soon as we learned who the other two bidders were, our confidence continued to soar. We had a strong feeling that ours was the most solid offer.

Then the unexpected happened; Dr Sant's government fell and, after a snap election, the Nationalist Party regained power after a short break of twenty-two months. Our optimism was jolted. We couldn't know whether the new administration would continue with the project and we resumed our nail biting. However, a few weeks after the election results, the government announced that the tendering process would continue as planned, and it wasn't long before we were asked to discuss our plans with the government evaluation team. A few weeks later, we were awarded the contract. We had further meetings with the evaluation team, during which we went into detailed explanations of the whole project, and at last we were given the official go ahead for the commencement of works. This was a God-given reward for the hard work the whole team had put in to realise the dream and I thanked Him for it. Thanks to Him, the government realised that the consortium I had put together had come up with the best option.

I was determined to prove myself and develop this derelict and abandoned part of the Grand Harbour to its full potential. It took almost nine months for the very detailed sixty-five-year lease contract to be drafted. In the meantime, we prepared the necessary building permit application and, as soon as this was issued, we immediately started on the €35 million investment programme.

Although I was the largest single investor, I still had to follow the bureaucratic procedures that good corporate governance entails. However, this was my first experience of not being the majority shareholder in a large organisation and I had to adapt myself to following and respecting a few board decisions that I wasn't in agreement with.

Even while the construction works of the Valletta Waterfront, as the project was aptly named, were going at a fast pace, marketing it internationally was already in full swing. This beautifully projected landmark, now generally considered one of Malta's loveliest, was scheduled to open for business in July 2001. When completed, it was hailed as an achievement by both parties in Parliament. Both had a hand in it; therefore, both had a good enough reason to laud it. And the government was so loudly full of itself about it that the Maltese have been made to believe that it was a state-funded project.

It immediately made a positive impact abroad and Europa Nostra presented awards to the consortium for the immaculate restoration works carried out on the vaults and the old quay, and also for the stupendous architectural features. It has also been voted as the best European Cruise Liner Terminal.

Being involved in a number of developments practically simultaneously, however, meant that I needed to raise more funds. At the time the Malta Stock Exchange was in its infancy and only one state-controlled bank, government stocks and two other well-established companies were being quoted. We, therefore, had long discussions about whether we should raise funds through a public bond issue. The regulations were still, then, very stringent and not very inviting, however, which could have been the reason that so very few companies were listed on the stock exchange. We were not allowed to offer a public bond issue to be listed by the stock exchange without incorporating at least a 20% share issue as well. I was hesitant to release part of the shareholding of my largest investment so far, namely the Suncrest Hotel. But I wanted to go for public funds and so I had no option but to sell the 20% shareholding. Thus, we became the first leisure industry company to be listed on the stock exchange. All bonds and shares, issued for the value of €3 million and €1.5 million respectively, were taken up within forty-eight hours, which was much earlier than the anticipated seven days. We had to be more careful with regard to corporate governance now that we were listed, especially since a daily update was quoted at prime time on the main TV channel.

This last initiative caused me an unsavoury experience, which could have had dire consequences for the small investors who had put their trust in my business operations. A local supplier wished to submit a bid to furnish our group with his products. To put himself at an advantage over his rivals and, most of all, get in our good books and, or so he thought, increase his chances of selling his wares to us, he bought a substantial amount of our shares. His bid, however, was not competitive at all and he was easily beaten by another supplier. He took it all very badly and wanted to take revenge for what he considered an unreturned favour.

He approached a friend of mine and told him, 'Would you do me a favour and pass on this message to Angelo? Tell him that he'll soon know how I'll get back at him.'

He was very true to his word because, just a month after the shares were listed on the stock exchange, he sold a few worth just €250.00 at a loss. Although the amount of shares was very little, it still affected, albeit slightly, the overall share value. He kept repeating this, week after week, always selling a few shares every time, causing the share value of the listed company to continue to plummet. This caused uncertainty among the other investors, especially the smaller ones. Over a period of two years, during which he continued with his weekly sales, the share value was 50% of the original although the bond value was still doing reasonably well on the market.

Strictly speaking, there was nothing illegal in his actions. They were simply underhand and vindictive, causing much stress and concern to the hundreds of innocent small investors who had wanted to augment their small capital and income. I had to do something drastic to halt this artificially induced devaluation, but, unfortunately, financial regulations prohibited me from intervening by buying shares at a higher price to reverse somewhat the negative trend, thereby protecting the small investors and assuring them that the situation wasn't as bleak as reflected in the daily quoted value. Still, I decided to buy back the shares and delist my company from the stock exchange. I did this when the exchange relaxed its stringent restrictions that had prohibited the sale of shares with any bond issue. I, therefore, launched another bond issue and paid back all the original 20% shareholders. To these I also offered a premium to enable them to recoup their loss on their original investments. Although I wasn't obliged by law to do this, I felt I had to repay them for the trust they had shown in me.

In Chapter 12, I mentioned the golf course application, which started picking up momentum during 2003. It was, in fact, slowly but surely, becoming a hot national issue.

It had taken the Planning Authority three years to assess a report professionally prepared by world renowned golf consultants, even after the final favourable recommendation was deleted at its insistence. After these three years, the Authority instructed us to hold public consultation meetings and prepare descriptive leaflets for distribution to the general public. I was so positive about the project's contribution to the area's environment that I had no hesitation whatsoever in informing the public about all aspects of the developments – negative or positive.

Even prior to these public consultation meetings, I had already contacted each of the part-time farmers, about ninety of them, who were supposedly working the fields in the designated area. Not a single full-time farmer, whose livelihood depended on the land, was among them. Only seven had other small pockets of land in other areas and could be considered genuine part-time farmers. The rest, among whom there were lawyers and other professionals, picked up the occasional farm tool as a hobby. Only 10% of the lot, however, were against the development of a golf course, but when I offered them a larger and better area in the same locality, they refused. They approached members of the media to whom they fed a pack of lies. After all, they had nothing to lose. They even had the gall to go to the Archbishop, a very influential and respected head of the Catholic Church in Malta, with the story that there were 200 families whose livelihoods depended solely on the harvest of these fields. The Archbishop was understandably shocked. He must have been painted a vivid picture of 200 destitute families thrown out of their properties by an unscrupulous and insatiable capitalist. I was being vilified and pictured as the ultimate land grabber. The Archbishop transferred his worries to the politicians who really should have known better, but, suddenly, my golf course application became a political ball game with every member of the house wanting a kick at the ball.

Following this, a number of presentation and public consultation meetings were held to discuss the issue. One such meeting, held in a prominent building in Valletta, went moderately well and the people who attended listened attentively and put intelligent questions in the most civil manner. They were even invited to put down their comments and reservations in writing in a visitors' book prominently placed in the hall.

The public consultation meeting at Rabat, however, where the golf course was proposed to be located, was a totally different kettle of fish. The hall was packed, mostly by objectors to the project and their legal advisors. I felt just like the Biblical Daniel in the lion's den, but I wasn't sure I would be as lucky. It was evident from the very start that the 'farmers' packing the hall were not there to understand what the development was all about, but to derail any possibility of an agreement.

I started the meeting with a short introduction, after which it was the turn of the leading consultants to explain the technical details of the proposed project. As soon as the first one opened his mouth he was greeted with a cacophony of shouts of 'We're Maltese! We don't understand English! We want the discussion in Maltese or nothing at all!'

I immediately asked one of the Maltese technical consultants to act as interpreter, but some technical words are not translatable or are very difficult to render in Maltese. This holds true in any other language, but every time the interpreter struggled to find a Maltese equivalent to a technical word or phrase in English, those present created uproar, demanding a change of interpreter. Their intentions became more obvious by the minute, but I was determined to see the presentation through come what may. If I had to die, I would die fighting. So, I sat there for three solid hours watching the charade through to its conclusion until the hall emptied of the crowd of hecklers. All the time, a Planning Authority representative sitting among the crowd, took note of everything that was being said for onward transmission to his bosses at the directorate.

The result of this meeting was that the 'farmers' gained public support. Maltese farmers have always been considered the most hardworking among the population and the least paid for the long hours they put in. Their livelihood depends on the whims of the weather, and a shortage of rain in winter always spelt disaster and hardship for them and their usually large families. This is all very true and people in general look upon them with sympathy, and more so when an unscrupulous developer threatens to usurp their lands. They are depicted as victims trodden upon by an evil and rich money-grabber who could corrupt everybody, including politicians, to attain his goal. In my case, the 'farmers' managed to attract the sympathy of the people, especially when it was bandied about that 200 farmers, whose livelihoods depended wholly on their fields, were on the verge of being ruthlessly kicked out to make way for a golf course for the 'rich capitalists'.

This was very far from the truth. As I said earlier, there wasn't a single full-time farmer among the lot whose livelihood depended on those fields. The majority of the parcels of land involved were tilled on a part-time basis. Moreover, a good percentage of the whole area was abandoned or uncultivated land.

There had to be a solution and I was determined to find it. I was raised on farms and among farmers, and I had learned to speak their language. I spoke to all the people who had holdings in the area and managed to come to an agreement with a good 90% of them. Thanks to my childhood and adolescent experience, I knew exactly each field's potential annual yield and income, and I offered various alternative proposals to each farmer. What I offered was always better than what the farmers would have given up. I even included in the deal a large sum of money which, if deposited in a bank, would have paid them interest higher than the total annual turnover from the field. In spite of all this, the remaining 10% adamantly stood their ground and created so much noise and opposition that they managed to win over the sympathy of the media, the church and clergy, and, subsequently, the party in opposition and the general public. These 10% managed to depict themselves as the oppressed while I became the modern day Simon Legree. Surprisingly, the government suddenly declared itself against the development after ten years of intensive discussions, plans and reports.

Two months later, the Planning Authority invited us to present our case at a public hearing scheduled for 9th September at two o'clock in the afternoon, in front of the deciding board for a final decision after those many years of hard and painstaking exercise, meetings and expense. The irony of it all is that the Planning Authority was set up specifically as an autonomous entity, unaffected by political pressure. But is it really?

When the golf course application was finally brought up before the deciding board for a public hearing, the chairman told us that our architect and golf consultant had only ten minutes each to present our case. How could we present such a complicated case in such a short time? How could we summarise ten and a half years of work and thousands of pages of reports in twenty short minutes? How can one explain that, in comparison, five minutes was allowed to every Tom, Dick and Harry who thought he had something to say about the development? Not exactly the level playing field one expects from an authority that boasts impartiality.

I knew it was a lost cause, even though it was only later that we learned that the Director General had done his homework well. He and members of his directorate had organised a four-hour-long, informal presentation to the members of the board on the same morning of the hearing, during which all the reasons for refusal were outlined and amplified in the most thorough manner.

The public hearing was a total farce, and that's putting it mildly. In fact, it's funny how body language says it all; it was a mime, with the members going through the motions like robots with their heads down, scribbling nonsense on their notebooks to give the impression that they were attentively noting everything that was being said that would help them come to a fair and honest decision. We couldn't help noticing their antics and kept our eyes glued on them throughout the whole session, noting especially the way they acted during the representations by the objectors. Not one of them looked up from the sheets of paper on the table in front of them. Not one of them paid any attention to what the objectors were saying. Not one of them said a single word or asked a question of clarification. They sat there, eyes down, scribbling and sometimes whispering among themselves. They were even oblivious to the favourable comments made by respected NGOs, such as Birdlife, Fondazzjoni Wirt Artna (Malta Heritage Trust) and others.

When, after two hours of circus acts dominated by able acrobats, the chairman went for a vote, all the members voted against the development except for one abstention. It was just a confirmation of what had been decided during the morning's presentation by the Director General. Anyway, it was abundantly clear that the cabinet of ministers had succumbed to public opinion and would be voting against the development during one of its regular weekly meetings.

Our disappointment at the injustice of the unfair hearing and final decision was total, but we immediately applied for a reconsideration of the case. The Planning Authority, however, to prevent us from presenting our case to the ombudsman (who had, in the meantime, been established by Parliament), sat comfortably on the application and, to date, has not brought it up for reconsideration. Until this happens we are unable to appeal or to refer the case to the ombudsman, the law courts, or even the European Court of Justice.

In the meantime, the pending problem of the 'reserved matter' of the elevation of the hotel was still brewing. But I shall come to it in a later chapter.

Valletta Cruise Port

15

My Patriotism

(2002–2004) 50–52 years

People my age cannot boast of having gone through the most destructive of wars in world history, the privations, the bombings, the loss of life and the devastation our parents returned to at the end of it. We were luckier. We were the active witnesses of our country's rise from the ashes after four years of continuous bombing and this is something for which I am eternally grateful. However, as I approached my fiftieth birthday, I realised that there's nothing really special about attaining the age of fifty. It's just twelve months after the forty-ninth and twelve months away from the fifty-first. But, some people take time to come to terms with the passing of time. At twenty, young people realise with a shock that their carefree teenage years are over. At thirty, they have to work harder and longer hours to pay their home loans and their children's education fees. At forty, they realise that they're getting close to middle age and that their children are too carefree for their liking. And at fifty? At fifty one can look back at half a century of experience.

I consider each decade a sort of threshold; an opportunity to look back and appreciate the experience garnered, which makes one that little bit more mature. I would be a hypocrite if I said that at each of these thresholds I didn't stop and wonder how quickly ten years passed. And each subsequent decade seems to pass ever more quickly.

My life has always been too active to allow me the luxury to wonder for too long. But, on my fiftieth birthday, I had already slowed down a little thanks to my children's involvement in the group, thus reducing the burden I singlehandedly carried on my shoulders for decades. And I realised that my scope in life would be incomplete if the experience and wisdom accumulated over half a century was not passed on to the younger generation. I have also always tried to encourage the general public through my articles in the papers and my participation in conferences and debates on TV.

My life has always revolved around the business world and, as with others my age, I have been an active witness to my country's economic growth. As a young boy I experienced the hardship of raising a large family when unemployment was rife; the economy depended solely on the whim of the British Government, factories were practically non-existent and tourism was just another word we learned to spell at school. Unfortunately, many still don't appreciate what the country has managed to achieve during the decades since World War II and especially after Independence in 1964 when Malta started fending for itself. Some people today take everything for granted as though success and progress are manna from heaven.

I love my country and am proud of my patriotism. This is why some people's lack of appreciation of their country hurts me deeply. Malta's extensively rich and historic architecture, together with its long and turbulent history, deserves much better. Not many people around the globe are aware that we have the most ancient free-standing structure in the world. The megalithic temples, built between the fifth and second millennia B.C., pre-date the pyramids by a thousand years and are certainly older than Stonehenge. Malta and Gozo are dotted with small and large temples, and they are all bunched together as one World Heritage site. All this proves that a fairly large settlement had existed on the Islands as far back as 5,000 years before Christ. Four of the temples, Hagar Qim, Mnajdra and Tarxien in Malta, and Ggantija in Gozo, are so monumental that they must have catered for large populations. I compare their role to that of a large, modern cathedral in some large European city, catering for a large population.

This uniquely rich heritage in such a tiny nation fascinates me and all foreigners who visit. In fact, some describe Malta and Gozo as an open air museum. But, what fascinates me even more is that such a small island with no mineral resources to think of and with very little water has managed to survive and sustain a population that is always on the increase. The only resources Malta can boast of are its workers and the beautiful limestone that makes our buildings so uniquely different. We have one of the world's densest populations – over 400,000 people crowded inside 300 square km of land – and our forefathers managed to survive centuries of foreign domination. We had the Greeks around 700 BC. Then came the Phoenicians, followed by the Carthaginians, Romans, Byzantines, German tribes (mainly the Goths and the Vandals), Arabs and Normans. Then we became part of the Kingdom of Sicily as part of the Holy Roman Empire, following which we were governed by the Aragonese, the Angevins, the Knights of St John, the French under Napoleon and finally the British until Independence in 1964. The list alone leaves one breathless, but every conquering nation left its mark on the culture of the inhabitants, including the language with its Semitic roots, and our architecture. Malta has 60 km of fortifications, mostly built by the Knights of St John who also built some of the most beautiful palaces around the island and especially in Valletta.

Malta is strategically placed in the very centre of the Mediterranean, thus making it a prime target for any foreign power with ambitions to dominate Southern Europe, North Africa and the Middle East. Britain was no exception and never shied from referring to Malta as an island fortress with a population that 'accidentally' happened to be living within its walls. No wonder Hitler wanted to obliterate us from the map; according to many military historians, had Malta fallen, World War II would have been lost. Being such an important 'fortress', Malta was the most bombed island in the world. With Independence, however, Malta's role in world affairs changed completely and it's now an important hub between Africa and Europe. It's no wonder I feel proud of being a descendent of a people who have endured untold hardships throughout the ages so that we, today, can boast of an economy that is the envy of much larger countries.

My pride in Malta has sparked a deep fascination for our history and there isn't a book that deals with Malta's history that hasn't found its place in my ever-expanding library. However, when I started attending forums on Maltese history and the environment I noticed the look of surprise on many faces. Others would whisper in ears and grin, wondering what a major developer like me was doing in the opponents' den. Many still associated development as the enemy of the environment. But others, less blinkered, were pleased to see me among them. They realised that at least one building contractor and developer appreciated Malta's culture and environment and, in time, I was accepted by one and all as a genuine lover of everything that is Maltese, including the defects and shortcomings.

As previously explained, my articles in the newspapers were attracting wide attention. However, a particular editor thought it fit to write, 'I do not believe that these articles are written by Angelo.'

I felt very offended and immediately phoned him.

'What makes you conclude that the articles are not written by me?' I asked him angrily. 'Are you implying that I'm incapable of writing articles? I assure you that I never sign one unless it's written by me!'

This same editor was often a key spokesman on environmental issues on TV and radio. I often crossed swords with him during debates because many, including him, still considered me the spokesman for sustainable development, which was considered by some with tinted glasses as an enemy of the environment. The funny thing was, however, that most times he ended up agreeing with my reasoning.

On one particular occasion, during a short commercial break

during a radio debate, he turned on the presenter and said, 'I can't understand why, in spite of preparing myself well to oppose Angelo, I always end up agreeing with him.'

Suddenly his face turned pale and he continued, 'We're still off the air, aren't we?'

When the presenter reassured him, he continued, 'Imagine your listeners hearing me say these things about Angelo!'

In time he too came to appreciate my commitment to Malta's environment, in spite of my being a building contractor and developer, as my articles regularly reflected my strong feelings for my country, its history and environment. In fact, very often I would end them with special bullet form messages like the following:

• Together we can polish this Jewel of the Mediterranean.
• Let us all work collectively to leave a better Malta for our future generations.
• Let us make our forefathers proud of today's action by creating sustainable development.
• Let us instil pride and patriotism in our children, as in a few years' time they will be the leaders of our country.
• Do not ask what your country can do for you, but what you can do for your country.

As mentioned previously, this last quotation, from John F. Kennedy, is one of my all-time favourites and I keep it in mind during every action I take, so much so that it was my main inspiration in establishing my Group to become synonymous with quality projects. Every project we have been involved in ended up improving even the immediate surroundings. The Valletta Waterfront is a typical example; I was the promoter behind the idea of this outstanding project and the leading individual shareholder. The whole area is so beautiful that, as I said before, both parties in Parliament vie with one another to take full credit for it, and this convinced the people that it was a government-funded project.

Owing to my passion and love for my country and my business interests in both the construction and tourism industries, I set up a joint committee between the Federation of Building Contractors (FOBC – of which I was president) and the Malta Tourism Authority (MTA). The aim was to mitigate the conflicting aspects of construction and tourism, especially in tourist zones. The MTA welcomed this initiative wholeheartedly, more so since it was put forward by a federation representing the 'main culprits' where tourism was concerned. My intention was to reduce and possibly eliminate the general public's bias against construction. My first action as Chairman was to insist that all construction works in tourist zones would be limited according to the new regulations, which were drafted by the ad hoc committee. I admit, however, that I'm not wholly satisfied with the general adherence to these regulations, especially when the main offender is the government, with its lack of sensitivity when insisting on carrying out unnecessary road works that disrupt tourist zones during the peak tourist season.

It was around this time that Dad suffered a stroke that left him half paralysed. For a long time, Dad had been spending most of his waking hours with Mum, seeing to all her needs and supporting her as best he could. Every morning he would pick her up in his arms from her bed in the nursing home, walk slowly to his car and place her gently in the passenger seat. Then he would take her for a drive around Malta, returning her to the nursing home at lunchtime. In the afternoon, after she had rested, Dad would again pick her up in his arms and take her for another drive. He performed this act of love and dedication every day without fail until tragedy turned her attention on him. None of us could believe that he, strong as an ox, could so suddenly and without the least prior warning become an invalid. He, like Mum, would now require constant professional assistance, which could only be given in hospital. And so we accommodated him at the same special nursing home right next to Mum at Palazzo Capua. We gave them both the best medical assistance possible including the constant presence of a nurse throughout the day. This, however, couldn't reduce the trauma suffered by the whole family. We could hardly communicate with Dad. He understood every word addressed to him, but his mouth was unable to form the message he so wanted to convey. We could see the look of frustration and desperation each time he struggled unsuccessfully to make us understand him. It hurt us to see him reduced to that condition – a man totally independent throughout his life now reduced to that helpless situation. By the time I had finished writing this book both my parents were relieved of their suffering – Mum on 14 January 2011 and Dad a year later on 21 January 2012.

This period was highlighted also by Richard's marriage to Charmaine and Claire's to Duncan. Suddenly, our villa was empty, or so it seemed, with only Jessie, Denise and I left. Furthermore, Denise was spending most of her time abroad to continue with her advanced studies. Jessie and I decided to sit down and discuss the situation, and it didn't take us long to arrive at a decision. None of us were getting any younger and keeping such a large villa spotlessly clean was becoming too much for Jessie, who also had her philanthropic organisation keeping her busy most days of the week. It necessitated more domestic help, thereby reducing our privacy considerably. We, therefore, decided to move into the large and beautiful penthouse we had built on top of our luxurious Verdala Mansions at Rabat, very close to Mdina, the old capital city of Malta. The penthouse commanded a breath-taking view of most of the island with its beautiful landscapes and far towns and villages all the way to the Mediterranean. Occasionally, on a clear day, we could even see Sicily, a hundred km away. The penthouse has a large interior spread over one floor and 350 square metres of terraces.

Jessie breathed a sigh of relief. It was less work for her. It also meant more time for relaxation together and, therefore, more time for sport and leisure. Jessie could now devote more hours to her tennis and other active sports, while I took up golf and also started exploring the surrounding countryside on my beloved mountain bike. We also took the opportunity to take more frequent short breaks on mainland Europe.

Our children's deeper involvement in the Group's management considerably reduced the day to day pressure that, for decades, had ended up on my desk, but I didn't give up my twelve-hour working day, five and a half days a week; this regime had become too much a part of my life to give up so easily. However, it became less hectic for me at the office and I was less mentally drained at the end of the day. I could now dedicate more hours each day to planning, which was my lifelong favourite hobby, though it's also one of my responsibilities as CEO. I still, in fact, spend enjoyable weekends sitting down at my desk at home with a blank sheet of paper in front of me, a scale rule, sharpened pencil and rubber eraser at the ready to help me absorb myself happily creating our in-house projects and refurbishments – and there was still a lot to create.

Already having the four-star Victoria right in the central part of Sliema, I didn't want to miss the opportunity of also going for a large vacant property right next to it. The easiest and quickest profit-making development would have been a prestigious block of residential apartments. But, I realised that a real estate project would permanently block the possibility for a future extension to The Victoria. Should I opt for the latter, it would mean a long-term investment with no quick return as in real estate. It wasn't an easy decision to make. What finally tipped the scales in favour of a hotel development was Claire's keenness and enthusiasm for hotel management. But then there was the issue of planning permission.

Getting the Planning Authority's approval for any major project anywhere in Malta was always an ordeal. Getting one for a project in the city centre of busy Sliema was much worse. The first building permit application was submitted in 1998. The site was very restricted and, while drawing the plans, we realised that a larger one would suit us much better for the up-market development. Furthermore, some of the buildings adjacent to the site were quite dilapidated and would have jarred with our finished product. I, therefore, decided to acquire the surrounding half-dozen properties and initiated negotiations with the various owners. Some of the properties were occupied for perpetuity and, knowing the reasons I wanted them, the owners jumped at the opportunity of asking for sky-high compensation. Although their 'take it or leave it' attitude irked me considerably, I had no option but to pay. There was an eighty-five-year-old woman, however, who would not give up her first floor miniscule apartment. Not even for all the gold in the world.

'You see, Mr Xuereb,' she told me in a feeble and gentle voice, 'I was born right here, in the next room, and have always felt safe here, surrounded by the things I'm familiar with. I would feel safer and happier to die here than anywhere else.'

I couldn't help appreciating her attachment to and love for the place, but I had a hotel to build and, in spite of offering her full board and accommodation at the retirement home next door to where she was born and top-notch hospital treatment a few paces away for the duration of her life, she wouldn't budge. Not even her children's entreaties to accept my most generous offer could move her.

In the end I had to give up. This meant that I had to plan the hotel in such a way that it would have to go around and over her small house. It also meant excavating the rock all around her for 15 metres in order to accommodate the underground car park and services. This meant a huge additional cost in order to surround the foundations around her house with a chain of concrete piles to protect her and the building from any damage. The revised plans were duly submitted to the Planning Authority and, as soon as they were processed and approved, the old lady suffered a stroke and became completely immobile, requiring round the clock attention. Her family was now free to accept our offer plus an additional large sum to relinquish the perpetual tenancy. Once again, we went back to the drawing board to redesign the plans to resubmit to the Planning Authority.

After all was nearly done, Claire came up to me with yet another proposal.

'Pa, why don't you take this unique opportunity and consider developing a new five-star instead of an extension to The Victoria?'

I sat back to listen to her explain how the new development would allow conference delegates the choice of a hotel to fit their budgets. She sat in front of my desk while I pondered on this fresh idea. I began to see the advantages of having a four-star hotel within walking distance of a five-star, and the more I thought about it the more advantages I could see. I told Claire that it was an excellent idea and she was over the moon. This, however, would entail the scrapping of five years of constant haggling with the Planning Authority and the Malta Tourism Authority, and the writing off of the long hours spent on constantly revising the plans. While all these thoughts were racing through my mind, Claire remained sitting across the desk, probably afraid I would have second thoughts. She was still twenty-eight, but three years of managing The Victoria had matured her. She had managed to prove herself even beyond my expectations, elevating the hotel to the highest performing four-star in the Maltese Islands.

'Let me tell you what, Claire; since this is your idea and you did well at The Victoria, why don't you manage both? I don't see why –'

'Oh, Pa, do you really mean it? Do you really have so much faith in me?'

I smiled and nodded my head.

'Then I promise I won't let you down. I promise I will face the challenges of this new responsibility with the same dedication.'

I did not waste any time and set the ball rolling by recruiting one of the best interior designers in Malta and, together with Claire, we started meeting every three days to exchange views on new concepts and throw ideas around. We three formed a perfect team with Claire presenting proposals on how to have the best operations at minimum costs, the interior designer putting forward ideas on how to create the most charming hotel in Malta, while my contribution was to create a good and practical plan to save on construction costs and time while respecting all the new hotel regulations.

At first, and as expected, our official project's architects weren't so pleased with these frequent changes, but when they studied the attractive solutions we were coming up with, they accepted our plans and, in the end, presented them to the authorities for processing and approval. The rigid and excessive bureaucracy that still reigned supreme was another stumbling block, however. The Tourism Authority refused to grant a five-star hotel licence unless it had a swimming pool at ground floor level. Trying to explain what we had in mind was totally frustrating.

'But how is it possible to have a swimming pool at ground level overshadowed by tall buildings?' I tried to explain to officials of the authority during a consultative meeting. 'What tourist would want to sunbathe beside a pool perpetually in the shade?'

I argued and tried to explain the advantages of a pool at roof level.

'Try to imagine a pool at roof level with a knife edge allowing a panoramic view of both harbours, including Valletta. Can you imagine the pleasure of going through this unique experience without having to move out of a swimming pool?'

'We appreciate all this, Mr Xuereb, and can see the advantages,' one of the officials said. 'But what can we do? We have our regulations which we have to follow. We simply can't budge from them.'

'Okay. I'll grant you that. A five-star is clearly out of the question. How about classifying it as a boutique hotel instead?'

'A boutique hotel? How can we when we don't even have a policy for this classification?'

'So as policies and regulations stand, I can apply and get a licence for a four-star while, if I apply for a five-star and therefore be in line with government policy to upgrade our tourism product, I get a straight and unequivocal no. Is that it?'

The officials could see the stupid reasoning behind the existing policy, but could do nothing about it, however embarrassing for them. At last, and following another long meeting, it was agreed that we submit an application with the same plans, but for a four-star hotel licence. Later, we could apply for upgrading to a five-star when policies were reviewed and amended to comply with government strategy. During the following twelve months this issue was resolved and a licence to operate a five-star hotel was issued.

The construction phase started at the beginning of 2006, but with the frequent upgrading of plans, the project manager was finding it difficult to keep up with the constant pressure. Therefore, two months into the works, I decided to take direct responsibility of the project management and would be free to amend and make decisions on the spot while work was in progress.

It wasn't the easiest of challenges to complete the fourteen floors in eighteen months right in the very centre of Sliema, completely surrounded by third party buildings. But, we did our utmost to keep inconveniences to our neighbours to the barest minimum possible and not to prolong them longer than necessary by working at the fastest rate possible.

I had planned the opening for my fifty-fifth birthday on 15th June 2007. The usual scepticism that greeted this targeted date did not bother me in the least. Confounding my critics was a regular feature in every project I undertook and to make certain that this hotel wouldn't be the exception, I started spending at least ten hours a day on site, especially with the opening date fast approaching. As I planned, my birthday was celebrated with the soft opening, while the final finishing was completed during the following few months.

These few months were an ideal opportunity to introduce Denise into the project management team and she helped in the finishing of this outstanding five-star hotel. Again, she didn't let me down. Her quick grasp of my on-site management skills encouraged me to let her take over the project management from the soft opening to the final completion. This new experience further increased her interest in the job and opened her eyes to the advantages of further training in this field. This experience prompted her to read for a master's degree in the subject at a university in Paris.

Claire suggested 'The Palace' as a name for the new hotel.

'It would emphasise its high quality, Pa,' she added proudly, and The Palace now prides itself as being one of the most elegant modern city hotels in Europe, featuring large suites, some of which are specially themed, making it unique in its class. All those who have been involved in the project feel proud now that they were able to see what their contribution had helped to create. In fact, a number of top international fashion magazines have chosen The Palace as their background for photo shoots and in 2011, we won the *Design Et Al* best award for medium-sized hotels. The award is hosted by leading interior design magazine, *Design Et Al. The International Hotel and Property* awards reward the best in hospitality interior design and architecture from around the world. The citation states, 'Design is a gift, and those who can unleash it effectively are worthy of praise.'

Palazzo Capua

16

A Politician

(2005–2008) 53–56 years

Malta is one of few democratic countries with only two political parties represented in Parliament. This situation has now prevailed since the election held in 1966, two years after Independence. In fact, the 1962 general elections saw five parties represented in Parliament. The Nationalist and Labour parties were always the largest and the situation in 1962 was rather unique for various reasons.

The 1960s were dominated by the bitter conflict between the Catholic Church and the Labour Party led by Dom Mintoff. The 1962 election, as explained in Chapter 1, came about following four years of direct rule from the Colonial Office in London. Both leading parties in Malta were clamouring for Independence from Britain. But, while the Labour Party was demanding a complete amputation, the Nationalists opted for Independence within the Commonwealth, with a Governor General representing the Queen.

The Labour Party's quarrel with the Church had its political consequences when the Archbishop imposed an interdict on all those who were involved in the publication of the party's newspaper and those who read it. The Church further compounded matters when it imposed the infamous 'mortal sin' on all those who voted for Labour. Many Labour supporters were staunch Catholics, but would never bring themselves to vote for the Nationalist Party.

This would have resulted in a high percentage of abstentions, which the political parties, under the Church's 'umbrella', couldn't afford to lose. The Church, therefore, saw to it to use its influence for the establishment of a new workers' party that didn't see eye to eye with Mintoff's hard-line policies. So, the Christian Workers Party (CWP) was born.

The Nationalist Party had its own problems as well. Herbert Ganado, a lawyer and long-time member of the party hierarchy, a staunch Catholic, a former editor of the Church's official newspaper and a former President of the Catholic Action Movement, was totally opposed to early Independence because he thought that Malta would not survive for long without the British services spending. Party leader Dr George Borg Olivier thought otherwise and a clash of personalities within the party was inevitable. This resulted in a split and Ganado formed his own party, which he named the Democratic Nationalist Party (DNP).

Another element in this fray was the Progressive Constitutional Party led by Mabel Strickland, daughter of the once-powerful Lord Gerald Strickland, party leader of the original Constitutional Party and Prime Minister during the turbulent 1920s. The PCP was just a remnant of the once-dominant Constitutional Party led by Miss Strickland's father. It was adamantly imperial in its policies and totally against Independence from Britain.

The 1962 election was contested in the most confused conditions possible and, while the Nationalist and Labour Parties were still dominant, the CWP and the DNP managed to win four seats each, while the PCP managed one. In four years, the small parties had vanished from the scene and Parliament began to be dominated by just two parties. Since then, Malta has experienced the alternation of power fairly regularly until 1987 when, apart from the twenty-two months of Labour Government between 1996 and 1998, the Nationalist Party has always been in power. The difference between the two parties has always been minimal except in the 1992 election and again in 1998, when the Nationalists won by an astounding 13,000 votes majority out of 264,027 votes cast. The

Nationalist Government we have now enjoys a wafer thin, 1,600 vote majority.

The system in Malta is very unlike that of other European countries. It is practically unthinkable that a member votes against his party in a Parliamentary vote (Mintoff's toppling of Dr Sant's Government in 1998 was a rare occurrence, if not unique). Furthermore, with the country so equally divided between these two large parties, decisions that could lose votes for the government are rarely, if ever, taken. The country is so polarised that everything is given a political hue. We practically breathe, think and talk politics all day, though the situation has eased a little during these last two decades. Rivalry is so intense that the party in opposition hardly ever cooperates with the government on matters of national importance and, in the end, it is the people who suffer. Come election time, both parties mobilise their militants and each and every vote is fought for like two dogs over a juicy bone.

Propaganda wise, both parties are well equipped and organised. Both have their own daily and Sunday newspapers, their radio and television stations, and enormous headquarters. Each has its own clubs in every town and village where people gather every evening for a drink, a chat and very often to grumble. These clubs also serve as offices where candidates and Members of Parliament meet with constituents, hear complaints or requests and give promises of action. Some of the more affluent candidates and MPs can afford their own offices where they meet constituents in more privacy and comfort.

Both political parties are well organised at grass roots level. They have local committees in every town and village and they keep tabs on supporters and even non-supporters through informers at street level. All information is channelled to the party headquarters where it is analysed and action is taken mostly through house visits by Members of Parliament and candidates. The clubs also serve as venues for political and social activities organised for party members and supporters, and which MPs and candidates attend. These activities serve as further opportunities for people to meet their representatives in Parliament at grass roots level.

Their headquarters are so enormous and richly furnished that they are the envy of many European political parties. To maintain such large and imposing edifices, however, the parties require enormous funding, which comes from loyal supporters, but mostly from businessmen.

Eventually, the time came when I couldn't accept the situation any longer. I couldn't come to terms with a situation where one is branded a Nationalist or a Socialist for the simple reason that one doesn't contribute cash to any one of the parties, or to both (as many often do to have the best of both worlds). It had also become openly obvious that politically connected private companies were being preferred to others, sometimes more professional and with a better track record, when government tenders were being awarded. Back in the 1970s and 80s everyone grumbled about the blatant and clumsy way the Socialist Government wanted to take over companies that didn't belong to its henchmen, and it always preferred Socialist-leaning businessmen to all others. The Nationalists in opposition used to condemn this attitude (and rightly so), calling it 'institutionalised corruption'. The situation had now been reversed. It is now the Socialist opposition that is pointing fingers.

Except for a short interval of twenty-two months, the Nationalist Party has been in government for twenty-three years. During the twenty-two months of Socialist rule, Dr Sant, an economics graduate from Harvard, tried to govern practically single-handed, thus distancing himself from his ministers and the general public. He possessed a unique single-mindedness that alienated him from ex-Prime Minister Dom Mintoff, a similarly hard-headed politician. This led to Dr Sant's downfall and fresh elections in 1998, three years prematurely. Since then the Nationalists have won all general elections, culminating in 2008, which saw them win by fewer than 1,600 votes – down from 13,000 in the previous two.

It was clear that the people were fed up by the arrogance of the Nationalist Government. Cabinet ministers thought that nothing could remove them from power – not with Dr Sant still leading the Labour Party. People's needs were simply ignored and ministers surrounded themselves with their henchmen and yes-men vying for endless favours. But people are not easily duped – at least not all of the time. Thousands of traditional Nationalists stayed home on voting day and now we have a Nationalist Government that, at the time of writing, hasn't yet done anything to win back lost sheep.

I had friends in both camps and I often discussed my vision for a joint effort by both parties with them, to reduce their petty political bickering for the good of the nation. My motto as Mayor of Naxxar, that 'together we can make a better place for the next generation', should have been taken up by both political parties. But, the division between them was too wide to bridge so easily and I thought I should do something about it. I had attained all I wanted in my business career and so I had nothing to lose. My interest in politics was not for personal gain. I had no financial interest by involving myself in politics. I'm a patriot and, as such, my only interest is the welfare of my country and a better future for the next generation. I felt confident that my vast experience in business and the vision and style of leadership I practiced throughout my career would stand me in good stead should I be in a situation where I could influence both parties. I thought that if I could just achieve this one aim, which I considered a mission, to get the two main parties to work together in matters of importance for the welfare of the people, I would be the proudest of Maltese for having contributed towards the betterment of my country, thus guaranteeing a better Malta for future generations.

My only previous political experiences were my two runaway victories in the local elections at Naxxar. My two terms as mayor were very successful both for me and, more importantly, for my locality. I considered all this seriously and thought that if I could dedicate the same energy I could prove that what could be achieved for the people at local level (when political party representatives put aside their partisan interests where the welfare of the people was concerned) could also be achieved at a national level if the people's representatives in Parliament put the country's interests before their parties'. I, therefore, decided that to achieve this end I would have to contest the general elections and get elected.

Contesting a general election as an independent candidate isn't the same as contesting a local election. The odds against success are enormous. One's chances would be much greater if one was backed by a political party with its effective and sophisticated propaganda machine. I could, therefore, have chosen one of the two big parties, thereby increasing my chances considerably. But my intention to bring the two parties together would have been defeated as the opposing party would definitely consider my proposals suspect and accuse me of ulterior motives.

One day, during a casual conversation with Dr Josie Muscat soon after he had purchased my private hospital, I brought up this political dilemma of mine.

Dr Josie Muscat was elected Member of Parliament for the first time in 1962 on the Nationalist Party ticket at the age of twenty-two when still a medical student, becoming the youngest ever MP. He was always returned in every election, the last one being that of 1981, after which he decided he had had enough.

'In fact, Angelo, I often wonder about the present political situation and where it would lead us if it prevails. Like you, I think that something needs to be done and I'm toying with the idea of forming a new political party to contest the next election.'

These words made my heart miss some beats. This was the opportunity I had been waiting for and, from that day, Dr Muscat and I forgot all other subjects and continued talking politics. We were both convinced that the country needed the presence of a credible third political party in Parliament to inject more justice and unity into the governance of the island. We decided there and then to set up this political party ourselves and contest the next election scheduled for the year after. Both of us were much aware of the enormity of the task we had set ourselves and of the short time available to start everything from scratch and make

A weekend passion.

Skiing in Austria with our German friends Helmut and Ingeborg Wittman.

The Victoria lobby.

The Victoria Hotel.

Sunny Coast Holiday Complex

Verdala Mansions with Mdina in the background.

Capua Hospital.

Palazzo Capua.

The Suncrest by night.

The Palace.

Valletta
Cruise port.

The Valletta Waterfront.

An artist's impression of Simblija Gardens.

Aerial view of Sliema properties.

Reading a book with Jessie on our terrace.

With our friend the great missionary Dun Gorg Grima.

At Claire and Duncan's wedding.

Proud grandparents of Jack and Millie.

an impact on the electorate. It was a difficult challenge indeed and we wanted our party to be as credible as possible.

The persons we decided to approach as possible candidates had, in the past, already been involved in politics and came from both political spectrums. Their track record was impeccable and they were well known and respected for their integrity and genuineness.

Malta adopted the proportional representation system and (together with Gozo) is divided into thirteen electoral districts or constituencies. Although the system is much fairer than, for example, the 'first past the post' system, as practiced in Britain, it still requires some changes to really make Parliament truly representative of the will of the people.

Each district elects the first five candidates that attain the established quota of votes. The quota is a sixth of the number of valid votes cast plus one. For example, in a district where 18,000 valid votes are cast, the quota would be 3,001. Therefore, only 15,005 votes out of a total of 18,000 are in fact utilised. This leaves 2,995 'useless' votes or 16.6%. This percentage on thirteen districts add up to many thousands and, in a country like Malta where over 97% voter turnout is regular, the system leaves much to be desired.

Talks between the two main parties (with little involvement of the negligible Green Party) to find ways to make every vote count have been on-going for years. But, it seems that the Nationalists and Socialists are in no real hurry to find solutions and are always 'disagreeing' on some small detail or other. It's obvious that the present system suits both because any solution would benefit a small party rather than them. The only solution for our new party to have a chance at all was to concentrate our efforts on electing one or possibly two candidates. In order to achieve our aim, we decided to field candidates in just six districts – those districts where our candidates were popular among the grass roots.

The Nationalist Party has been around for a hundred and thirty years, while the Labour Party, at the time of writing, is celebrating the ninetieth anniversary from its founding. These two parties' roots are so deeply embedded in the Maltese way of life that our task seemed nearly impossible. We would be a puny David against two super gigantic Goliaths.

Dr Muscat and I immediately set about writing a statute and christened our party *Azzjoni Nazzjonali* (National Action). It was agreed that Dr Muscat would act as leader with me as his deputy until a general meeting confirmed or otherwise these positions. Both of us were, however, willing to renounce our positions should we succeed in our endeavours to attract renowned political figures better suited to lead the party.

As I said earlier, Dr Muscat was notorious for his outspokenness. But he had a clear vision of what our country's aspirations should be. He could deliver a ninety minute speech on just a few short notes scribbled on a notepad. However, a character like Dr Muscat's has its pros and cons. It's always good for a political party to have a leader who could deliver a rousing speech practically off the cuff and keep his listeners spellbound on the spot. On the other hand, he could easily get carried away and start firing away ideas and beliefs totally beyond and sometimes in complete contrast to the party's principles as declared in the opening paragraph of the party statute, formulated and approved just a few days earlier. This was exactly what journalists would be looking for and they had a field day jotting down what would make sensational headlines rather than the real message in the party's beliefs. The two main parties, with their sophisticated and influential media, did not miss their chance to make hay while the state-run TV station gave that subtle slant in its report, just enough to put our party in a bad light.

I felt I had to personally inform the recently elected Prime Minister, Dr Lawrence Gonzi, about the real intention behind my decision. I didn't want him to hear some biased report in the media and arrive at the wrong conclusion about my genuine intentions. I had known Dr Gonzi for a long time and he knew

I was a lifelong supporter of his party. I sincerely believed in his honesty and capabilities, but I felt he was losing control of some of his ministers' actions, thereby risking losing the election to the Labour Party. I asked him for an appointment by email and, as is his practice, he answered within the hour. He told me he was at some conference in Helsinki, but that he would see me as soon as he was back in Malta. This quick reply convinced me that he had already heard something about my involvement in a new political party.

Dr Gonzi is not a habitual early riser, but makes up for it by extending his working day well into the early hours of the morning. He kept his word by giving me an appointment for Monday morning at nine o'clock, just hours after landing.

Punctually, at nine o'clock, I walked into his office.

'Good morning, Angelo,' he said while vigorously shaking my hand. His eyes were tired from the long flight and lack of sleep. 'So, what's up this early in the day?'

Though he was visibly tired, his words lacked none of his natural bonhomie and spontaneous accompanying smile.

'Good morning, Prime Minister. I thank you for seeing me so soon after your arrival, especially since what I have to say is rather important.'

'Go on, Angelo. I'm listening.'

'It's just that I wanted to tell you personally about it so you won't get the wrong impression from media reports. Dr Josie Muscat and I have formed a new political party and intend to contest the next general election.'

'But why, Angelo? What made you take a decision like this?'

'That's why I wanted to talk to you, Prime Minister. I want to tell you the truth and hold nothing back. You know I've always been a Nationalist Party supporter and I believe strongly in your honesty and capabilities, and that you're the best person to lead the party. But I'm afraid you're losing control of your ministers, Dr Gonzi. The man in the street has lost confidence in them and this reflects on the popularity of the party. I sincerely fear you're risking losing the election to the Labour Party. Our intention is to attract respectable persons as candidates and, if we manage to elect one or two of them, we would seriously consider your government's policies and support them after possible amendments to guarantee real justice for the people.'

'But don't you see, Angelo, that there's no way your party could win a seat in Parliament? And don't you realise you would only be risking taking some of our supporters with you, thus guaranteeing the very thing both of us want to avoid at all cost? Don't you realise you'd be helping the Labour Party win the election?'

We continued to argue for twenty minutes, after which he asked me to reconsider my decision. I declined and he graciously respected my decision.

Dr Muscat and I decided that the party would be officially launched some time during the following two weeks. The launching of the Party was well attended. Dr Muscat as leader, publicly declared that we would be fielding candidates in all districts. My mouth fell open. This decision was taken unilaterally and committed us to much more than we could chew. How could we manage to find the right candidates for thirteen districts?

The media belonging to the two main parties ignored us completely and the state-owned TV station barely mentioned us. This continued to render our task harder still because media coverage is of paramount importance in a political campaign. There were two other TV stations, both privately owned, which we could exploit. But both enjoyed very limited audiences.

We hurriedly set about preparing an action plan for the party's election campaign which, according to the electoral law, could not start earlier than five weeks before polling day. It normally starts as soon as the Prime Minister announces the date and dissolves Parliament. It's the Prime Minister's prerogative to decide upon the date. Therefore, practically no one could know about the exact date although it is an open secret that the party in government would be alerted well beforehand by the Prime Minister, so that its propaganda machine would be well oiled in advance of its rivals.

The electoral law stipulates that no candidate can spend more than €1,400 on his or her personal campaign unless sponsored by third parties. This puts candidates of the smaller parties at a great disadvantage compared to their rivals in the big parties who have enormous media resources at their disposal.

In the short time remaining, we had to sell our party's official name to the electorate. We had to prepare all the advertising material and billboards well in advance not to be caught napping in case the Prime Minister called an early election. We planned media exposure, but the Broadcasting Authority's regulations are very strict where political campaigns on TV and radio are concerned; we weren't allowed by law to organise political debates on TV even if we bought air time and on a private station. The amount of air time was given by the authority according to the support enjoyed by the parties. It was, therefore, obvious that the Nationalists and Socialists would enjoy hours of exposure compared to the few minutes given to small parties like ours. The little time allowed to us made it difficult to project our political beliefs and explain our electoral manifesto.

The two big parties completely ignored us, concentrating instead on the great rivalry between them. We were treated, rather, as though we didn't exist and were never invited to a direct debate with the two big parties.

There were various occasions when Dr Muscat as party leader, or I as Deputy, attended public functions at which party leaders were invited and which were covered by the media. However, the three main TV stations always edited their filming in such a way that neither Dr Muscat nor I were ever featured in the evening news. As an option, we submitted an application to the Broadcasting Authority for permission to buy one hour's airtime once weekly on one of the private TV stations. The Broadcasting Authority, however, would hear none of it. And no wonder, because we later found out that the board was composed of four members each from the two big parties with the chairperson appointed by the government after consultation with the opposition. This made it impossible for our proposal to go through.

We complained about the fact that since the two main parties had their own TV stations they could dish out partisan propaganda twenty-four hours a day and seven days a week. However, the Authority informed us that these stations were considered political TV stations and, therefore, were not breeching any law or regulation.

'So what if we applied for a new political TV station?' I asked the Authority's chairman. 'Would you issue a licence?'

'By all means,' he replied. 'You file an application and after we process it we'll be able to issue a licence.'

'Any idea how long this would take?'

'I should think it would take between four and six weeks.'

'Okay, then. You'll be receiving an application inside two weeks.'

At the next executive committee meeting, a proposal that the party should invest in its own TV station was approved unanimously. It was also decided that we should not waste time searching for the right people to run the station. We, therefore, formed a joint venture with a local company already experienced in the media business. Then we placed an order for the necessary technical equipment. In the meantime, we also submitted our application to the Broadcasting Authority and started recruiting the necessary personnel, which included cameramen and journalists to cover the daily events for the newsroom. We carried out all this on the premise that the Broadcasting Authority chairman's timeframe would be honoured. Our members were enthusiastic about this breakthrough and that, at last, they could see a light at the end of the tunnel.

We discussed all sorts of options on how best to project our vision and explain the electoral manifesto to the general public in a way that they could easily understand and appreciate. Having our own TV station would make it so much easier than having to cram everything in the few minutes allocated on the National TV once every few weeks. The Broadcasting Authority, however, was not as enthusiastic. All feedback from the Authority was negative and it brought up all possible excuses to delay the processing of our application. The Authority's Board met once a month and postponing the decision from one session to the next meant that by the time something was done about our application, the election would have been over and done with. Some of the excuses brought up were hilarious and pathetic, and would have been treated as such had not our situation been so desperate.

The many silly excuses we received from the Authority for delaying the process varied from, 'The board did not have enough time to discuss your application,' to 'Your building approved permit does not cover a TV station.' (In actual fact, it is the Planning Authority which would require a copy of a TV station licence in order to process a change of use of a building to a TV station.) Other collectable excuses include, 'The board did not approve the weekly TV programme schedule submitted with your application,' and 'The board does not agree with the projections of your feasibility study.'

The board was certainly in no hurry to process our application. Its members treated it as just a minor item on their agenda, possibly among 'other matters', and our prompt replies to any of their queries were discussed during their next meeting a month later. This went on and on until many months passed with the election getting closer and closer. The TV station equipment had long since arrived, been installed, tested and made ready for our first transmission. But still we had no licence to operate it.

Suddenly, the Nationalist Party came to life and started placing large blank billboards on concrete bases at strategic places all around Malta and Gozo – a sure sign that the election was round the corner. This activity spurred the Labour Party into frenzied action by placing similar structures as close as possible to their rivals'. Most government ministers started their campaign all over the country, sending attractive and quite large booklets in full colour, highlighting their achievements during the previous five years. Almost every page carried a picture of a smiling and satisfied minister. The official intention behind the publications was to highlight the government's achievement. It was, in fact, nothing but a blatant piece of partisan propaganda 'sponsored' by the taxpayer. This put all other political parties, including the Labour Party, at an unfair disadvantage.

At last, the Prime Minister announced the date of the election and dissolved Parliament. The date was set for 8th March 2008 and it gave us exactly five weeks to convince as many of the electorate as possible with the limited resources at our disposal.

Our AN (*Azzjoni Nazzjonali*) party leader stuck to his fixation of fielding candidates in each of the thirteen districts. I tried one last time to dissuade Dr Muscat from this suicidal jump in the dark, since such wastage of energy would definitely cost us in the half dozen districts where we stood a chance of winning a seat in Parliament. I reminded him that our only chance of success depended on fielding our best candidates in as few districts as possible and concentrating all our resources on these very few. But he wouldn't budge.

At last, when the final list of candidates was submitted to the Electoral Commission, it was too late to argue any longer. The die was cast and whether I liked it or not, I had to do my best to push forward all our candidates. I was given the responsibility of organising and overseeing the party's campaign promotion while Dr Muscat took over the role he was best at – that of main speaker at public meetings and addressing press conferences.

We at last gave up chasing the Broadcasting Authority for a TV station licence and decided instead to partly make up for this lack by designing the right billboard that would best project our policies and beliefs. I carried out some research and discovered that the Nationalist Party had installed sixty large billboards during the previous election campaign. We decided to match that figure and erect them as close as possible to the largest billboards of the opposing parties. One of our candidates had a knack for art work and came up with some very attractive images and accompanying slogans, most of them very eye catching and definitely more so than those produced by the other parties. Our messages on the billboards were aimed at promoting our innovative ideas, and not criticising the other political parties, as the others were doing. We had no doubts whatsoever that ours would be the first to attract drivers' and public transport commuters' attention.

Another ploy we resorted to was the door-to-door distribution of an attractive A3 leaflet in full colour, together with another leaflet to introduce the candidate for a particular district. Our promotional material lacked nothing in its presentation and was considered of an equal standard to those produced by the two big parties with their seemingly limitless financial backing.

The Electoral Law stipulated that during the official electoral campaign, the National TV station must allow the same coverage to every party contesting. The law also covered the rights of candidates running on an independent ticket. However, since every law has its loophole, the National TV station used the fact that there was no stipulation as to the times of the day (or night) when each party should participate in political debates. The same free hand was taken with regard to each party's own promotional message. Whereas the two big parties' participation in debates and their promotional messages were aired during prime time hours, our party and *Alternattiva Demokratika* (Alternative Democracy – the Green Party) were limited to late night hours when only insomniacs would be watching. The programmes we were invited to participate in were invariably aired as late as ten thirty and eleven o'clock at night when most people are asleep after a long, tiring day at work.

Whatever the appearance given to the general public, it was clearly evident that the party in Government was in full control of the National TV station. The whole campaign on TV was planned and conducted only to benefit the two main parties. Needless to say, the name of our party was never mentioned on the TV stations owned by the two political parties. As far as they were concerned, we did not exist. Every possible obstacle was created to restrict and sometimes even prohibit our appearance on the silver screen. In fact, the few invitations we did receive to appear on TV sometimes reached us just two days before a programme. Sometimes, they arrived as late as the day before and on occasions on the same morning of the scheduled recording. These limitations severely restricted our campaign to push forward our candidates to take part in debates on TV, and the little exposure allowed was availed only to Dr Muscat and myself. The two main parties could afford to put forward as many of their candidates as they wished during the disproportionate air time allowed them. They each had more than a hundred candidates and most of them managed to appear and talk on TV at some time or other during the final five weeks.

We planned a series of frequent press conferences on various subjects, spanning the whole spectrum of Maltese life, and preparations for these press conferences were time consuming. On top of this, there were days when I had to take part in three or four debates, the subjects for which were handed to me just hours before, giving me just enough time to jot some notes and drive fast to the TV station. This hectic schedule became a daily routine and, as the election drew nearer, I became more involved in public meetings at different locations all over Malta and Gozo, during which I was always one of the speakers. Dr Muscat was always the main speaker, however. He was a born speaker and he would make the most of this God-given ability to speak for hours on end if given the chance. I wasn't as good, but I soon got used to the many impromptu debates I was pushed into. Sometimes I would sit back and think about this complete change in me and wonder what had happened to that shy country boy who never answered back and the young man who turned red and speechless in the presence of beautiful girls.

'Look at me now,' I would say to myself. 'I'm now an outspoken politician unafraid to cross swords with the best.'

Apart from being the deputy leader, and with full responsibility for the promotion of the campaign, I was also given the additional task of presenting the party's many infrastructural and tourism plans for the country. Josie Muscat may have been gifted with a natural flow of words, but my gift for coming up with good plans and innovative ideas was no less providential. These were the things I enjoyed doing most and they had proved to be fundamental to the success of my business career. Sketching was one of my stronger points and it was to give us the edge over the other parties. I was able to design new concepts or embellishments for local districts, which we launched during press conferences on site. The launch press conferences were aided by impressive detailed plans and designs on large billboards. These included a master plan for Valletta and for the reform of the general public transport system. The latter included plans for mass transportation on a monorail system, partly underground and partly elevated, as well as traffic management, a super yacht hub centre at Sliema, a master plan for the Grand Harbour, and a similar plan for the south tourist zone for a number of yacht marinas around Malta and Gozo. We also covered proposals on how we could mitigate the negative impact of construction activities on the surrounding neighbourhoods and the tourism industry, a plan on how to improve the quality of tourism and how to replenish our sandy beaches to qualify them for the Blue Flag certification, and many other plans. All these I managed in the few weeks leading up to the election.

The obstacles created for us, and which limited the projection of our party to the electorate, were reflected in the election results. The target of obtaining more than 16.6% of the votes in at least one district proved elusive. It was impossible to match the two big parties' mammoth fundraising activities, which generated millions of Euros annually, mostly through large donations by businessmen. The party in government enjoyed the further advantage of using taxpayers' money for extravagant propaganda material just in advance of the election period proper. We had tried our best to somewhat make up for this by matching them in the media sector, but the Broadcasting Authority's foot-dragging tactics put paid to our only chance of reducing the imbalance that existed and this, more than any other factor, diminished our chances of winning a seat in Parliament.

The Nationalist Party was again the winner – but only just.

With a wafer-thin majority of 1,580 votes it was the first time since the party won in 1987 that it could only form a minority government. The disgruntlement among the Nationalist supporters – the thing I had feared most – nearly unseated Dr Gonzi. The voters' turnout of 93% was the lowest since 1971. It was a protest vote the Nationalists could ill afford to ignore. Many simply stayed home hoping that their party got a real thumping for not learning from past lessons. In the end, the Nationalists had to be content with 49.33% of the valid votes cast. But this also meant that, by the end of the new legislature, the Nationalists would have governed Malta for twenty-five years except for a short interval of twenty-two months between 1996 and 1998.

The two small parties – ours and *Alternattiva Demokratika* – did not manage to get enough votes to elect one candidate and none made it to Parliament. Ironically, the long-awaited TV station licence was granted to us a few weeks after the election and, since we now had no use for it, we sold it to third parties.

Our intention to elect a member to Parliament to help guarantee unity in the interest of the nation was totally genuine. Neither I nor anybody else within the party had any intention of building a political career. But I had learned my lesson. I had to respect the will of the people for voting according to family tradition and for wanting to stick to a two-party Parliament.

I decided to call it a day. Later, even Dr Muscat, who shared my clear vision about Malta's needs, decided to give up politics for good and wound up the party. In the end, it was a new and great experience both for me and for the party. It helped me to better understand the ruthlessness that goes on behind all the smiles, cheers and backslapping. It also taught me that, however intense the rivalry between the two big parties, they ultimately share the same agenda that puts paid to the possibility of a third party driving a wedge between them at least in the foreseeable future, unless one of them experiences another split similar to those of the 1960s. When, one day, a credible third party manages to make it to Parliament, our future generations will then enjoy the diffusion of our politically dominated way of life.

I have often compared Malta to the unpolished Jewel of the Mediterranean and I am confident that, with less political interference, we can make this jewel reflect the brilliance of all the Maltese people. Only then can we be proud of our achievements. Only then can we be assured of our future generations' respect for our legacy to them.

At the time of writing, three years after the experience, I can calmly analyse our actions objectively and pinpoint the mistakes we could easily have avoided. Undoubtedly, fielding so many candidates, most of whom were practically unknown in the districts they contested, was a major error. This decision forced us to try and eat more than we could chew. Our organisation was makeshift, owing to the non-existent traditional base of the party. Concentrating on just two or three districts would have given us a better chance of attracting reputable and experienced political personalities with the chance of one of them making it to Parliament. Our one satisfaction is that some of our ideas have been taken up by the government and executed.

We were a new and very young party with resources too limited to face the insurmountable obstacles, some of which were put purposely in our way. Compared to the big parties, we were like a new-born baby. But the baby made enough noises to scare the big party leaders, especially the Prime Minister who had told me months prior to the election that there was a real fear that we might 'steal' many of the party's votes and thus compromise its chances of winning. Had the goal posts not been shifted as suited the big parties, we might just have managed it. This unfair treatment of small parties would dishearten any genuine new political party with the capabilities to generate changes for the betterment of the country. An amendment in our constitution regarding this unfair political competition may give a chance to a third party to make it to Parliament. An amendment is also needed to allow governments to appoint technocrats if they realise that they do not have the required quality among those elected to be appointed as ministers.

As I have already explained, the Electoral Law makes it amply clear that no candidate may spend more than €1,400 on his election campaign and that no party may start campaigning before the Prime Minister announces the date for the election, which is usually five weeks from the date of the announcement. However, all this does not impede the two big parties from spending millions of euros each year for the five-year-long legislature. As far as the two big parties are concerned, the election campaign is always on and is accelerated during the few weeks before the election. Both organise weekly political activities in various localities at which the party leaders are always the main speakers. Fundraising activities take all forms, culminating in a day-long phone-in TV programme, during which supporters pledge sums of money. The amounts collected run into hundreds of thousands or even millions. Party radio and TV stations, together with their daily and Sunday newspapers, bombard the electorate with non-stop partisan propaganda.

Managing such an enormous organisation, together with the maintenance of both parties' state-of-the-art headquarters, requires unlimited funding and I believe that all this should be considered part of their election campaign. Considering all the above, restrictions on the candidates' expenditure during the 'official' election campaign, lasting a mere five weeks, are all the more ridiculous. And, anyway, few if any still believe that candidates stick to this legal restriction.

The result disappointed me greatly, I must admit, but there's still life beyond politics and I had to move forward once I had admitted my mistakes and learned from them. One positive outcome of all this was that I became more popular and my credibility with the general public did not suffer. During my campaign, I was very careful not to criticise or attack my opponents on a personal level. I had no need to. My aims and interests weren't parochial or personal. All the party and I wanted to do was to promote our vision for Malta and Gozo, and to show that we had the capabilities to do things differently and better for the people of this country. My campaign never offended or alienated any of my rivals and this was proven by the intact friendships that I still enjoy with most senior members of all political parties.

Shortly after the election, the Labour Party elected a new leader. Dr Joseph Muscat, a thirty-four-year-old former Member of the European Parliament, whom I consider a friend, is also a man with a vision and I think he could be the catalyst for the changes the Labour Party needs to effect in order to be successful in the next election.

The Palace Hotel

17

The Future and Beyond

(2009–2012) 57–59 years

At fifty-seven and with both feet planted solidly on the ground, I decided to allow myself more free time to fill my days. It was the time to spend less time at the office and more time on the green practising my golf and on my bike exploring the maze of country lanes that lead from one breath-taking view to another within the shortest of distances. I also bought a new and larger fifty-five-foot power boat, which I aptly named Vision, and which I could easily handle on my own and sometimes with some assistance from Jessie. Together with close friends Joe and Josette, we enjoy two short breaks in Sicily every summer and, when I'm not too busy, we spend Sundays cruising around Malta's clear, blue waters.

My other great leisure interest was still for sports cars and speed, but not since my first Toyota Dad had given me for my 18th birthday have I had the time and pleasure to really enjoy slamming the accelerator all the way down to the floor. Parting with that beautiful machine was heart-breaking but necessary. With more time for me to enjoy such pleasures, one winter Sunday morning, during my regular coffee with my brothers, I hinted that I might exchange my Mercedes 500S for a four-door Maserati. My brothers are also mad about sports cars and all of them tried to talk me out of my idea.

'Angelo,' they told me, 'the Maserati doesn't reflect the real you and your position.'

I couldn't understand what they meant and didn't notice my brother Manuel's son, Clive, who runs a bookshop, get up from the table and run to his shop around the corner. He returned breathless just a few minutes later with a big smile and handed me a large colour photo of an Aston Martin DB9.

'This is what they mean, uncle,' he told me. 'This is the real car for you.'

I looked at it and liked what I saw. I looked up at my brothers and they were all smiling their agreement with Clive's opinion.

'But this is a two-seater,' I said, frowning. 'Where would my friends sit?'

'There's enough space in your new BMW, isn't there?' they said, referring to my 5 Series model while smiling in a benign manner as if I was their junior brother.

I took another look at the Aston Martin and the more I looked the more I liked the shape.

The next day, Clive came over to my office with all the details and information to enable me to buy it. A few months later, I was driving it all the way from the UK and I have to admit that it has become my favourite toy. I often refer to it as 'The Beauty and the Beast'. The 'beauty' is when Jessie is sitting in the passenger seat while I drive it at a sedate pace, while the 'beast' is when I'm driving alone with the accelerator pressed all the way down. Driving on the German Autobahn, I touched 190 mph! I felt like a youth on my first fast drive in my Toyota. There's nothing that could beat the excitement and thrill of speed. When I'm alone, sitting behind the wheel, I feel young again and, for a few hours, I completely forget my age.

Aston Martins and similar powerful sports cars are not built for Malta's roads. We have no highways or racing circuits where the engines could show what they're really capable of. Therefore, every so often I join a group of mutual enthusiasts and book a race track in nearby Sicily where we can drive our engines to their full potential around bends and down straights very similar to a Formula One circuit. It's only there, on that track, that the

Aston Martin lives up to its nickname. It doesn't only seem like a beast, but a roaring beast of prey savaging all rivals intruding into its territory. The first time I drove on the track I was rather apprehensive, unconvinced about the safety measures around it. But a few warm up laps convinced me that it was equipped with more and better safety precautions than motorways.

The 2009 recession hit the world with a vengeance. We witnessed the collapse of huge financial institutions and large, reputable banks. Iceland went completely bankrupt and other countries with a strong economic base only just made it to safety. Malta didn't go unscathed. We were hit quite badly and my three business sectors were affected as negatively as everybody else's. Building permit applications slowed down to a trickle, slowing construction activity to a level unheard of throughout my thirty-seven years of experience. It also hit the property market and Malta ended up with an oversupply, which forced some developers to call it a day.

Having already had previous experiences of global recessions during my career, I could foresee this from two years back. I was, therefore, very cautious and prudent about my investments and held back from real estate, thus relieving the group from undue financial constraints. I sadly watched inexperienced investors in this field buying old houses to convert into blocks of apartments with substandard quality finishing, trying their luck by asking for unrealistically high prices. They did quite well initially, but as the recession began to really bite, they found themselves stuck with hundreds of thousands of euros worth of unsaleable property, forcing the banks to call in their loans.

The fragile industry of tourism was another victim. The number of tourists from European countries, where unemployment was high and salaries slashed, went alarmingly down. I had just finished my new five-star hotel and I was left with no option but to try and fill it at low room rates, still a challenge when considering the fewer tourists coming to Malta and the intense competition from other hoteliers in the same hot waters. Cruise liner passengers were also fewer, affecting my share in the VISET Consortium. It was a time when, faced with such daunting difficulties, the worst of my career, I had to be at my ultimate best at facing probably the biggest challenge in decades, and guiding all sectors out of it all would be my greatest feat yet. I have always believed and preached that 'you test the capability of a ship captain in rough seas not in calm waters'. I think Winston Churchill was First Sea Lord when he coined this saying! He also said that 'kites fly highest against the wind, not with it'. He should know. He was at his best when leading his country against the Axis during World War II. Unfortunately, and against what my heart dictated, I had to shed a number of workers in the construction sector. I also had to put all new development on hold and, thanks to Claire's excellent handling of our hospitality sector, operational costs were reduced to the barest minimum without affecting the excellent service my hotels have always provided.

I have been through this repetitive economic cycle approximately every decade, and the natural reaction by all concerned, including the government, has always turned the downward cycle back to gentle comeback inside three years. After a few more years, the economy has always picked up its normal cycle and this time round won't be an exception, even though I have to admit that this recession was the worst I can remember. Tourism started picking up again during 2010 and, thanks to our management and staff training in cost economising, we have seen all our hotel operations flourishing again. Although still slightly behind on the average room rates, the advantage of having good locations, good service and a good management team guaranteed our being back to the normal healthy cycle.

The local tourism industry performed very well during 2011, and 2012 is expected to be a record year including the cruise liner sector. Again, I was proven right that the economy is a cycle and that, in bad times, one must be more courageous and determined to continue to struggle against all odds to overcome all the difficulties that one has to encounter. As an entrepreneur, one has to look at a glass half-full rather than a half-empty glass. In difficult times, many executives look at the negative side and you see them all coming with their problems. Unfortunately, few will provide solutions to these problems. Others look at the huge mountain of problems in front of them, without realising that by climbing carefully and taking calculated risks, the mountain will start looking like a hill. The real entrepreneur will continue to climb the never-ending way with pride and confidence as things begin to look positive, and then stronger he will be when faced with other huge mountains to be tackled again in the same manner.

The recent recession is not as bad as that of pre-World War II and I can sense that the international economy will soon pick up again. Together with my children and my Group's Executive team, I am already planning to engage in further expansion, both locally and internationally – including finally constructing The Simblija.

You will remember in earlier chapters I wrote about my plans for a retirement home complex which delivered dignity – Simblija Gardens. After twenty years of constant battling and harassment my project has been finally approved. This is further proof that, with persistence and determination to succeed, any objective can be achieved. The other project for development will hopefully terminate the seventeen-year Verdala Hotel Complex saga. The process of trying to get the project off the ground has become an addiction. The more obstacles placed in my way, the more determined I become to persuade the Planning Authority, Government Ministers and even the Prime Minister. In reality, this whole saga has been ever-present throughout half my entire working life. As I have said, I am unwavering in my mission to restore the status of this complex as a major economic contributor to the group and indeed to the Maltese economy, just as when it was the flagship hotel in the five-star hotel sector in Malta way back in the early 1970s.

It is indeed a pity that the Government is barring the

redevelopment of a hotel which represented the commercial hub of the Rabat and surrounding communities for many years and which, following a form of requisition by the Government, was left to rot without any investment for over 10 years. The whole application process was full of stops and starts, with the initial application filed in 1994 and full development permission received in 2001, albeit with a reserved matter on the elevation rendering redevelopment impossible. I have submitted various proposals for this elevation; however, the procrastination by the high officials involved remains unabated for reasons which defy logical explanation.

I have, at a greatly increased cost, complied with the Authority's recommendation to demolish the existing hotel and re-develop it following a terraced architectural design concept that would greatly improve the existing highly sensitive skyline. In spite of the numerous schemes submitted and notwithstanding the nature of the proposal the path is always firmly barred.

Recently, I wrote to the Prime Minister, Ministers, Chairman and Directors of the Planning Authority, begging them to take a definitive decision, presenting them with the only two feasible options at this stage: either to approve one of the various proposed elevations to my existing full development permit, having seven floors above street level (if need be, they can design the elevation themselves) or to allow me to demolish the structure and re-construct in keeping with the same volume of the valid building permit I possess, into a more pleasing terraced elevation enjoying a wider footprint but with a reduction of the highest level to five floors, putting it at the same height as the adjacent, recently-built properties.

I still live in the hope that Malta's highest authorities will change their stance from one of persistent bureaucracy and procrastination to an approach conducive to finding an end to this never-ending saga. I keep my fingers crossed in the hope that a permit is issued and construction works will be well underway by the time this book is published.

Once these two projects (and the other projects we have in the pipeline) are completed, the Group will be launched into a new and exciting era.

Maybe at my age I should rest on my laurels and consider retiring to a life of sitting back to enjoy a life of pleasure and relaxation. But I simply can't. I can still feel the urge of that thirteen-year-old boy who wanted to succeed in business. I still possess the determination of that thirteen-year-old boy who surprised his elders with his prompt answer, but wasn't taken seriously on that Sunday afternoon, so long ago. My enthusiasm and urge for further growth have not diminished one iota with the passing of time. I shake my head in disgust and resist the very thought of retirement, at least in the foreseeable future – not when so many exciting opportunities still lie ahead. What would Jessie do with a restless man playing at being a lazy husband watching television all day?

Even if I did quit business, which is definitely not on my agenda, I don't envisage staying completely idle. I'm quite frequently asked to participate in public discussions and conferences on diverse subjects, especially on infrastructural projects. In fact, I have already gone public about various proposals to the government to consider more projects of national importance on a Public Private Partnership (PPP) or Built Operate and Transfer (BOT) basis. The government has expressed interest in the suggestions, but, as expected, all governments have bureaucratic systems which have to be navigated.

An ideal opportunity to forget about a life of relaxation came along when our consortium (led by one of my construction companies) was awarded the contract for the construction of the new Parliament Building in Valletta. The plans for this prestigious building, designed by world renowned architect Renzo Piano, command very detailed specifications and conditions which demand high management skills to complete and execute on a fast-track basis. My successful career was built on my ability to complete turnkey projects on time and to the required high standards, and I thought that this most important and prestigious project would add another feather in my cap. I would also be extremely proud of executing an idea from such a famous architect. I have, therefore, decided to take the whole matter in hand and take on the role of project manager.

I immediately realised that this could be the baptism of fire for Denise to act as my assistant project manager. I enrolled her on this prestigious and unique project and we formed a perfect team. While I have thirty-seven years of practical experience, Denise has all the latest knowledge in theory and administrative capabilities.

Prior to the commencement of works I was called to attend a high level meeting during which I was repeatedly warned about the importance of keeping to the schedule. It was also emphasised that the standards must be the highest possible and that the most stringent health and safety measures were to be followed throughout. I was aware of the polemic generated by the project and, for months on end, the daily papers dedicated whole pages to letters and articles criticising and sometimes lauding Renzo Piano's concept. I therefore appreciated the concern voiced by those present, and the responsibility thrust on my shoulders.

'Gentlemen,' I answered confidently, 'throughout my long career I have been involved as project manager in a number of bigger and more demanding projects, and have never failed to make a success of them. I assure you that I shall dedicate my knowhow and energy to rendering this prestigious project to your satisfaction. I understand the importance of this project and appreciate its national value. And I also know that all the media will be monitoring the progress day by day as will the people entering Valletta. I assure you, gentlemen, that I won't let you down.'

My confidence managed to ease the stress on the faces around me and I even noticed some smiles. But I didn't speak just to please the people at the meeting. I spoke out of conviction and confidence in my ability to stick to my commitment.

After the meeting I called another with my joint venture partners to inform them about what was expected of us, and then went on to brief our supervisors and foremen.

While works were in progress, a delegation from the government paid us a visit. I gave them a tour of the site and explained in detail what was going on, again reassuring the members that I would stick to the conditions of the contract that the project would be completed by the end of February 2012. When the delegation left, Chris, CEO of the Government Corporation, came over to me wearing the mischievous smile I knew so well.

'Angelo,' he said, 'I know you'll finish in time to honour your commitment. But, as a personal favour, why don't you finish by the end of January instead? I know you can do it. And so do you.'

I smiled back and he understood that I had taken up the challenge.

Towards the end of November 2011 I was again approached by the top executives and one of them said, 'Look, Angelo, we know you're well ahead of the time-frame stipulated in the contract and we appreciate that. Now we're asking you to accelerate works even further and finish by the end of December. You see, we've decided on some additional works which we want completed by the end of January.'

I looked at the men in front of me and then at the men working hard on site. The building was already taking shape and it was obvious that works were much more advanced than envisaged when the contract was signed. I looked again at the top executives.

'Well, gentlemen, this is far more challenging than I had imagined. You haven't given me enough time to plan ahead with only a month to go to the end of the year. You know it's the season when we expect bad weather and to top it all it'll soon be the festive season. Give me some time to think about it.'

But it took me only ten minutes to decide to take up this seemingly impossible challenge.

I smiled at them. 'Okay, gentlemen. I shall do my utmost and God willing I'll finish by the end of the year.'

We shook hands and I left them to start planning in detail the works for the following thirty days. This meant total commitment from all concerned including the workers. It was all the more tough considering the restricted site area which can only take one tower crane, thus causing the least inconvenience to the large crowds that flock daily to Valletta. All this restricted us to the use of small mobile cranes to service the perimeter areas.

Two days later the CEO and I met again. We smiled knowingly at one another. We both understood the irony of it all. His challenging me to finish works by the end of January had been out-bid by the top executives!

'Chris,' I said, 'you know that once I've given my word I will honour it. You know me well by now.'

'You don't have to remind me, Angelo. You know I have full confidence in you, and I thank you for taking it up.' Then he smiled and continued, 'And by the way, have a peaceful Christmas.'

I sensed the irony in his voice and laughed. 'Thanks for your good wishes, Chris. We shall be spending Christmas peacefully together here, on site. No Christmas shut down for us this time round!'

We enjoyed taking this challenge and we managed to complete our contract eight weeks ahead of programme and with the highest quality standards and difficult specifications. This achievement augurs very well for even more challenging projects for the coming years.

And after this? In fact, I've been doing much thinking. It's true that I love rambling around the countryside on my mountain bike. It's also true that I love travelling and that during the course of writing these memoires I discovered the joy of reading a good book. But my life won't be complete unless I indulge myself in my lifetime hobby. I have always been a visionary and a good planner. Planning is my lifelong hobby which I practised with a passion, and I intend to spend my increasing leisure time working on a long-term master plan for the Maltese islands, comprising sixty-seven localities. I intend to plan in sketch form the infrastructural works, which I foresee as the best solutions to the present issues and, also, how we could make our islands more beautiful.

While writing this paragraph, I laid down my pen and thought about the ten-year-old village boy drawing plans on blank paper and constructing small rubble rooms in the fields. And here I am, now, so many years later, planning and drawing a master plan for the whole country.

Some of my ideas may seem outrageous to many. But I'm used to being pooh-poohed and later proven right. My vision is based on my acquaintance with the localities at ground level coupled with my experience in various sectors of the Maltese economy and social life. I have visited countries the world over, keeping an eye for detail. The more I saw, the more I became convinced about the potential of my Malta, which I love so much. I feel that this enjoyable exercise is another challenge to prove to myself that I have the capabilities to further help my country become the Jewel of the Mediterranean. I shall give this the title, 'Vision for Malta 2050'.

Throughout my career, I have learnt that many of my ideas were considered outrageous when published, but, after ten or twenty years, these were implemented. Then, hopefully after my lifetime, some would look up my master plan and say, 'Well, Angelo already had this vision many years ago.'

The time will come, however, when I shall gently ease myself out of the action. I shall not be here forever, let alone behind my desk in the group building. When this happens I shall rest, certain that the Group is in strong hands.

When I was much younger and totally immersed in expanding my business and diversifying, with my three children still very young and wholly dependent on their mother, I never gave a thought about the fact that one day they would be old enough to start thinking about careers of their own. In time, however, seeing them grow taller and in the secondary stage of their education, I realised that one day I would be gone and, for all

I knew, my business would go along with me unless my children followed in my footsteps.

It is only now, closer than ever to the age of sixty, that I realise how lucky I am in Richard, Claire and Denise. It was just a few years ago that I thought it opportune to broach this subject with them and make them realise their father was not immortal, and neither was his business unless they carried it on to the next generation.

Gradually, I started passing on my experience to them, giving them small doses in the art of conducting business as I went along. I call this 'succession process planning' and it was imperative that my children learn very early on from my successes and, more importantly, from my failures, thus letting them understand that, when the time is right, they will be the ones who take full control.

I dread to think about what could have happened had I not acted as I did. I have known many people work hard at their business till well past their pensionable age and still retain a strong hold of their enterprise. I have seen their enthusiastic children eager and qualified for their turn to take over, but completely overruled by their domineering fathers. In the end, they leave the family business and either offer their experience to a rival company or start on their own. This could easily spell the end of a business painstakingly built over decades. In fact, statistics show that only 30% of family businesses continue to be successful during the second generation. This shrinks to just 11% during the third.

This was a nightmare I was determined to avoid. And that is why I count myself lucky. None of my three children wished to opt out and the three of them did their utmost to specialise in one of the three sectors that are the pillars of my enterprise. It put paid to the most dreaded possibility in a businessman's life – that of having to sell to third parties. Thanks to my children's decision, I never lost the urge to keep on working hard and to guide them in their endeavours to become successful in their field. This, however, wasn't the easy task I'm making it out to be. As always, there's the gap one has to bridge. The mentality of every new generation is different from the previous. The difference in the upbringing, education, culture, social life, living environment, lifestyle and political environment all, in a small or larger extent, affect the way one views life in general. Diverse views create different opinions and attitudes.

The only important advantage we of the older generation have on the next is wisdom, because wisdom can only be attained through experience. And experience can only grow with the passing of time. Wisdom teaches patience and tolerance. Tolerance is the key to understanding and sometimes embracing the new generation's view, however alien it may seem to us. Whenever I come across uncertainty, most times I give the benefit of the doubt to the new generation. I wasn't as lucky when young and it is only when I am certain that their opinion is wrong and detrimental to the Group's interests that I put my foot down, certain that, in time, when more mature and wise, they will look back and understand the wisdom of my decisions. This approach has benefitted the four of us and I hope it will continue to do so.

Although one may consider my business a family affair, I never discuss it with my children outside the office. Family and business, as with oil and water, should never mix. Outside the office we enjoy each other's company and this helps to keep the family bond that we are so proud of intact and ensures an excellent relationship. This approach has worked well so far and I hope it'll last until I decide to call it a day.

I am also extremely proud of the fact that I am now a grandfather. Claire and Duncan were first to extend the family tree to the third generation with the birth of their twins, Jack and Millie, who bring along more love and happiness. Jessie and I are so proud to be grandparents for the first time and are looking forward to making time to play with them. I will try to make up for the time I did not have when our children were growing up. My children have excellent relationships with their spouses and their families. It's not often that in-laws, coming from a different environment, integrate so easily with a family whose life is absorbed so deeply in business. But I thank God that my three children have been wise and lucky in their choices.

The succession process of a family business is quite a delicate operation, especially when the final decision about who would eventually become CEO is taken. I believe that the best person for the job should be an enterprising and knowledgeable family member whose sole and genuine interest is the advancement of the business. The alternative is the appointment of a qualified outsider with an excellent track record for managing business enterprises with strict and good corporate governance.

In Mexico they say, 'Father, founder of company, son rich and grandson poor.' This is a dangerous pitfall that has spelt the ruin of many big businesses where the founder works hard to build a successful business while the son, when taking over, fails through mismanagement to keep the momentum, bent only on enjoying the wealth left him by his father while, in the end, the grandson inherits a failed enterprise and an empty bank account. This is exactly what I'm doing my best to avoid, but it would be sadistic and senseless to force my children through the same hardships I went through to understand this. It would be wrong, however, not to make them realise that nothing comes easy in life, and that even the most successful business could be ruined through laissez-faire. Difficulties crop up around every corner and I have, slowly but surely, taught my children how to face them and patiently solve them. I never tire of reminding them that 'to be successful requires hard work while to be unsuccessful requires no effort whatsoever' and that 'it's always that extra effort that makes one a winner'. It's like a 100 metres track race where a hundredth of a second spells success or failure.

I have instilled in my children the above dictums since they were relatively young so that by the time they were ready to join the Group they were already prepared for the challenges awaiting them. They entered the Group fully equipped with the necessary courage and optimism required to face the big challenges ahead of them.

It is my sincere wish that what Jessie and I have taught them will help them further enlarge the business they shall inherit and also to have a happy and successful married life, thus ensuring the continuation into the third generation what I started decades ago.

Richard, a graduate with an MSC in Construction Management from Manchester University, is fully involved in our construction companies. Claire, with a Glion Bachelors Degree in Hospitality and Tourism Management and a Bachelor of Science (Hons) in International Hospitality Management (University of Wales), is at the helm of our hotels operations and has already made a name for herself in the tourism industry. Denise, recently graduated in Project and Programme Management and also with a Masters in Business Administration from an International Business school in Paris is already very active in the group's business developments as an executive at head office. Her baptism of fire didn't take long in coming, as I appointed her my assistant in the new Parliament Building project mentioned earlier. All three are now directors of the Group.

Now, after thirty-seven years of hard work and constant growth, I feel happy and satisfied to see our hardworking children follow in my footsteps and I wish them the best in their careers. I feel happy and satisfied that, although I had to face excessive bureaucracy every step of the way and without which I could have achieved more, I have still managed to make a success of my career. My achievements throughout the years are there for all to see and appreciate, and for my family to be proud of. For all this, I thank God. And with His help I shall continue for as long as He wills it.

 Valletta
 Mdina

18

The Tragedy

1st January 2012

I had intended to end this history on 31 December, 2011. There was nothing to add to the story, but after what happened on 1st January, my mind instinctively recalled the opening words of the epilogue: *'But is it really an epilogue?'* and *'Does my life story deserve an epilogue just now?'*

I couldn't have been more prophetic because on New Year's Day my family was made to pass through the most horrible tragedy imaginable: a tragedy that shook the whole nation. At 7 a.m. on 1 January an intruder broke into the residence of my daughter Claire and her husband Duncan, both still asleep with their three-month-old twins in their cots close to their bed. A twenty-six-year-old intruder, probably after overdoing it drinking on New Year's Eve, broke into the penthouse and made straight for the kitchen where he selected the two longest knives. Then he entered the bedroom and inflicted a deep wound on Duncan's body.

Duncan, now rudely awakened and badly wounded, somehow managed to struggle with his aggressor and even to push him away from the twins, to shift the fight from the bedroom to the dressing room, where he managed to disarm the intruder of one of the knives. This gave him a fairer chance to fight for his life, though he was weakened from loss of blood from the various wounds already sustained. He, somehow, managed to fight back, trying hard to keep the aggressor away from the bedroom. And he succeeded, albeit dying in the process. Both died in the struggle, leaving Claire a widow and their two little angels fatherless.

Duncan's robust health, physical strength and his love for his family made it possible for him to fight back though seriously injured and still being stabbed repeatedly with those lethal knives to his death. But he died a hero: a hero to his family until the very last breath. I have no doubt whatsoever that, had Duncan not fought back, this assailant would not have spared Claire and, possibly, the children. The aggressor wore no balaclava or gloves to hide his identity, and although the police have not yet found a motive for this horrible act, I am fairly certain that his sole intention was to kill, and kill himself in the process. If what I think is correct, the annihilation of a whole family wouldn't have mattered to him. Not in the mental state he was in. It was only through the Lord's mercy and Duncan's heroism that the lives of Claire and their two angels Jack and Millie were spared.

Duncan and Claire made an exceptional couple, madly in love and wholly dedicated to their family. He was also a great chef and had been very supportive of Claire from the very first day they met in 2005. I equate their passion for one another with the eternal love story of Romeo and Juliet. When Claire found out she was pregnant, the happy news spread like wildfire among their many friends, relatives and business associates.

Ten weeks into her pregnancy Claire was told she was expecting twins. The news thrilled Claire and Duncan and filled their parents with indescribable joy. Soon enough Claire started to keep a diary, recording her every week's actions and experiences. She even wrote about the time she and Duncan first met, and how they fell in love. She wrote about his and her families; their upbringing and the values they inherited from their parents. She wrote all this and more, so that the twins would one day know and understand how blessed they were to have Claire and Duncan as parents. She wanted to present it to Jack and Millie when they were old enough to understand it. Reading sections of the diary I was impressed with the happiness and love contained in every handwritten paragraph. Duncan was no less enthusiastic, and lovingly helped Claire select pictures to include in the diary together with the results of the monthly ultrasound 4D images.

Duncan wasn't only well known and appreciated in the catering business, but he was also respected as a true photography enthusiast. This further assisted Claire in her busy schedule as the Group's Hospitality Director and as Chairperson of the ITS (Institute of Tourism Studies). He had set up his own business unique to Malta, naming it Uphotomalta, taking tourists on guided tours off the beaten track around the Maltese islands to show them the hidden charms missed by the mainstream tours while teaching them photography and ensuring they take great photographic souvenirs back home with them.

With a keen photographer husband it was only natural that Claire was the subject of hundreds of pictures taken during her pregnancy and after. Very often Jessie and I would invite them for lunch at our home, and Duncan and I would spend many happy afternoons playing snooker. He was also very good at billiards and on the rare occasions I managed to beat him I always made it a point that the whole family would know. He had so much charm. He was talented and friendly, and so much fun to be with. I shall sorely miss him, and can never erase his honest smile from my memory.

Many times he used to come up to me and say, 'Hi Boss,' (that is what he always called me) 'I had a very busy week with many tourists from various hotels, and I really enjoyed it.' Then we would settle down and talk, and he would ask for my advice and I would naturally encourage him to expand his business, seeing that his heart was in it.

One day he came up with the idea of offering a more personalised taxi service. I was impressed and encouraged him to develop this concept. He soon bought an existing company and his business flourished in just a few months. He managed and operated his business on a 24/7 basis. This reminded me of my early years in business when I never wanted to miss one single opportunity.

From early pregnancy, Claire and Duncan embarked on the transformation of one of their four bedrooms into a children's bedroom and playroom. It's a large room and the happy couple spent many hours decorating it in as much detail as possible. They even hung empty photo frames on the walls, to be filled later with their children's pictures! They left nothing to chance. They planned everything meticulously and perfectly, eagerly awaiting their loved ones' arrival. They even bought a brand new four-wheel-drive Land Rover that could easily fit two especially designed baby carriers and a long wheelbase pram – all this to make the vehicle as secure as possible for the little ones.

It was on the 7th of October 2011 that Claire gave birth to the two lovely little angels. Jack, I'm proud to say, resembles me while Millie is Duncan's double. I've never known a happier couple than Claire and Duncan, and their happiness was contagious.

I've already said in my book that my happiest moment in life was the birth of Richard, our first born. My only regret is that I was so busy with my hectic early business life, when everything depended on me, that I couldn't then afford to spare a few days off work to enjoy Richard's early days. This contrasts sharply with what Duncan and Claire decided. Although totally committed to their work they decided that the family came first and took three months off so they could give their full attention to their tiny loved ones.

When the little ones were about six weeks old I thought I'd phone Claire to ask her about her plans and whether she was planning to return to work, at least on a part-time basis. I was in for a nasty surprise.

'Look, Pa. I want to dedicate the full three months to the little ones. These are the most precious months in my entire life. I want to give them my fullest attention.'

After a short pause, she continued, 'I shall be working from home and I promise I shall return fully charged on 1st January.'

What could I say? She was adamant about it and I had no other option but to bow my head and let her have it her way. But later, when thinking about it, I realised how right she was. The twins were the fruit of her love for her husband, and she had a right to enjoy them to the full.

Who would have imagined what was in store for the happy couple on 1 January 2012?

Duncan was very busy throughout the whole of December, including the festive season. But he was a family man, and he believed that important dates like Christmas Day and New Year's Eve should be family celebrations. So instead of making the best of New Year's Eve business opportunities, he gave his employees the whole evening off so they could celebrate it with their families.

He had planned another surprise for us as well. He and Claire had invited Jessie, myself and his parents Frank and Maria to celebrate the coming of the New Year with them at their penthouse. Jessie and I were looking forward to this occasion. 'What better way to celebrate this day?' I told Jessie. 'Claire and Duncan have already blessed our new year with two little angels. It's much better to celebrate with our closely knit family than the usual gala dinners and celebrations we're used to.'

We had already celebrated the Christmas period with parties thrown by friends and business associates. Therefore we were looking forward to this intimate and special evening. That evening at eight Jessie and I were heartily welcomed by Claire and Duncan at their large and beautifully decorated penthouse, at the top of Falcon House, right in the centre of Sliema, around the corner from The Palace Hotel. Frank and Maria were there as well and after a pre-dinner drink, Duncan and Claire happily presented us with a specially prepared album of photographs of Jack and Millie. It was their Christmas present for their parents. The photos were professionally taken by Duncan, of course, and mounted in the most exquisite manner. Duncan was so proud of his handiwork and so happy to see the four grandparents overjoyed.

The meal was delicious. We then moved to their warmly

decorated sitting room, where they showed us their video of their beloved little ones, from a few weeks before birth till a few days back. This last video clearly demonstrates their love for each other and for their little angels. Afterwards, Duncan, Frank and I spent some time playing snooker, with Claire taking pictures of us and filming us enjoying ourselves while playing with Jack and Millie. At the stroke of midnight Duncan opened a bottle of champagne and we all hugged each other. Duncan played The Beatles' '*All You Need Is Love*', the young couple's wedding song and theme.

At 1.30 am we hugged each other for the last time and we reminded Claire and Duncan about New Year's Day lunch at our place. Shortly afterwards Duncan drove his parents home, a few blocks away.

At seven in the morning I was rudely woken up by the shrill noise of the telephone. It was Claire, and she was hysterical.

'Pa, come immediately. A man carrying two knives has entered our apartment and there's blood all over the place. Come now, Pa. Come now!'

I managed to ask, 'Do you know who he is?'

'No, Pa. No.'

'We're coming right away.'

Jessie became hysterical and wanted to know what was happening. I tried to call the hospital emergency line and I got through in a few minutes. I could hear the lady at the other end giving instructions to somebody on how to get to Claire's home. So Claire had managed to get through before me, I said to myself. I gave the operator more precise details about the location and told her to instruct the paramedics to break down the front door if necessary. They had to get inside as quickly as possible.

A few minutes later Jessie, Denise and I were on the road. It was a fifteen-minute drive to Sliema and I had no time to lose. Claire phoned Jessie to tell her that the police were already in the apartment and that Duncan was injured. Jessie went hysterical at this news and I drove like a madman, ignoring traffic lights, speed cameras and road speed calmers. We rushed up to Claire's apartment and the police led us into the children's room, where our daughter was crying forlornly and hugging the twins. We were instructed not to leave the room until the paramedics finished their job of attending to Duncan and the intruder. Claire, however, begged me to find a way to go and check Duncan's condition. I could not find an excuse to leave the children's room until the twins started crying for their feed.

I told the police officer guarding us that we couldn't keep the twins hungry, and that I had to go and fetch their milk bottles from the other end of the apartment. He acceded to my request and escorted me all the way. I had a glimpse of the area where the two men were lying on the corridor floor and had the shock of my life. Duncan and this aggressor were lying on the floor in a pool of blood! I felt my blood run cold. Until then none of us knew that they were so badly injured. Claire had no inkling that Duncan's injuries were fatal. The last time she had seen him he was lying on top of his adversary and she assumed that her husband had managed to get the better of him and was pinning him to the floor. I was rooted to the spot and stared at Duncan and the intruder. I could not make out any sign of breathing. I don't remember how I managed to locate the feeding bottles. I was fighting down tears and trying to look normal for Claire's and Jessie's sakes.

'How's Duncan, Pa?'

She was crying and holding one of the twins tightly to her while the other lay peacefully next to her.

'Tell me, please, pa. How is he?'

I had to think fast. 'The paramedics were in the way, Claire. I couldn't make out anything.'

Denise looked at me and met my eyes. I made a sign with my eyebrows which she immediately understood. A few minutes later I managed to alert Jessie as well and it was difficult for us three to keep back the tears. We had to for Claire's sake. She must not know about the tragedy.

I had another opportunity to go out of the room again and the escorting police officer told me that we had to make Claire aware of what had happened as officers from the Forensic Unit were on their way and the duty magistrate would be coming over to interview her.

I took some time outside the room to compose myself and build up courage. As soon as I returned to the children's room I was met with three pairs of hungry eyes, eagerly waiting for my first words. But I didn't say anything. I couldn't. I simply went over to Claire and hugged her with all my strength.

She screamed. 'It's Duncan! Tell me, Pa. Tell me please.'

I couldn't talk. I tried but couldn't. I could only hug her more tightly and sob uncontrollably.

I did not need any words. She understood, and Jessie and Denise joined me hugging her. It was too much for her. She went hysterical, crying and screaming as the shock hit her strongly like a tidal wave. Her sorrow and grief overwhelmed us and we couldn't control her. She wanted to get up and go near her beloved Duncan, and it took all our strength to restrain her.

I had already phoned Duncan's parents and told them that their son was injured by an intruder. They had immediately rushed to the block of apartments but were refused entry by the police outside. Frank and Maria were still unaware of the seriousness of the situation and I felt it my duty to inform them of the real facts.

When I went downstairs and was walking towards them I could see that they and their other son Gordon were restless, hungry for news.

'How is he? How's Duncan?'

I couldn't answer. I just lowered my head, started crying and hugged the three of them.

Frank understood and pulled away. 'What?' he shouted.

I just nodded my head.

'They killed my son! They killed my son!'

The shock devastated them. I couldn't hold Maria and Gordon on their feet and had to get help from the police officers. I couldn't believe I was living through this nightmare. I have never passed through such a terrifying time. I had to act strong when torn to shreds inside, and face the daunting task of having to prop up Claire, Jessie, Denise and Duncan's family. In those few minutes I thought that this harsh reality was going to break me. But I had to remain strong, somehow. No more for myself than for the three families around me.

We set about trying to find out who this homicidal intruder was, but no one seemed to know him, or ever have heard of him. After ninety minutes of police investigations, officers asked me whether the name Nicholas Gera, aged twenty-six, rang a bell. Neither I nor the members of the three families affected by the tragedy had ever heard of him.

News of the tragedy spread like wildfire all over Malta and the media immediately took it up. In the meantime Claire was being questioned by the duty magistrate and special police investigators, and this went on for a long time.

Bits of information about the intruder started trickling in. It seems that, as an eleven-year-old refugee from war-torn Bosnia, he and three brothers were adopted by a Maltese woman. He was a loner with very few friends. He worked at a restaurant and at half past two on the night of the incident he had joined his work colleagues and restaurant management for the customary end of year drink. Afterwards he drove the chef home in Sliema, a few doors from the Gera residence, and continued on his way to a bar to resume his celebrations.

It seems that by then he was already over the limit because the patrons noticed him acting abnormally. He made some rude gestures at two young ladies present and even passed obscene remarks. Some time later he smashed a glass on the floor and the management decided that it had had enough of him bothering the patrons. He was calmly but forcibly shoved out of the establishment. He then moved to two other bars in the area where he continued to consume more drinks.

At around five in the morning he tried to return to the first bar, but found the door closed. He phoned a friend working in the same bar to intercede with the management on his behalf so that he would be re-admitted. But he was refused entrance. He was so furious that he was caught on CCTV smashing a bottle outside this bar. Having nowhere else to go he decided to return home; or so everybody presumed, since his car was parked in front of his mother's house. In fact even his mother thought he was asleep when he probably must have made his way on foot towards Falcon House, just two blocks away. He managed to go up on the roof and jump onto Claire's large terrace, a leap of three metres. From there he gained access to the penthouse.

The police investigators, including the Commissioner, interrogated a number of people to try to establish a motive. They even checked all mobile phones, computers and everything that could give them a clue, but they could find no connection whatsoever between him and Duncan or Claire. They analysed over 35,000 mobile calls and messages, and other digital contacts that Claire, Duncan and the assailant had during the previous nine months, but they did not find even one single contact between them. The Commissioner of Police was understandably baffled. He told me that in his thirty years of police service, many of which as a crime investigator, he had never come across such a double tragedy without leaving the least clue of the assailant's motive. The police interviewed Claire a number of times for very long hours to try and find some form of link. But the truth is there is none. Up to the time of writing the police are still digging deep, trying to find a motive for this horrific tragedy which has shocked the whole nation.

The first week of the year is normally news free. Parliament is still adjourned and, except for the odd traffic accident, there are few items that catch the media's attention. This unique double killing, the first ever to happen in Malta and on the very first day of the year, fuelled all the media's hunger for something to write and speak about.

The police were still very busy investigating every bit of possible evidence and therefore did not issue any statements to the press. Unfortunately this gave free rein to all sorts of speculation and conclusions, some of which were so outlandish and cruel that they further increased the grief of the families involved in the tragedy. The media was hungry for news and not getting any from the police, so some irresponsible journalists went for the sensational by interviewing people from the general public and in no way linked to the story. This further added to the speculation. On the other hand, hundreds of those who knew Duncan and Claire wrote passionate comments in the digital newspapers expressing their sincere sympathy. They wrote about Duncan's charismatic character and about their shock that such a horrible tragedy could happen to such a loving family.

My family couldn't stand it any longer and I, as the natural spokesman in the circumstances, had to go through the additional torture of facing the cameras to try to calm things down and appeal for common sense, especially since the police had not yet arrived at any conclusions. I tried to be as discreet as possible so as not to hinder police investigations, but I couldn't let damaging and irresponsible rumours continue to spread and hurt my family. The tragedy never left the front and centre pages of all the newspapers for a whole week and was generally the first item on TV news bulletins. Our phones wouldn't stop ringing with messages of condolence, and likewise our mobile phones and emails. We received countless sympathy cards, and we're all thankful for the many words of comfort we received.

A week after the tragedy we made it strongly clear to the media that all speculation and rumours must stop as they were obstructing police investigations. Then the unexpected happened. On 9 January the Prime Minister announced a Cabinet reshuffle. Suddenly the limelight was shifted and we breathed a sigh of relief.

Some people, however, live on sensationalism. A person blessed with God's gift of omniscience went so far as to write that I had persuaded the Prime Minister to effect a quick Cabinet reshuffle as a personal favour so that the people's attention would shift from the tragedy!

There were many who wrote and spoke, condemning the media for fuelling people's imagination. One such person was a prominent

Maltese member of the European Parliament who wrote an article entitled '*The week the media went wild*'.

The autopsy results showed that Duncan had twenty-five stab wounds while the intruder had fifteen. Both died from heavy loss of blood. These results further confirm Duncan's courage and selfless love for his family. One cannot arrive at conclusions without proof, but I cannot help wondering how many stab wounds Duncan had already received before he managed to disarm the intruder of one of the knives. And I cannot help imagining him attacking the intruder when already mortally wounded but determined to save his wife and the little ones. If that isn't unconditional love and blind courage, I don't know what is.

The fight to the death was over in less than five minutes. Duncan died so that others may live. He is a real-life hero not only for those whose lives he saved, but for all those who knew him and consequently loved him.

The respect Duncan enjoyed was manifested during the funeral. Two thousand mourners packed the church and spilled onto the steps and pavement outside. Claire wouldn't leave the children behind. They slept in their large pram beside her, on the front row. The trauma she went through has left her so scared for their lives that she wouldn't let them out of her sight. Not for a single moment. She has become so over-protective that she wouldn't dream of leaving them with anyone, not even with her closest and trusted friends.

The celebrant delivered a moving homily that brought tears to the eyes of the people inside and outside the church. Aware of the rumours and speculation that abounded, he compared Claire to the Mother of Jesus standing beneath the cross. He urged the people to do what St John the Evangelist did when he described the Crucifixion. St John was unmindful of the rumours that went around Jerusalem at the time. He was mindful only of the suffering of Jesus' immediate family, sharing the suffering of Mary's son who, like Duncan, died so that others may live. The celebrant referred to the forgiveness offered by Claire and Duncan's family, and compared it to Jesus' *'Forgive them for they know not what they do'*.

Jessie sat next to Claire, doing her utmost throughout to support her suffering daughter. Claire has much courage and will power. She wished to mount the steps to the altar, face the people and read a love letter she wrote to her dead beloved. But the Church had lately refused such manifestations of grief. Claire, however, did read it before Duncan was gently put to rest, and distributed copies to all those around her.

A choir sang wonderfully in church and Duncan's friends made it a special occasion by singing some of his favourite songs, including The Beatles' *'All You Need Is Love'*. The coffin was carried out of church by six of Duncan's closest friends, his brothers and our son Richard. When the coffin was lifted shoulder high, all the people inside and outside the church burst out in spontaneous and rousing applause.

The worst moment was at the cemetery. It was so hard and heartbreaking to say a final farewell to someone I loved so dearly. My family, his family... Claire. There were so many people around me, crying openly. And I imagined him, lying inside the coffin with two little teddy bears next to his head, reminders of the beloved babies he left behind.

At last it was over and I had a look around me. It was only then that I realised what a large crowd had accompanied Duncan to his final resting place. There were so many flowers that the surrounding graves resembled a garden in spring. Before turning to leave I had a last look at the grave. There lies a thirty-two year old who has loved until it hurt, I said to myself. May God reward him a hundredfold.

The next few days were a continuous nightmare for his immediate family and close friends. Claire and the little ones moved into our residence. She was still suffering from shock and before she goes to sleep we have had to bring down all the security shutters and lock all doors. Sometimes she imagines an intruder lurking somewhere in the house. But she is courageous. She fought hard to get over this very difficult time. She knew that life had to go on, if not for her sake, for their angels'. She prepared herself mentally to get back to normal life. She already had my assurance that I would act as the twins' father figure and that I would give them all the attention and good upbringing my health allows me to. Jessie and Denise had also assured her of their total support.

The household routine has changed drastically. I now return home an hour earlier to have more time to play with Jack and Millie. It's already becoming a regular family routine to take the little ones out for some fresh air in the countryside. It's becoming a pleasure for me to push this rather cumbersome pram and look at Jack's and Millie's smiling faces. Duncan has left us two angels to remember him by.

Claire asked me to design a commemorative tombstone to be placed on Duncan's grave. I designed it lovingly immediately. Claire wanted more than Duncan's details engraved on the plaque. She insisted on a figure of a dove carrying an olive branch, the symbol of peace. She also wanted the words: REST IN PEACE OUR DEAR DUNCAN; UNCONDITIONAL LOVE and ALL YOU NEED IS LOVE. She told me that all these represented the love and peace that overflowed from Duncan's character and their relationship.

I have prepared two boxes that contain many photos and some of the many videos they took throughout their beautiful years full of love, Claire's diary, friends' comments, a number of newspaper articles, TV coverage, Claire's final love letter to Duncan and a personal letter from me to Jack and Millie. These boxes are now sealed and won't be opened until Jack and Millie reach adulthood. We want them to understand who their father really was. They will never know him as a person, but at least they will know that their father lived and died for them, and that they should honour him as the hero he truly is.

It is very hard to get over this trauma. My family and Duncan's are still trying to understand this new reality and to cope with it. But I'm an optimistic person and always look at the half-full part of the glass rather than at the other half. This tragedy was a physical and mental blow for all of us. But we have to believe that every dark cloud has a silver lining. The fact that Claire's and the twins' lives have been spared is already a blessing, and gives us the necessary strength to go on with life while keeping in mind that only Duncan's heroism made this possible. He wasn't just a son-in-law. In the few years I had known him, his charisma had entered my heart so deeply that I shall never, for as long as I live, forget our dear friendship.

For Claire this was another trauma. I can still see her, as a thirteen year old, unable to walk for three dreadful months, so long ago. God was with her then and a miracle made her whole again. That experience made her tougher. She's a very tough character, determined to fight again for her survival as a whole person, and the survival of her twins, as Duncan would have wished it. She says: 'My love for Duncan does not end here. My greater love starts now!'

Thankfully, my father was spared all this suffering and I thank God for that. Lately his condition had so deteriorated that his few minutes of consciousness were few and far between. But in those few minutes, his enquiring look seemed to show that something was not completely right. His eyes hovered around the room as though expecting to see somebody who should be there, but wasn't. And then he would close his eyes, with sadness all over his face.

He passed peacefully away in the evening of Saturday the 21st of January, surviving Duncan by just twenty-one days.

AX Hotels

Epilogue

But is it really? An epilogue, I mean? Not after everything I've written in the last chapter it isn't. And does my life story deserve an epilogue just yet?

When I sat down at my desk months ago with a pen in my hand and a sheaf of blank paper in front of me, I had not yet read one single book, let alone written one. Now, many ballpoint pens later, I'm again sitting at the same desk looking at a 4-inch-thick manuscript filled with thousands upon thousands of words that recount the many adventures, joys, heartbreaks, suspense, successes, disappointments, tears and triumphs that came alive while my pen raced across the pages, trying to keep up with the memories that my subconscious started regurgitating with astounding clearness.

What is inside this book are the ingredients of a life fully lived, but a life that is not unique. Thousands before me have trodden the path I chose to take. Most of them have succeeded and are remembered for the legacies they left to their families, communities and countries. Others, however, did not last the whole course and faltered somewhere along the way. It is my sincere wish that my book serves to reduce the number in the latter group.

While I was writing this book and recalling my humble beginnings, I realised more than ever how hard I had to struggle to overcome the obstacles I faced every step of the way. It was only when I delved deeper into my memory that the minute details of my life surfaced in the most vivid manner. I laughed out loud at happy memories, cried when recalling the tragedies that nearly broke me, seethed with anger when I remembered the injustices, and I thanked God for always being there with me and my family when the going was tough. I relived it all, minute by minute, and felt satisfied that I have had a full life.

It wasn't easy. Nothing comes easy. And I couldn't have done it without the vision, determination and persistence that I was adamant about holding on. Even food requires working hard for. It doesn't fall like manna from heaven. Ask any living creature on earth. Food is survival, and man, as any other creature, has to go out and look for it. If he doesn't at first succeed he has to try and try again until he does. Otherwise, he'll weaken and drop to the ground to become carrion for the vultures hovering overhead and the opportunistic jackals always lurking around, sniffing for just such an opportunity.

Life is one big challenge and giving up means death. A man who gives up will be as dead as those who fell at the wayside on the road to success, his early efforts forgotten and buried with him in a mass grave for the anonymous. Man has to believe in himself and in his aspirations in order to make it to the top. He has to persist in order to achieve results, and the harder the body blows, the sweeter the fruits of success. Real success requires hard work and sacrifice. Becoming a loser is much easier. It doesn't require hard work and sacrifice. One has just to whine self-pityingly about one's problems without lifting a little finger to solve them, while a winner talks about solutions. Winners never look at the empty half of the glass. That's for the losers to notice. They wake up in the morning already counting the hours to bedtime while the winners' day is never long enough. Perceiving oneself as a sure winner is the right first step to becoming one.

Experience has made me realise that the bigger the difficulty encountered, the greater the determination to succeed. And the greater the effort, the sweeter the taste of success. Not all men hold to this philosophy. Men are different and have different attitudes towards life. They have different ways of dealing with problems and, ultimately, still arrive at the same success I achieved.

My attitude is not the only winning formula, but it has worked for me and I hope it will work for others.

Success in business, however, is just one of man's many aspirations. Some aspire to become great sportsmen. Others wish to be remembered as great politicians or writers or musicians. Whatever the ambition, determination and hard work are the main ingredients. The important thing is to remain totally focused, but flexible enough to meet changing circumstances. Very often, when one's vision reaches beyond the horizon, the way ahead may seem impossible to charter. That's no reason to give up or aim lower. Once you know the direction you want to take, all you need is to adjust your bearings along the way. It's very much like using a GPS (Global Position System) when driving over unfamiliar terrain. The GPS gives you the general way to your destination, showing only the main roads leading to it. But once you zoom in, capillaries of secondary roads and even simple narrow pathways appear as if you're looking at human flesh through a microscope. Sometimes a main road is blocked due to works or traffic pile-ups and you have to veer into a secondary road. In the end, however, you would make it even if it meant driving into potholes, over bumps and unmade roads.

Success doesn't grow on trees. We're sometimes tempted to go for the easy money and it could work for some, but it's a dangerous course. I'm proud that I've never fallen for it, preferring to go the whole way assured of my capabilities and endurance. My sincere advice is to shun such temptations as they could easily end in disaster. I liken it to driving at reckless speed on a motorway; one momentary lapse of concentration and you end up part and parcel of the wreckage. I have always preferred the longer and safer route. Aspiring entrepreneurs must remember that success is 80% sweat and only 20% inspiration, not the other way round. There exists no magic wand to turn lead into gold, and achieving success does not mean winning every deal that comes your way. A success of 10% on your business opportunities means you're doing very well. In real life, opportunities are hard to come by, but they are there, nevertheless. It's your determination to search for them that spells success.

Sir Winston Churchill was correct when he said that 'kites rise highest against the wind, not with it'. He should know. His and his country's finest hour was when the odds were totally against the defeat of Nazi Germany. It is when you succeed against heavy odds that the rewards are the greatest. Making money may be one of the main motivators, but, for me and many others, the prime motivator is the pride in our achievements and the challenges we faced along the way. Sometimes goals seem beyond our grasp, but if we truly believe in ourselves and our aspirations, we will arrive where we want to, maybe a little bruised, but stronger, hardier and more experienced to face the next challenge.

It is true that competition always exists, but keen rivalry is the name of the game. This doesn't have to turn into paranoia, thinking that everything and everybody is there to destroy you. The important thing is to be wary about who you associate with. I have been lucky in the people I chose to form the team around me. A winning team with the right partners or associates with whom the trust is mutual and sincere is a sure way to success.

Your natural charismatic approach is more effective than rhetoric. It will radiate from you and act as a magnet for others to join your winning team. A smile is never out of place; neither is a sincere and warm handshake. Body language speaks louder than words and is part of the art for successful negotiations. First impressions last long, sometimes forever, and, therefore, are of the utmost importance. The clothes you wear give the first wrong or right impression. You wouldn't ask your bank manager for a loan dressed in a soiled boiler suit. Neither would you sit around a conference table in a jogging suit.

Honesty and integrity are the two main pillars on which a satisfying and successful career is built. Never treat anybody as an inferior. Every human being has dignity and, once this is respected, the respect is reciprocated. True humility is not grovelling. Neither is it keeping your eyes downcast, playing the holy. True humility is treating everyone your equal. Underestimating other people's talents and dignity could spell disaster to a promising career. Although it is said that men are born equal, it is a true fact that some are born more gifted than others, but no human being is bereft of some special talent which makes him unique as an individual, and it is up to an aspiring entrepreneur to bring out the best out of people, giving them dignity and a better life for them and their families.

Parents are the first teachers. Education starts at home and parents should be the first to notice and appreciate a child's natural inclinations. When still a young boy, I had a passion for building small rooms with rubble stone and later I made it clear to my parents that I wanted to become a businessman. As you well know, my aspirations were not taken seriously, but I managed to succeed because I was determined to go my way whatever the obstacles. But how many potentially successful businessmen were thwarted by parents' misguided plans and ended up having to change careers midway through their adult life? Parents should guide rather than impose. It's not their career that is at stake. Fortunately, nowadays, my generation is more receptive to their offspring's ideas and offer encouragement, which is so vital for the young, inexperienced, but promising, would-be entrepreneurs. All this would prepare our young to learn to face the hard life of cut-throat competition where no quarter is given.

Many successful entrepreneurs I know have, like me, had no university education. Some are barely literate. And yet they all made it to the top and are still climbing, proving that education can be done without for a successful business career. I am not saying or advocating that a university degree isn't an asset and doesn't enhance your business career and lifestyle. But no university degree can take the place of the natural instinct you've been born with, which is the main ingredient for success. This reminds me of a joke about an illiterate, rich contractor who wanted to cash a hefty cheque at the bank. When asked by the cashier to put his signature on the back of the cheque, the contractor answered, 'Sorry, but I can't write.'

The cashier answered, 'Imagine if you had a proper education how much richer you would have been.'

'Well,' answered the contractor. 'I guess that if I had a proper education I would have become a bank clerk.'

A young entrepreneur with a real vision would have to undergo the frustration of facing blank stares when trying to explain an original concept that does not fit the authorities' orthodox and blinkered way of thinking. An original idea that doesn't fit snugly in some straitjacket policy is rejected without much ado. Or even worse, it would be made impossibly difficult through the maze of bureaucracy that is practised with dedicated passion and scruple by the people in power. Having passed through countless labyrinths and dead ends throughout my career, I can well sympathise with somebody coming up with an original idea, which has first to pass through the eye of the needle for it to happen. We, the older generation, need to give youth a chance. We cannot risk losing our talented young people by not giving those with a vision the opportunity to develop their creative powers. On the contrary, we need to pass on to them our experiences in order to achieve the continuity between one generation and the next.

The challenges I've had to face throughout my life prove that nothing that's good comes easy. I can't emphasise more, even if I repeat it ad nauseam, the importance of vision, hard work, facing challenges head on, efficiency and determination as the key words to success. Some people say that luck should be added to the list. I don't believe in luck, or if there's luck it's you who have to make it happen. After all, some others say that luck favours the brave, which means that you have to be alert and make sure that the first opportunity finds you in the right place at the right time. If people wish to call that luck... Well, let them. In the end it won't lessen the merit of your achievements.

Opportunities are there if you look hard for them, and once, through your tenacity, you come upon one, don't ever lose your focus. Work hard at it and follow it through to the end. That's the way to achieve your objectives and become a winner. Business is very much like athletics; it only needs that extra effort to beat your rivals. Some world records are bettered by a mere hundredth of a second, but that small fraction of a second assures a windfall for the record breaker.

Remember that life is not a ball, and business life is even less so. You can't dance around the risks, big or small. Risks are there to be faced and taken. But the rewards always lead to further progress. The rewards are like fruit hanging at the end of a branch; the thinner the branch, the greater the risk. But once you manage to pick your fruit, the great risk involved makes the fruit taste sweeter.

Business deals resemble a game of golf. With the first shot, the player tries to drive the ball as close to the hole as possible. He might manage a hole in one, but that's a rarity, more a fluke than perfect play. As in playing golf, it is almost impossible to conclude a business deal at the first attempt. But once you conclude a deal, get it signed and get on with the work as soon as possible, thereby keeping a fast momentum going and not giving the other side a chance for back paddling.

Life is full of experiences and I can't say mine was an exception. I've had some very good experiences while others were quite bad, but I've never let the latter pull me down. On the contrary, I considered them part of my education in life. Each bad experience has taught me something new – something I never knew before – and this attitude has helped me retain my positive approach to life. In a country the size of Malta, where opportunities are limited and where everybody knows everybody else, it is much more difficult to overcome the everyday obstacles, but I can't grumble. In the end, I managed quite well and am satisfied with my achievements. I cannot, of course, say that I managed everything I set out to do. The previous pages attest to this. But I won't let my few failures discourage me in any way, even at this stage of my life. I still look forward to new challenges, which I shall face with the same vigour, courage and optimism.

I never tire of quoting Kennedy's 'Do not ask what your country can do for you, but what you can do for your country'. Unfortunately, very few of our politicians possess a business background. Most are well qualified academically, but find it difficult to understand this entrepreneur's vision. I have always believed that ACTION moves faster than WORDS, while politicians find it easier to indulge in beautiful rhetoric that impresses but rarely produces. It is the politicians, however, who ultimately possess the power to make the good things happen in this country. It is they who should act the parents who listen to the people and give the necessary support. They should economise on lip service and dedicate more energy to concrete action. We entrepreneurs, and the population at large, are so used to their complimentary and beautifully worded statements for the benefit of the media that we are never surprised when nothing actually happens and everything is forgotten practically overnight.

Finally, I have always worked very hard and my achievements have given me pleasure and satisfaction. But the highest reward life has given me is my family. I have been blessed with a wife who stood by me through thick and thin. She believed in me on the very first day we met so long ago, but seeming like yesterday, and she has never wavered. I have also been blessed with three hardworking offspring who appreciate the maxim that nothing in life comes easy. It is true that they have found a successful enterprise, but they work as hard as ever to keep it growing and make it more successful. They give me the courage and incentive to continue to work hard so that their endeavours find the just rewards.

Every member of my family has found a niche in which to develop their talents. Richard has found his footing as construction director, Claire has found fulfilment as the group's hospitality director, while Denise is fast getting to grips with the development and operations activities. And Jessie? Jessie's love affair with AX Foundation, which supports people with special needs, though well past the honeymoon stage, has never faltered but is a strong as ever.

As already stated, retirement is far off in the future, but I'm now finding more time to spend with Jessie, my lifetime companion. We both deserve it. We both made the sacrifices necessary to make our dream come true.

The recent global economic slowdown has also left me with some idle time on my hands. Not being the type to sit at my desk and contemplate the opposite wall or spend hours watching TV, I decided that it was time to start jotting down my life story in longhand. It was Jessie who, once again, had to put up with a husband who spent his short breaks from the office and whole weekends absorbed filling page after page with reminiscences. Her patience knows no limits and I thank her for it.

I also thank my parents for the strong dose of discipline in my upbringing. This helped me become a mature businessman at a very early age. Throughout my business life I have never tried to forget my humble beginnings. Neither have I tried to hide it. In fact, I'm proud of my early days and have always tried to remain the humble Angelo who helped his mother in the kitchen and his father in the fields. Appreciating how hard it was for me to make it in the business world, I have never shirked from assisting others during their time of need. I shall always be proud of my roots in the village of Naxxar. I thank God for inspiring me to always keep my feet firmly on the ground and for rewarding me so handsomely for it.

I am satisfied with my achievements so far and I honestly believe that my innovative ideas throughout the years have contributed towards making Malta what it is today. This Jewel of the Mediterranean has certainly become brighter these past few decades and I want to be there when it becomes the brightest of them all.

Angelo Xuereb